SOCIAL JUSTICE
MULTICULTURAL PSYCHOLOGY
AND COUNSELING

Social Justice Multicultural Psychology and Counseling

2ND EDITION

Rita Chi-Ying Chung and Frederic P. Bemak

OXFORD
UNIVERSITY PRESS

OXFORD
UNIVERSITY PRESS

Oxford University Press is a department of the University of Oxford. It furthers
the University's objective of excellence in research, scholarship, and education
by publishing worldwide. Oxford is a registered trade mark of Oxford University
Press in the UK and certain other countries.

Published in the United States of America by Oxford University Press
198 Madison Avenue, New York, NY 10016, United States of America.

Library of Congress Cataloging-in-Publication Data
Names: Chung, Rita Chi-Ying, author. | Bemak P., Fred, author.
Title: Social justice multicultural psychology and counseling / Rita Chi-Ying Chung, Frederic P. Bemak.
Other titles: Social justice counseling
Description: Second edition. | New York, NY : Oxford University Press, [2023] |
Earlier edition published as: Social justice counseling : the next steps beyond multiculturalism. |
Includes bibliographical references and index. |
Identifiers: LCCN 2023017320 (print) | LCCN 2023017321 (ebook) |
ISBN 9780197518267 (paperback) | ISBN 9780197518281 (epub)
Subjects: LCSH: Cross-cultural counseling. | Psychiatry, Transcultural. | Social justice.
Classification: LCC BF636.7.C76 C48 2023 (print) | LCC BF636.7.C76 (ebook) |
DDC 158.3—dc23/eng/20230615
LC record available at https://lccn.loc.gov/2023017320
LC ebook record available at https://lccn.loc.gov/2023017321

Printed by Marquis Book Printing, Canada

CONTENTS IN BRIEF

CONTENTS

ACKNOWLEDGEMENTS

I (Rita Chi-Ying Chung) dedicate this book to my parents: Jack Tai Hing Chung and Daphne Chung (Young Lai Yung) who taught me to embrace my culture, instilled in me the passion, the strength, the courage, and the fearlessness to speak up and out against human rights violations and injustices. To my nieces and nephews – the next generation to challenge social injustices. To my students who embraced the challenges that I posed to them in class, and evolved into social justice warriors. Lastly, to my partner both personally and professionally (Fred Bemak) for his continuous support, encouragement, and sharing and riding the social justice roller coaster together. What a ride!

I (Fred Bemak) dedicate this book to my parents, Walter and Ruth Bemak, who taught me at an early age about social justice, integrity, responsibility, and standing up for one's beliefs and my daughters, Amber Bemak and Lani Tourville, who continue to carry the torch of life, vibrancy, passion, social change, and social justice, and my grandchildren, Tennessee, Louie, and Mandarava, who are our hope for the future to carry human rights forward. And to my students for their bravery to challenge themselves, challenge others, trust the process of social change, and share their stories. And finally, to my partner, Rita Chi-Ying Chung, my deepest appreciation and gratitude for sharing this journey.

CHAPTER 1

INTRODUCTION TO SOCIAL JUSTICE MULTICULTURAL PSYCHOLOGY AND COUNSELING

Rita Chi-Ying Chung and Frederic P. Bemak

Injustice anywhere is a threat to justice everywhere.

—Martin Luther King

It is in justice that the ordering of society is centered.

—Aristotle

The future belongs to those who prepare for it today.

—Malcolm X

We were excited by the prospect of writing the second edition of this book, but as we (Rita and Fred) embarked on this journey our hearts became heavy and deeply saddened as we witnessed multiple social injustices in our community, the nation, and the world. We have rewritten this introductory chapter a number of times as these injustices occurred, aware that these events impacted our and others' personal and professional lives and, subsequently, our writing. Astoundingly, each violation of human rights and social and racial justice was as profoundly devastating, disturbing, and shocking as the one that preceded the injustice one month, one week, one day, or even one hour before.

Subsequently, these social injustices we are experiencing and writing about will significantly impact generations to come. Therefore, we strongly believe that it is important to capture these injustices in this edition to maintain ethical social justice integrity and document the truth about the wrongs so many are now facing. At the same time, we acknowledge that we cannot include every injustice that occurs, otherwise the book will never be completed. Due to the gravity, severity, and enormity of some of these injustices, we cannot ignore these momentous events since these situations underscore the urgency and dire need for us, in the mental health profession, to include social justice and human rights as an integral aspect of our practice and training.

Given the times we are living in, we decided to begin this book by highlighting three major social injustices that caused us to significantly pause in our writing and made us rethink and rewrite this Introduction. These three events will provide a framework for this volume and set the stage for examining social justice and multiculturalism in the mental health field. The three events, in chronological order, are the 2020 worldwide racial injustice protest; the coronavirus (COVID-19) global pandemic that resulted in the loss of millions of lives and crippled economies worldwide; and the January 6, 2021, attack on the U.S. Capitol, a beacon of democracy not only for the United States but globally. Each of these events placed us in an existential conundrum and forced us to rethink our personal and professional priorities. As we began writing this edition, the first social issue that created a social justice heartache for us was witnessing the racism and ensuing protests and violence that were, and still are, ripping the United States apart.

Although there were multiple Black Lives Matter demonstrations after the numerous murders by law enforcement officers of unarmed African Americans, it was media coverage showing the inhumane and senseless murder of George Floyd on March 25, 2020, that sparked global racial justice demonstrations. Media showed a Minnesota police officer place his knee on Mr. Floyd's neck for nine minutes and twenty-nine seconds as Mr. Floyd pleaded that he could not breathe and three other police officers watched without intervening (Carlisle, 2020). The police officer was arrested and charged with second-degree murder (and later convicted). This incident generated mass protests throughout the United States and globally, not only demanding justice for Mr. Floyd, but also decrying the ongoing and continued murder of African Americans by law enforcement and instances of racism toward people and communities of color and Indigenous First Nation populations worldwide. Mr. Floyd's case is one of many senseless murders of unarmed African Americans by law enforcement. The list of people of color who have been killed by police without probable cause is extensive. In fact, due to the degree of racial injustices and violations, the May 31, 2020, *Time* magazine front page stated "America has its knee on people of color" (Alter, 2020). We suggest readers undertake research to investigate the horrendous past, present, and ongoing racial injustices against people of color by law enforcement.

Unfortunately, even as we write this, yet another peaceful protest against racial injustice escalated into rioting and looting. The media shifted attention from the original purpose of the protest to the violence and destruction of property. The change of focus reinforced the stereotypical connection between race and violence, falsely accentuating the negativity between civil protests by people and communities of color and lawlessness. As social justice conscious psychologists and counselors, it is important that we not give in to political countertransference (Chung et al., 2008) but instead have the ability to deconstruct media and political messages to discern protestors from rioters and looters and to understand the historical and sociopolitical roots and importance of civil disobedience and protest to combat injustices. Although we remain hopeful that these racial violations and the need for protests may diminish and be dated by the time you, the readers, are reading this book, we are concerned as we watch historical and modern-day sociopolitical and psychopolitical trends exemplifying systemic racism and xenophobia, in the United States and globally, continue and escalate. This underscores the need for social justice–minded psychologists and counselors to proactively advocate for racial justice in conjunction with other social injustices.

It is disconcerting that in the midst of violence, tension, and a lack of understanding about racial justice, the world also is in the throes of the COVID-19 global pandemic. The last pandemic occurred in 1968 with the influenza A (H3N2) virus. With stay-at-home and lockdown orders, mandatory mask wearing in some parts of the United States and many other countries, coupled with repeated resurgence of the virus and its variants around the world, it is indeed an interesting time in history to be writing about the relationship between mental health professionals, social justice, and diversity. Although early information about COVID-19 identified those with preexisting conditions and the elderly as the most impacted, later data showed that no-one is immune: COVID-19 is an "equal opportunity" disease resulting in nondiscriminatory deaths. As the United States and the world were desperately trying to gain control and minimize the effect of the pandemic, social justice concerns emerged. Issues such as racial/ethnic and socioeconomic status differences in access to health resources in testing, treatment, and vaccinations; questions regarding the racial origin of COVID-19 raised by a number of politicians and news media (who called this the "Chinese virus" and "kung flu," actions which in turn precipitated a global escalation of hate crimes, racism, and violence toward Chinese/Asians); findings that exposed the interrelationship between race, racism, poverty, health, and well-being, with higher numbers of people of color testing positive for COVID-19; and those who do not believe in COVID vaccinations becoming violent toward proponents of the vaccines.

The Centers for Disease Control and Prevention (CDC, 2021) COVID-19 data show that Black/African Americans, Latinx, American Indians, and Alaska Natives in the United States experience higher rates of COVID-19–related hospitalization and death compared with White populations. These disparities persist even when accounting for other demographic and socioeconomic factors. The disparity is associated with both historical and current experiences of racism and discrimination that lead to mistrust of the healthcare system and wariness of vaccines, vaccination providers, and institutions making recommendations for the use of vaccines (CDC, 2021). For example, African Americans are 12% of the U.S. population, yet, according to the CDC, account for more than 26% of COVID-19 cases and 23% of deaths (Alter, 2020). Similarly, the impact of COVID-19 on the economy is found to be more devastating to communities of color where there is higher employment in unskilled positions, frontline healthcare workers, and those classified as "essential workers" even though COVID-19 affects all groups and communities (Alter, 2020). Therefore, in this volume, when we talk about social justice clients, we alternately use the term "clients" and "stakeholders," the latter term referring to all those who are directly or indirectly impacted by injustices.

In addition to the above two major social justice situations that have overwhelmed us while writing this second edition, an attack occurred on the U.S. Capitol while Congress was meeting to certify the 2020 U.S. presidential election results. The assailants were U.S. citizens who believed that the 2020 election was "stolen"—a belief proved to be untrue and identified as the "Big Lie." The Big Lie has been perpetuated by conspiracy theorists, some Republican senators, Fox News anchors and hosts, journalists, allies of the former U.S. President, and, sadly, the former president himself who continues to insist that he is the rightful president. Lives were lost during the attack (Cohen et al., 2021; *Washington Post*, 2021). What the United States and the world witnessed on January 6, 2021, was not just an implausible and violent attack on the U.S. Capitol, a symbol of U.S. democracy, but also a direct attack on democracy worldwide. Along with rest of the world, former U.S. presidents and world leaders reacted with disbelief, shock, horror, and anger, condemning the violence (BBC, 2021). The sitting president at the time of the January 6, 2021 attack did not tell the rioters to stop the violence or acknowledge the assault but rather pledged his "love" for the attackers and reinforced that the election was "stolen." Despite being impeached for a second time, he falsely continues to insist he only lost the election because of corruption (Cohen et al., 2021; *Washington Post*, 2021).

Considering all three of these events slowed down our progress in writing the second edition as we reflected and reconsidered social justice, human rights, diversity, and mental health. What is our role as social justice–oriented practitioners when we witness and directly and indirectly experience injustice? As we contemplated this question, we have written the second edition feeling more determined than ever that we, as social justice–oriented psychologists and counselors, play a crucial role in addressing injustices and human rights violations. We are more committed than ever that our profession must engage in healing through social justice advocacy, activism, action, and change. We also want to stress that highlighting these three major events in no way minimizes, dismisses, discounts, or suggests that these three injustices are more important than other injustices, but rather we note these three injustices as poignant examples at this moment in time. We strongly believe that an injustice is an injustice, not prioritizing, judging, comparing, or contrasting inequities and human rights violations.

In addition, we fully acknowledge that social injustice is not one-dimensional, and there is intersectionality when individuals, families, and communities experience multiple injustices simultaneously (e.g., the individual who may be disabled, living in poverty, and an immigrant). Consequently it is important to acknowledge the wide range of social injustices and human rights violations that impact individuals', families', and communities' physical safety, psychological and economic well-being, and quality of life and address the complex intersectionality of other social issues such as racism, xenophobia, poverty, discrimination, global warming, gender-based violence, gun violence and mass shootings, sexual abuse, assault and violence, religious intolerance, sexism, and so on that are an essential part of our clients' experiences.

Although this Introduction begins in a somber manner, these are the realities of doing social justice work. Our hope in sharing these incidents is to encourage you, the reader, to become committed, passionate, motivated, and inspired to proactively address social injustices and promote social change. At the same time, we neither want to "sugar coat" the realities of social injustice and human rights violations nor minimize or romanticize the challenges and hard work it takes to be social justice–oriented mental health professionals. In our experience, social justice work at times requires us to "dig deep" and find the courage, stamina, tenaciousness, resiliency, and fortitude to face the challenges and despair that are present for our clients and ourselves. Maintaining the hope and belief that we can make a difference is important in this work. As Michelle Obama (the first African American U.S. First Lady) said, "you will not always be able to solve all of the world's problems at once but don't ever underestimate the importance you can have because history has shown us that courage can be contagious and hope can take on a life of its own" (2018).

Inspiration, hope, and encouragement can emerge from injustices. As I (Fred) always say in teaching psychology and counseling classes, "trust the process." For example, the U.S. racial justice protests that are occurring as we write this book have comprised the most varied group of protesters in U.S. history, including intergenerational demonstrators from diverse racial, ethnic, and cultural backgrounds, genders, religions, and socioeconomic groups. African Americans are protesting alongside their brown, yellow, red, and white brothers and sisters; young and old; gay, straight, and transgender; and of varied religious and socioeconomic groups, all raising their voices in unity demanding racial justice. Furthermore, the demonstrations are not solely focused on U.S. injustices but involve countries around the world protesting, both in solidarity with the United States and against their own racial injustice issues. In the United States, we have witnessed the remarkable: police officers throughout U.S. cities "taking a knee" as they hold up their shields against protesters, shaking hands and hugging protesters, and sharing hand sanitizers with protestors (due to COVID-19 safety issues) and chiefs of police in various states marching with protestors (Silverman, 2020).

This is also the first time in U.S. history that the House and Senate Democrats gathered at the U.S. Capitol's Emancipation Hall to kneel in silence for 8 minutes and 46 seconds in memory of George Floyd prior to announcing the details of their proposed major legislation on reforming U.S. police departments and combatting racial bias, with demands for a ban on chokeholds, a creation of a national police misconduct registry, and mandated racial bias training (McEvoy, 2020). Multiple organizations, companies, and businesses have made public statements supporting anti-racism and racial justice, such as Macys, Ben and Jerry's ice cream, North Face, United Airlines, and the American Psychological Association; see Box Text 1.1). In addition, Kennedy Mitchum, a 22-year-old who was tired of people referring to the dictionary's narrow definition of racism, managed to persuade the U.S. publisher Merriam-Webster to change its dictionary's definition of racism to include not just individual racism, but also structural and systemic racism, incorporating the complex and multidimensional aspects of historical; sociopolitical; psychopolitical; psychosocial; macro, meso, and micro levels; and ecological views about realities of racism in the United States (Williams, 2020). Modifying the dictionary's definition of racism is an excellent illustration of how one person can make change.

In 2021, there appeared to be a change occurring in terms of awareness of and support to end racism and speaking up and out about racism, xenophobia, and racial justice. The kind of situations mentioned above provide social justice–oriented psychologists and counselors hope that change will occur, hope that we in the mental health profession must maintain and sustain throughout our social justice work and journey. As Martin Luther King, Jr. said, "We must accept finite disappointment, but never lose infinite hope." Unfortunately, not all social justice advocacy work will result in immediate change, and we may not see the fruits of our activism work in our lifetimes. However, this should not deter us from being tenacious and patient and continue to prevent and intervene in social injustices. It is important

BOX TEXT 1.1 AMERICAN PSYCHOLOGICAL ASSOCIATION ADDRESSING RACISM

On October 29, 2021, the American Psychological Association (APA) Council of Representatives passed three resolutions acknowledging and apologizing for the APA's role in promoting and perpetuating racism and racial discrimination in the United States; the role of psychology and the APA in dismantling systemic racism in the United States; and its role in advancing health equity in psychology. The following email was sent out to APA members.

Dear APA Members,

We are reaching out to share news about a historic moment for APA and the field of psychology.

During its October 29 meeting, our APA Council of Representatives adopted an apology for APA's role—and the role of the discipline of psychology—in contributing to systemic racism. The apology acknowledges that APA "failed in its role leading the discipline of psychology, was complicit in contributing to systemic inequities, and hurt many through racism, racial discrimination, and denigration of people of color, thereby falling short on its mission to benefit society and improve lives."

The resolution, which passed unanimously, acknowledges that the association should have apologized sooner. "APA, and many in psychology, have long considered such an apology, but failed to accept responsibility," the resolution says.

The APA Council of Representatives also adopted two accompanying resolutions, one delineating APA's and psychology's role going forward in dismantling systemic racism and the other pledging to work to advance health equity in psychology. The former directs APA's CEO to develop a long-term plan to prioritize, operationalize, and ensure accountability for achieving real action toward the goals identified in the resolutions. This plan is to be presented to the Council at its meeting in August 2022.

These three resolutions reflect a monumental undertaking involving a broad cross-section of APA's members, including our elected and appointed leaders. The work was spearheaded by the APA Task Force on Strategies to Eradicate Racism, Discrimination, and Hate and its five-member Apology Advisory Subcommittee and the APA Presidential Task Force on Psychology and Health Equity, all composed of eminent psychologists who were chosen for their knowledge and expertise.

The apology and dismantling racism resolutions represent a significant milestone in APA's commitment and promise to examine the role that the field of psychology and the association itself have played in promoting and sustaining racial inequity. By affirming these resolutions as association policies, APA is in a much more informed position to take meaningful action, and ultimately, diversify and strengthen the organization and field of psychology.

The apology and resolutions are just the beginning of the work we must do to eradicate racism and discrimination within our field and build an equitable and diverse discipline. This requires our membership and profession to work together as allies.

We want to engage our members, learn from your lived experience, and harness the research you conduct, the services you provide and the advocacy in which you engage. We invite you to join us for one or more of the following member town halls to learn more about these historic resolutions and to share your ideas.

The town halls are an important part of this ongoing dialogue, and we look forward to your participation.

As psychologists, we have the power to bring about profound change—not only to our field but also to our broader world.

Sincerely,
APA Board of Directors
https://www.apa.org/about/apa/addressing-racism

as social justice–oriented psychologists and counselors to stay focused on our goals. Rather than focus on immediate gratification, we need to have faith and "trust the process" that the social justice action we do will led to tomorrow's change. As I (Rita) tell my students, we're "planting social justice seeds."

As we reflect back to the first edition of this volume, *Social Justice Counseling: The Next Step Toward Multiculturalism* (Sage, 2012), the field of psychology and counseling has advanced immensely by recognizing and acknowledging the necessity of providing our clients and their communities with effective social justice culturally responsive services and treatment interventions. Therefore, we have renamed this second edition *Social Justice Multicultural Psychology and Counseling*. When we first introduced the first edition for publication with a major publisher (not Sage), the prospectus was received with high expectations and a substantial advance. When we submitted the manuscript in early 2001, there were concerns about the content and its relevance to psychology. As a result, the manuscript was intentionally sent out to many more than the typical number of reviewers for a blind review. Ten reviewers responded, with a majority criticizing the social justice orientation as not being relevant to the profession. The writing style and presentation were praised, but the reviews ranged from distasteful to absolute outrage. Reviewers questioned and attacked us (the authors), condemning our character and voicing concerns that individuals who emphasized that a core component of psychology and counseling be social justice and diversity should be banned from the profession.

The publisher became nervous with the reviews and asked us to "tone it down." Dismayed by the highly personal and highly charged (blind) reviews, we decided to table the book. Although I (Rita) was shattered by the response, I also knew that the reviewers' furious and vicious attacks were signs that we (Fred and I) were on the right track. After all, doing social justice multicultural work is all about constructively challenging the status quo, rocking the boat, intentionally advocating for new and healthier positions and ideas that promote transparent, open dialogue and discussion. Since social justice mental health work is also about timing, 10 years later we approached Sage Publications with our ever-present book idea. Sage gladly published the book in 2012, and now, once again, in 2023, we are proud to be working with Oxford University Press.

As we did with the first edition, we would like to acknowledge the social justice giants and warriors whose shoulders we stand on. Their bravery, courage, tenacity, creativity, passion, and motivation inspire us to do the work that we do. In addition to the everyday heroes and heroines, we would like to acknowledge the well-known social justice and human rights warriors such as Mahatma Gandhi, Stephen Biko, Ida B. Wells, Martin Luther King, Cesar Chavez, Harriet Tubman, Sojourner Truth, Malcolm X, Yuri Kochiyama, W. E. B. Du Bois, John Lewis, Larry Itliong, Philip Vera Cruz, Harvey Milk, Marcus Garvey, Booker T. Washington, Frederick Douglass, Mary McLeod Bethune, Howard Zinn and many more. In addition, we would like to recognize those in the mental health field who have paved the way and continue to make strides in and contributions to the social justice multicultural mental health perspective. Although the names of these mental health giants are too many to list in this Introduction, we do mention these individuals throughout this volume.

In the first edition, we learned that the volume was used not only by psychology and counseling training programs, but also in social work, public health, nursing, and other helping professional training programs. The second edition is also written with an interdisciplinary perspective, using the term "mental health professionals" and "psychologists and counselors" interchangeably throughout. Furthermore, although the volume focuses primarily on U.S. demographics to illustrate social justice issues, we believe that the book is not U.S.-centric but instead generic, for global use with the appropriate insertion of statistics, data, and social justice and human rights information and examples within the context of the reader's own discipline, culture, and country. This was seen in the translation of the first edition into Korean and Turkish.

This second edition consists of a combination of updated chapters with new ideas and concepts and new chapters that focus on the effective implementation of social justice and multicultural work. Feedback from the first edition encouraged us (Rita and Fred) to place our own social justice journeys at the beginning of this volume. Thus, we begin by providing you with an understanding of how and why we became dedicated and passionate about doing social justice multicultural psychological work, as well as the origin of our ideas and concepts. After this introductory chapter, Chapter 2 is Rita's social justice narrative and Chapter 3 is Fred's social justice journey. Chapter 4 is an updated overview of social justice psychology and counseling, providing a brief historical background about the development of social justice multicultural psychology and counseling. Chapter 5 presents social justice and human rights as the fifth force in psychology and counseling. We believe it is important to know and understand the roots of social justice psychology and counseling and the events, situations, and variables that have shaped and moved psychology and counseling to address social injustices that impact our clients and their families and communities.

In the first edition, we clustered all of our graduate students' social justice journeys into one chapter. Feedback from those who used the first edition in their graduate classes suggested that we separate students' individual social justice narratives and intersperse them throughout the volume. The rationale for this suggestion was that, after reading different chapters, it would be inspirational to read about the social justice journey of a peer. We have taken their advice and interspersed the social justice narratives of ten graduate students throughout the volume, beginning with Chapter 6. Other students' social justice narratives are found in Chapters 9, 11, 13, 15, 17, 20, 22, 24, and 25. The other chapters of the volume (7, 8, 10, 12, 14, 16, 18, 19, 21, 23, and 26) relate to the skills, insight, awareness, and knowledge required for effective social justice and multicultural work, with graduate students' social justice journeys inserted between these chapters.

Chapter 7, "The Role of Social Justice Mental Health Professionals," is a new chapter focusing on an introspective self-examination of reasons why one becomes involved in social activism. The chapter challenges the reader, regardless of whether you are beginning or are already doing social justice–oriented mental health work, to undergo an in-depth self-reflection and self-examination about the motives for incorporating social justice into your professional life. Including this chapter was prompted by our witnessing mental health professionals doing social justice–oriented work with hidden agendas for personal gain, leading us to believe that honest, open, and courageous introspection is an important component to efficacious social justice and human rights mental health work. Chapter 7 ends with a discussion on what we call "social justice integrity and civility" that coincides with our belief that psychologists and counselors play an important role in modeling tolerance, respect, and civility. Modeling is especially important in an age of disrespect and intolerance of those who are different from us and in a time when character assassination, gaslighting, and even inciting and condoning violence toward those who have different values, beliefs and viewpoints is cultivated and accepted. Thus, the chapter explores ways to do effective social justice work in a divided and divisive time, examining how we maintain social justice integrity and civility when faced with negativity and hostility and challenging social justice mental health professionals to take the "social justice high road."

Chapter 8, "Unpacking the Psychological Barriers that Prevent Social Justice Action," is also a new chapter, and it continues with the theme in Chapter 7 of introspection, focusing on self-examination of the psychological barriers that prevent mental health professionals from becoming socially active in their work. The chapter discusses a number of critical obstacles that prevent mental health professionals from doing social justice–oriented work, including imposter syndrome, nice counselor syndrome, the culture of fear, the fear of litigation, the fear of failure, personal apathy, and professional paralysis. The chapter explores how, after the 9/11 terrorist attacks in the United States, a growing culture of fear spread to many facets of society, including the mental health field. Chapters 7 and 8 address how to better "know thy self" as social justice–oriented mental health professionals. Both chapters are placed early in the book so that you can identify, recognize, and understand what may hold you back from doing social justice–oriented work. Critical reflection on and consciousness about your purpose, aim, and goal of doing social justice work, as well as your own psychological barriers, are an important start in minimizing the barriers to doing social justice mental health work.

Chapter 10 is a discussion about the principles and rationale for developing the Multiphase Model (MPM) of Psychotherapy, Counseling, Human Rights, and Social Justice. The MPM is a culturally responsive model that we developed to address social justice and human rights issues in mental health. Chapter 12 provides a detailed description of the MPM.

Chapter 14, "The Critical Intersection of Social Change and Social Justice," discusses the importance of identifying, recognizing, and understanding challenges and resistance in the change process. With this knowledge, social justice–oriented mental health professionals can become savvy in adapting and developing skills, strategies, and techniques to be effective social justice change agents and advocates. The chapter explores how psychologists and counselors training to work with resistance can be utilized when facing resistance in doing social action work.

In Chapter 16, "Leadership and Social Justice," we discuss leadership styles and skills that are helpful in social justice–oriented mental health work. The chapter describes proactivity rather than reactivity and inactivity and the importance of having the skills, courage, and vision to assume leadership roles in addressing social issues that impact the psychological well-being of our clients. We also discuss social justice courage and risk-taking as major components of being a social justice leader, advocate, and change agent. Chapter 18, "Social Justice and Human Rights Advocacy in Mental Health," begins with a brief overview of the history of advocacy in psychology and counseling followed by an exploration of how to work with, rather than for, clients. Chapter 19, "The Myths and Realities of Empowerment," discusses a critical outcome of advocacy that we call *authentic empowerment*. This chapter presents 10 factors involved in fostering authentic empowerment and a case study example of social justice and authentic empowerment.

The importance of working across disciplines in doing social justice action is discussed in Chapter 21, "Interdisciplinary Collaboration as a Means of Achieving Social Justice." The chapter outlines four considerations for doing cooperative work with colleagues from other disciplines and presents guiding principles for interdisciplinary work. Chapter 23, "Creativity and Social Media as a Tool for Social Justice Advocacy and Action," is a new chapter that discusses creative social action strategies and techniques that can be utilized with diverse segments of society, such as how to work with different generations in promoting racial justice or preventing sexual assault. The chapter also includes a discussion on the use of technology and social media in doing social justice work.

Finally, we end with Chapter 26, "Self-Care: Feeding Your Soul." This chapter explores how we exercise self-care while being flexible, creative, and employing civility and integrity in the delivery of our social justice and human rights agenda. The chapter discusses how there will be times when doing social justice mental health work that we will encounter strong resistance, gaslighting, character assassination, and being devalued for our social justice values, beliefs, and efforts, thus highlighting the importance of being proactive in doing self-care. We believe self-care in social justice work is critical, so we wanted the volume to close with this theme.

We have added box texts throughout the book to prompt consideration about personal priorities that link to social justice and multicultural mental health work, and we've included inspirational stories of advocacy and change. Although not all the examples in the various box texts are directly related to mental health, they do provide suggestions and examples of social action and activism in which mental health professionals could participate and collaborate with others and/or adapt for use in their mental health work.

As the book moves into the production and publishing process we were fortunate enough to have an opportunity to do final edits. Taking full advantage of this opportunity we would like to underscore three additional social injustice and human rights violations that are occurring and again highlight the critical need for us in the mental health field to do, and continue to do social justice advocacy, action, and change. Although these events are happening in three different countries they do have a global impact and psychological repercussions regardless of where you live. The first situation is the unprovoked 2022 invasion of Ukraine by Russia. This has created major disruptions, displacement, and loss of lives for multitudes of people. Although much of the world has responded by condemning Russia and providing support to Ukraine as well as establishing quick visa access for escaping Ukrainians, it has not stopped Russia from continuing its violent attack, which has resulted in millions fleeing the country and thousands dying.

The second injustice that we would like to highlight is continued mass shootings and gun violence in the United States. Although we mention in Chapter 14 ("The Critical Intersection of Social Change and Social Justice") that there had been 693 mass shootings in the United States in 2021, the current statistics as of November 22, 2022, are similar at a figure of 601 (Ledur & Rabinowitz, 2022), or almost 13 mass shootings a week. These senseless acts of violence create fear, instability, distrust, and significant psychological distress that affects everyday life and is becoming more common as an everyday occurrence.

The third social justice situation relates to the number of Iranian women who have been murdered, raped, and sexually assaulted and are on the forefront of putting their lives at risk for actively protesting for women's rights, equality, and freedom in Iran. Their bravery has inspired numerous groups to address these issues and has brought global attention to women's rights. The 2022 protest includes schoolgirls, university students, and women and men from various ethnicities marching on the streets protesting and chanting in Kurdish and Farsi "Woman, Life, Freedom" (Begum, 2022). As the world watches these incredible girls, women, and men daringly confronting Iranian police and government officials, knowing that their action may result in death, we are in awe and inspired by their courageous action while simultaneously holding our breath in hope that they will remain physically and psychologically safe.

All three events and the others that we mentioned in this chapter and throughout the book have major impact on psychological well-being, quality of life, democracy, and physical safety. These injustices and human rights violations have a major influence on the work that we do as mental health professionals. With grave and dire events and situations such as the three mentioned here, we in the field of psychology and counseling cannot and should not turn our backs on incorporating social justice action, advocacy, and change into our culturally responsive mental health work. Certainly, new and more current human rights violations and social injustices will continue to emerge. We encourage you to reflect on these issues as you are reading this book.

Finally, we wish you success in your social justice work and journey and would like to close with two quotes. One quote is from Jane Goodall who said, "What you do makes a difference, and you have to decide what kind of difference you want to make." The second quote is from Mahatma Gandhi who said, "A small body of determined spirits fired by an unquenchable faith in their mission can alter the course of history." So always have faith that you can create social justice and change. We wish you well as you embark on your social justice human rights journey.

REFERENCES

Alter, C. (2020, May 31). America has its knee on people of color. Why George Floyd's death was a breaking point. *Time*. https://time.com/5845752/america-has-its-knee-on-us-george-floyds-death-was-a-breaking-point-protests/

BBC. (2021, Jan 7). U.S. Capitol riots: World leaders react to "horrifying" scenes in Washington. https://www.bbc.com/news/world-us-canada-55568613

Carlisle, M. (2020, May 29). Former Minneapolis police officer Derek Chauvin charged with third-degree murder and manslaughter in George Floyd's killing. *Time*. https://time.com/5844816/derek-chauvin-arrested-george-floyd-minneapolis/

Centers for Disease Control (CDC). (2021, Nov 30). Health equity considerations and racial and ethnic minority groups. https://www.cdc.gov/coronavirus/2019-ncov/community/health-equity/race-ethnicity.html

Chung, R. C-Y., Bemak, F., Ortiz, D. P., & Sandoval-Perez, P. A. (2008). Promoting the mental health of migrants: A multicultural-social justice perspective. *Journal of Counseling and Development, Multicultural and Diversity Issues in Counseling, Special Issue, 38*, 310–317. https://doi.org/10.1002/j.1556-6678.2008.tb00514.x

Cohen, Z., Grayer, A., & Nobles, R. (2021, Nov 17). What's next in the investigation of January 6. CNN. https://edition.cnn.com/2021/11/17/politics/january-6-whats-next/index.html

Ledur, J., & Rabinowitz, K. (2022, Nov 20). There have been more than 600 mass shootings so far in 2022. *Washington Post*. https://www.washingtonpost.com/nation/2022/06/02/mass-shootings-in-2022/

McEvoy, J. (2020, Jun 8). Democrats take a knee for Floyd, unveil police overhaul legislation. Forbes. https://www.forbes.com/sites/jemimamcevoy/2020/06/08/democrats-take-a-knee-for-floyd-unveil-police-overhaul-legislation/#49f4bfdf319d

Obama, M. (2018). *Becoming*. Viking Press.

Silverman, H. (2020, Jun 2). Police officers are joining protesters for prayers and hugs in several U.S. cities. CNN. https://www.cnn.com/2020/06/02/us/police-protesters-together/index.html

Washington Post. (2021, Dec 4). The attack: The Jan. 6 siege of the U.S. Capitol was neither a spontaneous act nor an isolated event. https://www.washingtonpost.com/politics/interactive/2021/jan-6-insurrection-capitol/

Williams, D. W. (2020, Jun 9). A Missouri woman asked Merriam-Webster to update its definition of racism and now officials will make the change. CNN. https://www.cnn.com/2020/06/09/us/dictionary-racism-definition-update-trnd/index.html

CHAPTER 2

JOURNEY OF AN ASIAN WOMAN HUMAN RIGHTS AND SOCIAL ACTION WARRIOR

Rita Chi-Ying Chung

Every great dream begins with a dreamer. Always remember, you have within you the strength, the patience, and the passion to reach for the stars to change the world.

—Harriet Tubman

The time is always right to do what is right.

—Martin Luther King, Jr.

WHY HUMAN RIGHTS AND SOCIAL ACTION AND NOT A DOCTOR?

I was once told by a White male friend that I had three strikes against me: (a) being Chinese, (b) being a woman, and (c) growing up in a British colony. I grew up in a traditional Chinese family where the sole ambition for girls was to get married into a respectful family. Girls getting an education was not viewed as a top priority, and if you were going to get an education, then you should be doing a degree in law, medicine, or engineering. It was difficult for my parents to understand why I wanted to study psychology: "What is psychology?" they asked, "What do you mean, you talk about emotions (which is going against cultural norms), and how much do you get paid?" Ironically, it was the values that were instilled by my parents that led me into psychology, human rights, and social justice.

This chapter contains portions of a reprint from Rita Chi-Ying Chung (2009), "Reflections of an Asian Woman Human Rights and Social Action Warrior," *Journal for Social Action in Counseling and Psychology*, 2(1), 36–43. Reprinted with permission.

I did not realize that my social injustice lesson came at such an early age until recently. I was watching a television show where someone was doing an exercise about earliest memories. At that time, I thought, "What a great exercise to do with my class." I began to think about my earliest memory. My earliest memory was a wonderful one, of holding my grandfather's hand and only being able to see his knee as I was learning how to walk. That warm memory suddenly shifted to confusion and pain. As we walked to the door of our family's fruit shop I saw my parents and aunties and uncles serving the White customers. I was probably around 18 months old and did not understand the interaction I was witnessing. But one thing was clear, even at 18 months: I was aware of how painful it was to observe the demeaning, sniggering, patronizing, and belittling behavior exhibited by the White customers to my family. This was my first memory! Unfortunately, it would not be my last memory or experience of racism, racial injustice, and oppression.

Similar to other people of color, I have had numerous experiences of racism, discrimination, and oppression. For example, my father, as a young adult, was denied entry to a movie theater, since the sign outside stated: "no dogs or Chinese," or the time when my sister was told that she could not be the valedictorian of her high school class despite her standing as the top student. The school principal harshly told my sister: "We all know that you're the best student in the school, but we can't give this status to a Chinese." The repeated messages of being inferior to White people and not seen as a human being were strongly imprinted in my mind. When it was time for me to go to school, I struggled to learn English since we spoke only Chinese at home. Being the only non–English speaker (apart from my older brother and sister) in the school, staff were not equipped to deal with this issue. With my older siblings rapidly excelling in learning English, the teachers concluded that I was cognitively impaired and told my parents that I was "slow." My parents, with minimal English, did not understand the concept so the teacher said I was "retarded." I was placed into classes with girls who were identified by the school as slow learners. The school's expectation was that we would all drop out of school by age 15, get pregnant, and get married. In that order. So, the focus of our education was to prepare us for our future as wives, teaching us how to cook, sew, clean, and grocery shop.

I did, however, manage to get into a history class, feeling excited and thinking that it was a way to change what was destined for me. Unfortunately, that decision backfired. I still have vivid memories of being 13 years old and being the only Asian student in the class. I became anxious when the teacher talked about World War II. Anticipating that there would be discussion about the Japanese participation in World War II, my main concern was that the White students would think that I was Japanese. Well, that was the least of my concerns when the history teacher asked the class, "Why do you think Chinese are yellow?" I knew immediately that this was not going to be a positive discussion. The history teacher then proudly announced to the class that "During World War II the Chinese men did not want their women and girls to be raped, so they put them in the barrels where people would urinate in and hence they became yellow."

Despite these insults and injustices, my parents, who were both refugees who escaped from the Japanese invasion in China during World War II to New Zealand, which was a British colony, instilled in my siblings and me the core values of being humble, always helping those who are less fortunate than you, treating everyone respectfully and equally regardless of their identities, and not be judgmental, selfish, arrogant, or egocentric. Coming from a Confucius and Buddhist background, we were taught the yin-yang approach to social injustices, where we were educated to be open, empathic, and humble. We learned not to complain about being ridiculed or about our experiences of racism, discrimination, inequities, and unfair treatment. Some may interpret this as passive acceptance, but the Chinese approach, which I did not understand until I was older, sees that, from this perspective, comes harmony, balance, and energy to strategize on how to effectively combat these injustices.

Being an immigrant and living in a migrant community, I became a cultural and language broker for newly arrived Chinese immigrants and Southeast Asian refugees. Not surprisingly, my personal experiences led me to help my community with the aim to minimize racism, discrimination, and oppression so that the next generation would not have to endure such injustices. To understand more about my experiences and those of my family and community, I decided to do a degree in psychology. And the psychological concepts, theories, and models of racism, hatred, prejudice, discrimination, stereotypes, forgiveness, liberation psychology and restorative justice gave me the tools, skills, strategies, and courage to combat human rights violations and social injustices. My experiences define who I am, what I stand for, and what I am willing to fight for.

Since I was a child I fought for human rights and social justice so it naturally evolved into my professional work as a psychologist. My name is Chi-Ying, literally translated, "bestowed from heaven courage," she who courageously endures nature's hardships by harmonizing with her environment (Aria & Gon, 1992). It is my karma to have experienced and endured racism, discrimination, and oppression, and I will continue to do so. But it is also my karma to learn from my experiences and move out of my traditional Chinese woman's role and cultural expectations to take a leadership role and proactively combat human rights violations and social injustices. It is my karma to weave my Asian cultural values and teachings into social action, blending the yin and yang of knowledge and action. I do not have special skills, nor am I different from other people: all I have is my passion and commitment to fight against the injustices and human rights violations I encounter for I cannot and will not be silent about these injustices. What follows is my humble story of my lessons learned as an Asian woman fighting for rights, equity, and fair treatment for *all* people.

EIGHT KEY LESSONS LEARNED AS AN ASIAN WOMAN SOCIAL JUSTICE WARRIOR

The successful outcome of social justice work does not necessarily happen within days, weeks, or months. This may take years. I truly believe in the *planting the social justice seed* analogy. I have learned to be patient and trust that what I am doing will lead to change. Change that I may never witness—and that's fine because social justice work is not about feeding my ego. So, instead of dwelling on whether I can make a difference, I trust the process and accept and feel at peace that I've done my best, regardless of the outcome. Sometimes one is unaware of the change they have made. Personally, I am endlessly surprised and humbled by emails, cards, and letters I receive from students and community members about the impact of our interactions and the change this has produced. The following are eight key critical lessons I have learned in doing social justice and human rights work, lessons that have impacted me personally and professionally: Patience, Perseverance, Tenacity, Creativity, Flexibility, Compassion, Forgiveness, and Hope.

PATIENCE, PERSEVERANCE, AND TENACITY

No one said that social justice work is easy. Change is hard for most people. The Chinese word for crisis translates into "danger and opportunity," which describes the essence of change for people and systems. Change represents a sense of fear and danger of the unknown. To be a social justice advocate requires patience along with perseverance and tenacity and the ability to continue the fight against injustice. It is all too easy to give up. When I feel that I'm not getting anywhere or don't have the energy or time to do social justice work I am reminded of the people I met after the devastation of Cyclone Nargis in Myanmar (Burma) in May 2008. The young man I worked with who lost his entire family, or the young boy who told me that while he was looking for his family member he began counting the dead bodies and gave up after he counted 200. Both of them, even with their loss of family members and the total destruction of their entire village, volunteered at a local international nongovernmental organization (INGO) to help protect orphaned minors who had lost or were separated from their families as a result of the cyclone. The courage, strength, and resilience they displayed provides me with the strength to persevere and be tenacious and patient when fighting for social justice and human rights.

CREATIVITY AND FLEXIBILITY

Thinking out of the box and being creative and flexible is another lesson I have learned. For example, working with refugee families to help access services and trying to educate host communities about the realities and needs of refugees is a challenging task. Going through traditional mainstream channels often doesn't work. Change may require one to be creative in one's attempts to receive fair treatment and equal access to resources and opportunities. For example, after spending numerous hours trying to educate social services, health and mental health professionals, teachers, and social service providers about culturally responsive practices for refugees, I realized that I was not getting anywhere. No one was willing to listen, especially since my recommendations sometimes contradicted mainstream media reports of refugees' successfully adjusting, showing photos of refugees wearing Western clothes and standing outside their new apartments, smiling and seemingly content.

Frustrated with the stereotypes and myths, I decided to use the same source, media, that created these misperceptions to promote social change and action. Looking through the major newspapers I identified and contacted journalists who reported on social justice stories and asked them if they were willing to write a more accurate account of the post-migration challenges facing refugees. After some discussion and negotiation journalists agreed to write updated stories. We (the refugee community, journalists, and myself) collectively agreed that journalists would write a series of articles over a period of several months since one article would not be enough to create the desired impact. The articles would focus not only on the challenges, but also on the strength and resilience of this population and the contributions of refugees to their communities. As the result of the newspaper articles I was approached by the Departments of Health, Education, and Social Services to conduct a series of workshops and training for health and mental health professionals, social services, and other care providers regarding culturally responsive services for refugees.

Another social justice situation that required creativity involved traditional indigenous approaches to health and mental health. Some Asian cultures use "coining" as a healing method, which is a form of dermabrasion therapy. This ancient treatment method is still widely used to rid the body of "heat" or "negative energies." The method uses a coin to rub on the person's body, resulting in marks and bruises on the skin. These marks have been misinterpreted by mainstream Western health and mental health and educational professionals as signs of abuse. I have been asked numerous times by the Asian community to assist in situations where a child had been removed from their parent's home because teachers mistakenly identified the coining marks as physical abuse, or physicians saw coining marks on the elderly and perceived this as signs of elder abuse. To avoid erroneous interpretation of coining, in collaboration with community members and medical providers, a training video was produced to educate service providers about this Asian healing method (see Box Text).

COMPASSION AND FORGIVENESS

A difficult lesson for me regarding human rights violations and social injustices is to have compassion and forgiveness for perpetrators. I have learned from sex trafficking survivors a valuable lesson of forgiveness and compassion. I'm truly humbled when they share with me their ability to forgive their perpetrators for the atrocities that they have endured. This demonstrates for me genuine kindness and an authentic sense of humanity. It is not for me to judge others, but instead to understand the behaviors and motivation in why and how people participate and engage in injustices. If the survivors I work with can forgive and have compassion for their perpetrators, then I, as a social justice–oriented psychologist, also need to have those qualities and must embrace the value of wide-ranging forgiveness and compassion. This, I must admit, I'm still working on.

HOPE

A major lesson I have learned is the degree of hope individuals have, as well as the need for psychologists and counselors to instill hope in clients. Time and time again, working with clients who have survived genocide, atrocities, traumas of war, human trafficking, or devastating natural disasters such as, tsunamis, cyclones, hurricanes, earthquakes, and wildfires, I am always surprised and humbled by the degree of hope and resiliency shown by survivors. For example, driving up to the American Indian reservation in San Diego, California, where a large portion of the reservation was totally destroyed by the 2007 wildfires, there was a sign written in charcoal at the entry saying "We Believe in Miracles." The same degree of

BOX TEXT 2.1 COLLABORATIVE PARTNERSHIP AND EMPOWERMENT IN EDUCATING ABOUT TRADITIONAL HEALING PRACTICE

A major concern was raised in the Asian community regarding reports of child and elderly abuse as a result of bruises on the body that were discovered by teachers, doctors, and social workers. As a result, some children were taken from their parents' homes by social welfare and child protective services (CPS) and investigations were initiated for elderly abuse. The bruises were found to be a result of *coining*, a traditional healing method used in some Asian cultures. Coining does leave bruises on the body and may be misinterpreted by some as abuse. To ensure that this situation did not reoccur, the Asian community decided that an educational video would be made and distributed. I contacted film companies and asked if they could make the video at a reduced fee. Having read the article in the newspaper regarding challenges in psychosocial adjustment with refugees, a film company agreed to make the video and copies for distribution free of charge. I worked in partnership with the community to make a 15-minute video to educate teachers, health professionals, CPS, law enforcement, and other service providers about coining and its potential for misinterpretation. The video included medical experts and community and spiritual leaders describing the long-standing tradition of coining, as well as teachers talking about their experience with coining and how it could be mistaken for abuse. The video also showed a child being coined by a community member. Community members were involved in the video to explain the coining process and how its patterns of bruising differ from those of child abuse and other forms of violence. The video was used for training in community agencies and by local universities in their medical, social work, counseling, psychology, public health, and teacher training programs.

In addition, with the assistance of a local nonprofit agency, I developed lists of culturally sensitive health and mental health professionals, bilingual and bicultural translators, and other relevant resources within the area. The lists were translated into various Asian and other languages and distributed to community members.

This case study is an example of using multiple strategies in social justice work. It illustrates the importance of working in partnership with individual clients, families, and communities. Also, with community input and major involvement in making the video, community members felt empowered by using their voices to educate about their traditional healing methods. It is while working with this cooperative involvement that workers for human rights and social justice can effectively address prevention and intervention from a holistic and ecological standpoint.

hope was also witnessed in Mississippi after Hurricane Katrina. Driving to areas most severely hit by the hurricane, I saw signs on the road that said "Together, We will rebuild our community, Together, We will support each other, Together, We will lead the way." Outcome research attributes hope to 15% of successful counseling and psychotherapy (Lambert & Bergin, 1994). Having witnessed the degree of hope with the populations that I have worked with, I would say that hope is, in many cases, much more than 15%. Psychologists and counselors can contribute to their clients' hope and resiliency by having hope in and for their clients, their families and communities as well as having the ability to instill hope.

IMPLEMENTATION OF THE EIGHT LESSONS TO SOCIAL JUSTICE WORK

Working with girls who have been trafficked into the sex industry promotes the same themes of resiliency, strength, hope, and forgiveness. I had the privilege to be asked by an INGO to work on the prevention of child trafficking and child protection. For three years, I have worked in urban cities and rural villages in Myanmar. where there are minimal resources. Much of my time was spent in villages without electricity, running water, toilets, or showers. In these villages, people have never seen anyone who is not Burmese. The living conditions are minimal, with people sleeping on mats on dirt or rough wooden floors. Some huts just have a roof and no walls or doors. Not being a fan of camping, this experience has led me to put aside my personal comforts in life and focus on the purpose of my work.

I have been holding village-wide meetings with 100–300 people on issues of human trafficking and child protection. For some villagers, this is the first time they have heard of these concepts, although human trafficking and child abuse and violence are widespread. Patience, perseverance, tenacity, flexibility, and creativity are needed in educating illiterate people living in constant and extremely high poverty at the edge of humanity, people who regularly beat and—to survive—sell their children. The INGO taught the children to use political theater to educate their parents and village members about their experiences of physical abuse and being sold. As the children acted out their experiences to the entire village, there were tears and emotional reactions by villagers. This was the first time that children voiced to their parents, elders, and village members their experiences of violence, trafficking, and abuse. Utilizing my cross-cultural skills in communication, group dynamics, and group process, I worked in collaboration with the children and village members to further educate and promote prevention of child trafficking, child labor, and violence.

After the children performed their social justice theater, we (the children, village members, INGO staff, and myself) would sit on the ground for hours as I facilitated a community brainstorming session focused on how parents could stop beating their children. Mothers sat crying, realizing for the first time the effects of their beatings on their children. The community talked and shared ideas on alternatives to beatings if their children were naughty. Children shared their ideas with their parents about what they believed could be effective discipline as an alternative to beatings and gave suggestions about how parents could interact with them if they were naughty. Leaving the village there were promises of child protection rather than child abuse. This all takes patience, and the results are not necessarily immediate. After a few months, on going back to one village for follow-up, a mother rushed toward me and, in front of the entire village, proudly announced "I no longer beat my child five times a week, I only beat him three times a week." For the child, the mother, and the villagers, that was progress. Both mother and child have hope that things will be different. The child forgives the mother for all the previous severe beatings he endured and now promises to try to be a better child. This was a lesson for the entire village.

The mother began talking to other parents about alternative ways of releasing anger and frustration rather than beating their children. There is collective hope, collective forgiveness, and community healing in the village. Children in the village were given a voice, both adults and children know of the United Nations Child Rights Convention (CRC), and there is a collective and genuine intention to implement the CRC at the village level. A child protection committee was formed in the village that consisted of elders, village members, and children to ensure that the CRC is upheld. This is just one example of how change can occur on individual, family, and community levels as an outcome of social action. On a systemic level, in collaboration with the INGO, we held meetings with village leaders, spiritual leaders, township authorities, the local police, and the Myanmar social welfare and health officers on prevention of child trafficking and child protection.

In summary, I will not mislead you and tell you that doing social justice is easy and that you will not encounter barriers or resistance. Social justice advocacy works to intentionally challenge the status quo, the "usual" ways of doing things, and to "rock the boat," which will elicit fear, uncertainties, anxieties, and evoke strong negative emotional reactions from others. Not everyone will understand what you're doing, nor will they agree with you. You may lose friends, family members, and colleagues, and experience disappointment when those you think will "have your back" and stand by your side fail to support you. There may be frustration and exhaustion, raising questions like, "Why am I doing this?" At these moments I find it is important to remind myself of the simple answer: "I'm working toward creating a socially just world for all. Not just for my generation, but my children's generation, and generations after that." The important thing is to keep an eye on the prize and trust that change will come, even though you may not see it in your lifetime. Trust the social justice process. At the same time surround yourself with social support systems and always remember to "feed your soul" by practicing self-care. I hope my narrative has provided ideas for you on how to move social justice and human rights knowledge and passion to action. I pass on to you the eight key valuable lessons I have learned from my social action work: Patience, Perseverance, Tenacity, Creativity, Flexibility, Compassion, Forgiveness, and Hope. I wish all the best on your social justice journey, planting social justice seeds and developing the social justice warrior within you.

REFERENCES

Aria, B., & Gon, R. E. (1992). *The spirit of the Chinese character: Gifts from the heart.* Chronicle Books.

Lambert, M. J., & Bergin, A. E. (1994). The effectiveness of psychotherapy. In A. E. Bergin & S. L. Garfield (Eds.), *Handbook of psychotherapy and behavior change* (pp. 143–189). Wiley.

CHAPTER 3

THE ROOTS OF SOCIAL JUSTICE

The Personal Journey of a Human Rights Advocate

Frederic P. Bemak

> Injustice anywhere is a threat to justice everywhere.
>
> —Martin Luther King, Jr.
>
> A "No" uttered from the deepest conviction is better than a "Yes" merely uttered to please, or worse, to avoid trouble.
>
> —Mahatma Gandhi

When I reflect on my lifetime work in social justice I realize that the values and sense of action were simply underpinnings of my life from a young age. Although "social justice" was not the term that was used to characterize my earlier life, it was the essence of the values that I had been brought up with and that were espoused in my family. My grandfather, a Russian immigrant, had been a union organizer, fighting for worker's rights. Interestingly, he maintained the values of concern and fairness for workers even when he later became a manager and owned his own shoe factories. His beliefs and his tenacity about fairness, equity, human rights dignity, and privilege remained the heartbeat of my family ethos.

Along with my grandfather's core beliefs were those of my parents', who were young and rebellious. We learned not to care about material goods, enjoyed protest singers such as Pete Seeger, and learned to question things that did not make sense. Already, at the age of 11, I had been reading and thinking about the merits of socialism and communism that

This chapter contains portions of a reprint from Fred Bemak (2009), "The roots of social justice: The personal journey of a human rights advocate," *Journal for Social Action in Counseling and Psychology, 2*(1), 36–43. Reprinted with permission.

might be helpful to those less fortunate in the United States and had already identified my favorite magazine as *National Geographic* and one of my favorite books as a Time/Life *Book on World Religions*, both of which provided fascinating exposure to other cultures and diverse viewpoints. An early experience occurred when there was a clash with these values in my advanced 6th-grade class. All the students in the class knew we were different from other 6th graders, and we received constant messages that we were being primed for successful futures. It was clear to the entire school that those in the advanced class were identified as future leaders and were being given special treatment, special coursework, and special attention. It was also clear that we were to become leaders who would maintain the status quo. Interestingly the teacher selected to teach us was a devout and overly zealous former U.S. Marine officer who saw very little beyond his U.S. military view of the world and U.S. philosophical, scientific, and military domination. An example of his worldview was his selection for the class annual field trip. Rather than visit a famous museum or historical site or attend a cultural event in New York City, 1 hour away, he chose to visit the U.S. Naval Academy in Annapolis, Maryland, which was a 10-hour round-trip journey.

In class one day, my teacher was once again berating cultures, religions, and political thinking not consistent with U.S. mainstream thought as "horrible, bad, and evil." Reflecting about my readings and discussions at home with my parents and thinking about my grandfather's Russian background, I raised my hand and shared a different point of view about other cultures. Questioning my teacher resulted in difficulties for me for the remainder of the school year. Despite being popular and having many friends, my teacher from that point on clearly felt that I would not make a "good Marine" and should not be part of the "club." The sense of devaluation and criticism did little to diminish my strong social network or critical thinking, thus laying a foundation for continued reflection, an even greater conviction in not taking statement as fact, and questioning that which did not make sense. This 6th-grade experience set the tone. Several years later, in 11th grade, I found myself in the midst of a controversy in my high school. All my classmates were complaining about the lunchroom food. While I was eating horrible-tasting cafeteria food filled with sugar and starch, I was also learning about leaders and heroes, such as Martin Luther King Jr., Mahatma Gandhi, and John F. Kennedy, who were fighting for civil rights and human rights. They were standing up to make a difference in worlds much larger than my high school. To top it off, astronauts had reached the moon, so anything seemed possible. Leaders, change, rights, justice—all of these concepts were swirling around in my 16-year-old mind, giving me a glimpse of higher mountains and the possibility of dreams actually coming true! With this in mind, and facing the daily dread of lunch with my classmates, I organized my high school's first sit-in to protest the lunch food.

Amazingly I couldn't find one classmate who disagreed that we were eating horrible, tasteless food, and that "Yes, we should do something about it!" Many of my peers joined in the protest, sitting in the high school campus courtyard, refusing to go to class, testing the parameters of possibilities, and flexing our muscles to see if we might also be able to change the world. Very quickly an irate school administration squashed our protest, ordered students back to class under the threat of suspension, singled out the ring leaders (two others and me), called my parents, and angrily brought me to the office. With a serious threat of high school suspension hanging over my head, a new awareness about personal commitment to one's strongly felt beliefs and convictions, a sense of isolation (yes,

my classmates all scurried back to class while I remained protesting), an evolving understanding about power in action, a new level of experiencing some of the ins and outs of
leadership, and the accompanying knowledge that the cafeteria food was still, in fact, horrible, I began to more clearly define what I believed in, what I stood for, and who I was as a
person. As my classmates complained about their impotence and lack of ability to change
things, I was formulating my own path and sense of self as it related to fighting for equal
rights, fairness, equity, and social justice. Thus, my social justice march crystallized at the
age of 16 with bad food and autocratic administrators, as I began to learn lessons about social change, equity, equal rights, dignity, tolerance, and human rights. It is no surprise that
I soon became involved in civil rights, working with African American youth and families in
Roxbury, Massachusetts, during the late 1960s, as a university student. My work in Roxbury
was accompanied by protesting against civil rights violations and the Vietnam War, a personal refusal to fight in an unjust war in Vietnam, and working as a summer counselor at the
University of Massachusetts (UMass), Amherst, Upward Bound Program, which was a project that was part of President John F. Kennedy's national War on Poverty. Upward Bound
was a fertile ground in which to live and breathe interracial understanding and tolerance
and figure out how to create an intensive 8- to 10-week summer cross-cultural community
residential program with low-income academically failing Black, Hispanic, and White high
school students, many of whom had never been in contact with people from other races or
ethnicities. We were a microcosm community struggling with interracial tensions, Black
Power, migrant Hispanic communities, English language learners, the devastating effects of
poverty, and generations of racism and discrimination as we worked daily with the struggles
of the youth and staff in the program and our community's trials and tribulations.

After receiving my undergraduate degree, I was invited to work full time in the Upward
Bound Program, expanding the student focus of my summer counseling job to working
directly with the families, communities, and schools where, on a daily basis, I encountered
issues of poverty, injustice, discrimination, and racism. Simultaneously I attended graduate
school at UMass, where I tried to meld the world of higher education with the daily realities
of the Upward Bound experience. The merging of work life and graduate student life was
fascinating. One day I would find myself in Washington DC in meetings on Capitol Hill
to negotiate budget and project parameters, or in the University President's office talking
about the program's achievements and community initiatives. The next day I would be at
a local community center in the inner city with Upward Bound students and their parents
and grandparents to discuss advocacy strategies for their children at the local high school
when they were denied services, resources, or enrollment access to college-bound classes.
In the middle of days like this, I would attend classes where many of my classmates had neither experience with nor knowledge about the real workings of social justice, human rights,
human dignity, multiculturalism, racism, or oppression.

Five years into this experience, at the age of 26, I found myself as one of the youngest
Upward Bound Project Directors in the country with an earned doctoral degree. The Upward
Bound experience set the stage for my life's work. Moving between high-level national and
state policy and budget meetings to grassroots organizing and community work became
a necessary and critical skill to promote social change and the values of social justice that
were now part of my being. Understanding differences, the pain and anger associated with
injustice, the firm conviction to take risks, and my growing skills as a leader and advocate

were all formed during my years in Upward Bound. This experience was enriched by other major personal and professional journeys, such as leaving Upward Bound and spending one year with a backpack traveling on local buses and trains in developing countries around the world, helped me gain a far deeper appreciation of cultural differences and a much broader worldview.

Other experiences followed in which I carried the same convictions and values, such as directing a model national mental health pilot community-based project for deinstitutionalized youth; assuming the position as Clinical Director for a National Institute of Mental Health (NIMH)-funded consortium providing national consultation and training to a wide variety of community-based programs; creating Counselors Without Borders, a nonprofit organization to do post-disaster counseling work (see Box Text 3.1); and receiving several significant cross-cultural international awards to undertake research and scholarship in other countries (e.g., Fulbright Scholarships in Brazil, Scotland, Turkey, and Malta; International Exchange of Experts Research Fellow in India; Kellogg Foundation International Leadership and Development for two and half years throughout Latin America and the Caribbean; Visiting Faculty appointments in Australia, Brazil, Canada, Malta, Mexico, and Taiwan). These experiences helped solidify a long-term commitment for my life's social justice work. I have done consultation and training throughout the United States, as well as worked in 65 countries, focusing on issues of mental health and social justice. My research and scholarship continue to focus on mental health, social justice, and human rights related to youth and families at risk and migrants and has been conducted both throughout the United States and internationally. The key focus of my research has been an intersection in the areas of social justice and human rights, cross-cultural mental health, poverty, human trafficking, refugees, academic achievement and equity for all students, homelessness, separated and vulnerable children, immigrants and refugees, street children, child soldiers, and post-disaster mental health.

It remains somewhat unclear how this happens, but, at any given time in my career, there are multiple activities on my plate, all related to my work and rooted in social justice. Each of us must find our own style and pace, and I have always felt comfortable with having multiple activities going on at one time.

In hopes that it might be helpful for you in crafting out your own social justice journey and commitment, please allow me to describe what is going on for me currently in terms of my social justice work. I should also add, before sharing what I am doing at this moment, that this is a fairly standard pace I typically maintain, although as Professor Emeritus I could easily have chosen not to do this work. It is also striking to me that I rarely seek out these activities but that, most often, they come in the form of invitations or requests. I imagine that the bottom line is the passion and commitment to change and improve the human condition, rather than any other extrinsic reward, which has been a fairly constant theme during my career and is, in my opinion, related to the continued stream of invitations and opportunities. My firm conviction and belief is that this will be true for your work as well, that, as you pursue social justice for the work itself, opportunities expand and snowball so that you are able to contribute more and help with changes that are beneficial on multiple levels.

That being said, here is what is happening at the moment in my social justice work as a recently retired professor. As I write this chapter, the second visit to Malta has been

BOX TEXT 3.1 COUNSELORS WITHOUT BORDERS POST-DISASTER WORK IN HAITI

Counselors Without Borders (CWB) is a nonprofit organization that I had founded in 2005 to respond to Hurricane Katrina. It later expanded to address other national and international crises, such as the California wildfires, Cyclone Nargis in Myanmar, the earthquake in Haiti, the tsunami in Thailand, Hurricane Maria in Puerto Rico and working with asylum seekers along the Texas and Mexican border. This example will focus on CWB's work in Haiti.

The 2010 Haiti earthquake is listed as one of the top five deadliest earthquakes in the world, affecting the entire country, destroying buildings, killing and injuring hundreds of thousands of people, and leaving well over 1 million people homeless. Following the earthquake, there was a tremendous need for psychosocial support focused on working with trauma and posttraumatic stress disorder (PTSD). I was asked and funded by USAID three months after the earthquake to take a CWB team to Haiti to do post-disaster training for school personnel and mental health community-based professionals as well as to provide counseling to those living in make-shift disaster tents.

We began our training in a Port-au-Prince school, where only a portion of the school buildings remained standing. Invited to the training were directors and head masters from eight schools around the capital city and numerous school administrators. Since there are no mental health professionals in Haitian schools, it was common practice for the administrators to provide counseling for students. The training reviewed how to provide psychosocial support for traumatized students, parents, and staff and helped design a plan of intervention. Simultaneously, as frequently happens in post-disaster situations, we also helped administrators cope with their own personal and family trauma. The two-day training was followed by direct counseling interventions by the CWB team for the next few days. While the CWB team was doing counseling interventions, they were shadowed by school administrators who observed how to implement the Disaster Cross-Cultural Counseling (DCCC) model (Bemak & Chung, 2011). The direct counseling was done with students (individuals, families, and groups), parents (individuals, families, and groups), and staff (individuals and groups). Following the direct counseling interventions, CWB staff met with school administrators to provide supervision and consultation.

Similar training was done at other community sites with psychologists and social workers who, although they were trained in their respective disciplines, did not have any training in or skills for working in post-disaster situations. In addition, we were also asked to counsel those living in the make-shift disaster tent communities who were identified as having extreme trauma and difficulty coping with the aftermath of the earthquake. All of the training and counseling was done within a culturally responsive social justice framework, taking into account reactions to the anger and frustration at the lack of political response to the disaster, the economic concerns that were raised, apprehension about housing and medical care, cultural beliefs and practices about healing, and interest in advocating for better, more responsive services and support.

Sources: https://www.counselorswithoutborders.org/
Bemak, F., & Chung, R. C-Y. (2011). Post-disaster social justice group work and group supervision. *Journal for Specialists in Group Work, 36*(1), 3–21. https://doi.org/10.1080/01933922.2010.537737

confirmed for a Fulbright Specialist Award to work with the University of Malta and the Malta Ministry of Health and Ministry of Education to provide consultation, training, and presentations related to the mental health treatment of North African refugees; have received an appointment at the University of Malta as Affiliate Professor; am providing weekly clinical supervision for a psychologist in Dubai; am co-investigator of a Simon Fraser University, Canada, grant funded by the Canadian government doing global research on refugee mental health and disabilities that involves international consultation and research in Jordan, Kazakhstan, and Canada; am preparing to deliver a keynote address for a national conference on healing in a broken world in the United States; recently published an article in the *International Review of Psychiatry*; am considering a part-time appointment at a university in New Zealand to help infuse ideas about social justice and human rights into its curriculum; confirming a visit and possible faculty appointment at a university in Malaysia to provide training in post-disaster counseling; finalizing a grant to provided culturally responsive mental health training in Kenya; and have been providing consultation to establish mental health programming and support in Ukraine and Turkey.

In summary, I truly enjoy my professional life and continue to be active in retirement. It is no longer work, but a melding of social justice work and life. Days unfold that provide an avenue for my commitment and passion to social justice and social change that will play a small part in trying to help and improve our world. I would like to leave you with a small story that had significant impact on my social justice work and that may have some relevance for you. It is a story that I often come back to when thinking about what we each can do and how each of us can contribute to social justice work. Earlier in my career I was working in Nicaragua, providing consultation to the Ministry of Health. This was after the civil war in Nicaragua, and, as always happens, there were many orphans as a result of the war. I was sitting with the national Minister of Health and the national Director of Mental Health discussing staffing structures that would be most helpful in meeting the needs of orphaned children. It was quite an experience, feeling like I was having a national impact and helping to craft a national strategy.

The very next day, staff from the major mental health hospital wanted to take me out to a remote village to observe the success of an aftercare program and meet a former inpatient client. Our drive took us on smaller and smaller roads until we finally stopped at the edge of a jungle. Leaving the car, we began walking through banana groves, through rice fields, past small shacks, and over muddy rivers. As we walked I remember vividly thinking that I was truly in a remote corner of the world and surely near the "end of the earth." When we finally arrived at a small village, I met the former client and his family. He had been given a scissors and comb and taught how to cut hair while in the mental health institution. Upon returning to his community, he set up a small barbering practice with the help of an old weather-beaten chair and broken mirror under an old tree that provided a little shade. As I spoke to him and his family, villagers quickly gathered around, and the encounter quickly turned into a family therapy/community intervention session.

As our time ended, the former client and his family expressed tremendous gratitude for our discussion and talked about how much better they felt after our meeting. It was at that moment that I had a profound realization: it truly did not matter if I was speaking with the Minister of Health to develop an entire national system or helping one single person living in the jungle at the "end of the world." The experiences, the work, the emphasis on social justice were exactly the same—one person or an entire country. Whatever and wherever we have the capacity to help is exactly where we need to be. This lesson was a lesson well learned: I am fine sitting in a corner speaking with an individual in need of mental health and social justice support, help, and assistance or working with a national government to craft policy change about major global social justice issues. Social justice is social justice is social justice, and each of us has a part to play. Peace be with you.

FURTHER READING

Bemak, F., & Chung, R. C.-Y. (2011). Social justice group work and group supervision in post-disaster situations. *Journal for Specialists in Group Work, 36*(1), 3–21. https://doi.org/10.1080/01933922.2010.537737

Bemak, F., Chung, R. C.-Y., & Sirosky-Sabdo, L. A. (2005). Empowerment groups for academic success (EGAS): An innovative approach to prevent high school failure for at-risk urban African American girls. *Professional School Counseling, 8*(5), 377–389. https://www.jstor.org/stable/42732475?seq=1

Conyne, R., & Bemak, F. (2004). Teaching group work from an ecological perspective. *Journal for Specialists in Group Work, 29*(1), 7–18. https://doi.org/10.1080/01933920490275312

CHAPTER 4

SOCIAL JUSTICE MULTICULTURAL PSYCHOLOGY AND COUNSELING

Theories and Concepts

Rita Chi-Ying Chung and Frederic P. Bemak

The Constitution itself. Its language is "we the people"; not we the white people, not even we the citizens, not we the privileged class, not we the high, not we the low, but we the people; Not we the horses, sheep, and swine, and wheel-barrows, but we the people, we the human inhabitants.

—Frederick Douglass

If you want happiness for an hour—take a nap. If you want happiness for a day—go fishing. If you want happiness for a year—inherit a fortune. If you want happiness for a lifetime—help someone else.

—Chinese proverb

Justice will not come ... until those who are not injured are as indignant as those who are.

—Thucydides (c. 460–400 BC)

REFLECTION QUESTIONS

1. When you were a high school or secondary school student, did you ever observe a social injustice? Do you remember what you thought and felt? Did you do anything? Why or why not?
2. Are there social injustices that you wish you could change? If so, what are they?

3. Civil rights leaders; outspoken critics of war, slavery, and oppression; leaders of the women's movement; advocates for the poor and disenfranchised; activists promoting LGBTQI rights; environmental activists; and so many others have taken major steps that frequently placed themselves in danger and at high levels of risk. To what degree would you "step out" and place yourself at risk to fight for a social justice issue you believe in?

Many of us who enter the mental health profession arrive with an awareness of a variety of social injustices such as xenophobia, sexism, poverty, discrimination, racial injustice, gun violence, global warming, environmental racism, and gender-based violence, etc. Our intent entering the helping profession is to assist clients, their families, and communities to heal from painful problems, many of which involve violations of justice and human rights. To keep up to date, the psychology and counseling fields promote continuous education and discussions regarding best practices in meeting the changing needs of our clients. For example, as the United States became more racially and ethnically diverse, the American Psychological Association (APA) and the American Counseling Association (ACA) developed and incorporated multicultural guidelines and competencies. As we strive to be relevant for current and future clients, it is essential that we in the helping profession are aware, recognize, understand, and acknowledge the lived experiences of clients, their families, and communities within a macro ecological social justice and human rights context. This involves examining clients' issues and concerns from psychopolitical, cultural, historical, and psychosocial perspectives.

Social justice has been coined as the "fifth force" in psychology and counseling (Pack-Brown et al., 2008; Ratts et al., 2004), with psychodynamic counseling as the first influence, cognitive-behavioral the second, humanistic-existential as the third, and multicultural counseling as the fourth force (Singh et al., 2020). As we incorporate issues of social justice and human rights into our work, it requires us to move beyond the traditional therapeutic framework to proactively prevent and intervene in injustices encountered by our clients. When writing the first edition of this volume, the term "social justice" was not found in the mental health vernacular or dictionaries. Now, 10 years later, social justice is defined by Merriam-Webster online dictionary (n.d.) as *a state or doctrine of egalitarianism*. As the definition suggests social justice work in the helping professions addresses issues of power, privilege, prejudice, and biases with an aim to establish an equal and equitable playing field that promotes fair access to resources and opportunities for all. Thus, it is important to address issues of equity, equality, and fairness on the individual micro level, as well as on the meso (community) and macro (society) levels, by intentionally and proactively challenging the status quo, with the goal of dismantling oppressive structural and systemic systems that perpetuate unfairness and injustice and negatively impact psychological well-being.

As we discuss the critical need to incorporate social justice into our work it is important to gain an understanding of the origins and history of social justice in psychology and counseling. Social justice became more prominent after multicultural counseling was identified as the fourth force in the field and following the establishment of multicultural guidelines and competencies. Given that social justice is at the very heart of multicultural psychology and counseling, the next section provides a brief overview of multicultural psychology and counseling, the development of the multicultural guidelines and competencies, and the relationship between multicultural psychology and counseling and social justice.

BRIEF HISTORICAL OVERVIEW OF MULTICULTURAL PSYCHOLOGY AND COUNSELING IN RELATION TO SOCIAL JUSTICE

Multiculturalism is not a new or recent concept. For centuries, dating back to ancient civilizations, people recognized barriers, challenges, and potential problems in communicating and interacting with those from different cultural backgrounds (Jackson, 1995). One difference with the past is that cultural diversity has expanded globally and can be found in varying degrees throughout the world. Given globalization, global warming, and the advancement of technology, there is a rapid expansion of cultures across national and international borders, with vast movements of people voluntarily and involuntarily migrating to different states, regions, and countries. Consequently, multiculturalism is not only a worldwide phenomenon, but also a multifaceted and multidimensional issue, and it can result in xenophobia and intolerance of differences. With the recognition of the dramatically changing racial, ethnic, and cultural demographics in the United States and around the world, the mental health field has paid increasing attention to the influence of culture on clients. Given that our families, communities, schools, and areas where we live will be affected by growing cultural differences, there is a greater likelihood that we, in the mental health field, will see clients from racial, ethnic, and cultural backgrounds that differ from our own, making it essential that we are recognize and understand the complexity and influence that multiculturalism has on both our clients and ourselves as mental health professionals.

The history of multicultural psychology and counseling spans several decades. In the 1950s, there were few journal articles on this topic. During that period, scholars of color faced barriers to publishing in professional journals that were dominated by a small group of European American, nationally known authors, coupled with a general lack of interest in multicultural and cross-cultural issues (Walsh, 1975). In the 1960s and 1970s, psychopolitical and sociopolitical events and conscious raising grew throughout the United States and in some parts of the world as a result of simultaneous events during that time, such as the anti-Vietnam War, civil rights, gay rights, and the feminist movements. A new political and social critical consciousness of racism, prejudice, biases, discrimination, privilege, and power influenced counselors and psychologists to reexamine the mental health field in relationship to social injustices, thus generating increased professional interest in the development of multicultural psychology and counseling. Notions such as the inferiority of people of color, differences of diverse groups, and the superiority of the majority White culture were questioned (Jackson, 1995). During this era, multicultural psychology and counseling blossomed, in part due to support and cooperation by White mental health professionals who had acquired a new sense of awareness and sensitivity to unfair treatment, inequities, and racial injustice. Questions were raised regarding whether psychological and counseling theories, models, strategies, interventions, and techniques that were based on European American traditions could be applicable to clients from different ethnic, racial, and cultural backgrounds.

Adding to this awareness and cultural sensitivity were increased higher education opportunities for people of color and culturally diverse groups, as well as a growing interest in working in the helping professions by these populations. This resulted in a group of racially and culturally diverse helping professionals trained during this time period raising questions about the responsiveness of the profession to cultural differences in an increasingly diverse population (Aubrey, 1971). The impetus established in the 1960s continued into the 1970s, with researchers increasingly investigating multicultural and cross-cultural issues in counseling and psychotherapy. Funding from the federal and state governments and private foundations promoted a surge of rapid growth in cross-cultural and multicultural research in the 1980s and 1990s. This growth continued into the 21st century, with professionals conducting research and writing about diversity and multicultural issues in record numbers (Jackson, 1995).

At the same time, communities of color and diverse populations were gaining a heightened awareness and understanding of the challenges they were encountering (Atkinson & Hackett, 2004). This critical consciousness led to mental health professionals developing greater knowledge and skills to more effectively respond to cultural differences, thus gaining a better understanding of how clients' and therapists' cultural backgrounds, power, biases, prejudice, and privilege contributed to the therapeutic relationship. As a result, there was an increase in multicultural psychology and counseling training (Kiselica et al., 1999), with a rapid emergence of new courses from 1991 to 1995 (Hollis & Wantz, 1994), leading us to our current practices in the 21st century. Given the importance and profound impact of multicultural psychology and counseling, the term "fourth force" was coined to describe the profession's theory (Pedersen, 1991). This underscored the importance of culture as central and complementary in relationship to the other three major theories or "forces." The steady growth in research and the recognition of the importance of culturally responsiveness to all psychological work lays a clear foundation for multicultural psychology and counseling as the fourth force.

The interest in developing culturally responsive and inclusive psychological interventions grew from criticism of the Western colonization of psychology. This is illustrated when we examine the evolution of multicultural psychology while considering three models with differing cultural viewpoints and belief systems. The *genetic deficiency model* purports that people of color are intellectually inferior to White European Americans. Initially, this view was supported by Arthur Jensen's studies (e.g., Jensen, 1969; Nyborg & Jensen, 2000) who examined differences between African Americans' and Whites' levels of intelligence and was later supported by the concept of the *bell curve* (Hernstein & Murray, 1994). Although these theories promoting a view of inferior intelligence based on race were very popular at one time, it is important to be aware that Jensen's studies have been discredited, while Hernstein and Murray's findings are disputed (Valencia & Suzuki, 2001).

The *cultural deficiency model* takes a monocultural view that assumes all people are the same (or should be the same) and hold similar cultural beliefs, values, attitudes, and worldviews. In this model, the majority European American White cultural group in Western developed countries is considered the baseline for comparisons with all other culturally diverse groups. Standards for all other cultural groups are viewed as culturally deprived or deficient if they do not measure up to the baseline standards of European Americans. Hence, people of color, immigrant and refugee populations, those with linguistic differences, LGBTQI populations, those with differing abilities, those who identity with non-Christian religions, and other diverse populations who are not part of the European American mainstream, are seen as culturally deprived and lacking the attributes of the majority culture. This perspective provides a basis for therapeutic encounters that are highly ethnocentric, with narrow beliefs that reinforce and advocate for the superiority of one group.

The third model, the *culturally diverse model*, supports the concept of multicultural counseling and cultural differences. Being from a cultural group other than the mainstream dominant culture is not seen as a limitation or disadvantage. In this model, one is not judged from the perspective of White European Americans or the majority culture, so that differences are not viewed as deficiencies, weakness, or flaws. Instead, diverse cultural perspectives are valued, respected, and appreciated. Therefore, the culturally diverse model, with its focus on multiculturalism, does not view cultural differences as debilitating, as the two previous models do, but rather as positive, healthy, vital, and indispensable components of society (Robinson & Howard-Hamilton, 2000). The culturally diverse model embraces multiculturalism, supporting, valuing, respecting, and appreciating racial, ethnic, gender, sexual orientation, religion, abilities, socioeconomic status, and other cultural differences. Helping professionals who adhere to this model recognize that cultural differences should be acknowledged and celebrated, and they bring this value into their work.

THE DEVELOPMENT OF MULTICULTURAL GUIDELINES AND COMPETENCIES

During the past few decades there has been a substantial increase in the literature about multicultural psychology and counseling training, practice, and research. The world of counseling and psychotherapy has been comprehensively examined and critiqued through a multicultural lens. For example, authors have addressed issues such as acculturation (e.g., Berry, 2015; Chun et al., 2002; Sam & Berry, 2006); cultural barriers to accessing mainstream mental health services (e.g., U.S. Department of Health and Human Services [U.S. DHHS], 2001); cross-cultural trust and empathy (Chung & Bemak, 2002); the concept of worldviews (Ibrahim et al., 2001); racial, ethnic, and White identity (e.g., Cross, 1995; Cross & Vandiver, 2001; Helms, 1995; Phinney, 1992); sexual orientation development (e.g., Dube & Savin-Williams, 1999; Espin, 1994); biracial and multiracial identity (e.g., Root, 1992, 1996; Winters & DeBose, 2003); culturally responsive prevention and intervention programs and theories based on multiculturalism; and culturally embedded skills and techniques (e.g., Constantine et al., 2007; DeLucia-Waack et al., 2004; Gielen, 2004; Herlihy & Corey, 2015; Leong et al., 2007, 2013; Pedersen et al., 2015; Sue et al., 2019; Toporek et al., 2006). This body of research has focused on how we, as mental health professionals, can be culturally responsive to clients from different racial, ethnic, and cultural backgrounds.

As mentioned previously, the 1980s and 1990s brought greater consciousness and spurred a movement to help mental health professionals become aware of the need to be culturally responsive to clients from different cultural backgrounds. It was during that time period that the profession began to establish multicultural guidelines and competencies. These competencies are important to understand because they provide a context for our work and a foundation for integrating social justice into training, practice, research, and service.

BRIEF OVERVIEW OF MULTICULTURAL GUIDELINES AND COMPETENCIES

Both the APA and ACA, as well as other helping professions, have adopted and continue to update the multicultural competency guidelines. For example, in 2017, the APA Council of Representatives adopted revised multicultural guidelines for psychologists (*Multicultural Guidelines: An Ecological Approach to Context, Identity, and Intersectionality*), while in 2015, the ACA endorsed revised multicultural competencies (*Multicultural and Social Justice Counseling Competencies*). The updated APA and ACA multicultural guidelines include issues of intersectionality, social justice, and advocacy that provide an evolutionary understanding of the foundation for our current social justice work. We refer readers to their own professional organizations and their respective divisions within the organizations for updated guidelines and competencies.

Familiarity with the history and development of the multicultural guidelines and competencies is helpful to understand the evolution of diversity issues in psychology and counseling that are the foundation for our social justice work. The development of the multicultural counseling competencies (known as MCC) originated in 1981, when APA Division 17 (Counseling Psychology) established a committee to develop a position paper defining multicultural competencies. The position paper identified 11 competencies (Sue et al., 1982) and was accepted—but, interestingly, was not endorsed by the Division 17 Executive Committee. However, it was published in *The Counseling Psychologist* (Sue et al., 1982), providing helping professionals with the first set of guidelines on requirements for becoming a competent multicultural psychologist and counselor. The position paper was important as a baseline for later work, serving as a template for subsequent refinement and expansion of the competencies (e.g., Arredondo et al., 1996; Sue et al., 1992, 1998).

Ten years after the publication of the position paper, a list of 31 MCC was published (Sue et al., 1992). The 1992 competencies were endorsed by three APA divisions (currently the Society of Counseling Psychology [Division 17], Society for the Psychology of Women [Division 35], and the Society for the Psychological Study of Culture, Ethnicity and Race [Division 45]) and six ACA divisions (Association for Adult Development and Aging [AADA]; Association for Counselor Education and Supervision [ACES]; Association for Gay, Lesbian, and Bisexual Issues in Counseling [AGLBIC]; Association for Multicultural Counseling and Development [AMCD]; American School Counselors Association [ASCA]; Association for Specialists in Group Work [ASGW]; and the International Association of Marriage and Family Counselors [IAMFC]). Although the APA did not immediately endorse the competencies, the APA Board of Ethnic Minority Affairs did publish the Diversity Guidelines (APA, 1993). Furthermore, recognition of the importance for psychologists to utilize MCC when working with clients from different ethnic, racial, and cultural backgrounds resulted in changes in the APA Ethical Principles of Psychologists and Code of Conduct, so that the MCC were included (APA, 1992).

Notably, it took 20 years for the MCC to be endorsed by the Executive Committee of Division 17 (Arredondo et al., 1996; Sue et al., 1992). There were three professional organizations that played a major role in establishing the MCC: APA's Divisions 17 and 45 and ACA's division the Association for Multicultural Counseling and Development (AMCD). The original 11 multicultural competencies (Sue et al., 1992) evolved into the 31 multicultural competencies (Sue et al., 1992) that were operationalized (Arredondo et al., 1996), as well as, two additional competencies that addressed issues of racial identity (Sue et al., 1998), making a total of 33 competencies. These 33 MCC served as a template for the APA Multicultural Guidelines (APA,1993). It was not until 2002 that the APA Council of Representatives finally endorsed the multicultural competencies (Arredondo & Perez, 2003), while ACA endorsed them in March 2003 (ACA, 2003).

Since there is substantial literature and comprehensive descriptions of the MCC (e.g., Arredondo et al., 1996; Pope-Davis & Coleman, 1997; Sue, 1995; Sue et al., 1992, 1998) and revised and updated guidelines and competencies, only a brief summary of the original MCC will be discussed. MCC have been defined as counselors' attitudes/beliefs, knowledge, and skills in working with clients from a variety of ethnic, racial, and cultural groups (e.g., groups defined by gender, social class, religion, sexual orientation, abilities, etc.) (Sue et al., 1992, 1998). The MCC are structured into a three-by-three matrix consisting of three levels (attitude/beliefs, knowledge and skills) and three dimensions comprising (1) therapists'/counselors' awareness of their cultural values and biases, (2) therapists'/counselors' awareness of the client's worldview, and (3) culturally appropriate intervention strategies, which includes integration of traditional cultural healing methodologies. The MCC focused not only on being aware, acknowledging, accepting, and understanding the impact of culture on clients and their historical, psychopolitical, and psychosocial experiences, but, just as importantly, also focused on therapists' and counselors' own cultural backgrounds as they impact their beliefs, values, worldviews, biases, prejudice, and power. Essentially this required that the "counselor know thyself" (Sue & Sue, 2008). An example of this is when a graduate student told me (Rita) that she thought to be culturally competent all she needed to do was work on her skills. However, after taking the multicultural counseling course, she realized that no matter how skillful she might become, she would not be culturally responsive if she did not undergo an in-depth examination of her own cultural biases, prejudices, privileges, and power.

It is noteworthy that the APA and ACA have been attentive to the issues of diversity and inclusion and have kept up with the changing times by making important updates and revisions to the guidelines and competencies (e.g., Constantine, 1997; Hills & Strozier, 1992; Ladany et al., 1997; Pedersen, 1991; Ponterotto, 1997; Quintana & Bernal, 1995). For example, both the APA and ACA developed competencies and guidelines for additional diverse populations. In 2011, the APA adopted the revised *Guidelines for Psychological Practice with Lesbian, Gay and Bisexual Clients*, and, in 2009, the ACA adopted the Association for Lesbian, Gay, Bisexual, and Transgender (ALGBTIC) Issues in Counseling. Again, we encourage readers to refer to their own professional associations to access the updated multicultural guidelines and competencies. The substantial research, training, and interest in diversity have paralleled the marked attention paid to multiculturalism within the helping professions over the past few decades. Research by Hooks et al. (2013) has been an

BOX TEXT 4.1 HOW MUCH STUFF DO WE ACTUALLY OWN?

- In the average U.S. home, there are approximately 300,000 items.
- The average size of the U.S. home has nearly tripled in size over the past 50 years.
- The U.S. has more than 50,000 storage facilities, equating to 7.3 square feet of self-storage for every person in the U.S.
- 1 out of every 10 Americans rents offsite storage.
- 25% of people with two-car garages don't have room to park cars inside them, and 32% only have room for one vehicle.
- The average 10-year-old child owns 238 toys but plays with only 12 toys daily.
- 3.1% of the world's children live in U.S. but they own 40% of the toys consumed globally.
- The average U.S. woman owns 30 outfits, 1 outfit for every day of the month. In 1930, the number of outfits was 9.
- The average U.S. family spends $1,700 on clothes annually.
- The average American throws away 65 pounds of clothing per year.
- About half of American households do not save any money.
- U.S. homes have more televisions than people, turned on for more than a third of the day.
- Americans consume twice as many material goods today compared to 50 years ago.
- 12% of the world's population that lives in North America and Western Europe account for 60% of private consumption spending, while 33% of the population living in South Asia and sub-Saharan Africa account for only 3.2% of consumption.
- Americans donate 1.9% of their income to charitable causes while 6 billion people worldwide live on less than $13,000 per year.
- Americans spend $100 billion on shoes, jewelry, and watches, which is more than money spent on higher education.
- Shopping malls outnumber high schools, and 93% of teenage girls rank shopping as their favorite pastime.
- Women will spend more than 8 years of their lives shopping.
- Over the course of the American lifetime, a total of 3,680 hours or 153 days will be spent searching for misplaced items.
- Americans spend $1.2 trillion annually on nonessential goods.
- The $8 billion home organization industry has more than doubled in size since early 2000, growing at a rate of 10% each year.

Source: Becker, J. (2019). 21 surprising statistics that reveal how much stuff we actually own. http://www.becomingminimalist.com/clutter-stats/

important addition, adding the concept of cultural humility to ensure that psychologists and counselors remain culturally responsive. The overwhelming support for these multicultural guidelines and competencies underscores the importance of integrating cultural diversity as a fourth force and a core to our work and training as psychologists and counselors.

RELATIONSHIP BETWEEN SOCIAL JUSTICE AND MULTICULTURAL GUIDELINES AND COMPETENCIES

As the original MCC were being developed, Arredondo (1999) explored how oppression and racism were addressed, identifying topics such as personal awareness of privilege, values, stereotyping, and oppression; knowledge about the effects of sociopolitical influences on self-concept and identity; and understanding institutional obstacles and diagnostic cultural biases as impediments to social justice. Arredondo's work points to the importance of professionals having an awareness and understanding of both their own and their clients' cultural backgrounds, value systems, beliefs, prejudices, biases, power, and privileges. At the same time, as healers and social change agents, it is important to understand the context of systems and institutions that provide a basis for working with individuals, groups, families, and communities. We concur with Arredondo that the original MCC established a foundation for social justice and human rights and truly is the core of ongoing and future work in the integration of mental health with social justice and human rights.

Even so, there has been criticism for not satisfactorily incorporating social justice principles (Vera & Speight, 2003). Derald Wing Sue and his colleagues (1998) clearly stated, "Multiculturalism is about social justice, cultural democracy, and equity" (p. 5). Others (e.g., Arredondo & Perez, 2003; Chung & Bemak, 2012; Constantine et al., 2007; Helms, 2003; Speight & Vera, 2004; Toporek et al., 2006; Vera & Speight, 2003) have agreed and advocated for social justice in the mental health field. Helms' (2003) criticized that the multicultural psychology and counseling literature focused on integrating social justice principles at the micro level while ignoring the larger systemic levels. We agree with Helms, in that a commitment to multicultural guidelines and competencies also involves a commitment to social justice at both micro and macro levels. Interestingly, it should be noted that although the ACA did not endorse the MCC until March 2003, the organization (then known as American Association of Counseling and Development) did publish a significant position paper in 1987 on human rights, calling for counselors to be advocates for social change. With revisions and updates of multicultural guidelines and competencies to include social justice by the ACA in 2015 and APA in 2017, there is a clear acknowledgment of the importance of addressing social justice concerns in our work as psychologists and counselors.

Multicultural guidelines and competencies have clearly set the stage for professionals to "open their eyes" and examine presenting problems, behaviors, and responses not only from the individual's point of view, but also from the macro, ecological, and contextual viewpoints. The revisions to the guidelines and competencies have highlighted the importance of analyzing clients' behaviors and presenting problems within a broad scope of variables inclusive of the interaction of the family, community, historical, cultural, and political perspectives as well as the surrounding ecosystem. These are all important elements that contribute to clients' lives and influence our assessment and intervention strategies. Thus, social justice is at the very core of multicultural guidelines and competencies, making it essential that professionals have the ability to accurately perceive ecological factors that influence clients as well as the skills to challenge and address systemic barriers that impede the client's growth, development, physical safety, quality of life, and psychological well-being (Constantine et al., 2007; Fondacaro & Weinberg, 2002; Hage, 2003; Peters & Luke, 2021; Prilleltensky & Prilleltensky, 2003; Vera & Speight, 2003). Consequently, we believe that it is our moral, social, and ethical responsibility to address these issues proactively rather than ignore larger contextual issues that affect our clients' psychological well-being and safety. We emphasize being proactive since we contend that, as social justice advocates, it is important to focus on prevention and intervention rather than fall into a pattern of re-activity after the fact. To fully understand and appreciate how the field has moved from an individual perspective to broader social justice issues, a brief overview of the historical perspective of social justice is discussed below.

SOCIAL JUSTICE–ORIENTED PSYCHOLOGY AND COUNSELING: A BRIEF HISTORICAL OVERVIEW

Although the issue of social justice is not a new concept in the field of psychology and counseling, it has taken a long time to be recognized in training and practice. The concept of social action was identified in the writings of Frank Parsons and then, later, Carl Rogers, both of whom advocated that the profession respond to social injustices at individual and societal levels (Hartung & Blustein, 2002; McWhirter, 1998). During the same time period, Clifford Beers was advocating for more humane treatment of individuals with mental illness (Tenety & Kiselica, 2000). Early feminist and multicultural scholars criticized the absence of approaches to oppression and inequities in traditional psychological work (Espin, 1994; Sparks & Park, 2000; Sue & Sue, 2008). As mentioned in the previous section, in the 1960s, strong political movements in the United States raised the social and political consciousness of many people, including psychologists and counselors. As a result, ethnic and race-specific associations were developed that responded to erroneousness, so-called scientific hypotheses about the intellectual inferiority of Blacks (Jensen, 1969) and the cultural deprivation of minorities (Arredondo & Perez, 2003; Riessman, 1962). In May 1971, the *Personnel and Guidance Journal* published a special issue entitled "Counseling and the Social Revolution" edited by Michael Lewis, Judith Lewis, and Edward Dworkin and highlighting social injustices in the counseling profession. It raised questions regarding the psychology and counseling profession's role and suggested that psychotherapists and counselors must not assume a passive role by simply understanding injustices without becoming active participants in the movement for social change.

BOX TEXT 4.2 FOOD WASTE

- 40% of food in the United States goes uneaten, equating to more than 20 pounds of food per person every month.
- Food production uses 10% of the total U.S. energy budget, 50% of U.S. land, and 80% of freshwater consumed in the U.S.
- The average U.S. consumer wastes 10 times as much food as an individual in Southeast Asia, an increase of 50% from 1970s.
- Per year, there is an estimated 132 billion pounds of food waste, equating to $162 billion worth of food.
- Approximately 70 billion pounds of food waste goes into landfills, where it decomposes and emits methane, a greenhouse gas. Globally, this accounts for about 7% (3.3 billion metric tons) of the total emissions of greenhouse gases annually.
- 30% of food in the world goes uneaten, which equates to $400 billion each year.
- Food waste is a concern in other countries as well:
  o In England, consumers throw away approximately 30% of food purchased, including more than 4 million whole apples, 1.2 million sausages, and 2.8 million tomatoes.
  o In Sweden, consumers throw away about 25% of purchased food.
  o In certain parts of Africa, reports show about 25% or more of crops go bad before they can be eaten.
  o In New Zealand, Wellington households generate an estimated 39 million liters of food waste each year.
- Food wasted in developed countries could feed all the world's 870 million hungry people.
- The food waste problem is expected to worsen as the world's population increases. By 2030, consumer food waste will cost $600 billion a year.

Sources: Gunders, D. (2012, Aug). Wasted: How America is losing up to 40% of its food from farm to fork to landfill. Natural Resources Defense Council. http://www.nrdc.org/food/files/wasted-food-ip.pdf

Martin, A. (2008, May 18). One country's table scraps, another country's meal. New York Times. http://www.nytimes.com/2008/05/18/weekinreview/18martin.html?pagewanted=all

Nixon, R. (2015, Feb 25). Food waste is becoming serious economic and environmental issue, report says. New York Times. http://www.nytimes.com/2015/02/26/us/food-waste-is-becoming-serious-economic-and-environmental-issue-report-says.html?_r=0

Woolf, A. (2020, Jan 1). Three new community composting hubs to be created in Wellington. https://www.stuff.co.nz/environment/climate-news/118544309/three-new-community-composting-hubs-to-be-created-in-wellington

As the psychology and counseling field began to recognize and acknowledge the prominence of social justice issues impacting clients, discussion began on whether social justice should be the fifth force in psychology and counseling (Ratts, 2009; Ratts et al., 2004). To reflect the increasing acknowledgment of social justice issues encountered by clientele and to ensure that psychologists and counselors provided effective services, both the APA and ACA included social justice, intersectionality, and advocacy in their updated and revised guidelines and competencies. In February 2021, the APA passed a human rights resolution that was a culmination of decades of research on psychology's responsibility to address issues of human welfare and social justice (APA, 2021). Highlights of the resolution noted in Box Text 4.3 underscore how important it is for psychology to respect and advocate for human rights; apply knowledge to a greater realization of human rights; and incorporate in training (high school to postdoctoral) human rights, racism, and bias against marginalized groups. (Please refer to the APA website for the entire resolution (https://www.apa.org/about/policy/resolution-psychology-human-rights.pdf).

Mental health professional journals continue to publish special issues focusing on social justice and human rights. We recommend readers to regularly update themselves on current social justice research in their respective fields and associated disciplines in order to get a broader perspective of interdisciplinary macro and ecological approaches to doing social justice work. To better understand how psychology and counseling have assimilated social justice and understand the progression and implementation of social justice–oriented psychology and counseling, a brief summary of the social justice philosophy, models, and theories that have influenced social justice psychology and counseling is discussed below.

SOCIAL JUSTICE PHILOSOPHY AND MODELS

Social justice philosophy has origins in John Locke's ideas about liberty and equality (Hartnett, 2001; Nozick, 1974; Stevens & Wood, 1992). His libertarian justice model proposes that it is the responsibility of individuals to make their own decisions and determine their own destiny, with the premise that there is equal opportunity and freedom for every individual to determine their own lives and outcomes. Two major criticisms of this premise are the assumptions that everyone has the opportunity to choose and that everyone is on an equal playing field. In essence, this means that as long as individuals have opportunities to change, then inequalities in issues of class, race, ethnicity, gender, abilities, sexual orientation, etc., are inconsequential. Others have challenged and expanded on Locke's assertions. Rousseau argued that the freedom of choice should not create unequal opportunities in a society and become institutionalized as the status quo (Rawls, 1971). He claimed that government should play a major role in preventing social inequalities while supporting freedom of choice. The *communitarian approach* to social justice highlights the interaction between power, privilege, and oppression (Young, 1990), emphasizing the danger that these dynamics may lead to inequities. *Distributive justice* (Prilleltensky, 1997) describes the importance of working within the larger sociopolitical context, rather

BOX TEXT 4.3 APA RESOLUTION ON APA, PSYCHOLOGY, AND HUMAN RIGHTS (FEBRUARY 2021)

The report of the American Psychological Association (APA) Task Force on Human Rights proposes a definition of human rights in relation to psychology; reviews the relationship between human rights and the concepts that have historically guided APA (e.g., human welfare, public interest, and social justice); proposes an analytical Five Connections framework to assess the connections between psychology and human rights and uses that framework to review APA's recent and ongoing human rights activities; and makes recommendations for organizational mechanisms that can ensure APA's ongoing and visible commitment to human rights. The Five Connection framework is as follows:

- Psychologists possess human rights by virtue of being human as well as specific rights essential to their profession and discipline;
- Psychologists apply their knowledge and methods to the greater realization of human rights;
- Psychologists respect human rights and oppose the misuse of psychological science, practice, and applications and their negative impact on human rights;
- Psychologists advance equal access to the benefits of psychological science and practice; and,
- Psychologists advocate for human rights.

Source: https://www.apa.org/about/policy/resolution-psychology-human-rights.pdf

than emphasizing the individual as the means to overcome injustices. This requires the redistribution of power, with equality and fairness as an essential component that fosters cultural diversity. In turn, *liberation psychology* proposes that the field prioritizes what has to happen in the future, rather than focus on the discrimination and oppression of the past (Martin-Baro, 1994).

Collaborative models of change aiming for greater equity have been driven by systemic and feminist theories that restructure the power relationship and reshape the dynamics of the therapeutic encounter. It has been argued that changing oppressive and unequal power structures in the therapeutic relationship requires a belief in and commitment to social obligation. Lewis et al. (1998) presented a model to work with issues of oppression that incorporated consulting, advocacy, education, and being an agent of change into public policy. Similarly, Atkinson et al. (1993) developed a multicultural model to more effectively deal with oppression, expanding the counselor's role to embrace being a change agent, advocate, advisor, and consultant. These models, regardless of their approach, all strive to effectively deal with inequities and unfair treatment by changing the role of the mental

BOX TEXT 4.4 THE NEED FOR BEES

- More than 90% of the leading global crop types are visited by bees.
- Honeybees add more than $15 billion in value to U.S. farming each year.
- In a single trip, a worker bee can visit up to 100 flowers and carry more than half its weight in pollen.
- 35 UK bee species are under threat of extinction, and all species face serious threats.
- One-third of honeybees died or disappeared during the 2012–2013 winter, which was a 42% increase over the year before and well above the 10–15% losses beekeepers usually experience in the winter.
- Since 2006, an estimated 10 million beehives have been lost, at a cost of $2 billion.
- One-third of the food in our diet relies to some extent on bee pollination (U.S. Dept. of Agriculture).
- £1.8 billion is how much it would cost UK farmers to pollinate their crops without bees.
- Neonicotinoid pesticides are deadly to bees and are used on more than 140 different crops and in-home gardens, resulting in countless chances of exposure for any insect that lands on these treated plants.
- Loss of pollinators could lead to lower availability of crops and wild plants that provide essential micronutrients for human diets, impacting health and nutritional security and risking increased numbers of people suffering from vitamin A, iron, and folate deficiency.
- The impact of the loss of bee pollination on the farm:

Crop	%	Crop	%
Almond	100%	Cucumber	80%
Apple	90%	Grape	1%
Asparagus	90%	Lemon	20%
Avocado	90%	Onion	90%
Broccoli	90%	Peanut	2%
Blueberry	90%	Plum/Prune	65%
Celery	80%	Tangerine	45%
Cherry	80%	Watermelon	65%
Cotton	20%		

Sources: Walsh, B. (2013, August 19). The plight of the honeybee: Mass deaths in bee colonies may mean disaster for farmers and your favorite foods. *Time Magazine.* https://content.time.com/time/subscriber/article/0,33009,2149141-2,00.html
https://friendsoftheearth.uk/nature/why-do-we-need-bees

health professional in a way that goes beyond traditional counseling and psychotherapy. Building on the social justice theories, philosophical concepts, and models and criticism of these models, we developed the *Multiphase Model of Psychotherapy, Counseling, Human Rights, and Social Justice* (MPM) that synthesizes other models of social change, based on our work experiences in social justice and human rights. The MPM (discussed in depth in Chapter 12) directly targets social justice and human rights in a culturally responsive way and presents a definitive outline for how we, as mental health professionals, can redefine our traditional roles to more effectively and proactively respond to social injustices and potential human rights violations. The MPM includes various phases that incorporate culturally responsive social justice and human rights interventions at ecological, micro, meso, and macro levels in an effort to clearly define the application and implementation of social justice and human rights work in the mental health field.

THEORIES THAT INFLUENCE PSYCHOLOGICAL SOCIAL JUSTICE WORK

DECOLONIZATION OF WESTERN PSYCHOLOGY

Traditional psychological and counseling theories and concepts are based on Western Eurocentric male paradigms, which are not culturally responsive and often not applicable to other groups. In the face of changing U.S. racial, ethnic and cultural demographics, the fields of psychology and counseling have discussed this issue at length, resulting in the changes in both APA (2017), ACA (2015), and many of their divisions developing guidelines and competencies to addresses multiculturalism and social justice. Even so, psychology and counseling training programs are still heavily based on traditional Western theories that are entrenched in issues of power, marginalization, and oppression (Singh et al., 2020). In most cases, master's and doctoral-level training programs only address multiculturalism and social justice in a single multicultural psychology or counseling course, meeting the minimum requirement to address cultural responsiveness and, more insidiously, upholding and reinforcing the status quo by perpetuating colonialist and imperialist structure of power, beliefs, and values (Pieterse et al., 2009).

The colonialist power structure maintains cultural beliefs of superiority and normalcy, inferring that "others" need to fit into the dominant values and beliefs held by those who are White, Anglo-Saxon, Euro-American, heterosexual, and Christian. Overt and covert societal messages and structures are in place to pressure, shape, socialize, and reinforce cultural and diverse groups to conform to the colonialist's viewpoints, without consideration, integration, or appreciation of other cultural worldviews, values, and strengths. The power of these direct and subliminal messages often silences the voices of culturally diverse groups. Belief in superiority reinforces the dominant culture's structural power and privilege, fostering a system of "haves" and "have nots" and the "in-group" versus "out-group" mindset that promotes the continuance of marginalizing and oppressing of diverse groups.

Pedersen (1987), who coined multicultural counseling as the fourth force, described a number of frequent assumptions of cultural biases in traditional Western counseling. One assumption he noted was colonial viewpoints being the basis for normal behavior. What is "normal" in one culture may be viewed as "abnormal" in another culture. He also described how the Western emphasis on individualism resulted in an overemphasis on independence and competition. Given that 70% of the world population comes from collectivistic cultures that value family, community, dependence, and cooperation (Triandis, 1994), assumptions from approximately one-third of the world's population about the culturally dominant norms of individualistic societies is erroneous. Subsequently there are challenges for collectivistic cultures to conform to individualistic behavior that focuses on I, me, myself, rather than on the group, family, and community. Another assumption Pedersen described is the focus in traditional psychotherapy and counseling on changing the individual rather than viewing the source of the problem as a broader systemic issue. As mentioned previously, social injustices do not occur only on an individual intrapsychic level but also on a societal level. Therefore, as mental health social justice activists and advocates, our work is not only focused on the individual but also on dismantling the structural and systemic barriers that create oppression, marginalization, inequalities, and inequities that impact individuals', families', and communities' psychological well-being.

Decolonization is a cornerstone of social justice psychology and counseling (Goodman et al., 2015). Decolonization requires an in-depth examination of power and inequities and involves intentionally dismantling structural and systemic systems of oppression and inequities, with an aim of giving voice to those who have been marginalized, ignored, and dismissed. To do social justice–oriented work is to examine aspects of psychology and counseling from a decolonized perspective, simultaneously working with disenfranchised and marginalized groups to (re)construct psychological and counseling skills, techniques, strategies, and interventions that are both culturally responsive and address issues of injustices.

SOCIAL JUSTICE THEORY AND PRACTICE AND LIBERATION PSYCHOLOGY

The term "social justice" is not only used in psychology and other social sciences, but is also increasingly popular in mainstream society given the multiple social injustices that are occurring today. Some individuals refer to social justice as a "liberal" concept, dismissing and belittling the importance and urgency of addressing social injustices. Actually, one foundation of social justice psychology and counseling is rooted in theology or *liberation theology*. Twentieth-century theologians claimed that the liberation of poor populations was a theme emphasized throughout the Bible (Tate et al., 2013). Catholic priests and nuns in developing countries actively fought against oppressive regimes that negatively impacted those who were underprivileged and oppressed. Evangelical activists participated in political activism in response to economic injustice, poverty, and human rights violations of the poor, creating a bottom-up grassroots social justice movement and hence the rise of *liberation psychology* (LP) and social action (Martin-Baró, 1994). Thus, LP is derived from liberation theology and stresses understanding the etiology of the harmful lived experiences of oppressed, marginalized, and disenfranchised populations and actively changing sociopolitical and sociocultural systems to improve mental health and psychological well-being.

LP contributes to the foundation of social justice mental health work even though it has not been part of mainstream Western Eurocentric psychological theories.

In concert with social justice–oriented psychology and counseling, LP emphasizes the decolonization and de-ideologizing of the oppressed groups' perceptions, beliefs, and values. The colonially imposed history and narratives about the oppressed are similar to Paulo Freire's (1970) *banking concept*. The banking concept refers to individuals and the oppressed as passive empty vessels that are filled with only the oppressor's information about who they are; who they can be; how to talk, think, feel, and behave; and when to talk and act. An example of colonial dominance that resulted in being discounted, silenced, and not having a voice can be seen in the U.S. historical documentation regarding the building of the first U.S. transcontinental railways. It is now a well-known fact that the Chinese were instrumental in building the railway, but the massive contribution by Chinese workers to U.S. society in constructing railroad tracks was largely ignored. In fact, when photographs during that period were taken, they portrayed a very different story, featuring prominently White American males (the Chinese were told to step aside when the photos were taken) and thus reinforcing the power structure and dominance of the majority culture (Wang, 2014). This major contribution by Chinese workers was not recognized during that time, thus denying their voice, contribution, and presence in U.S. society.

The goal of LP is to break free from the banking concept and dismantle and decolonialize structures and systems that are oppressively imposed on individuals. Our role as social justice–oriented psychologists and counselors is to foster empowerment by assisting individuals in becoming authentically empowered, helping them to develop tools, language, and a safe and brave space in which to attain what Freire (1970) calls *critical conscientization*. Freire describes critical conscientization as an in-depth awareness and understanding of the systems that have oppressed, shaped, and reinforced peoples' lives. Becoming authentically empowered involves deconstructing and reconstructing one's lived experiences rather than having colonial self-imposed narratives that define who one is and what was one's lived experiences. The process of achieving authentic empowerment and critical consciousness involves understanding systemic oppression and identifying those in power who perpetuate the oppression, acquiring an awareness of one's rights, and having the language to frame and articulate one's lived experiences.

De-silencing and finding a voice to express, in one's own vernacular, a personal narrative not based on the dominant systems definition of marginalization and oppression is an important step toward healing and liberation. This creation of personal history, cultural and social identity, and narrative using one's own language based on one's own truth leads to power in liberation and social change. An excellent example of providing space for finding one's voice and creating an authentic narrative is my (Fred) former professor, Howard Zinn, a renowned civil rights activist and democratic socialist, who in class lectures described U.S. history through lived experiences of marginalized groups. His book *People's History of the United States* (Zinn, 1980) described U.S. history through the eyes of African Americans, Asian Americans, Americans Indians, Latinx Americans, and other marginalized groups, focusing on their viewpoints as a minority group experiencing histories of oppression, discrimination, slavery, genocide, internment camps, etc.

Another example of the power of having language to describe lived experiences was the reactions of my (Rita) students of color when I used the term "White privilege" long before it was customary to use this term. Students of color were both excited and distraught. Excited because I provided them with language and affirmed that there were concepts about racial injustice that supported their experiences. Distraught because there is language about the racism and racial injustice that describes their experiences on a daily basis. Acquiring the language to describe their own and others' experiences of racial injustice led the students to feel compelled to fight against racism. These examples illustrate the importance in social justice–oriented mental health work to assist clients in finding the bridge to move from passively accepting what life is and has been to what life will and can be. As an African proverb states "until the lions have their own historians, tales of hunting will always glorify the hunter" (Quinn, 2013).

An effective tool that social justice–oriented psychologists and counselors can employ to assist clients, their families, and communities in constructing and reconstructing their histories based on their lived experiences and move toward LP and social justice principles is *social action research* and *participatory* or *community-based participatory research* (e.g., Fine & Torres, 2021; Greenwood & Levin, 2006; Janes, 2015; Wallerstein & Christens, 2021). This tool requires the development of partnerships with marginalized individuals and groups to cultivate supportive safe spaces for them to find their voice and use their own language to describe their lived experiences. Acknowledging and writing personal human rights narratives helps develop authentic empowerment and critical conscientization, along with the motivation and desire to promote social change. Adding to this, the strength-based foundation of LP enhances coping strategies such as hope, strength, and resiliency, which are so important when working within oppressive environments. Building on these techniques is conducive to discovering new transformative tools as strategies toward liberation, social justice, and human rights (Bemak & Chung, 2011).

It is clear that social justice psychology and counseling is aligned with LP, placing social issues, social change, and activism in the forefront rather than as a secondary issue. As Martin Luther King, Jr. stated, "A time comes when silence is betrayal" (Scruggs, 2017). There is no such thing is an "arm-chair social justice advocate" who endlessly talks without movement, nor is there a place or room for neutrality toward injustices. Not proactively addressing the social injustices impacting our clients and their families and communities is to support and reinforce oppressive systems, "Band-Aiding" situations, and creating and reinforcing the "therapeutic revolving door of injustice." As Bishop Desmond Tutu said: "If you are neutral in situations of injustice, you have chosen the side of the oppressor. If an elephant has its foot on the tail of a mouse and you say that you are neutral, the mouse will not appreciate your neutrality" (Ratcliffe, 2017).

UNITED NATIONS UNIVERSAL DECLARATION OF HUMAN RIGHTS

It is appropriate at this point to briefly mention the Universal Declaration of Human Rights (UN, 1948). Although the United Nations may seem far removed from the work you do in your local community, region, or even nationally, its broad international perspective has implications for our work as social justice–oriented counselors and psychologists. The thread that connects the Human Rights Declaration to psychology and counseling, particularly when we assume a position of incorporating social justice into our work, is the fundamental theme of equality, equity, human rights, and social justice for all people. Inherent in both the Declaration and the practice of psychotherapy and counseling is an individual's or a group's basic needs and rights to food and nutrition, accessible housing, education, medical care; the right to be in a physically safe environment; the opportunity to vote and participate in the democratic process; the right to a safe and productive life free of discrimination and oppression; and the opportunities to exercise free choice and free speech.

In addition to the APA and ACA guidelines and competencies, the Universal Declaration of Human Rights offers appropriate guiding principles that can help define our work. The helping profession's fundamental aim is similar to that of the Declaration in ensuring, first and foremost, that individuals and groups have the right to meet their basic needs, which are underscored by physical and psychological safety and protection. Once this fundamental baseline of human rights is achieved, then individuals can move on to address more complex levels or stages of development, fostering optimal personal, cultural, and social growth and development and psychological well-being. Similar to the focus of the UN Declaration, an important focus of the mental health professional is to be proactive and purposeful in preventing and intervening in situations that create inequities and injustices for individuals and groups of people. The Declaration provides a framework from which mental health professionals can address issues of injustice and equity and promote the social, psychological, physical, and spiritual health of individuals, families, communities, and organizations. This relates to cultivating diversity, inclusion, and acceptance of all individuals despite their socioeconomic status, age, abilities, gender, ethnicity, sexual orientation, identities, and religion or racial background, and it is imperative in ensuring maximum growth and the development of potential for individuals and disenfranchised and marginalized groups of people.

For example, psychologists and counselors can assist individuals in accessing their right to education, their right to social services, their right to due process of the law, or their right to accessible housing. In any of these areas, individuals have the right to equal opportunities to achieve success, grow, and access services despite diverse backgrounds, beliefs, values, and worldviews. In summary, while the UN's Universal Declaration of Human Rights and the fields of psychology and counseling are vastly different, there are distinctive parallels and overlap between the two. The Declaration provides guidelines regarding social justice and mental health, offering the potential to help us think differently about our role as mental health professionals who are striving for equity and opportunity for optimal growth and development within a safe environment for all. Although the 30 Articles of the Declaration are presented in this chapter's Appendix, we also recommend that readers further investigate the Declaration on the UN website.

SUMMARY

To successfully work with clients, families, stakeholders, and communities, culturally responsive social justice–oriented counselors and psychologists must have knowledge about how their clients perceive and relate to the world. Clients' and stakeholders' worldviews may differ from that of the helping professional. Regardless of the differences in perspectives, mental health professionals must respect clients' and stakeholders' worldviews and acknowledge that this is pivotal in fostering social change. Justice and rights advocates can be effective only when they understand, recognize, acknowledge, and accept their clients' and stakeholders' perspectives and lived experiences so that change is approached from within their worldviews. Again, fully applying and implementing the social justice multicultural guidelines and competencies is a critical starting point for understanding clients' and their families' viewpoints. A "quick-fix" multicultural or cultural sensitivity training workshop will not be enough. To be aware of diversity, inclusion, and injustices requires the practice of cultural humility, which involves life-long deep self-reflection, examination, and exploration of our biases, privilege, and power along with an honest and genuine commitment to social justice, diversity, and inclusion.

DISCUSSION QUESTIONS

1. Think of a social justice issue that you would like to address as a psychologist or counselor. What would be the first step that you would take to address this issue?
2. Approach someone in your family and one of your friends and ask them what they believe about social justice.
   a. Do they have similar or different definitions of social justice?
   b. Do they have definitions that are different from yours?
3. Find a local issue that you believe describes an injustice for an individual or a larger group of people.
   a. Is the injustice clearly understood by those who are affected by this issue or not?
   b. What do you imagine would be the role of a mental health professional in this situation?
4. Your client is Mrs. Fox. She is a 72-year-old African American woman. Her family doctor referred her to the community agency you work for. Mrs. Fox seems to be forgetting things; she is very sad, irritable, and "bored." It seems Mrs. Fox has been having arguments with her relatives more frequently, and she does not feel she is useful anymore. Mrs. Fox used to help to take care of her grandchildren, but she started to get sick and forget important things, and she got very impatient. Her family doctor prescribes ibuprofen for her complaints. Her insurance does not cover any type of psychological assessment, and her family seems to struggle financially. Her doctor thinks she might be developing some sort of dementia or depression.
   a. Can you identify some of the social injustices in this case? List them.
   b. What are some of those injustices that are institutional or part of the system? Are some of them based on race, age, or gender?
   c. What do you believe is your ethical and moral role as counselor/psychologist?

5. The chapter discusses how the MCC have set the stage for professionals to "open their eyes" to face real problems from a systemic and ecological perspective.
   a. How is social justice "opening your eyes" to human rights?
   b. What are some of those prejudices and barriers you still need to work on?
   c. How will this new information help you to challenge the status quo of today's systems?

APPENDIX 4.1

UNITED NATIONS UNIVERSAL DECLARATION OF HUMAN RIGHTS—10 DECEMBER 1948 (GENERAL ASSEMBLY RESOLUTION 217A)

Preamble

Whereas recognition of the inherent dignity and of the equal and inalienable rights of all members of the human family is the foundation of freedom, justice and peace in the world,

Whereas disregard and contempt for human rights have resulted in barbarous acts which have outraged the conscience of mankind, and the advent of a world in which human beings shall enjoy freedom of speech and belief and freedom from fear and want has been proclaimed as the highest aspiration of the common people,

Whereas it is essential, if man is not to be compelled to have recourse, as a last resort, to rebellion against tyranny and oppression, that human rights should be protected by the rule of law,

Whereas it is essential to promote the development of friendly relations between nations,

Whereas the peoples of the United Nations have in the Charter reaffirmed their faith in fundamental human rights, in the dignity and worth of the human person and in the equal rights of men and women and have determined to promote social progress and better standards of life in larger freedom,

Whereas Member States have pledged themselves to achieve, in co-operation with the United Nations, the promotion of universal respect for and observance of human rights and fundamental freedoms,

Whereas a common understanding of these rights and freedoms is of the greatest importance for the full realization of this pledge,

Now, therefore,

The General Assembly,

Proclaims this Universal Declaration of Human Rights as a common standard of achievement for all peoples and all nations, to the end that every individual and every organ of society, keeping this Declaration constantly in mind, shall strive by teaching and education to promote respect for these rights and freedoms and by progressive measures, national and international, to secure their universal and effective recognition and observance, both among the peoples of Member States themselves and among the peoples of territories under their jurisdiction.

Article 1.

All human beings are born free and equal in dignity and rights. They are endowed with reason and conscience and should act towards one another in a spirit of brotherhood.

Article 2.

Everyone is entitled to all the rights and freedoms set forth in this Declaration, without distinction of any kind, such as race, colour, sex, language, religion, political or other opinion, national or social origin, property, birth or other status. Furthermore, no distinction shall be made on the basis of the political, jurisdictional or international status of the country or territory to which a person belongs, whether it be independent, trust, non-self-governing or under any other limitation of sovereignty.

Article 3.

Everyone has the right to life, liberty and security of person.

Article 4.

No one shall be held in slavery or servitude; slavery and the slave trade shall be prohibited in all their forms.

Article 5.

No one shall be subjected to torture or to cruel, inhuman or degrading treatment or punishment.

Article 6.

Everyone has the right to recognition everywhere as a person before the law.

Article 7.

All are equal before the law and are entitled without any discrimination to equal protection of the law. All are entitled to equal protection against any discrimination in violation of this Declaration and against any incitement to such discrimination.

Article 8.

Everyone has the right to an effective remedy by the competent national tribunals for acts violating the fundamental rights granted him by the constitution or by law.

Article 9.

No one shall be subjected to arbitrary arrest, detention or exile.

Article 10.

Everyone is entitled in full equality to a fair and public hearing by an independent and impartial tribunal, in the determination of his rights and obligations and of any criminal charge against him.

Article 11.

(1) Everyone charged with a penal offence has the right to be presumed innocent until proved guilty according to law in a public trial at which he has had all the guarantees necessary for his defense.

(2) No one shall be held guilty of any penal offence on account of any act or omission which did not constitute a penal offence, under national or international law, at the time when it was committed. Nor shall a heavier penalty be imposed than the one that was applicable at the time the penal offence was committed.

Article 12.

No one shall be subjected to arbitrary interference with his privacy, family, home or correspondence, nor to attacks upon his honour and reputation Everyone has the right to the protection of the law against such interference or attacks.

Article 13.

(1) Everyone has the right to freedom of movement and residence within the borders of each state.

(2) Everyone has the right to leave any country, including his own, and to return to his country.

Article 14.

(1) Everyone has the right to seek and to enjoy in other countries asylum from persecution.

(2) This right may not be invoked in the case of prosecutions genuinely arising from non-political crimes or from acts contrary to the purposes and principles of the United Nations.

Article 15.

(1) Everyone has the right to a nationality.

(2) No one shall be arbitrarily deprived of his nationality nor denied the right to change his nationality.

Article 16.

(1) Men and women of full age, without any limitation due to race, nationality or religion, have the right to marry and to found a family. They are entitled to equal rights as to marriage, during marriage and at its dissolution.

(2) Marriage shall be entered into only with the free and full consent of the intending spouses.

(3) The family is the natural and fundamental group unit of society and is entitled to protection by society and the State.

Article 17.
(1) Everyone has the right to own property alone as well as in association with others.
(2) No one shall be arbitrarily deprived of his property.

Article 18.
Everyone has the right to freedom of thought, conscience and religion; this right includes freedom to change his religion or belief, and freedom, either alone or in community with others and in public or private, to manifest his religion or belief in teaching, practice, worship and observance.

Article 19.
Everyone has the right to freedom of opinion and expression; this right includes freedom to hold opinions without interference and to seek, receive and impart information and ideas through any media and regardless of frontiers.

Article 20.
(1) Everyone has the right to freedom of peaceful assembly and association.
(2) No one may be compelled to belong to an association.

Article 21.
(1) Everyone has the right to take part in the government of his country, directly or through freely chosen representatives.
(2) Everyone has the right to equal access to public service in his country.
(3) The will of the people shall be the basis of the authority of government; this shall be expressed in periodic and genuine elections which shall be by universal and equal suffrage and shall be held by secret vote or by equivalent free voting procedures.

Article 22.
Everyone, as a member of society, has the right to social security and is entitled to realization, through national effort and international co-operation and in accordance with the organization and resources of each State, of the economic, social and cultural rights indispensable for his dignity and the free development of his personality.

Article 23.
(1) Everyone has the right to work, to free choice of employment, to just and favourable conditions of work and to protection against unemployment.
(2) Everyone, without any discrimination, has the right to equal pay for equal work.
(3) Everyone who works has the right to just and favourable remuneration ensuring for himself and his family an existence worthy of human dignity, and supplemented, if necessary, by other means of social protection.
(4) Everyone has the right to form and to join trade unions for the protection of his interests.

Article 24.

Everyone has the right to rest and leisure, including reasonable limitation of working hours and periodic holidays with pay.

Article 25.

(1) Everyone has the right to a standard of living adequate for the health and well-being of himself and of his family, including food, clothing, housing and medical care and necessary social services, and the right to security in the event of unemployment, sickness, disability, widowhood, old age or other lack of livelihood in circumstances beyond his control.

(2) Motherhood and childhood are entitled to special care and assistance. All children, whether born in or out of wedlock, shall enjoy the same social protection.

Article 26.

(1) Everyone has the right to education. Education shall be free, at least in the elementary and fundamental stages. Elementary education shall be compulsory. Technical and professional education shall be made generally available and higher education shall be equally accessible to all on the basis of merit.

(2) Education shall be directed to the full development of the human personality and to the strengthening of respect for human rights and fundamental freedoms. It shall promote understanding, tolerance and friendship among all nations, racial or religious groups, and shall further the activities of the United Nations for the maintenance of peace.

(3) Parents have a prior right to choose the kind of education that shall be given to their children.

Article 27.

(1) Everyone has the right freely to participate in the cultural life of the community, to enjoy the arts and to share in scientific advancement and its benefits.

(2) Everyone has the right to the protection of the moral and material interests resulting from any scientific, literary or artistic production of which he is the author.

Article 28.

Everyone is entitled to a social and international order in which the rights and freedoms set forth in this Declaration can be fully realized.

Article 29.

(1) Everyone has duties to the community in which alone the free and full development of his personality is possible.

(2) In the exercise of his rights and freedoms, everyone shall be subject only to such limitations as are determined by law solely for the purpose of securing due recognition and respect for the rights and freedoms of others and of meeting the just requirements of morality, public order and the general welfare in a democratic society.

(3) These rights and freedoms may in no case be exercised contrary to the purposes and principles of the United Nations.

Article 30.
Nothing in this Declaration may be interpreted as implying for any State, group or person any right to engage in any activity or to perform any act aimed at the destruction of any of the rights and freedoms set forth herein.

Source: https://www.un.org/en/about-us/universal-declaration-of-human-rights

REFERENCES

American Association for Counseling and Development. (1987). *Human rights position paper.* Author.

American Counseling Association. (2003, Mar). *ACA governing council meeting minutes.* Author.

American Counseling Association (ACA). (2015). Multicultural social justice counseling competencies. https://www.counseling.org/docs/default-source/competencies/multicultural-and-social-justice-counseling-competencies.pdf?sfvrsn=20

American Psychological Association. (1992). *Ethical principles of psychologists and code of conduct.* Author. American Psychological Association. (2011). Guidelines for psychological practice with lesbian, gay, and bisexual clients. https://www.apa.org/pi/lgbt/resources/guidelines

American Psychological Association. (2017). Multicultural guidelines: An ecological approach to context, identity, and intersectionality. http://www.apa.org/about/policy/multicultural-guidelines.pdf

American Psychological Association. (2021, Feb). APA resolution on APA, Psychology, and Human Rights. https://www.apa.org/about/policy/resolution-psychology-human-rights.pdf

American Psychological Association, Office of Ethnic Minority Affairs. (1993). Guidelines for providers of psychological services to ethnic, linguistic, and culturally diverse populations. *American Psychologist, 48,* 45–48. https://doi.org/10.1037/0003-066X.48.1.45

Arredondo, P. (1999). Multicultural counseling competencies as tools to address oppression and racism. *Journal of Counseling & Development, 77*(1), 102–108. https://doi.org/10.1002/j.1556-6676.1999.tb02427.x

Arredondo, P., & Perez, P. (2003) Expanding multicultural competence through social justice. *Counseling Psychologist, 31*(3), 282–289. https://doi.org/10.1177/0011000003031003003

Arredondo, P., Toporek, R., Brown, S. P., Jones, J., Locke, D. C., & Sanchez, J. (1996). Operationalization of the multicultural counseling competencies. *Journal of Multicultural Counseling and Development, 24*(1), 42–78. https://doi.org/10.1002/j.2161-1912.1996.tb00288.x

Atkinson, D. R., & Hackett, G. (2004). *Counseling diverse populations.* McGraw Hill.

Atkinson, D. R., Thompson, C. E., & Grant, S. K. (1993). A three-dimensional model for counseling racial/ethnic minorities. *Counseling Psychologist, 21*(2), 257–277. https://doi.org/10.1177/0011000093212010

Aubrey, R. F. (1971). Historical development of guidance and counseling and implications for the future. *Personnel and Guidance Journal, 55*(1), 288–295. https://doi.org/10.1002/j.2164-4918.1977.tb04991.x

Bemak, F., & Chung, R. C-Y. (2011). Post-disaster social justice group work and group supervision. *Journal for Specialists in Group Work, 36*(1), 3–21. https://doi.org/10.1080/01933922.2010.537737

Berry, J. W. (2015). Acculturation. In J. E. Grusec & P. D. Hastings (Eds.), *Handbook of socialization: Theory and research* (pp. 520–538). Guilford Press.

Chun, K. M., Organista, P. B., & Marin, G. (2002). *Acculturation advances in theory, measurement, and applied research.* American Psychological Association.

Chung, R. C-Y., & Bemak, F. (2002). The relationship of culture and empathy in cross-cultural counseling. *Journal of Counseling & Development, 80,* 154–159. https://doi.org/10.1002/j.1556-6678.2002.tb00178.x

Chung, R. C.-Y., & Bemak, F. P. (2012). *Social justice counseling: The next steps beyond multiculturalism.* Sage.

Constantine, M. G. (1997). Facilitating multicultural competency in counseling supervision: Operationalizing a practical framework. In D. B. Pope-Davis & H. L. Coleman (Eds.), *Multicultural counseling competencies: Assessment, education and training, and supervision* (pp. 310–324). Sage.

Constantine, M. G., Hage, S. M., & Kindaichi, M. M. (2007). Social justice and multicultural issues: Implications for the practice and training of counselors and counseling psychologists. *Journal of Counseling & Development, 85*(1), 24–29. https://doi.org/10.1002/j.1556-6678.2007.tb00440.x

Cross, W. E., Jr. (1995). The psychology of nigrescence: Revising the Cross model. In J. G. Ponterotto, J. M. Casas, L. A. Suzuki, & C. M. Alexander (Eds.), *Handbook of multicultural counseling* (pp. 93–122). Sage.

Cross, W. E., Jr., & Vandiver, B. J. (2001). Nigrescence theory and measurement: Introducing the Cross Racial Identity Scale (CRIS). In J. G. Ponterotto, J. M. Casas, L. A. Suzuki, & C. M. Alexander (Eds.), *Handbook of multicultural counseling* (pp. 371–393). Sage.

DeLucia-Waack, J. L., Gerrity, D., Kalodner, C., & Riva, M. (Eds.). (2004). *Handbook for group counseling and psychotherapy.* Sage.

Dube, E. M., & Savin-Williams, R. C. (1999). Sex identity development among ethnic sexual-minority male youths. *Developmental Psychology, 35,* 1389–1398. https://doi.org/10.1037/0012-1649.35.6.1389

Espin, O. M. (1994). *Feminist approaches.* In L. Comas-Diaz & B. Greene (Eds.), *Women of color: Integrating ethnic and gender identities in psychotherapy* (pp. 265–286). Guilford Press.

Fine, M., & Torre, M. E. (2021). *Essentials of critical participatory action research.* American Psychological Association.

Fondacaro, M., & Weinberg, D. (2002). Concepts of social justice in community psychology: Toward a social ecological epistemology. *American Journal of Community Psychology, 30*(4), 473–492. https://doi.org/10.1023/A:1015803817117

Freire. P. (1970). *Pedagogy of the oppressed.* Continuum.

Gielen, U., Draguns, J., & Fish, J. (Eds.). (2004). *Culture, therapy, and healing.* Allyn and Bacon

Goodman, R. D., Williams, J. M., Chung, C-Y., Talleyrand, R. M., Douglass, A. M., McMahon, H. G., & Bemak, F. (2015). Decolonizing traditional pedagogies and practices in counseling and psychology education: A move towards social justice and action. In R. D. Good & P. C. Gorski (Eds.), *Decolonizing "multicultural" counseling through social justice* (pp. 147–164). Springer.

Greenwood, D. J., & Levin, M. (2016). *Introduction to action research social research for social change* (2nd ed.). Sage.

Hage, S. M. (2003). Reaffirming the unique identity of counseling psychology: Opting for the "road less traveled by." *Counseling Psychologist, 31,* 555–563. doi:10.1177/0011000003256434

Hartnett, D. (2001). *The history of justice.* Paper presented on the Social Justice Forum, Loyola University, Chicago, IL.

Hartung, P., & Blustein, D. (2002). Reason, intuition and social justice: Elaborating on Parson's career decision-making model. *Journal of Counseling and Development, 80*(1), 41–47. DOI:10.1002/J.1556-6678.2002.TB00164.X

Helms, J. E. (1995). An update of Helm's white and people of color racial identity models. In J. G. Ponterotto, J. M. Casas, L. A. Suzuki, & C. M. Alexander (Eds.), *Handbook of multicultural counseling* (1st ed., pp. 181–198). Sage.

Helms, J. E. (2003). A pragmatic view of social justice. *Counseling Psychologist, 31,* 305–313. https://doi.org/10.1177/0011000003031003006

Herlihy, B., & Corey, G. (Eds.). (2015). *Boundary issues in counseling: Multiple roles and responsibilities.* American Counseling Association.

Hernstein, R. J., & Murray, C. A. (1994). *The bell curve: Intelligence and class structure in American life.* Free Press.

Hills, H. I., & Strozier, A. A. (1992). Multicultural training in APA-approved counseling psychology programs: A survey. *Professional Psychology: Research and Practice, 23,* 43–51. https://doi.org/10.1037/0735-7028.23.1.43

Hollis, J. W., & Wantz, R. A. (1994). *Counselor preparation 1993–1995* (8th ed.). Routledge.

Hook, J. N., Davis, D. E., Owen, J., Worthington, E. L., Jr., & Utsey, S. O. (2013). Cultural humility: Measuring openness to culturally diverse clients. *Journal of Counseling Psychology, 60*(3), 353–366. https://doi.org/10.1037/a0032595

Ibrahim, F. A., Roysircar-Sodowsky, G., & Ohnishi, H. (2001). Worldview: Recent developments and needed directions. In J. G. Ponterotto, J. M. Casas, L. A. Suzuki, & C. M. Alexander (Eds.), *Handbook of multicultural counseling* (pp. 425–456). Sage.

Jackson, M. L. (1995). Multicultural counseling: Historical perspectives. In J. G. Ponterotto, J. M. Casas, L. A. Suzuki, & C. M. Alexander (Eds.), *Handbook of multicultural counseling* (1st ed.). Sage.

Janes, J. E. (2015). Democratic encounters? Epistemic privilege, power, and community-based participatory action research. *Action Research, 14*(1), 72–87. https://doi.org/10.1177/1476750315579129

Jensen, A. (1969). How much can we boost IQ and school achievement? *Harvard Educational Review, 29,* 1–123. doi:10.17763/HAER.39.1.L3U15956627424K7

Kiselica, M. S., Maben, P., & Locke, D. C. (1999). Do multicultural education and diversity appreciation training reduce prejudice among counseling trainees? *Journal of Mental Health Counseling, 21,* 240–254. https://psycnet.apa.org/record/1999-03701-004

Ladany, N., Inman, A. G., & Constantine, M. G. (1997). Supervisee multicultural case conceptualization ability and self-reported multicultural competence as functions of supervisee racial identity and supervisor focus. *Journal of Counseling Psychology, 44,* 284–293. https://doi.org/10.1037/0022-0167.44.3.284

Leong, F. T. L., Comas-Diaz, L., Nagayama Hall, G., McLloyd, V. C., & Trimble, J. (Eds.). (2013). *APA handbook of multicultural psychology.* American Psychological Association.

Leong, F., Inman, A. G., Ebreo, A., Yang, L., Kinoshita, L. M., & Fu, M. (Eds.). (2007). *Handbook of Asian American psychology.* Sage.

Lewis, J. A., Lewis, M. D., Daniels, J. A., & D'Andrea, M. J. (1998). *Community counseling: Empowerment strategies for a diverse society.* Brooks/Cole.

Lewis, M. D., Lewis, J. A., & Dworkin, E. P. (1971). Counseling and the social revolution. [Special issue]. *Personnel and Guidance Journal, 49*(9), 64–76. https://archive.org/details/sim_journal-of-counseling-and-development-jcd_1970-1971_49_index/page/n1/mode/2up

Martin-Baro, I. (1994). *Writings for a liberation psychology.* Harvard University Press.

McWhirter, E. H. (1998). An empowerment model of counselor education. *Canadian Journal of Counselling, 32*(1), 12–26. https://psycnet.apa.org/record/1998-00240-002

Merriam-Webster. (n. d.). Social justice. Merriam-Webster dictionary. https://www.merriam-webster.com/dictionary/social%20justice

Nozick, R. (1974). *Anarchy, state, and utopia.* Basic Books.

Nyborg, N., & Jensen, A. (2000). Black-white differences on various psychometric tests: Spearman's hypothesis tested on American armed services veterans. *Personality & Individual Differences, 28*(3), 593–599. doi:10.1016/S0191-8869(99)00122-1

Pack-Brown, S., Tequilla, T., & Seymour, J. (2008). Infusing professional ethics into counselor education program: A multicultural/social justice perspective. *Journal of Counseling and Development, 86*(3), 296–302. https://doi.org/10.1002/j.1556-6678.2008.tb00512.x

Pedersen, P. (1987). Ten frequent assumptions of cultural bias in counseling. *Journal of Multicultural Counseling and Development, 15*(1), 16–24. https://doi.org/10.1002/j.2161-1912.1987.tb00374.x

Pedersen, P. (1991). Multiculturalism as a fourth force in counseling. *Journal of Counseling and Development, 70*(1), 6–12. https://doi.org/10.1002/j.1556-6676.1991.tb01553.x

Pedersen, P. B., Lonner, W. J., Draguns, J. G., Trimble, J. E., & Scharron-del Rio, M. R. (Eds.). (2015). *Counseling across cultures* (7th ed.). Sage.

Peters, H. C., & Luke, M. (2021) Social justice in counseling: Moving to a multiplistic approach, *Journal of Counselor Leadership and Advocacy, 8*(1), 1–15. doi:10.1080/2326716X.2020.1854133

Phinney, J. S. (1992). The multigroup ethnic identity measure: A new scale for use with diverse groups. *Journal of Adolescent Research, 7*, 156–176. https://doi.org/10.1177/074355489272003

Pieterse, A. L., Evans, S. A., Risner-Butner, A., Collins, N. M., & Mason, L. B. (2009). Multicultural competence and social justice training in counseling psychology and counselor education: A review and analysis of a sample of multicultural course syllabi. *Counseling Psychologist, 37*, 93–115. https://doi.org/10.1177/0011000008319986

Ponterotto, J. G. (1997). Multicultural counseling training: A competency model and national survey. In D. B. Pope-Davis & H. L. K. Coleman (Eds.), *Multicultural counseling competence: Assessment, education and training, and supervision* (pp. 227–241). Sage.

Pope-Davis, D. B., & Coleman, H. L. K. (Eds.). (1997). *Multicultural counseling competencies: Assessment, education and training, and supervision.* Sage.

Prilleltensky, I. (1997). Values, assumptions, and practices: Assessing the moral implications of psychological discourse and action. *American Psychologist, 52*(5), 517–535. https://doi.org/10.1037/0003-066X.52.5.517

Prilleltensky, I., & Prilleltensky, O. (2003). Synergies for wellness and liberation in counseling psychology. *Counseling Psychologist, 31*, 273–281. https://doi.org/10.1177/0011000003031003002

Quinn, A. (2013, Mar 22). Chinua Achebe and the bravery of lions. NPR. https://www.npr.org/sections/the two-way/2013/03/22/175046327/chinua-achebe-and-the-bravery-of-lions

Quintana, S. M., & Bernal, M. E. (1995). Ethnic minority training in counseling psychology: Comparisons with clinical psychology and proposed standards. *Counseling Psychologist, 23*, 102–121. https://doi.org/10.1177/0011000095231010

Ratcliffe, S. (2017). *Oxford essential quotations* (5th ed.). Oxford University Press. https://www.oxfordreference.com/view/10.1093/acref/9780191843730.001.0001/q-oro-ed5-00016497

Ratts, M. J. (2009). Social justice counseling: Toward the development of a fifth force among counseling paradigms. *Journal of Humanistic Counseling, Education and Development, 48*(2), 160–172. https://doi.org/10.1002/j.2161-1939.2009.tb00076.x

Ratts, M., D'Andrea, M., & Arredondo, P. (2004). Social justice counseling: A "fifth force" in the field. *Counseling Today, 47*, 28–30.

Rawls, J. (1971). *A theory of justice.* Harvard University Press.

Riessman, E. (1962). *The culturally deprived child.* Harper & Row.

Robinson, T. L., & Howard-Hamilton, M. F. (2000). *The convergence of race, ethnicity, and gender: Multiple identities in counseling.* Prentice-Hall.

Root, M. P. P. (Ed.). (1992). *Racially mixed people in America.* Sage.

Root, M. P. P. (Ed.). (1996). *The multiracial experience: Racial borders as the new frontier.* Sage.

Sam, D. L., & Berry, J. W. (Eds.). (2006). *The Cambridge handbook of acculturation psychology.* Cambridge University Press. https://doi.org/10.1017/CBO9780511489891

Scruggs, A-O. (2017, Jan 13). Beyond Vietnam: The MLK speech that caused an uproar. USA Today. https://www.usatoday.com/story/news/nation-now/2017/01/13/martin-luther-king-jr-beyond-vietnam-speech/96501636/

Singh, A. A., Appling, B., & Trepal, H. (2020). Using the multicultural and social justice counseling competencies to decolonize counseling practice: The important roles of theory, power, and action. *Journal of Counseling and Development, 98*(3), 261–281. https://doi.org/10.1002/jcad.12321

Sparks, E., & Park, A. (2000, Oct). *Facilitating multicultural training of counseling psychology graduate students: Experiential learning in a diverse setting.* Paper presented at the First Annual Diversity Challenge Conference, Institute for the Study and Promotion of Race and Culture, Boston College, Boston, MA.

Speight, S. L., & Vera, E. M. (2004). A social justice agenda: Ready, or not? *Counseling Psychologist, 32*(1), 109–118. https://doi.org/10.1177/0011000003260005

Stevens, E., & Wood, G. H. (1992). *Justice, ideology, and education: An introduction to the social foundation of education.* McGraw-Hill.

Sue, D., Arredondo, P., & McDavis, R. (1992). Multicultural counseling competencies and standards: A call to the profession. *Journal of Multicultural Counseling and Development, 20*, 64–88. https://doi.org/10.1002/j.1556-6676.1992.tb01642.x

Sue, D. W. (1995). Multicultural organizational development: Implications for the counseling profession. In J. G. Ponterotto, J. M. Casa, L. A. Suzuki, & C. M. Alexander (Eds.), *Handbook of multicultural counseling* (pp. 474–492). Sage.

Sue, D. W., Bernier, J. B., Durran, M., Feinberg, L., Pedersen, P., Smithe, E., & Vasquez-Nuttall, E. (1982). Position paper: Cross-cultural counseling competencies. *Counseling Psychologist, 10*, 45–52. doi:10.1177/0011000082102008

Sue, D. W., Carter, R. T., Casas, J. M., Fouad, N. A., Ivey, A. E., Jensen, M., LaFromboise, T., et al. (1998). *Multicultural counseling competencies: Individual and organizational development.* Sage.

Sue, D. W., & Sue, D. (2008). *Counseling the culturally diverse: Theory and practice* (5th ed.). Wiley.

Sue, D. W., Sue, D., Neville, H. A., & Smith, L. (2019). *Counseling the culturally different: Theory and practice* (8th ed.). Wiley.

Tate, K. A., Rivera, E. T., Brown, E., & Skaistis, L. (2013). Foundations for liberation: Social justice, liberation psychology, and counseling. *Revista Interamericana de Psicología/Interamerican Journal of Psychology, 47*(3), 373–382. https://psycnet.apa.org/record/2014-45484-003

Tenety, M., & Kiselica, M. S. (2000). Working with mental health advocacy groups. In J. Lewis & L. Bradley (Eds.), *Advocacy in counseling: Counselors, clients & community* (pp. 139–146). ERIC.

Toporek, R. L., Gerstein, L., Fouad, N., Roysircar, G., & Israel, T. (2006). *Handbook for social justice in counseling psychology: Leadership, vision and action.* Sage.

Triandis, H. C. (1994). *Culture and social behavior.* McGraw-Hill.

United Nations. (1948, Dec 10). The universal declaration of human rights. http://www.un.org/en/documents/udhr/

U.S. Department of Health and Human Services. (2001). *Mental health: Culture, race, and ethnicity. A supplement to Mental health: A report of the surgeon general.* Author.

Valencia, R. R., & Suzuki, L. A. (2001). *Intelligence testing and minority students: Foundations, performance, factors, and assessment issues.* Sage.

Vera, E., & Speight, S. (2003). Multicultural competence, social justice, and counseling psychology: Expanding our roles. *Counseling Psychologist, 31*(3), 253–272. doi:10.1177/0011000003031003001

Wallerstein, N., & Christens, B. (Eds.). (2021). Special section: Engage for equity: Advancing the fields of community-based participatory research and community-engaged research in community psychology and the social sciences. *American Journal of Community Psychology, 67*(3–4), 249–504. https://doi.org/10.1002/ajcp.12430

Walsh, W. M. (1975). Classics in guidance and counseling. *Personnel and Guidance Journal, 54*(4), 219–220. https://doi.org/10.1002/j.2164-4918.1975.tb04227.x

Wang, H. L. (2014). Descendants of Chinese laborers reclaim railroad history. NPR. https://www.npr.org/secti
ons/codeswitch/2014/05/10/311157404/descendants-of-chinese-laborers-reclaim-railroads-history

Winters, L. I., & DeBose, H. L. (2003). *New faces in a changing America: Multiracial identity in the 21st century.* Sage.

Young, I. (1990). *Justice and the politics of difference.* Princeton University Press.

Zinn, H. (1980). *People's history of the United States.* Harper Collins.

CHAPTER 5

SOCIAL JUSTICE AND HUMAN RIGHTS

The Fifth Force in Psychology

Rita Chi-Ying Chung and Frederic P. Bemak

When you see something that is not right, not fair, not just, you have to speak up.
You have to say something; you have to do something.

—John Lewis

Striving for social justice is the most valuable thing to do in life.

—Albert Einstein

I'm no longer accepting the things I cannot change.... I'm changing the things I
cannot accept.

—Angela Davis

REFLECTION QUESTIONS

1. Do you believe you have power to change the conditions around you in any of
    the aspects of your life? If so, how do you imagine you could use this power? How
    would it feel to use this power and try to change the world around you?
2. How would you like to use your power toward gaining more justice for others?

Given the importance and critical need to respond to social and human rights issues, coupled
with a growing awareness of injustices, we believe that social justice and human rights is the
fifth force in counseling and psychology. This requires the mental health profession to chart
new territory and focus on social justice and human rights as it pertains to psychological

well-being. The American Psychological Association (APA) and the American Counseling Association (ACA) have acknowledged the importance of social justice and human rights in mental health practice and training, creating multicultural guidelines and competencies that include social justice. The inclusion of social justice in the practices of two major U.S. mental health organizations underscores the call for social justice and human rights as the profession's "fifth force." In effect, social justice is a response to social conditions that produce inequalities and inequities in how people in any given society gain access and rights to opportunities, resources, and advantages (Miller, 1999) so that, by definition, social justice includes concepts of justice, fairness, equity, and righteousness. The objectives of social justice work are to eliminate unfair treatment, inequities, and injustices, thus leading to a society where *all* members, regardless of their race, ethnicity, culture, sexual orientation, gender, religion, socioeconomic status, abilities, age, or other distinguishing characteristics, are on the same, equal, and equitable playing field. This means that *all* people, not just a privileged few, have equal and fair access to and distribution of resources and opportunity, and they are psychologically and physically safe and secure (Bell, 1997).

All of this leads mental health professionals to take on somewhat different roles than those that training and/or typical protocols have demarcated, as we redefine ourselves within a social justice and human rights paradigm that emphasizes being proactive and intentional in changing oppressive and discriminatory systems and establishing a more equitable distribution of power and resources so that all people can live with the same rights, dignity, safety, security, opportunities, and resources (Goodman, 2001). However, the extent and depth to which multiculturalism and diversity are addressed in psychology and counseling vary from program to program (Pieterse et al., 2008).

As mentioned previously traditional mental health interventions have focused on individuals and have been apolitical (Brown, 1997), ignoring and disregarding the influence of history, politic, culture, and environment on the experiences and behavior of clients and their families. Placing blame on the individual has discounted systemic injustices (Ryan, 1971). I (Fred) saw an example of this when working with a client who was experiencing racial discrimination at her place of employment. The client was in a work situation where she and others colleagues of color experienced microaggressions. For me to work with her by focusing only on intrapsychic issues and help her adjust to a hostile and oppressive environment would be to assist her with fitting into and adapting to a racist environment. To address the impact of the microaggressions as the client's problem would be sanctioning the racism she was experiencing and implicitly communicating to her that it was, in fact, her problem. To move beyond the traditional individual framework, I worked with the client on becoming her own advocate for changing the environment, and I helped her not only to deal with personal feelings and reactions to the situation, but to form partnerships with her colleagues to develop proactive strategies to change their discriminatory and hostile work environment. As this example shows, recognizing the interplay between the client's own individual problems and the larger social, political, historical, economic, and ecological world is key in social justice mental health work.

Given the national and global inequity of resources, opportunities, and access and the historical, psychopolitical, cultural, psychosocial, and ecological factors involved in discrimination and oppression, counselors and psychologists can no longer focus only on the intrapsychic dynamics and behaviors of their clients. When considering social justice in the mental health field, we are examining a broader perspective that incorporates social issues involving the individual, the family, the community, the wider society, and even the global community. Social injustice refers to injustices, unfair treatment, and inequities that result from racism, xenophobia, sexism, socioeconomics, ableism, and other "isms," all of which affect quality of life and the psychological well-being of individuals, families, and communities. Thus, we maintain that social justice and human rights be the fifth force in mental health.

As mental health professionals integrating social justice and human rights into our work as the fifth force we should be mindful about the wide range and impact of injustices. Social injustices may be experienced in a variety of different ways, ranging from personal affronts to broader violations that are institutionally and systemically based. A social injustice may be a clear and overt inequity, such as denial of entry to a private club based on race, gender, socioeconomic status, or religion, or a hate crime directed at the person, such as the word "Jap" (a derogatory term for Japanese) seen by us (Rita and Fred) scratched onto the hood of a parked car (see Box Text 5.1). Other forms of social injustice may manifest more covertly and subliminally, such as unwritten institutional policies that prevent people of color and/or women from advancing to senior positions or discrimination that results in lower pay raises for those who are physically challenged or identify as LGBTQI.

BOX TEXT 5.1 CAR VANDALIZED WITH A DEROGATORY NAME FOR JAPANESE

Although there are various definitions of social justice psychology and counseling (e.g., Bell, 1997; Smith et al., 2003; Sue et al., 2019), all definitions include issues of promoting equitable distribution of resources, access, and opportunities that are required to meet basic human needs for enhancing growth and development; eliminating oppressive and discriminatory barriers and disparities that interfere with the quality of life; and ensuring physical and psychological safety and security. In working toward social justice and human rights, it makes sense that psychologists and counselors be equipped to challenge unfair and inequitable systems through assessing clients from ecological, micro, meso, and macro perspectives that include historical, psychopolitical, economic, cultural, and psychosocial viewpoints. We strongly believe that any definition of social justice counseling and psychology should not just contain a description or definition of social justice, but also involve an action component incorporating advocacy and empowerment. One of the first exercises I (Rita) used in my graduate-level social justice class was to ask students to develop their own definition of social justice. Table 5.1 provides examples of social justice definitions from my classes in various semesters. Note that each definition consists of mental health professionals proactively participating in eliminating injustices, thus underscoring that social justice and human rights is indeed the fifth force in psychology and counseling.

The prevalence of national and global social injustices, which led to social justice and human rights being conceived as the fifth force in our field, correlates with mental health professionals having an ethical and moral obligation to address these issues within the therapeutic context. This requires an understanding of the relationship between clients' cognitive and affective functioning and their behavior and their engagement within their larger world milieu. Thus, the environmental issues that negatively impact a client's life, the broader systemic factors that influence a client's psychological health and well-being, and the effect of institutions, organizations, and systems (e.g., schools, the workplace, legal and political systems) must all be viewed within the larger perspective of psychological well-being. When working toward social justice and human rights, these ecological variables provide a broad context that shapes and contributes to an individual's psychological well-being. Within a social justice mental health context, these variables play a key role in the therapeutic interventions of helping professionals, again leading to social justice and human rights as the fifth force.

Some years ago, Humphreys (1996) argued that psychologists can effectively provide more in-depth, sustained benefit to society through the betterment of social institutions and changes in social policy rather than through psychotherapy. Seven years later, Vera and Speight (2003) further enhanced this idea, arguing that counseling psychology was uniquely positioned to shift gears toward social justice work, given its emphasis on personal strengths and resilience and on psychoeducational practices, interactions, and dynamics within the larger ecological context that fosters a generally broader, more holistic view of people. We would concur, and we suggest that client problems are frequently reactions and responses to deep-seated issues rooted in the historical, social, cultural, political, and economic world of the client. Hence, it is important that we, as psychologists and counselors, look at the larger macro-ecological context.

The importance of acknowledging social justice and human rights as a fifth force is illustrated in Figure 5.1, which demonstrates the influence and impact of societal and environmental factors on individuals, their families, and communities. As the diagram shows,

TABLE 5.1 George Mason University (GMU) social justice and counseling class definitions in different semesters

Semesters	Definitions
Spring 2015	Social justice counseling is advocating for equity and educating all stakeholders while working with systems to change policies and empower individuals, families, and communities marginalized due to different forms of discrimination, active oppression, and victimization. By bringing suppressed issues into public consciousness, we can bridge the gap between individuals and their environment. AKA: Advocation!
Fall 2016	Social justice counseling is a process to ensure equity, fairness, opportunity, empowerment, and basic human rights to all people through advocacy and action.
Spring 2017	Social justice counseling is seeking equity and equality through the process of CARE:
	Create access and collaborate
	Advocate for human rights, social change, and acknowledge differences
	Respect through compassion, acceptance, appreciation, and dialogue
	Educate and empower marginalized groups to fight for change.
Summer 2019	Social justice counseling is working alongside clients and stakeholders to advocate and address needs at the individual, community, and institutional levels to create a more just and equitable society by empowering clients to advocate for themselves and eliminating barriers through providing resources, education, access, and support.
Spring 2019	Social justice counseling encompasses working with others to proactively empower, support, advocate, and provide quality resources while taking actions to change oppressive systems. Social justice counselors have the responsibility to educate themselves and others about cultural competencies, social, political, economic, and global injustices.

individuals and their families do not live in isolation, so what affects society may also influence them directly or indirectly. For example, being discriminated against due to religious differences may be experienced on multiple levels, such as direct verbal or physical abuse; negative community responses that are public and condoned; harassment; attacks on religious places of worship; differential treatment in the workplace or school; stereotypical portrayals by media; unfair treatment in the health, financial, and legal systems; or differences in the quality of received services. Each of these situations impacts not only the larger community but also the individual's psychological well-being, quality of life, and sense of safety and security. To illustrate this point further using the school environment as an example, Figure 5.2 describes how external variables both within and outside the school environment may influence students' academic achievement (Bemak et al., 2014). Note that both diagrams are not necessarily an exhaustive list of variables impacting clients, but rather these underscore how individuals and families are affected directly and indirectly by what goes on in their environments.

We suggest that reducing client problems to intrapsychic, behavioral, or isolated personal issues without consideration of the larger systemic issues is "Band-Aiding" and doing

FIGURE 5.1 Macro Approach to Social Justice & Human Rights

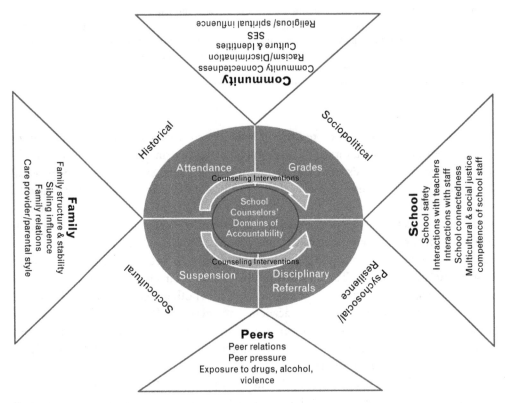

FIGURE 5.2 Variables Effecting Students' Academic Performance

Adapted from Bemak, et al., 2014.

a "quick-fix" without focusing on the root causes of the problem. This results in short-term solutions at the expense of addressing deeper-rooted social issues, subsequently running the risk of insidiously reinforcing and perpetuating the circumstances that created the problem in the first place. For example, when a client came to me (Fred) to discuss his frustration and anger about being poor, it was unacceptable to only help him come to terms with his feelings about living in poverty. Taking a deeper look at the historical, political, social, cultural, and economic circumstances that contributed to this client's long-standing poverty, I worked not only with the presenting feelings but also helped the client employ strategies to get himself out of poverty, assist his family in breaking the cycle of poverty, and facilitate skills that would promote successful ways to become an advocate for himself and his family to change his situation. I took this tack in psychotherapy rather than simply helping the client come to accept feelings of frustration and anger about being poor. This example highlights the critical need for psychologists and counselors to integrate social justice and human rights as the fifth force in their mental health work.

RELATIONSHIP BETWEEN POWER AND SOCIAL JUSTICE

It is important to deconstruct the relationship between the fifth force in psychology, social justice and human rights, and power. People in positions of power can perpetuate social injustices and human rights violations, intentionally or unintentionally, if they are intolerant, hold prejudicial beliefs, harbor a desire to maintain an inequitable status quo, and lack awareness, understanding, and openness about economic, racial, political, cultural, and social injustices. They can maintain their power, positions, and wealth by both consciously and unconsciously and intentionally and unintentionally treating designated groups of people unfairly and unjustly. At times, people in positions of power and privilege may disregard those who are less powerful. This may be due to ignorance, lack of awareness, or simply not being concerned about the lives of people who are powerless. These types of actions frequently contribute to a continuation of unfair treatment and inequity in services, resources, access, and opportunities, resulting in continued oppression, personal behaviors, and decisions that support and cultivate discrimination and unequal and inequitable institutional access to opportunities and resources, as well as established discriminatory policies and practices. The perpetuation of the power differential is underscored by the fact that many of those in power have social capital, with vast professional and social networks, information, knowledge, and skills through which to access resources and information, and peers, colleagues, family, and friends who have the ability to influence organizational, state, and governmental policies and funding priorities that could promote greater equity and fairness.

A good example, and one that has significant impact on psychological well-being, is the inequity in wealth and power in the United States and globally, with 2021 marking historical gains for the wealthy. The result has been the biggest leap in wealth disparity in recent history, with the world's richest people owning 11% of global wealth (Goodkind, 2021); the world's wealthiest people collectively gaining $1 trillion (with Elon Musk, one of the world's richest people, alone gaining nearly $118 billion in 2021); and the combined net worth of the 500 people in the Bloomberg billionaire index now exceeding $8.4 trillion, which is more than the gross domestic product of any single country in the world except the United States and China; while simultaneously, in the same year, the United Nations estimating that 150 million people fell into poverty (Morrow, 2022). With continued growing disparity between the rich and poor, 2019 Nobel prize economists Abhijit Banerjee and Esther Duflo wrote that we are living in a world with an "extreme concentration of economic power in the hands of a very small minority of the super-rich" (Goodkind, 2021).

Furthermore, the world's richest 1% (i.e., those with more than $1 million) own 44% of the world's wealth (Credit Suisse, 2019). In 2019, the world's billionaires (2,153 people) had more wealth than 4.6 billion people (Oxfam, 2020). In contrast, adults with less than $10,000 in wealth make up 56.6% of the world's population but hold less than 2% of global wealth (Credit Suisse, 2019). Similarly, in the United States, only a very small number of citizens own most of the wealth. The top 1% has approximately 16 times more wealth than the bottom 50% (Leonhardt, 2021). The top 10% own 70% of the country's total wealth, and, since 1989, wealth distribution shows that the rich have gotten richer, with the top 1% expanding their wealth share from 24% to 32% (Buchholz, 2021). Moreover, the United States has the world's largest millionaire population (18.61 million), accounting for 40% of total millionaires, with 40% of those in the top 1% of global wealth distribution (Credit Suisse, 2019).

In fact, in the United States, the top 1% *alone* has more wealth (>$25 trillion) than the middle class ($18 trillion), exceeding the wealth of the bottom 80% and equivalent to more than all the goods and services produced in the U.S. economy in 2018 (Sawhill & Pulliam, 2019). Before 2010, the middle class owned more wealth than the top 1%, but there has been a steady decline since 1995 of the amount of wealth held by the middle class, coupled with a steady increase by the top 1% (Sawhill & Pulliam, 2019). Clearly, the gap between those who have (the rich) and those who do not have (the poor) wealth, resources, and power is widening (Buchholz, 2021) while the U.S. middle class is shrinking and joining the ranks of the poor (Sawhill & Pulliam, 2019). It has been projected that it would take just 1% of the top 1% of wealth ($250 billion annually and $2.5 trillion over 10 years) to rectify some of the United States' most demanding social justice problems (Sawhill & Pulliam, 2019). The inequities in wealth and power have human rights and social justice consequences for those who do not hold economic wealth or stability, impacting their psychological well-being, physical safety and security, and economic justice, thus once again denoting the importance of social justice and human rights as the fifth force in psychology and counseling.

Economic disparities lead to multiple social injustices. For example, in the United States, 10% of individuals and their related institutional bodies have the majority of wealth and power and subsequently substantially greater influence in society as compared to the 90% majority of the population who wield significantly less wealth and power. As a result of having greater wealth, they inherently carry more privilege and power in a society that allows them to use their position to establish policies that can enhance or limit opportunities for others and access to resources for disenfranchised groups. Examples of this can be seen in the millions of U.S. citizens who have limited health and mental health care, diminished social services, inadequate housing, lower-quality education in poorer urban and rural school districts, fewer employment opportunities, restricted political representation, unfair judicial treatment, fewer legal rights, and generally reduced human rights. As we write the second edition of this book, 17 U.S. states are currently enacting 28 new laws that limit access for people of color and poor people to vote, thus creating barriers to voting in state and federal elections (Boschma, 2021). The voting obstacles provide an example of how those with wealth and power can significantly impact the future of others by using their status and finances to maintain wealth and power while having a significant impact on the lives and psychological well-being of others.

Figure 5.3 illustrates the correlation between power and privilege in the United States, considering the intersectionality of socioeconomic status, race, ethnicity, and gender. The connection between power and privilege significantly influences who will be elected and determines policies related to social justice, human rights, and psychological well-being. The elected officials' decisions will affect disenfranchised groups and may have deleterious effects on human services, social services, education, and mental health services, all of which meaningfully impact our work as mental health professionals. (Note: Since the statistics we are sharing here and throughout the book change annually, we recommend that you research the latest statistics of your local area, state, and country.)

When we examine issues of race, ethnicity, and gender in relationship to positions of power by officials who determine policies and practices with implications for social justice and human rights, there are significant differences. This holds true for variances in earnings

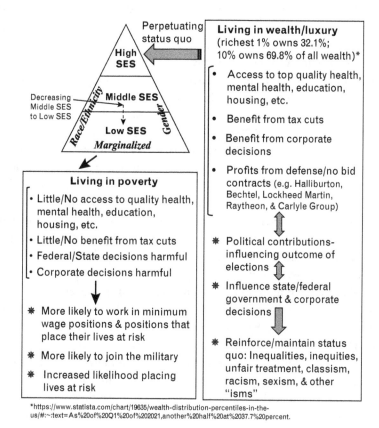

*https://www.statista.com/chart/19635/wealth-distribution-percentiles-in-the-us/#:~:text=As%20of%20Q1%20of%202021,another%20half%20at%2037.7%20percent.

FIGURE 5.3 Power & Privilege in the U.S.: The Intersectionality of Socioeconomic Status, Race/Ethnicity & Gender

Adapted from: Chung (2004).

as well. For example, in 2021, people of color and women were still underrepresented in the U.S. Congress and as chief executive officers (CEOs). To date, there has only been one U.S. president of color (Barack Obama, 2009–2017); one woman who ran for presidential candidate (Hillary Clinton, 2016); and one woman of color U.S. vice president (Kamala Harris, 2020–Present). Powerful positions in Congress remain dominated by White men even though women make up 50.8% and people of color account for 43% of the U.S. population (Boschma et al., 2021; Center for American Women and Politics [CAWP], 2020; Schaeffer, 2021). In 2020, 76.3% of the U.S. Congress was male: 74% in the Senate and 76.8% in the House of Representatives (CAWP, 2020). Although more women were being elected to Congress over the past decade, especially after the U.S. 2018 elections, when a record of approximately 102 women were elected to the House of Representatives and 13 to the Senate (Warner et al., 2018), there remains a gender disparity in representation. Breaking these figures down by race shows that approximately 78% of Congress members— 75% in the House of Representatives and 91% in the Senate—are White (Schaeffer, 2021).

Similarly, women and people of color are significantly underrepresented as heads of Fortune 500 companies, with only 37 (7%) headed by women and only 7 women running Fortune 100 companies (Hinchliffe, 2020). Similarly, 30% of U.S. college presidents are women, 9% are people of color, and only 5% are women of color (American Council on Education, 2017). Correspondingly, in 2019, women made up 49% of all law students, but only 23% of women are partners (Warner et al., 2019). Therefore, it is not surprising that there are significant gender and racial disparities in income. This can be seen with salaries, where, in the United States, women make only $0.82 for every dollar a man earns, creating a gender wage gap of 18%; by projecting that over 15 years, women will make just half (49%) of men's salaries. Examining the data further, African American/Black women earn $0.62 for every dollar a White male makes, Asian Americans $0.90, Latinas $0.54, and American Indian women $0.57 (Elsesser, 2020). (Note: The statistics quoted for Asian Americans throughout this section can be misleading given that this group is not monolithic and consists of more than 50 groups [Zhou, 2021]). Income gender disparity is not occurring only in the United States but globally (Szmigiera, 2021). Again, we recommend that readers investigate updated statistics in their own country, state, or region to examine the power inequities noted above. Economic and privilege imbalances continue to promote an unequal distribution of power and the likelihood to maintain, reinforce, and promote social injustices and human rights violations that impact psychological well-being. Hence it is crucial that we, mental health professionals, implement social justice and human rights in our work.

To further illustrate inequities and disparities, we examined poverty rates in the United States. Although there was a slight decline in poverty (0.5%) in the United States from 2017 to 2018, 38.1 million people (1 in 8) still live below the poverty line, with 1 in every 6 children (11.9 million, 16.2%) living in poverty. Linked to poverty has been a rise in those without health insurance, from 25.6 million people in 2017 to 27.5 million in 2018, including 4.3 million children (U.S. Census Bureau, 2019). Achieving economic justice is particularly acute for the more subordinate, disenfranchised, oppressed, and marginalized groups who are in greater need and face greater challenges in achieving economic stability and equity given little or no social capital and with less access, resources, opportunities, voice, and power.

To illustrate this point, in 2018, the median household income of the U.S. White American was $70,642, compared to Black/African American ($41,361) and Hispanic

($51,450) households (U.S. Census Bureau, 2019). The poverty rate of Whites was 8.1% compared to Asians (10.1%), Blacks/African Americans (20.8%), and Hispanics (17.6%) (U.S. Census Bureau, 2019). The poverty rates affect home ownership, so families of color were far less likely to own their own homes. Home ownership, which is tied to gainful employment, is 72% for Whites, 12% for Asian Americans, 14% for American Indian/Alaska Natives, 30–42% for Black/African Americans, and 25% for Latinx (U.S. Census Bureau, 2019). All of these statistics relate to the psychological well-being and mental health of our clients and are important for mental health professionals to understand as part of their work. Again, we encourage you to look at updated statistics related to these issues in your region, state, and country.

It is evident when we look at these data that issues of wealth and power are linked to race and ethnicity and connected to social justice and human rights as the fifth force. An example is highlighted by the late Gwen Ifill, the journalist who coined the term "missing white women syndrome" in 2004 (Robertson, 2021), referring to extensive U.S. national media coverage, reports, and documentaries about White women who are missing compared to missing women of color, who receive minimal coverage. For missing White women, the coverage is immediate, daily, and ongoing, so the issue becomes nationally known and in the forefront of national daily news, leading to a greater likelihood of finding the missing girls/women. Furthermore, police tend to believe reports on missing White girls/women and act immediately once they are informed of the situation (Robertson, 2021). Also, in some cases, money offered as rewards for information is more accessible. The result is that there is more time, energy, and resources spent in finding missing White women compared to missing women of color (Robertson, 2021).

The FBI statistics from the National Crime Information Center exemplifies this phenomenon. At the end of 2020, of the more than 89,000 active missing person cases 45% were people of color. Yet, according to an analysis by criminologist Zach Sommers, only about one-fifth of missing person cases involving people of color received media coverage (Eversley, 2021). To further illustrate the missing white women syndrome, I (Rita) do an exercise in my graduate multicultural counseling class, showing a list of missing girls/women of color (e.g., Tamika Huston, Keeshae Jacobs, Deidre Reid, Relisha Rudd, Stephanie Van Nguyen, Yvette Martinez). Sadly, as predicted, not one student had heard any of the names. Then I show a list of missing White girls/women (e.g., Elizabeth Smart, JonBenet Ramsey, Laci Peterson, Chandra Levy, Natalie Holloway, Gabrielle Petito). One hundred percent of students were aware of most names on the list as a result of repeated media coverage and television drama and documentaries. It is regrettable that any girl/women regardless of their race/ethnicity goes missing, but unfortunately the missing white women syndrome clearly demonstrates how bias toward race/ethnicity can influence the media and foster inequities and racial injustice based on racism, biases, power, and prejudice.

SOCIAL JUSTICE AND ETHICS

Traditionally in the United States, ethical standards for counseling and psychology are established based on legal precepts that guide moral behavior. In the United States, professional codes of ethics have been established for both counseling and psychology that are aimed at ensuring and protecting clients' rights. The ethical standards have been criticized for being too legalistic, accentuating linear thinking, being too objective at the expense of interplay between subjective and objective linkages, maintaining an emphasis on protection rather than growth, sustaining the status quo rather than focusing on change, and leaning too heavily on legal sanctions (Rowley & MacDonald, 2001).

Generally, ethical standards for psychologists and counselors have not addressed social justice or human rights issues, focusing more on overarching legal implications and the legal "do's and don'ts" in the practice of counseling and psychotherapy. The criticisms underscore the fear of being sued, resulting in hesitation to take risks that may be therapeutically beneficial to clients. More recently there have been modifications to this legalistic approach, with the ACA's ethical code noting the importance of promoting social justice and the APA's ethical principles including justice as a core principle, designating that everyone should have accessibility to and be able to profit from psychological practices. Even so, there has been criticism that the APA has not explored or clearly explained the implications of including the concept of justice (Hailes et al., 2021), which we would also note as a concern for the ACA's ethical guidelines. This is a critical point, related to social justice and human rights as the fifth force, and it requires clearer ethical guidelines and standards.

Although we appreciate the need and importance of a legalistic approach, given the general prevalence of litigation in the United States, we are concerned that the U.S. ethical codes do not sufficiently address the "human aspects" of mental health services in a proactive and positive manner. When I (Fred) served four years on a state licensure board for professional counselors, I was party to reviews of all the professional violations for counselors in the state. It was striking that there were no guidelines that promoted healthy client–counselor relationships, as are found in the United Kingdom (British Association for Counselling and Psychotherapy, 2018), but rather emphasized strict laws that guided ethical and professional behavior. Consequently, the professionals knew when they did something wrong, but they did not have guidelines for a more positive approach to their work or a framework for promoting the healthier and more positive psychological well-being of their clients. Our comments in this section about ethical guidelines present an expanded way of thinking about what we normally take for granted (in this case, ethical codes) and suggest that we could theoretically incorporate more comprehensive perspectives about including social justice and human rights into ethical principles, especially when viewing social justice and human rights as the fifth force in the field.

SUMMARY

In summary, it is indeed vital that mental health recognizes social justice and human rights as the fifth force as there is undeniably significant work for us to do as social justice–oriented psychologists and counselors. In this chapter, we discussed the importance of social justice and human rights as the fifth force, underscored by an examination of the issues that impact the mental health professional including the intersectionality of wealth, power, privilege, race, gender, and ethnicity. We also discussed ethical standards, and we present a number of statistics that help portray a context of justice and rights within contemporary society.

DISCUSSION QUESTIONS

1. Think about what social justice means to you. How would you describe social justice? After reading this chapter, has your definition of social justice changed?
2. How do you imagine wealth and power impacts psychological well-being? Please give specific examples.
3. Take a look at the ethical standards of your professional association. Do the standards adequately address social justice and human rights of clients? If so, how; if not, discuss where it would be helpful to include or add new standards.

REFERENCES

American Council on Education. (2017). American college president study. https://www.acenet.edu/Research-Insights/Pages/American-College-President-Study.aspx

Bell, L. A. (1997). Theoretical foundations for social justice education. In M. Adams, L. A. Bell, & P. Griffin (Eds.), *Teaching for diversity and social justice* (pp. 3–15). Routledge.

Bemak, F., Williams, J., & Chung, R. C-Y. (2014). Four critical domains of accountability for school counselors. *Professional School Counseling, 18*(1), 100–110. doi:10.5330/prsc.18.1.q40379257k35n1kx

Boschma, J. (2021, Jun 30). Seventeen states have enacted 28 new laws making it harder to vote. CNN. https://www.cnn.com/2021/06/30/politics/voter-suppression-restrictive-voting-laws/index.html

Boschma, J., Wolfe, D., Krishnakumar, P., Hickey, C., Maharishi, M., Rigdon, R., Keefe, J., & Wright, D. (2021, Aug 13). Census release shows America is more diverse and more multiracial than ever. CNN. https://edition.cnn.com/2021/08/12/politics/us-census-2020-data/index.html

British Association for Counselling and Psychotherapy. (2018, Jul 1). Ethical framework for the counselling professions. https://www.bacp.co.uk/events-and-resources/ethics-and-standards/ethical-framework-for-the-counselling-professions/

Brown, D. (1997). Implications of cultural values for cross-cultural consultation with families. *Journal of Counseling and Development, 76,* 29–35. https://doi.org/10.1002/j.1556-6676.1997.tb02373.x

Buchholz, K. (2021, Aug 31). The top 10 percent own 70 percent of U.S. wealth. Statista. https://www.statista.com/chart/19635/wealth-distribution-percentiles-in-the-us/

Center for American Women and Politics (CAWP). (2009). Women in the U.S. Congress 2009. http://www.cawp.rutgers.edu/fast_facts/levels_of_office/documents/cong.pdf

Credit Suisse. (2019, Oct). Global wealth report 2019. https://www.credit-suisse.com/about-us/en/reports-research/global-wealth-report.html

Elsesser, K. (2020, Mar 30). On equal pay day, what is the real gender pay gap? Forbes. https://www.forbes.com/sites/kimelsesser/2020/03/30/on-equal-pay-day-what-is-the-real-gender-pay-gap/#3851027d28ba

Eversley, M. (2021, Oct 4). When women of color disappear, who says their names? The Guardian. https://www.theguardian.com/us-news/2021/oct/04/when-women-of-color-disappear-who-says-their-names

Goodkind, N. (2021, Dec 8). World's richest people now own 11% of global wealth, marking the biggest leap in recent history. https://fortune.com/2021/12/07/worlds-richest-inequality-richer-during-pandemic/

Goodman, D. J. (2001). *Promoting diversity and social justice: Educating people from privileged groups.* Sage.

Hailes, H. P., Ceccolini, C. J., Gutowski, E., & Liang, B. (2021). Ethical guidelines for social justice in psychology. *Professional Psychology: Research and Practice, 52*(1), 1–11. https://doi.org/10.1037/pro0000291

Hinchliffe, E. (2020, May 18). The number of female CEOs in the Fortune 500 hits an all-time record. https://fortune.com/2020/05/18/women-ceos-fortune-500-2020/

Humphreys, K. (1996). Clinical psychologists as psychotherapists. *American Psychologist, 51,* 190–197. https://doi.org/10.1037/0003-066X.51.3.190

Leonhardt, M. (2021, Jun 23). The top 1% of Americans have about 16 times more wealth than the bottom 50%. CNBC. https://www.cnbc.com/2021/06/23/how-much-wealth-top-1percent-of-americans-have.html

Miller, D. (1999). *Principles of social justice.* Harvard University Press.

Morrow, A. (2022, Jan 4). The world's 500 richest people became $1 trillion richer last year. CNN Business. https://edition.cnn.com/2022/01/04/business/billionaires-gain-1-trillion-wealth/index.html

Oxfam. (2020). Extreme inequality and poverty. https://www.oxfamamerica.org/explore/issues/extreme-inequality-and-poverty/

Pieterse, A. L., Evans, S. A., Risner-Butner, A., Collins, N. M., & Mason, L. B. (2008). Multicultural competence and social justice training in counseling psychology and counselor education: A review and analysis of a sample of multicultural course syllabi. *Counseling Psychologist, 37,* 93–115. https://doi.org/10.1177/0011000008319986

Robertson, K. (2021, Sep 22). News media can't shake "missing white woman syndrome," critics say. New York Times. https://www.nytimes.com/2021/09/22/business/media/gabby-petito-missing-white-woman-syndrome.html

Rowley, W. J., & MacDonald, D. (2001). Counseling and the law: A cross-cultural perspective. *Journal of Counseling and Development, 79,* 422–429. https://doi.org/10.1002/j.1556-6676.2001.tb01989.x

Ryan, W. (1971). *Blaming the victim.* Pantheon.

Sawhill, I. V., & Pulliam, C. (2019, Jun 25). Six facts about wealth in the United States. https://www.brookings.edu/blog/up-front/2019/06/25/six-facts-about-wealth-in-the-united-states/

Schaeffer, K. (2021, Jan 28). Racial, ethnic diversity increases yet again with the 117th Congress. Pew Research Center. https://www.pewresearch.org/fact-tank/2021/01/28/racial-ethnic-diversity-increases-yet-again-with-the-117th-congress/

Smith, L., Baluch, S., Bernabei, S., Robohm, J., & Sheehy, J. (2003). Applying a social justice framework to college counseling center practice. *Journal of College Counseling, 6*(1), 3–13. https://doi.org/10.1002/j.2161-1882.2003.tb00222.x

Sue, D. W., Sue, D., Neville, H. A., & Smith, L. (2019). *Counseling the culturally diverse: Theory and practice* (8th ed.). Wiley.

Szmigiera, M. (2021, Apr 8). The global gender gap index 2021. https://www.statista.com/statistics/244387/the-global-gender-gap-index/

U.S. Census Bureau. (2019, Sep). Income, poverty and health insurance coverage in the United States: 2018. https://www.census.gov/newsroom/press-releases/2019/income-poverty.html

Vera, E., & Speight, S. (2003). Multicultural competence, social justice, and counseling psychology: Expanding our roles. *Counseling Psychologist, 31*(3), 253–272. https://doi.org/10.1177/0011000003031003001

Warner, J., Ellmann, N., & Boesch, D. (2018, Nov 20). The women's leadership gap. https://www.americanprogress.org/issues/women/reports/2018/11/20/461273/womens-leadership-gap-2/#:~:text=Women%20constitute%20a%20majority%20of,percent%20of%20all%20medical%20degrees.

Zhou, L. (2021). The label aspires to unify a wide range of communities with common cause and shared experiences. But many feel it flattens and erases entire cultures. Vox. https://www.vox.com/identities/22380197/asian-american-pacific-islander-aapi-heritage-anti-asian-hate-attacks

CHAPTER 6

STUDENT CHAPTER

An Advocacy Addict

Hollie Daniels

When I decided to become a school counselor, I never considered the idea of self-reflecting on my own personal biases and how that would completely change my life. I grew up in a small town in Southern Virginia where everyone was either Black or White and things were kept very simple. I moved to Northern Virginia, where I began my own life as a 22-year-old woman. I submerged myself in the diversity of the new area and enjoyed meeting people who were nothing like myself. Multicultural counseling was a class that changed my entire life. I began my graduate program viewing the world with blinders on, and, after reflecting on myself as a White woman during the multicultural counseling course, I realized that I had been terribly blind.

I remember sitting in my kitchen reading *A Race Is a Nice Thing to Have* (Helms, 1992), which had been assigned in the multicultural class. I cried and allowed myself to fill up with anger, guilt, embarrassment, and shame. All I could see during the reading was my father, my grandparents, my mother, and all of those who played a role in my life growing up. I was raised in a home that viewed the world through a very racist lens.

My sister had always dated African American men, and, being older, I always felt it was my job to help hide this from our father. Every time the issue was brought up for his approval, it was quickly shot down with an argument filled with disgrace and shame toward my sister. How could she possibly date a Black guy and go against her families' beliefs? I used this, along with the support from my classmates and Dr. Chung, to find the courage to speak out to my father about the issue of racism in our family. I became obsessed with educating him on social justice issues and would continuously call to talk or invite them up to attend a cultural experience I was attending in Northern Virginia. At first, they didn't hear me and were shocked that this was something I was "learning" at graduate school. My grandparents were also very appalled that this was my own developed view on social interaction. I was beginning to form my own values and beliefs, and, for my family, it was disappointing to see that my culture and world was developing into something very different from their own.

For the first time in my life, I realized that I was White. I understood that I was privileged in a way that others would never experience who were persons of color. I, too, held a color, and, along with the color White came privilege. I realized how others of color viewed me as a blonde, White, woman and reflected on how I was going to use this identity to connect to others. White privilege and race are not discussed because it makes people uncomfortable and defensive. My family spent some time being very uncomfortable, but soon realized that I was addicted to advocating and they had no other choice, but to hear me. After fighting through the guilt, the shame, and then finding the courage to confront my family affirmed for me that change happens over time and that, even if I am only planting seeds with them now, over time they will listen.

I had started the program in a committed, five-year relationship. After taking the multi-cultural counseling class, I realized that as a White woman who had developed such passion for social justice work, I also needed a partner in life who supported my views. My relationship ended six months after taking the course due to the differences in values and beliefs we had in life. I felt renewed and ready to begin my journey in the way I envisioned it to be. I had nothing holding me back, and I developed a strong support system of family and colleagues who were ready to listen and support my desire for advocating.

We choose not to see the ugly, unjust issues in life when we are living in the skin of a White privileged being. One of our privileges is that we don't have to look; we don't have to live it. Past generations of those who held White privilege often abused the power they had and continued to feed into discrimination. I've learned that as a White woman, people listen to me and will eventually hear me when I passionately advocate for students, those of color, and any social injustices that may arise. I have a voice and the ability to speak up. My entire purpose in life changed after taking this multicultural counseling class. I processed feelings of guilt, shame, selfishness, courage, anger, frustration, and determination. My family has taught me a lot. I have learned that in talking about the ugly that's hidden under the rug so that the public doesn't know you're quietly racist is tough, but it will bring a new realization to family members and an overall sense of respect will develop.

I am a 5'0", blonde, White, privileged woman, and I have voice that I have chosen to use to speak out against social injustices. I would hope that those who read this reflection can relate and be willing to admit to their own views or biases and know that it's okay to remove your blinders and really take a look at your own color. The question is, what are you going to do now that you can finally see?

I suggest processing on your own to begin. Take the time to cry and feel ashamed; ashamed that you weren't able to see until now. Admit to yourself that any biases you may have or that your family may have are okay. Give yourself permission to speak, because we only become who we allow ourselves to be. If we choose to look away and not speak out when discrimination occurs, then no matter what our values, we become the oppressor. Find courage through your classmates, your family, and professors. Living with White privilege is something many will never understand, but with this dispensation we can educate others about what it truly means to be living in our world as a White person of privilege. People who feel safe will be willing to disclose more. Connect to your colleagues, trust in them, and rely on them to help support you through this process. This is the process you must trust in order to successfully develop a true sense of multicultural awareness. Students of color should also know that being angry and filled with hate toward a White person is okay. Give yourself permission to be angry. Your challenge will be moving out of anger and into trust toward your White colleagues and peers. I suggest being as open as you can allow yourself to be.

Our world has chosen to continue unjust actions that just look different from the way they may have years ago. Oppression occurs every day, in every occupation, school, and life experience. We can all play a role in highlighting these actions and educating others on how a just system is something we all need to be advocating for. It begins with discussion, communicating, and talking about the pain we all have that racial differences have created. There is a lot of hurt in the world caused by discrimination and transgenerational trauma for all cultures. For those living in a White privileged world like me, we can all address this hurt if we simply find the courage to admit to what we've chosen not to see until now. Once you've found that courage to admit to these prejudices and then speak out to those in your life, you will begin to feel empowered, strong, and ready to speak out about issues you never even thought would be part of your life.

REFERENCE

Helms, J. E. (1992). *A race is a nice thing to have.* Associates, Inc.

CHAPTER 7

THE ROLE OF SOCIAL JUSTICE MENTAL HEALTH PROFESSIONALS

Rita Chi-Ying Chung and Frederic P. Bemak

If there is no struggle there is no progress.

—Frederick Douglass

Change will not come if we wait for the other person.... We are the ones we're waiting for. We are the change we seek.

—Barack Obama

Freedom and justice cannot be parceled out in pieces to suit political convenience. I don't believe you can stand for freedom for one group of people and deny it to others.

—Coretta Scott King

REFLECTION QUESTIONS

1. Do you believe mental health professionals should incorporate social justice and human rights work in their counseling and therapy? Why or why not?
2. What would be a hesitation you might have about doing social justice–oriented counseling or therapy?
3. If you were criticized or attacked at work for your beliefs in doing social justice work, how do you imagine you would respond?

In embedding social justice into the work of psychology and counseling, it is important to view clients from a holistic and ecological viewpoint. To omit environmental influences on clients' lived experiences of oppression and discrimination and to emphasize solely their intrapsychic or behavioral issues would be ineffective in addressing social justice and human rights issues and would essentially maintain and reinforce the status quo (Prilleltensky, 1997). To be effective in incorporating social justice into our work, it is vital that we form collaborative partnerships with clients to gain an understanding of their experiences of injustice and human rights violations. Client participation in the process of counseling or psychotherapy is fundamental to social justice and human rights work, whereby the professional is a highly engaged participant in the change process, partnering with equally active and highly engaged clients. This was highlighted more than 50 years ago in Freire's (1970) work, when he posed the question of whether or not the client is best prepared "to understand the significance of an oppressive society? And who suffers the effects of oppression more than the oppressed?" (p. 22). For mental health professionals and counselors to ignore or discount the rich wealth of knowledge that clients bring to the mental health encounter creates a power differential and a reliance on the professional for expertise. By doing so, we impose on clients (as discussed in Chapter 4) Freire's (1970) "banking concept," which implies that clients are helpless and passive recipients, reliant on the counselor or psychotherapist to "deposit" information and help change their personal world while disregarding the need for larger systemic interventions.

The banking concept engenders unhealthy dynamics between therapists and clients and, more insidiously, reinforces the traditional status quo, maintaining clients as dependent without equal or any power while professionals maintain a position of control over clients' lives. If we are to be successful in promoting social change aiming toward greater justice, fairness, and rights, then it is essential that we develop alliances with people who are marginalized and oppressed (Nelson et al., 2001). An example can be seen in a client who comes to counseling feeling disempowered by her husband and also experiencing discrimination and misogynistic behavior by her male supervisor at work. The social justice work with this client would be to foster her own power within and outside of the therapeutic relationship, so that she finds her voice and feels increasingly comfortable to assert herself with both her husband and her work supervisor. Thus, the dynamics are consistent: the client is powerful within and outside of therapy.

We cannot underscore enough the importance of psychotherapists and counselors going beyond traditional psychotherapy and counseling when addressing injustices by incorporating human rights advocacy, developing prevention and intervention and outreach programs, and promoting social action in partnership with clients, their families, stakeholders, and communities. These added dimensions of one's work are equally important to traditional roles, consistent with Sue's (1995) contention that engaging in proactive and preventative approaches is essential to address historical and current oppression. We concur and suggest that individual counseling and psychotherapy may offer only a superficial "Band-Aid" that neither heals the client nor addresses the deeper social and political problems, maintains professional passivity, and often focuses on remediation. In fact, Prilleltensky (1997) called therapeutic remediation reprehensible, while others (e.g., Chavez et al., 2016; Vera & Speight, 2003) have promoted incorporating social justice and human rights into therapeutic work.

Taking the example of the client just described: to ignore gender discrimination and simply discuss how she might feel better with her husband and work supervisor would not touch the deeper-rooted issues related to her experiences of sexism and misogyny. We would assert that her ability to advocate for herself and receive support for being a self-advocate is critical in the therapeutic relationship. Developing strategies and a partnership that help prevent feelings of helplessness in the future and help her to change the dynamics of relationships with her husband and supervisor should be regarded as equally important and not mutually exclusive to psychotherapy and counseling (Vera & Speight, 2003). Although we underscore the importance of forming collaborative partnerships with clients in social justice mental health work, we would mention one caution about determining their lived experiences of injustice and human rights violations. It is important that we consult and clarify with clients about what harmful psychological issues they are facing before making judgments and decisions about how to move forward with forming partnerships in the therapeutic work.

Mental health professionals are in an ideal role to take on social justice work. Psychological-based training sharpens communication and listening skills and an understanding of group dynamics and group process and system and organizational dynamics, thus providing an excellent foundation. However, additional qualities are needed for social justice and human rights work. In the next section, we describe the unique role of social justice–oriented counselors and psychologists.

MENTAL HEALTH PROFESSIONALS AS POLITICAL AND SOCIAL ACTIVISTS

As we have discussed, counselors and psychologists have a responsibility to address the social issues that affect our clientele. To simply ignore the social problems, political decisions, and life circumstances that provide a context for those social ills is to contribute to many of the problems that bring our clients to us in the first place. Gender-based violence, lack of access to clean water, food insecurity, substance abuse, racial injustices, discrimination, sexual assault, abuse and harassment, gun violence, intimate partner violence, environmental racism, economic injustice, poverty, etc., all lead to individual, family, and community mental health problems. For example, ignoring political decisions about policies and funding allocations impacting clients means that we are treating the symptoms, not the source. There are endless examples of such issues that are relevant for mental health professionals. Take, for example, a county budget for education that defines the quality and priority for funding in a school district. Funding has implications for afterschool programs, which in turn have ramifications for the opportunities that are available for students during afternoons and weekends. Districts with more expanded activities reach more children who then have options to participate in sports, arts, educational clubs, drama, and community service rather than be idle and unproductive after school and on weekends.

Another example was the controversy that erupted when psychologists used their training and skills to design, implement, and oversee torture and abuse programs with Central Intelligence Agency (CIA) detainees as a means to combat terrorism (Eidelsen, 2017). To stipulate that as mental health professionals we should not weigh in regarding our opinions on such issues and that we should maintain a neutral stance is to play a part in allowing and sanctioning the use of mental health–trained professionals to engage in the practice of torture. Similarly, by not speaking out and being a bystander witnessing the impact of immigration policies on forced child and family separation is again sanctioning that injustice. Our professional input about these and other issues is important.

Professional organizations such as the American Psychological Association (APA) and the American Counseling Association (ACA) have made public statements about the psychological impact of various U.S. governmental policies, as in December 2021, when the APA advocated that the Environmental Protection Agency incorporate psychological science in its work to reduce climate change, pointing to the impact that environmental health has on disadvantaged communities. It is important that social justice–oriented psychologists and counselors speak up and share our beliefs and opinions about injustices and human rights violations. To solely rely on our professional organizations to advocate and make political statements while we, as individuals, remain quiet is to silence our voices in the name of "neutrality," thus allowing behaviors, policies, and funding that may be unjust and psychologically harmful to clients. Providing input to our county, state, and national elected officials and to our professional associations has the potential to make a difference. Again, psychologists and counselors are in a unique position to see patterns and trends in social problems, and they have the potential to contribute to the discourse and direction of our local, state, and national social order. It is important for us to be proactive, take a stand, and have our voices heard about these types of political and funding situations if we are to address the social problems that underscore many mental health issues.

Now that we have described the role of social justice mental health professionals, we continue with a description of social justice training followed by an introspective discussion about what motivates you (the reader) to do social justice–oriented work. We believe that thoughtful self-examination is critical to ensure that our clients and their families and communities are the sole beneficiaries of our work. Unfortunately, we have witnessed mental health professionals who have not deeply reflected on working as social justice–oriented mental health professionals, who are motivated by personal benefit rather than benefit for others. From our perspective personal gain in social justice and human rights work borders on being unethical and may cause harm to clients and their families and communities. Thus, we raise some challenging questions in the next section in the hope that you will undergo honest, in-depth, and insightful reflection about your social justice work.

SOCIAL JUSTICE TRAINING

As mentioned before, we, as counselors and psychotherapists, must move beyond our traditional roles in individual counseling that historically have neglected social problems. It is important that our work incorporates promoting change through advocacy and social action for clients, families, and communities. This involves taking risks and having the courage to challenge injustices at organizational, institutional, and societal levels. Having the skills to take the risks is essential and hopefully embedded in one's training, which includes becoming socially aware and active. Although those who are studying or have graduated from accredited training programs have acquired basic awareness, knowledge, and skills in the multicultural social justice competencies, well meaning, well-trained, and well-intentional mental health professionals may still lack a comprehensive understanding of the profound historical, socioeconomic, psychopolitical, and ecological issues that impact and drive the need to include social justice and human rights work.

Understanding the profound, long-term, and intergenerational effects of social injustices and human rights violations on clients and their families and communities is an important prerequisite to knowing how to effectively incorporate social justice into one's work. As the first editors (Tod Sloan and Rebecca Toporek) of the *Journal for Social Action Counseling and Psychology* stated, "Our colleagues need more concrete examples of what social change work looks like and of how one might go about reflecting systematically on that" (personal communication, November 7, 2008). Although their comments were made in 2008, they are still relevant today. After providing trainings, workshops, and regional, state, national, and international presentations, we (Rita and Fred) are always bombarded with questions and a press for clarification by colleagues and students on "how to actually do social justice work." The same happens when we publish our research and scholarship: we are flooded with emails about how to actually implement social justice work in mental health.

The intensity, constancy, and hunger for answers prompted us to initially write this book, as well as other articles and book chapters about the implementation of social justice training and action (e.g., Bemak & Chung, 2008, 2011a, 2011b, 2018; Bemak et al., 2011; Chung & Bemak, 2013; Chung et al., 2008; Chung et al., 2018). Our experience has highlighted that a number of psychologists and counselors in training have not undertaken in-depth, rigorous examinations of their own cultural backgrounds, power, privileges, prejudices, and biases, all of which are essential in doing effective multicultural and social justice work. The gaps in self-exploration could result in the unintentional contribution and reinforcement of maintaining the status quo and perpetuating oppression and discrimination, particularly for people with histories of marginalization and oppression (Martin-Baro, 1994; Prilleltensky, 1997). Therefore, as we work with people who have experienced oppression and disenfranchisement and who are culturally different from us it is essential that our training teaches us how to integrate multicultural competencies with social justice and human rights work. Working with growing numbers of clients who are victims and survivors of oppression, discrimination, and human rights violations requires graduate programs to train students more effectively in social justice methods. We recommend that, to attain skills in effective social justice and human rights action, in addition to an in-depth and genuine self-examination of one's own power, privilege, prejudices, and biases, programs must include training in (a) organizational change and systems skills, (b) strategies to access systems, (c) different ways of practicing our trade as mental health professionals, (d) new models of supervision that go beyond traditional individual therapeutic precepts and incorporate perspectives on human rights and justice, (e) advocacy skills, and (f) the incorporation of associated research to substantiate evidence-based mental health and social justice outcomes.

SOCIAL JUSTICE INTROSPECTION

Part of the training for psychologists and counselors is to undergo an in-depth examination of our own issues, biases, prejudices, privilege, power, and positionality. The assumption is that by understanding oneself we will not do harm to clients. Similarly, to do effective social justice work while maintaining the same goal of not harming clients and their families and communities, we must also undergo a similar process of self-reflection, introspection, and critique about our motivation and reasons for promoting justice-oriented social change. The focus of this section is to challenge you to honestly reflect and examine your interest in doing social justice–oriented mental health work. We pose questions throughout this section so that you can challenge yourselves about where you are in relationship to culturally competent justice-oriented mental health practice. To begin, we pose several reflective questions: Why am I doing or want to do social justice work as a mental health professional? What is my intention, hope, and expectation for doing social just work? What do I hope to achieve? What do I get out of doing social justice work, and how much does that matter? Does the social action–oriented work I do as a mental health professional meet my clients' needs? Meet needs I have? What is the balance between meeting clients' needs and my needs? Are there any present or past personal issues that are linked to my doing social justice oriented mental health work? If so, will those issues get in my way doing this work?

BOX TEXT 7.1 RIGHTING THE WRONGS

The Reimann family is one of Germany's wealthiest families and owns well-known chains, including Krispy Kreme, Panera Bread, Peet's Coffee, Einstein Bros. Bagels, Keurig, and Pret A Manger. In March 2019, the family discovered that their ancestors, Albert Reimann and Albert Reimann Jr. (now deceased), were both active supporters of the Nazi Party and used the forced labor of approximately 800 Russian and French prisoners and prisoners of war during World War II. Reinmann Jr. was initially apprehended by Allied forces after the war, but his judgment was overturned by U.S. officials, which allowed him to resume his business ventures and build the family's wealth. After a report revealing the truth of their family's history, the Reimann family publicly acknowledged their ancestors' crimes and pledged to distribute €5 million (US$5.5 million) to agencies that support Holocaust survivors globally. They also pledged to give €5 million to find and support those who were forced laborers for the company during the war, as well as €25 million (US $27.8 million) annually for Holocaust education programs aimed at combating anti-Semitism. The pledged funds will be distributed by the family foundation, which was renamed the Landecker Foundation to honor a Jewish man killed by the Nazis, who is also a grandfather of family members who own a part of the company.

Source: Fortin, J. (2019, Dec 12). Family behind Krispy Kreme donates millions to Holocaust survivors. The New York Times. https://www.nytimes.com/2019/12/12/world/europe/reimann-family-holocaust.html

At times we (Rita and Fred) have witnessed mental health professionals' desire to do social justice work to meet their own needs and for their own satisfaction. The work is more to feed their own ego than to benefit clients. We have referred to this as *masquerading* social justice psychologists and counselors who do not shy away from telling colleagues, family, friends, and strangers about their work, hoping for praise, admiration, and accolades. Our experience has shown that sometimes the thrust of the work is for self-gain and acknowledgment at the expense of clients, and this, in some cases, may lead to reinforcing and contributing to already harmful situations. Almost as if wearing "social justice blinders," there is a lack of insight into how their actions may undermine and compound social injustices. For example, we took a team of counselors through Counselors Without Borders (CWB), a nonprofit organization created by Fred, to do post-disaster counseling in California after the wildfires. While working on an American Indian reservation with the invitation and permission of the Elders, we came across psychologists working on the reservation through a well-known international organization. These psychologists, who had parked outdoors in the central open area of the reservation, were seated comfortably on folding chairs and eating their lunches (food was scarce at the reservation because of the fires); they asked one of our CWB team members to take a photo of them, explaining that they wanted pictures of themselves "being on the rez."

Although we appreciated their generosity to volunteer their services through a major organization, as we spoke with them it was clear that their priority in working on the reservation was to nourish their social justice ego at the expense of those living on the reservation. In fact, they told the CWB team that there was no point being on the reservation because no-one came to them for assistance. In contrast, we (the CWB team) experienced the opposite. Asking permission of the Elders to be on the reservation and demonstrating cultural sensitivity and cultural humility fostered credibility and trust that resulted in being embraced by the community, invitations to peoples' homes and the school to provide counseling, and a backlog of people wanting to speak with our team. As psychologists and counselors, a major objective when incorporating social activism into our work is to remove individual, institutional, and systematic barriers so clients can achieve a better quality of life, physical safety, and psychological and economic well-being. It is *not* about us and what we do, or about the benefits from our work. To guarantee that we keep true to our work as social justice–oriented psychologists and counselors, we need to keep our "social justice soul intact" (soul intact is a concept taken from Kozol [2007]) through self-examination, self-critique, and introspection using the questions and concepts we raise in this section.

SOCIAL JUSTICE HUMILITY

To ensure that our "social justice soul is intact" and that we are doing social justice work for the "right" reasons—that is, for the benefit of clients—requires us to engage in constant social justice introspection. This involves taking time to reflect on understanding the multi-dimensionality and complexity of injustice, even though we may believe we have full understanding of the inequalities and inequities. Understanding the breadth of social injustice and human rights violations that involve victims, perpetrators, passive observers, and beneficiaries of injustices is essential in our work (Baumert & Schmitt, 2016) and requires social justice humility. Social justice humility is an extension of cultural humility. Cultural responsiveness and cultural humility are instrumental in acquiring a deep-rooted understanding of social justice and human rights (Toporek & Ahluwalia, 2020). The concept of cultural humility as applied to cross-cultural psychology and counseling is to be "humble" and unassuming, recognizing that our expertise and knowledge about others' cultures are limited (Hook et al., 2013). Extending cultural humility to social justice work, which we call *social justice humility*, involves an added dimension of exercising the same qualities to clients' lived experiences of injustice and human rights violations. We believe that social justice humility goes hand in hand with cultural competencies, both of which provide tools for social activism work with diverse populations and cultures. Employing cultural competencies in our work along with social justice and cultural humility is a life-long process of introspection and self-critique, of examining one's biases, prejudices, power, and privileges, and acknowledging historical, psychopolitical, and sociopolitical structural barriers that prevent racial and social justice (Hook et al., 2013). With social justice humility and ongoing self-reflection, we can establish open and authentic partnerships with stakeholders, sharing an equal voice at the table. Together we can respectfully acknowledge clients' lived experiences and cultural values and identities while reflecting on our mutual biases, power, privilege, and prejudices.

VOYEUR, SAVIOR, AND MARTYR VERSUS ADVOCATE, ACTIVIST, AND CHANGE AGENT

To further explore reasons for doing social justice work we would like to introduce the term that we coined, *social justice voyeurism,* to describe the concept of doing social action to satisfy our curiosity about what it is like be oppressed or socially and politically violated. We compare this to watching reality television shows where people's pain and anguish is displayed for viewers. The interest and inquisitiveness in oppression, poverty, violations, etc., becomes the driving force for social activism, one rooted in "romanticizing" both social injustices and participation in social action. Thus, the motivation of being involved in "quixotic and mysterious" social issues is that others may idealize, praise, admire, and perceive us as heroes/heroines, as champions of the people (Kleinman & Kleinman, 1977). This leads to a second concept of being a *social justice savior* (Flaherty, 2016; Toporek & Ahluwalia, 2020). Saviorism in social justice work is all about rescuing others as a means to fulfill our own needs. This equates to believing that we have the skills to "save the less fortunate," even though we may not fully understand or be knowledgeable about clients' lived experiences or life circumstances.

Social justice voyeurism and saviorism lead to a third related concept, one found in the human rights activist literature, called the *culture of martyrdom* (Chen & Gorski, 2015). The culture of martyrdom refers to making sacrifices for the "less fortunate." These three interrelated reasons for doing social action are all about ourselves and our egos. Although social justice voyeurism, saviorism, and martyrdom are not the reasons why we as mental health professionals should be incorporating social justice into our work, unfortunately, at times, mental health professionals may fall victim to these falsehoods and find themselves seeking respect, admiration, and praise, longing to be seen on a social justice pedestal. This desire for admiration may seduce us into, what I (Rita), call, the "dark side of social justice," that is, falling victim to our own needs and desires (Chung, 2017).

To prevent moving to the dark side of social justice and to ensure that our social justice soul is intact, we must also ask ourselves: (a) Am I entering into social justice activism as "the expert" with the answers and solutions to "fix" clients' problems? (b) Am I entering into social justice work with the view that people need rescuing and saving, and that I am in a position to do so (Toporek & Ahluwalia, 2020)? And, (c) am I doing the work thinking about the benefits I will get from it, rather than the benefits of the work itself? We then have to carefully reflect on how we can utilize our set of skills to assist clients in dismantling injustices without being the voyeur, savior, or martyr and to share our expertise with clients as collaborative partners. Thus, when we are tackling social injustices and human rights violations, we are working *with* our clients and not *for* them, avoiding unhealthy dynamics that contradict social justice work and lead us to being social justice saviors, voyeurs, or martyrs.

In addition to these three concepts is another that we encounter when mental health professionals feel sorry for clients, saying things like "those poor people," or "glad that at least we're here to help the clients out." As we all know too well, it is unhelpful and demeaning to feel sorry for others. As we wrote years ago, it is important to demonstrate culturally appropriate empathy (Chung & Bemak, 2002) to facilitate empowerment and healing conducive to helping others (re)claim their voice, dignity, respect, identity, and self-worth. Avoiding being seduced and falling into the dark side of social justice and ensuring that our social justice soul is intact is to practice ongoing self-reflection, self-critique, cultural empathy, and social justice humility that safeguards that we neither harm nor exploit clients' situations for personal and professional needs, gains, and recognition.

POSITIONALITY AND IDENTITY

Introspection and self-critique are also important in helping understand our lived experiences and positionality in relation to how our privilege, power, and identities impact doing social justice work. Social justice psychologists and counselors undertaking social justice activism are not all on equal footing with regards to their power and privilege. *Positionality* refers to the complex and multidimensional social and political relationships and interactions with others and society; it considers one's background with respect to race, ethnicity, culture, religion, sexual orientation, age, socioeconomic status, gender, abilities, etc. (Toropek & Ahluwalia, 2020). Positionality is influenced and shaped by society's historical, psychopolitical, sociopolitical, psychosocial, sociocultural, and economic realities, coupled with existing power and privilege structures and, in some cases, the impact of colonialism and imperialism. Our lived experiences shape our identities and positionality

BOX TEXT 7.2 SOCIAL SUPERMARKET GIVES PEOPLE DIGNITY IN CHOICE

Instead of giving food parcels to those who need food assistance, a social supermarket has been established by a charitable trust that gives people an opportunity to choose. There's dignity in choice and a sense of "normality" without feeling stigmatized by their circumstances.

The social supermarket is just like any other supermarket, with fruits and vegetables, sanitary products, pasta, cheese, and baked beans lined up along the aisles. Items are free and anyone in need can go to the supermarket. Staff and volunteers are also be on hand to help shoppers choose what to "buy" for themselves and their families.

Instead of paying with money, items were worth a certain amount of points, ranging from one (i.e., canned foods) to five (baby formula). Shoppers were given a number of points to spend depending on their family size and whether they were shopping for themselves.

"It's never just about food—it reflects other things and the big one is the cost of housing. There's so much pressure and stress to pay the bills that sometimes there's not enough money leftover to buy food. . . . For parents to be able to tell their kids they were going shopping, gave families respect and dignity," stated the charitable trust CEO.

Future plans are to house the social supermarket in a building that has a community cafe, kitchens, laundry services, public bathrooms and showers, a space for people to pray, and 35 housing units designed to accommodate people experiencing chronic homelessness.

Source: https://www.stuff.co.nz/national/124521584/wellington-city-mission-opens-social-supermarket-first-of-its-kind-in-new-zealand

and are partially determined by imposed barriers to opportunities and resources. Societal messages involve exclusion versus inclusion, superiority versus inferiority, oppressor versus oppressed, rich versus poor, power versus powerless, and privilege versus underprivilege, thus defining identities that correlate with privilege, power, and oppression (Toropek & Ahluwalia, 2020).

Awareness of our positionality is important when doing social justice work. For example, I (Rita) am a first-generation Chinese woman who arrived in the United States to do postdoctoral studies. I am also a first-generation college student and was brought up in a British colony. Being an immigrant woman of color with a British accent and English as a second language, who has an invisible disability (limited/low vision) and lived experiences of colonialism and other isms, my access to resources and the degree of power and privilege in conveying social injustices will differ from those of a White US-born heterosexual Christian male. Even so, my positionality and identity should not and does not prevent me from doing effective social justice work: it is a matter of being creative in circumventing the barriers associated with my positionality and identity. In some cases, perceived positionality can be used advantageously when doing human rights and social justice work. An example was a Latinx student who shared with me being upset that he can "pass for White," so people assumed he is a White male. My response to him was to utilize this perceived positionality to educate White peers, colleagues, and friends about racial and social injustices.

As in the case of the Latinx student, our identities and lived experiences influence the way we interact with and interpret others. As social justice–oriented mental health professionals it is vital to carefully evaluate messages, stereotypes, microaggressions, and implicit biases that are publicly presented about specific groups' identities, ensuring that we don't accept and internalize inaccurate and unsubstantiated messages about both our own and other groups. It is important to be cognizant of public portrayals of identities in relationship to privilege, power, and oppression while simultaneously understanding our own fit in relationship to privilege, power, oppression, and biases. For example, I (Fred) began my work as a residential summer counselor, later becoming Director of an Upward Bound program (a federal anti-poverty program for low-income high school adolescents) with predominately African Americans and Latinx adolescents. It was essential that I understood my identity and positionality and how these factors had bearing on my interactions with the youth and their families. Being a White male, the need to address issues of colorism, discrimination, racism, oppression, White privilege, power, and other privileges was essential to cultivate healthy and respectful working relationships.

The examples and themes noted above underscore the importance of understanding one's positionality and identity and working through the barriers that inhibit social justice–oriented work. The importance of social justice creativity and savviness to navigate and maneuver around barriers constructed by those in positions of privilege and power is important in our work. Further enhancing social justice work is the importance of gaining both ascribed and achieved credibility (Sue & Zane, 1987) that combines professional credentials and actual successful work, thus boosting our social justice positionality and adding to cultural and social justice competencies. Based on both of our experiences, we would like to introduce two terms: *racial countertransference* and *political countertransference* (Chung et al., 2008) as issues that social justice–oriented mental health professionals must keep in mind in understanding positionality and identity and that will lead to effective cross-cultural social justice work. Racial countertransference is particularly important given escalated public documentation of racial injustices in the United States and globally, underscored by heated debates about educational institutions teaching critical race theory. Similarly, political countertransference (Chung et al., 2008) refers to constant media-based political messages about specific cultural and diverse groups, such as espousing negative views of undocumented and documented migrants, associating Arab Americans with terrorism, or linking the COVID-19 pandemic to the Chinese. Awareness and understanding of the effects of racial and political countertransference on one's social justice and human rights work is critical.

SOCIAL JUSTICE HIGH ROAD: DOING SOCIAL ACTION WITH INTEGRITY AND CIVILITY

Another important issue faced by social justice–oriented mental health professionals involves how one infuses social action into one's work when injustices may be politically driven and when one is confronted with hostile reactions. As social justice–oriented mental health professionals we are, at times, passionate about putting forward our viewpoint to eradicate injustices; however, not everyone has the same perspective. This can be seen with issues such as same-sex marriages, abortion rights, and voter suppression. Educating others who have opposing views about equity and justice can be frustrating, distressing, and stressful, especially when we encounter antagonistic reactions that result in attacks on our character and gaslighting or manipulation that causes people to question their own reality. The APA (2015) notes that gaslighting causes people to doubt their own perceptions and understandings of their experiences and subsequent interpretations of the world around them. In fact, given the U.S. political climate from 2019 to 2022, the term "gaslighting" became so popular and frequently used that Merriam-Webster named it 2022 word of the year (Shammas, 2022).

We enter the mental health field with the goal of assisting in the healing of individuals, families, and communities rather than focusing on the political nature of our work. Since social justice issues are deeply rooted in politics it is important that psychologists and counselors don't ignore the root causes of inequities, inequalities, and injustices. In our experience, it has been important to be aware and acknowledge the political influence on mental health and our work, which has been helpful in reducing feelings of exasperation. The question is how to respond with integrity and civility to politically motivated and sometimes underhanded tactics to promote injustices, especially when met with hostile attacks that are personal and sometimes dishonest.

Twenty years ago, I (Fred) wrote a short piece describing the importance of personal integrity and taking the high road when faced with unethical, hostile, and dishonest colleagues (Bemak, 2002). Sadly, the concepts still hold true today as we watch political rhetoric and blatant political dishonesty occur in the United States and globally, often involving shaming, blaming, bullying, gaslighting, character assassination, and victimization—tactics that not only make us doubt what we are doing, but more insidiously also crush any form of dialogue, force individuals into silence, and diminish hopes and dreams of justice. The frequency of this style of communication and disagreement has created a "new normal" of acceptable behavior. Although it is tempting to fight back using similar techniques, these are not strategies we utilize in social justice–oriented work. The social justice–oriented work we do provides a model of behavior and congruency in advocating for justice by displaying ethical behavior, decorum, civility, and integrity.

Yes, it is often trying and infuriating when we present our social justice values, beliefs, and viewpoints and are met with strong resistance, a refusal to listen, laughter, demeaning and belittling comments, or even threats to our lives. These behaviors are evident in school board meetings across the United States, or where doctors and parents advocating for wearing masks as protection from the COVID pandemic were jeered and threatened (Lenthang, 2021;

Marcus, 2021). Although it is painful to encounter these adverse behaviors, it is also important to rise above hurt feelings and focus on the purpose of promoting human rights and justice. As I (Rita) say to my classes: "in doing social justice work you need to develop a thick tough social justice skin." The concerns about respectful and civil communication are so serious that the APA created guidelines for civility operational definitions (see Box Text 7.3).

The apprehensions raised by the APA resonated with me (Rita) in a recent interaction with a colleague who is known for her social justice contributions in her discipline. During the interaction there was a strong disagreement. My colleague, in the name of social justice, aggressively advocated for her stance on the issue, trying to force me and others to agree with her. She was relentless, refusing to consider other viewpoints. As she became increasingly frustrated and angry she began using bullying, gaslighting, and character assassination behavior. When I called her on her non–social justice conduct she finally stopped badgering others and angrily left the room after the meeting. The interaction disturbed me. I was not questioning her perspective, but more so the delivery of her viewpoint. The encounter paralleled the current U.S. political climate where national, state, and community leaders utilize similar aggressive and hostile techniques. Many leaders and politicians, who presumably are role models for citizens, are now adopting this type of communication as the "new normal" to achieve their goals. We strongly believe that the methods that we, as mental health professionals, employ in delivering our social justice messages and actions should be examples of justice, dignity, respect, integrity, and civility, representing the type of justice we are working toward.

During the same period as the interaction described above, I (Rita) was asked to do a keynote address at a national social justice conference. The incident described above, compounded by negative political divisiveness in the United States, motivated me to address the issue of social justice integrity and civility in my presentation (Chung, 2017). The following are excerpts from my speech which may help illuminate social justice integrity and civility:

> What is troubling to me is witnessing those who have social justice values, commitment, motivation, and passion, and who are doing great work in the field, yet when it comes to handling social justice disputes or disagreements in order to get their social justice views across, some social justice–minded people lose their social justice integrity and civility. I am not saying that we should not protest loudly, advocate strongly, stand up and speak our minds out loud, but what I have witnessed are people who call themselves social justice advocates blatantly manipulate and deceive others to get their views across to others, similar to the tactics of the current U.S. Administration. Unfortunately, some of our political leaders are role models on how to react or interact with individuals or situations that they don't agree on. The examples are all too frequent when we have politicians who are publicly denigrating others because of their different beliefs and values. What is worrisome to me is when someone disagrees with us, how easily we can transform into a nonsocial justice or anti-social justice mindset by, acting negatively, berating them, using bullying behavior, gaslighting and assassinating someone's character, all in the name of social justice. It reminds me of the Hollywood action movies in that the behavior of the "bad guys" who display unethical behavior causing the audience to "boo," yet when the "good guys" who use the same techniques, the audience cheers their approval because the good guy was on the right side of justice. How quickly we lose our social justice integrity.

BOX TEXT 7.3 AMERICAN PSYCHOLOGICAL ASSOCIATION CIVILITY GUIDELINE

The APA civility expectation and guidelines state the following:

> As psychologists, we seek to embrace and practice the ethical principle of "respecting the dignity and worth of all people" and create a climate of civility, respect and inclusion throughout the APA community. We strive to accomplish this goal by interacting and communicating with others in a spirit of mutual respect and an openness to listen as well as to consider all points of view. While we may disagree on important issues, we debate and express our ideas in a collegial, civilized and professional manner. Corrective feedback will be provided constructively, respectfully and compassionately whenever members don't behave civilly in order to maintain a comfortable, safe and professional environment in which to conduct the work of the Association. Finally, we understand that individuals from different cultures and groups may have varying customs and beliefs about what constitutes civil or uncivil behavior. We expect all to be respectful and mindful of these differences and norms.

CIVILITY OPERATIONAL DEFINITIONS

1. Think carefully before speaking.
2. Differentiate and articulate facts from opinions.
3. Focus on the common good.
4. Disagree with others respectfully.
5. Be open to others without hostility.
6. Respect diverse views and groups.
7. Offer a spirit of collegiality.
8. Offer productive and corrective feedback to those who behave in demeaning, insulting, disrespectful, and discriminatory ways.
9. Create a welcoming environment for all.
10. Focus corrective feedback on one's best and most desirable behavior.

INCIVILITY OPERATIONAL DEFINITIONS

1. Interrupting and talking over others who have the floor.
2. Overgeneralizing and offering dispositional character criticisms and attributions.
3. Using language that is perceived as being aggressive, sarcastic, or demeaning.
4. Speaking too often or for too long.
5. Engaging in disrespectful nonverbal behaviors (e.g., eye rolling, loud sighs).
6. Offering false praise or disingenuous comments (e.g., "With all due respect but . . .").

Source: https://www.psychologytoday.com/us/blog/do-the-right-thing/201708/even-psychologists-need-help-civility-guidelines

My concern is how rapidly we justified using anti-social justice behavior. We even turn against each other, pointing the finger and quickly judge our social justice colleagues, peers, family and friends, especially if we don't think they are doing anything or enough to fight against social injustices. It is so easy for us to justify our behaviors that violates others who are against what we perceive as social justice principles that we believe in, because we think we are on the side of "Justice," after all we have social justice values and beliefs and we are doing social justice work. But somehow along the way our social justice integrity and civility got loss. To make us feel better some of us reframe our nonsocial justice behavior as being passionate about social justice. And yet what we are really doing is sacrificing our social justice values and destroying our social justice integrity. To use the term from Star Wars movie, we're "going to the dark side," that is, abandoning social justice integrity and civility to the social justice dark side. I once saw a bumper sticker that said "When your halo is on too tight—It gives me a headache," which is a great reminder for me that we must constantly reflect on how we deliver our social justice message. So, we need to take care to maintain our social justice integrity while we are doing social justice action, and if you're going to have your social justice halo on that is o.k., but just make sure it is not on too tight. I think it is fine to have strong emotions and passion when we discuss social justice issues, however, by NOT maintaining social justice integrity and civility, we have lost the critical social justice message we are trying to deliver. By going to the social justice dark side and committing character assassination does not create allies. In my opinion, to maintain the fight against the injustices in these turbulent times we MUST always maintain our social justice integrity and civility, despite whatever the situation is and how frustrated we may be if we do not immediately see the outcome we hope for. So, doing social justice work now, and in the future, we should aim for the social justice integrity high road. This is an absolute foundation now and for the future of social justice work. We must protest loud and clearly, but with integrity and civility. As Michelle Obama said "when they go low, we go high." There will be times when we feel jaded and a little disillusioned . . . however, I strongly believe that by maintaining our social justice integrity, our level of commitment, passion and motivation will sustain, people will listen and change will occur. When you're involved in social justice battles it is normal to experience social justice battle fatigue, feeling low with the gravity and extent of social injustices can wear you down. But during those turbulence times I am reminded of what Maya Angelou (1978) wrote:

You may write me down in history with your bitter, twisted lies, You may trod me in the
     very dirt
But still, like dust, I'll rise.
You may shoot me with your words,
You may cut me with your eyes,
You may kill me with your hatefulness,
But still, like air, I'll rise'

I would like to end the presentation with two quotes: the first one by Roger Wilkins (2007): "The road to social justice cannot be done in a sprint, but in a long-distance relay, carrying the baton from those before us and passing the baton to those who have not yet been born."

And the second a Chinese proverb that says: "A journey of a thousand miles begins with a single step."

Both sayings illustrate that being a social justice advocate can be a long process and at times challenging; however, we need to make sure we do not lose sight of what we have done so far, even though we may feel that we have not achieved what we would hope to. To truly take on this enormous task during these turbulent times, takes time, so we need to be patient as we are undergoing this transformation, and at the same time not get complacent—and to always maintain our social justice integrity as the soul of what we do. So, let me end by asking you a question: What road and journey will you take to ensure that social justice stays on the forefront as mental health professionals: the road that leads to social justice integrity and your social justice soul is intact, or the road and journey of gaslighting, bullying, and character assassination?

SUMMARY

In summary, this chapter discusses the role and explores the values and actions of social justice–oriented mental health professionals. As you take on the task of doing social justice mental health work, we have posed challenging questions for you to reflect on, with the purpose of ensuring that your social justice work is for the benefit of your clients and their families and communities. We are hopeful that the chapter has helped you reflect on personal qualities and characteristics important in doing social justice work, as well as on your personal motivation for incorporating justice and human rights into your work. We encourage you to continue this type of self-reflection and self-critique as a cornerstone of your career and continue to do social justice work with integrity, civility, and respect. The next chapter will continue this exploration and discuss psychological barriers that may be encountered as you continue on your social justice journey.

DISCUSSION QUESTIONS

1. Do you agree or disagree with Freire's "banking concept"? Please discuss the rationale for your answer.
2. Share with others in small groups your own biases, prejudices, privilege, power, and positionality. Do you find yourself comfortable with your reflections and insights about where you are, or are there things you would like to work on?
3. How do you imagine your identity and positionality will impact your social justice–oriented work?
4. Have you ever thought about social justice voyeurism, saviorism, and martyrdom? Please share thoughts about these concepts.
5. How do you imagine, when doing social justice–oriented work, you will maintain integrity and civility when faced with hostility, dishonesty, and attacks on your character?
6. Please discuss two points you agree or disagree with in excerpts from Rita's speech.

REFERENCES

American Psychological Association. (2021, Dec 2). Applauding Environmental Protection Agency's implementation of President Biden's environmental justice initiative. https://www.apaservices.org/advocacy/news/environmental-justice-initiative

American Psychological Association. (2018). American Psychological Association (APA)

Civility Statement and Operational Definitions. https://www.psychologytoday.com/us/blog/do-the-right-thing/201708/even-psychologists-need-help-civility-guidelines

Angelou, M. (1978). *And still I rise.* Random Press.

Baumert, A., & Schmitt, M. (2016). Justice sensitivity. In M. Schmitt & C. Sabbagh (Eds.), *Handbook of social justice theory and research* (pp. 1–45). Springer.

Bemak, F. (2002). Personal integrity and the high road: Counselors finding their way. In J. A. Kottler (Eds.), *Counselors finding their way* (pp. 95–100). American Counseling Association.

Bemak, F., & Chung, R. C-Y. (2008). New professional roles and advocacy strategies for school counselors: A multicultural social justice perspective to move beyond the nice counselor syndrome. *Journal of Counseling and Development, Multicultural and Diversity Issues in Counseling Special Issue, 38,* 372–381. https://doi.org/10.1002/j.1556-6678.2008.tb00522.x

Bemak, F., & Chung, R. C-Y. (2011a). Post-disaster social justice group work and group supervision. *Journal for Specialists in Group Work, 36*(1), 3–21. https://doi.org/10.1080/01933922.2010.537737

Bemak, F., & Chung, R. C-Y. (2011b) Applications in social justice counselor training: Classroom Without Walls. *Journal of Humanistic Counseling, Education, and Development, 50*(2), 204–219. https://doi.org/10.1002/j.2161-1939.2011.tb00119.x

Bemak, F., & Chung, R. C-Y. (2018). Race dialogues in group psychotherapy: Key issues in training and practice. *International Journal of Group Psychotherapy, 69*(2), 172–191. https://doi.org/10.1080/00207284.2018.1498743

Bemak, F., Chung, R. C-Y., Talleyrand, R. M., Jones, H., & Daquin J. (2011). Implementing multicultural social justice strategies in counselor education training programs. *Journal of Social Action in Psychology and Counseling, 3*(1), 29–43. https://doi.org/10.33043/JSACP.3.1.29-43

Chavez, T. A., Fernandez, I. T., Hipolito-Delgado, C. P., & Rivera, E. T. (2016). Unifying liberation psychology and humanistic values to promote social justice in counseling. *Journal of Humanistic Counseling, 55*(3), 166–182. https://doi.org/10.1002/johc.12032

Chen, C. W., & Gorksi, P. C. (2015). Burnout in social justice and human rights activists: Symptoms, causes and implications. *Journal of Human Rights Practice, 7*(3), 366–390. https://doi.org/10.1093/jhuman/huv011

Chung, R. C-Y. (2017, Mar 16–19). Social justice integrity in challenging times (keynote presentation). Counselors for Social Justice. American Counseling Association 60th Annual Conference, San Francisco, CA.

Chung, R. C-Y., & Bemak, F. (2002). The relationship between culture and empathy in cross-cultural counseling. *Journal of Counseling and Development, 80,* 154–159. https://doi.org/10.1002/j.1556-6678.2002.tb00178.x

Chung, R. C-Y., & Bemak, F. (2013). Use of ethnographic fiction in social justice graduate counseling training. *Counselor Education and Supervision, 52,* 56–68. https://doi.org/10.1002/j.1556-6978.2013.00028.x

Chung, R. C-Y., Bemak, F., Ortiz, D. P., & Sandoval-Perez, P. A. (2008). Promoting the mental health of migrants: A multicultural-social justice perspective. *Journal of Counseling and Development, Multicultural and Diversity Issues in Counseling, Special issue, 38,* 310–317. https://doi.org/10.1002/j.1556-6678.2008.tb00514.x

Chung, R. C-Y., Bemak, F., Talleyrand, R. M., & Williams, J. (2018). Challenges in promoting race dialogues in psychology training: Race and gender perspectives. *Counseling Psychologist*, 1–28. https://doi.org/ 10.1177/0011000018758262

Eidelson, R. (2017, Oct 13). Psychologists are facing consequences for helping with torture. It's not enough. *Washington Post.* https://www.washingtonpost.com/outlook/psychologists-are-facing-consequences-for-helping-with-torture-its-not-enough/2017/10/13/2756b734-ad14-11e7-9e58-e6288544af98_story.html

Flaherty, J. (2016). *No more heroes: Grassroots challenges to the savior mentality.* AK Press.

Freire. P. (1970). *Pedagogy of the oppressed.* Continuum.

Hook, J. N., Davis, D. E., Owen, J., Worthington Jr., E. L., & Utsey, S. O. (2013). Cultural humility: Measuring openness to culturally diverse clients. *Journal of Counseling Psychology, 60*(3), 353–366. doi:10.1037/ a0032595

Kleinman, A., & Kleinman, J. (1977). The appeal of experience; The dismay of images: Cultural appropriations of suffering in our times. In A. Kleinman, V. Das, & M. M. Lock (Eds.), *Social suffering* (pp. 1–23). University of California Press.

Kozol, J. (2007). Letters to a young teacher. Education Week. https://www.edweek.org/leadership/opinion-letters-to-a-young-teacher/2007/08

Lenthang, M. (2021, August 30). How school board meetings have become emotional battlegrounds for debating mask mandates. ABC News. https://abcnews.go.com/US/school-board-meetings-emotional-battle grounds-debating-mask-mandates/story?id=79657733

Marcus, J. (2021, Aug 12). We will find you: Anti-mask parents threaten doctors and nurses at Tennessee school board meeting. Independent News. https://www.independent.co.uk/news/world/americas/tennessee-mask-mandate-school-board-b1901112.html

Martin-Baro, I. (1994). *Writings for a liberation psychology.* Harvard University Press.

Nelson, G., Prilleltensky, I., & MacGillivary, H. (2001). Building value-based partnerships: Toward solidarity with oppressed groups. *American Journal of Community Psychology, 29*, 649–677. https://doi.org/10.1023/ A:1010406400101

Prilleltensky, I. (1997). Values, assumptions, and practices: Assessing the moral implications of psychological discourse and action. *American Psychologist, 52*(5), 517–535. https://doi.org/10.1037/0003-066X.52.5.517

Shammas, B. (2022, Nov 28). How "gaslighting" became Merriam-Webster's word of the year. *Washington Post.* https://www.washingtonpost.com/arts-entertainment/2022/11/28/gaslighting-merriam-webster-word-year/

Sue, D. W. (1995). Multicultural organizational development: Implications for the counseling profession. In J. G. Ponterotto, J. M. Casa, L. A. Suzuki, & C. M. Alexander (Eds.), *Handbook of multicultural counseling* (pp. 474–492). Sage.

Sue, S., & Zane, N. (1987). The role of culture and cultural techniques in psychotherapy: A critique and reformulation. *American Psychologist, 42*(1), 37–15. doi:10.1037/1948-1985.S.1.3

Toporek, R. L., & Ahluwalia. M. K. (2020). *Taking action: Creating social change through strength, solidarity, strategy, and sustainability.* Cognella.

Vera, E., & Speight, S. (2003). Multicultural competence, social justice, and counseling psychology: Expanding our roles. *Counseling Psychologist, 31*(3), 253–272. doi:10.1177/0011000003031003001

Wilkins, R. (2007, Sep 24). *Racial equality in America: Will the struggle ever end?* George Mason University Vision Series.

CHAPTER 8

UNPACKING THE PSYCHOLOGICAL BARRIERS THAT PREVENT SOCIAL JUSTICE ACTION

Rita Chi-Ying Chung and Frederic P. Bemak

We can disagree and still love each other unless your disagreement is rooted in my oppression and denial of my humanity and right to exist.

—James Baldwin

It doesn't matter how often you fall. What counts is that you keep getting back up. That's what makes all the difference.

—Sonia Sotomayor

Let your dreams be bigger than your fears and your actions louder than your words.

—M. Scott Peck

Take criticism seriously, but not personally. If there is truth or merit in the criticism, try to learn from it. Otherwise, let it roll right off you.

—Hillary Rodham Clinton

REFLECTION QUESTIONS

1. What do you imagine might hold you back from doing social justice–oriented work? What would be the professional barriers? What would be the personal barriers?
2. What would be the rewards in doing social justice–oriented work? How do you imagine you would feel standing up for the rights of your client?

3. Have you ever observed someone experiencing an injustice and you remained quiet and inactive? Why did you "hold back," and how did that feel? Would you do anything different in that situation now?
4. Have you ever experienced the imposter syndrome? If so, what was that like for you?

The previous chapter examined why you want to do social justice work. Now that you have explored your motivation and reasons for doing social justice work, we would like to continue this chapter with a critical self-examination of the psychological barriers that may prevent you from doing social justice–oriented work that contributes to clients achieving optimal psychological growth and well-being. Understanding the source of internal barriers will lead to unpacking these psychological barriers and assist you in doing social justice–oriented work as a mental health professional. Psychologists and counselors are skillfully trained to work with clients; however, social justice mental health work requires moving beyond traditional training to be able to challenge individuals and systems that are oppressive, unjust, unfair, and discriminatory. This involves working with the range of all those who are involved in human rights violations and social injustices. Baumert and Schmitt (2016) identified four types of individuals who are involved in situations of social injustice: the victims/survivors of the injustices, the perpetrators who commit injustices, the bystanders/observers who witness injustice but do not intervene, and the beneficiaries who benefit from injustices. We agree with Baumert and Schmitt's designation of who is involved in social injustices, especially noting the inclusion of bystanders/observers since we believe that witnesses of acts of injustice who choose not to intervene are reinforcing, supporting, and contributing to injustices. In addition, we add a fifth category that we call the *guardians of injustice*. The guardians are those who are in positions of power or authority and who have the ability to change unjust policies, rules, and regulations in systems, organizations, and institutions yet choose to ignore or refuse to facilitate change (see Figure 8.1).

To create effective systemic social change and action it is important to consider working with all five types of involved individuals rather than focusing solely on the victim and perpetrator. This can be a daunting task since many mental health professionals are trained to work with victims and survivors of injustices and not with the other four participants. There are programs that focus on perpetrator treatment specific to family- and gender-based violence (Bellini & Westmarland, 2021; Pearson & Ford, 2018), and restorative justice programs that bring victims/survivors and perpetrators together to assist in the healing for survivors and recidivism reduction for perpetrators (Roche, 2004), yet perpetrators often face greater legal punishment and consequences rather than receive treatment and rehabilitation. This was evident when I (Fred) visited a super-maximum security prison located in a major U.S. city. My colleague, the state's chief psychologist, explained to me that inmates were in solitary confinement for 23 hours daily (1-hour exercise in isolation was required by law each day) and received no mental health treatment during their incarceration. Upon their release inmates would leave the prison, moving from 24-hour-a-day isolation (which sometimes lasted for many years), directly onto a bustling city street without receiving any psychological transitional therapy.

Working with bystanders/observers, beneficiaries, and guardians may be challenging. Due to their indirect involvement in injustices, this group may be highly resistant and refuse

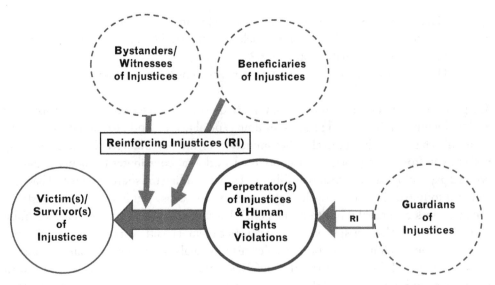

FIGURE 8.1 Individuals involved in social injustice and human rights violations

Adapted from Baumert & Schmitt, 2016.

to accept or take responsibility for their role in human rights violations or injustices. A study we did that was funded by the U.S. National Institute of Mental Health on Amerasian adolescent refugees (Vietnamese mothers and American fathers) underscored the significant mental health impact on the bystanders/observers (Bemak & Chung, 1998, 1999). Amerasian youth were ostracized and mistreated in Vietnam after the Vietnam War, with many children later migrating to the United States as refugees. The study found that those who observed other Amerasians in Vietnam being beaten, raped, tortured, and discarded experienced more psychological stress and trauma than those who were direct victims of the abuse (Bemak & Chung, 1998, 1999). The study highlights the impact of injustice on bystanders/observers and the need for social justice–oriented psychologists and counselors to work with this group of participants. Similarly, it is important to work with the beneficiaries and guardians of injustice since they may be unaware of or ignore the consequences of their benefits. Educating these two groups of participants about the impact on the survivors/victims may help motivate them to take a different stand about injustice. It is particularly important to work with the guardians of injustices who are often in positions of privilege and power and may have the leverage to change the status quo.

Daunting as it may seem to challenge all of those involved in instances of social injustice, it is important to not let these challenges discourage us or derail the focus on our goals of justice and human rights. We have found that some social justice–minded mental health professionals may be hesitant about and fearful of face-to-face confrontation but more comfortable with other forms of social justice activism, such as writing letters or emails to governors and senators or participating in demonstrations, such as the March for Our Lives (MFOL) against gun violence. It is important to underscore that all of these forms of activism can be effective tools in social change, even though this chapter will focus on social action that emphasizes face-to-face encounters with perpetrators, bystanders/observers, beneficiaries, and guardians of injustices. As psychologists and counselors, we are trained

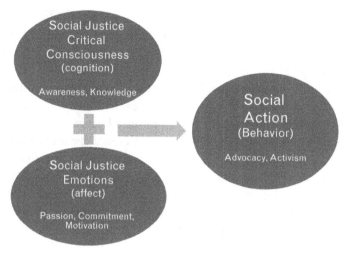

FIGURE 8.2 ABC's of social action and activism

in and have the expertise and skills related to effective communication, group dynamics, organizational dynamics, and dealing with resistance—all the ingredients necessary for conducting difficult, face-to-face dialogues, social justice discourse, and challenging unjust situations. To do effective social action we propose that there are three major psychological components to social justice action, which can be viewed as the ABCs to social action (see Figure 8.2). The first is the cognitive awareness and knowledge of social justice issues that we label *social justice critical consciousness*; second, the emotional aspects to social injustices, that is, the passion, commitment, and motivation that we call *social justice emotions*; and third, the behavioral aspect of social justice, which we call *social action*.

Witnessing graduate students in my (Rita) class who challenged family, friends, and colleagues about social injustices while their classmates with the same social justice critical consciousness and emotion were hesitant and fearful to do so led us to conduct a study exploring social justice courage, risk-taking, and barriers to social action (Chung & Bemak, 2023). The findings were interesting. As predicted, the results found both logistical and psychological barriers to taking social justice action. The logistical barriers included lack of resources (i.e., not having time, money, or organizational support) and fear of repercussions (i.e., loss of employment; being alienated and ostracized by family, friends, and colleagues; fear of retaliation not only for oneself, but also for one's family, community, and clients; and receiving threats to one's life) (Chung & Bemak, 2023). In this chapter, we focus on the psychological barriers that prevent mental health professionals from moving from social justice–critical consciousness and emotions to social justice action and activism. The purpose of addressing the psychological barriers is to understand their origin, with the goal of unpacking them in order to eliminate and minimize the obstacles that inhibit mental health professionals from integrating social justice into their psychological work. Similar to the previous chapter, we challenge you to reflect on your own psychological barriers that make you hesitant or prevent you from doing social justice work.

When students or colleagues share with us a reason why they are tentative about becoming socially active it is often what we (Rita and Fred) call *social justice negative self-talk*, which comprises internalized messages that individuals receive from family, friends, colleagues, society, and themselves. We have been told multiple times by students, colleagues, and mental health professionals that they do not believe they have the qualifications, skills, or experience to tackle problems of social injustice. We hear them say "I need more data to support my social justice point of view; I don't know what to say or do when I'm met with resistance; I'm not ready to do this work; I can't deal with people's strong emotions toward me when I challenge them; I feel like a fraud since I haven't had those (unjust) lived experiences; I have difficulty challenging people with more experience than me or those who are my parents' or grandparents' age." As we examine these concerns and challenges, it is clear that this hesitation is not a reflection of their social justice values and commitment. Acknowledging that these logistical barriers to social action exist led us to consider the psychological barriers that paralyze individuals and keep them from following through on their belief and commitment to human rights and social justice with hands-on, face-to-face social action.

We concluded from our study that the psychological barriers fell into four overlapping themes: (a) the imposter syndrome (IS), which includes the interaction with stereotype threat; (b) the nice counselor syndrome (NCS); (c) the culture of fear (COF), which includes the fear of failure; and (d) personal apathy and professional paralysis, which includes differentiating between urgent versus important tasks. In addition, we discuss Freire's (1970) concept of *false generosity*, which questions whether the type of social action we are doing contributes to dismantling unjust systems or aims at appeasing our own social justice guilt.

IMPOSTER SYNDROME

Imposter phenomenon or IS relates to a broad range of people and professions (Bravata et al., 2020). IS was first identified in a study of successful White professional women (Clance & Imes, 1978) who expressed difficulties in accepting and internalizing their success, believing that they were frauds and, subsequently, imposters. It was concluded that the IS was influenced by societal messages attributing women's competency and success to luck rather than to inherent abilities. Over the years people experiencing IS have expanded across professions, genders, and age groups. In a meta-analysis of 62 IS studies, it was concluded that employers and clinicians must be watchful for IS among the whole population, rather than just focusing on women (Bravata et al., 2020). Numerous IS studies were conducted with students ranging from middle school to graduate school, investigating fears about being imperfect and preserving social standing (Ferrari & Thompson, 2006) and feelings of pessimism and low self-esteem (Cozzarelli & Major, 1990). Levels of perfectionism in college students have steadily increased over the past 27 years, with the most recent generation having higher expectations of themselves and others and more determination to seek external sources of approval (Curran & Hill, 2019).

IS characteristics found in millennials and young adults (Lane, 2015; McAllum, 2016) include avoidant behaviors such as procrastination, withdrawing from participating and avoiding challenging tasks (Lane, 2015); vacillating between avoidant behaviors and overworking tendencies (McAllum, 2016); and hesitancy in risk-taking behavior resulting in the development of high levels of perfectionism and fear of failure (McAllum, 2016). Studies with students of color show that IS correlates with anxiety and depression with African American, Asian American, and Latinx college students (Cokley et al., 2015, 2017; McClain et al., 2016). A wide range of IS studies have also been conducted with people in the workforce ranging from supervisors, managers, accountants, teachers, and health professionals, finding that IS is associated with diminishing job satisfaction and performance on the job, augmented levels of stress and burnout over time, and delegation of challenging tasks (Bechtoldt, 2015; Crawford et al., 2016; Hutchins & Rainbolt, 2017; Vergauwe et al., 2015).

The insidious outcome of IS causes anxiety, lack of confidence, self-imposed perfectionism, feelings of self-doubt and fraudulence, feelings of being a phony, discounting evidence of competence, reliance on external validation, and difficulty identifying personal skills and accomplishments. Studies have also found that IS impacts one's identity, becoming more complex when individuals claim multiple identifies since each identity is associated with its own set of IS societal messages (Bernard et al., 2018). For example, for Black graduate students, the intersection of race and being a graduate student exhibits a complex set of IS messages (Stone et al., 2018). The IS feelings and behaviors may be reinforced by experiences of racial microaggressions, as well as by distrust perpetuated by individual, historical, institutional, and sociopolitical racism and racial injustice (Stone et al., 2018). However, having a strong racial identity has a significant impact on IS feelings and behavior since it counteracts some of the IS negativity (McClain et al., 2016). This speaks to the importance for our work as social justice–oriented psychologists and counselors in reinforcing and encouraging the building of strong racial identities in our students and clients of color.

These findings point to the interplay between IS and stereotype threat (ST; Steele, 1997). ST is closely related to IS in that both phenomena involve societal messages producing negative effects of self-doubt, lack of confidence, and fraudulence. The ST research focuses primarily on marginalized groups, such as people of color or women in science, technology, engineering, and mathematics (STEM) areas (Spencer et al., 1999; Steele & Aronson, 1995). Whereas IS attributes intelligence, abilities, skills, and capabilities to external factors such as luck, ST links these variables to genetics that categorizes people as superior or inferior, with marginalized groups falling into the latter category. Even with an understanding and awareness of ST it is so deeply ingrained in the societal mindset that we can fall victim to believing that ST relates to not only other groups, but also to our own group and ourselves. For people of color this leads to internalized racism (Pyke, 2010).

Regardless of our qualifications, skills, experiences, and professional status the overlap of IS and ST can undermine us in our social justice work. For example, Maya Angelou, a world-renowned poet, memoirist, and civil rights activist, once said "I have written eleven books, but each time I think 'Uh oh, they're going to find out now. I've run a game on everybody, and they're going to find me out" (BBC, 2016). Similar to Maya Angelou, social justice–oriented mental health professionals are not immune to IS even though we may have undergone in-depth self-examination of our personal issues as part of our training. We are no less susceptible to experiencing IS, and we are just as vulnerable to IS as anyone else. Being aware of and able to identify that you're falling victim to IS is an important first step in eradicating the social justice negative self-talk and experiences of IS, which leads to more effective social action. We would like you to reflect on the prevalence and effect of IS and ask yourselves: Does IS have an impact, or will it have an impact, on your behavior and your social justice work? If so, to what extent? And, if so, what would be your strategies to overcome IS in order to be effective in social justice and human rights work? -

NICE COUNSELOR SYNDROME

In addition to IS is NCS, a term that I (Rita) originally coined and that we have written about as a psychological barrier to social advocacy, action, and activism (Bemak & Chung, 2008). Individuals who enter the mental health professions come in the field to assist others in healing. Many mental health professionals are often viewed as "nice" people, who are pleasant, agreeable, good-hearted, kind, pleasing, enjoyable, friendly, courteous, well-mannered, considerate, and so on. All exceptional qualities of being an effective helping professional. We agree that people working in mental health should possess these characteristics; however, we have concerns that a lack of balance in these qualities may also lead to the NCS. We are not against psychologists and counselors being "nice," but we have concerns when the amiability and avoidance of conflict or tension with colleagues and organizations comes at the expense of helping clients, families, and communities. Too often, we have witnessed mental health professionals who are afraid to challenge or raise issues with colleagues, agencies, institutions, and systems even though there is harm being done to clients through direct clinical work or unjust policies. The concern is more about maintaining good relationships with colleagues and institutions and avoiding conflict than clients' psychological well-being, thus leading to the NCS. The NCS is typically exhibited by many good-hearted, well-intentional psychologists and counselors who are commonly viewed as being an "agreeable and nice" person at their agency or organization. These professionals live up to their reputation of being congenial people, constantly striving to promote harmony with others while avoiding and deflecting interpersonal conflicts or tensions in the workplace.

For example, the NCS in the school setting is evident in counselors who are noted to be comfortable assuming the roles of mediator and problem-solver when working with students, parents, and other school personnel. The value these counselors place on being viewed as good and nice people may prevent them from implementing social justice advocacy and organizational change that could lead to interpersonal disagreements and conflicts with other school personnel, especially those interested in maintaining the existing educational status quo (Bemak & Chung, 2008). Many counselors and psychologists experiencing the NCS may truly believe in the importance of promoting educational equity for all students, particularly students from marginalized groups. However, their overarching concern to be perceived as nice and friendly people who promote acceptance, peace, and interpersonal harmony at any cost leads them to shy away from addressing, initiating, and confronting issues of equity and from advocating for fair treatment and access to opportunities and resources for all. NCS may be a way of characterizing those counselors and psychologists who demonstrate a willingness to help perpetuate the status quo by conforming to expectations and the need for others to perceive them as the "nice person" (Bemak & Chung, 2008).

Thus, a primary concern of one exhibiting the NCS is on how others view them, apprehension about making enemies, and avoiding upsetting family, friends, and colleagues. Since a priority is to be a "people pleaser" and preserve good relationships personally and professionally, there unfortunately may be an impact on clients' psychological well-being. If we are effective in promoting social justice for our clients, then it is inevitable that some people will disagree and be upset. That is the reality. By speaking up about injustices and inequities we may be perceived by some as troublemakers who are rocking the boat. Social advocacy and action will disrupt the status quo and may be disturbing to colleagues. Maybe we need to change the script to reframe our mindset, instead saying something like "if people are not upset with us, then maybe we're not doing our job successfully as social justice–oriented psychologists and counselors."

An example of this can be seen when I (Fred) became Executive Director of the Region I Adolescent Treatment Program funded by the Massachusetts Department of Mental

Health. The program served youth identified as the "most disturbed" in the state, all of whom had been unsuccessful in multiple other treatment programs. The status quo for treatment had been containment and minimizing outbursts, with the highest-priority goal being to maintain sedate environments. As the new head of this program I was concerned with the status quo for this type of treatment being to maintain calm, avoiding at all costs any feelings of anger, pain, hurt, and sadness with volatile and emotionally upset clientele. The history of treatment with this population was to not challenge, confront, exacerbate, or aggravate the situation, which to me translated as not being "treatment." It was clear to me that it was important to change the treatment program since it was, in my opinion, a disservice and injustice to the adolescents in the program.

Knowing that changes to the treatment could create confusion, negativity, resentment, and tension among staff, it was important to keep in mind the best treatment for the clients. To change the treatment protocol, my emphasis and focus was to train staff to provide treatment by respectfully challenging, confronting, supporting, discussing, and questioning the youth in order to understand the source of flare-ups and outbursts that had been long-established patterns in relationships and situations. Staff at first were uncomfortable and resented me for instituting changes in treatment protocol, but, over time, as they became more skilled and witnessed change in the youth's behavior, they became more accepting, leading to a highly successful treatment program. If I had been concerned about being liked, being the "nice person," prioritizing a peaceful and harmonious environment over clients' growth and development, then I wouldn't have taken the steps that caused staff dissension, resentment, and resistance that was initially directed at me.

This example reinforces what I (Rita) have said to my graduate students: that to be effective social justice psychologists and counselors we must develop what I call a "thick tough social justice skin," with awareness of ourselves while keeping a focus on the goal of social justice work. This necessitates not personalizing resistance, surrounding oneself with individuals who understand and support the work, staying focused, and not being sidetracked or intimated by those who are negative toward social justice work. As you process the NCS, ask yourself: Do I exhibit NCS characteristics? If so, why? Why is there a need for me to be the nice counselor or psychologist? How would you overcome the NCS and balance doing social justice activism while keeping a good relationship with your colleagues, supervisors etc.?

CULTURE OF FEAR

The emotion of fear, which is part of the human experience, can expand to become collective fear or a "culture of fear" (Chung et al., 2008). The COF is similar to other psychological barriers in that it may prevent us from doing social justice work. For example, after the September 11, 2001 (9/11) attacks on the United States by a militant Islamic organization, a COF based on the fear of terrorism and Islamophobia emerged. The COF caused uncertainty and distress, producing anxiety, doubt, suspicion, helplessness, and hopelessness (Furedi, 2005). After 9/11, the COF was reinforced by periodic government announcements color-coding rises in the terrorist threat level, creating hypervigilance and anxiety in both the United States and globally. Interestingly, rarely were there public announcements when the threat level was lowered or no longer existed, which would have helped to reduce the COF.

Contributing to COF is anger. Mishra (2017) wrote that we living in the *age of anger*, describing how the global right-wing and reactionary political movements lead to isolationism, nationalism, secularism, and chauvinism. Misha explains how the age of anger is rooted in the pursuit of individualism and capitalism, the tenets of which promote rage and anger in a demoralized world and reinforce the COF. Underscoring the COF and the age of anger is the global COVID pandemic that has created major life disruptions, uncertainties, anxieties, anger, rage, and fear. The 2019 Gallup Global Emotions study documented this situation, reporting that 22% of U.S. citizens experienced frequent anger. Two years later, in 2021, the Gallup Emotions report surveyed adults in 115 countries and found 24% experienced anger the previous day. We suggest that the high degrees of anger add to the COF, affecting not only the individuals experiencing the anger, but also those in their communities and countries that precipitate collective anger and thus resulting in a collective COF.

The COF is continually being propagated and used as an effective political tool. Examples of the COF, such as xenophobia and the fear of outsiders, have been persistent long-term fears in the United States (Bennett, 1995; Risse, 2016). The COF is used to take advantage of individual's susceptibility as they displace and project their anxieties, concerns, and fears on others as threats to their safety and livelihood (Bennett, 1995; Risse, 2016). The COF can be proliferated by politicians to control and manipulate the general public and is associated with the concept of *fearmongering* (Glassner, 2010). An example of political use of the COF is the U.S. Trump administration's rhetoric about immigration and migrants threatening citizens' jobs security, physical safety, and the availability of resources and opportunities, as well as promoting xenophobia by calling COVID the "Chinese virus" or the "kung flu," resulting in increased hate crimes toward Asians (Fang, 2020).

The COF is also reinforced and accentuated through distortion or altered images and information by social media and mainstream news. For example, in 2020, Fox News perpetuated the COF and xenophobia by publishing on its website's homepage digitally altered and misleading images that showed anti-racists demonstrators in Seattle, Washington, making them appear violent and dangerous (Darcy, 2020). What was a peaceful Black Lives Matter protest, Fox News portrayed as a possible "armed takeover," publishing an altered and deceptive photo collage that included armed gunmen and shattered storefronts. Media misrepresentations led to Trump calling protesters "domestic terrorists" and threatening to use federal force to clear the demonstrators out of the area (Darcy, 2020). The combination of Fox News and Trump's statements persuades, encourages, and reinforces the COF. To counteract the COF, it is important that social justice–oriented psychologists and counselors are politically savvy, not just accepting information about injustices at face value, but rather validating the data and reports through multiple sources. In addition, since it is apparent that we live in an age of anger, to avoid "drinking the COF Kool-Aid," we must also take extraordinary precautions and engage in an ongoing honest self-reflection and self-critique to ascertain the source of existing fears while utilizing cultural competencies and cultural and social justice humility in understanding our biases and prejudices.

FEAR OF FAILURE VERSUS BADGE OF HONOR

As social justice–oriented psychologists and counselors who live in a world where the COF is present, we may be confronted with our own fear of failing. The word "failure" has negative connotations that impact if, how, and when we take steps toward social justice in mental health work. Failure may lead to questions regarding our abilities, intelligence, and capabilities, causing us to have questions and doubt, feel foolish and inadequate, and fear being laughed at and ostracized by family, friends, and colleagues. These negative thoughts and feelings can diminish confidence about doing social justice work. In some cultures, the negative thoughts and feelings equate to "saving face," so that failure is perceived as shameful, not just for the individual, but for their entire family and, in some cases, the extended family. Regardless of one's cultural background, it is human nature to want fit in and be accepted. Thus, for mental health professionals doing social justice–oriented work, it is important to reduce the fear of failure by creating socially supportive environments where courageous risk-taking promoting justice is encouraged and supported.

This creates a transformation from stigmatizing failures in social justice work to celebrating successes and rethinking failures as attempts to succeed, similar to Silicon Valley companies' support for innovation and experimentation. The Silicon Valley companies encourage risk-taking behavior and celebrate failure by wearing "failure as a badge of honor" and by having "failure parties" (Gallo, 2017). Mental health social justice–oriented professionals could do well to adopt this perspective, celebrating social advocacy, activism, and action not only when there are accomplishments, but also when attempts are unsuccessful. We suggest celebrating social action failed attempts as *planting social justice seeds* that are part of a history of developing a foundation and the momentum that will lead to future success and social change. Clearly, not every social action will be efficacious, but the fact that we have the courage to take the risk to challenge injustices should be viewed as a "social justice attempt badge of honor." Embracing and reframing failure can help diminish and eradicate negative psychological social justice self-talk and the fear of failure. As Nelson Mandela said, "I learned that courage was not the absence of fear, but the triumph over it. The brave man is not he who does not feel afraid, but he who conquers that fear" (CNN, 2008).

FEAR OF LITIGATION AND ETHICAL CODES

Even with the American Psychological Association (APA)'s and the American Counseling Association (ACA)'s inclusion of social justice as a core principle promoting the idea that everyone should have accessibility to and be able to profit from psychological services, there is criticism that the APA and ACA have not explored or explained the implications of including the concept of justice (Hailes et al., 2021). The lack of clarity about ethical guidelines for doing mental health social justice work leads to confusion and hesitancy about social action. For example, numerous colleagues and students have shared with us that they are hesitant and fearful to promote or advocate for social justice because of the fear of legal consequences. The fear of being sued may restrict psychologists and counselors from taking risks to promote social justice. The prevalence of fear in the threat of lawsuits in the mental health profession has actually led the medical field to recognize this as a disorder, the *medical malpractice stress syndrome*, characterized by a sense of worthlessness, depression, physical illness, psychological dysfunction, and anxiety (Scibilia, 2020). In reality, according to the APA, approximately 2% of psychologists actually had a malpractice suit filed against them at some point in time (GoodTherapy, 2019), which is a low percentage given the high degree of fear of litigation.

The low proportion of lawsuits against psychologists may relate to the overwhelming majority of mental health professionals following established ethical standards. We have always believed in taking professional ethical standards very seriously and agree with the psychological and counseling codes of ethics of ensuring and protecting clients' rights and doing no harm. At the same time, the U.S. ethical standards have been criticized for being too legalistic (Rowley & MacDonald, 2001). The criticisms must be weighed as one does therapeutic social justice–oriented work that is based on values, principles, change, morality, and legality, all of which require sometimes taking chances to promote social justice, fairness, and equity.

Keeping in mind the codes of ethics and the concerns about the fit between social justice work and ethical codes, combined with the fact that only a very small number of psychologists and counselors face legal problems, may be helpful in diminishing the fear of ligation as a basis for not doing social justice work. Although we appreciate the need for and importance of a legalistic approach, we are concerned that the U.S. psychology and counseling ethical codes do not sufficiently address the "human aspects" of services in a proactive and positive manner. Our comments in this section about ethical guidelines present an expanded way of thinking about ethical standards and suggest that we further incorporate social justice and human rights into ethical principles, ones that are conducive to psychologists and counselors doing social justice–oriented work. We would pose the following questions for your consideration: Are you afraid of being sued over actions to promote equity and equality for clients? Can advocacy that eliminates unjust and unfair circumstances for clients be unethical? Why do you imagine some mental health professionals use ethics as an excuse for not being advocates for their clients?

PERSONAL APATHY, PROFESSIONAL PARALYSIS, URGENCY, AND IMPORTANCE

Another barrier to social justice work is *apathy*. Personal apathy helps counselors and psychologists avoid controversy and conflict with coworkers and may lead to complacency and support of the status quo even if it negatively effects clients. Similarly, *professional paralysis* is a barrier (Bemak & Chung, 2008) that results in psychologists and counselors being overwhelmed and confused by the magnitude and complexity of social injustices. This may lead to the professional thinking, "What can I do to make a difference? After all, I'm just one person." Our response to this has been to remember that social change comes in all shapes and sizes. Social justice advocacy and action do not imply that we need to generate world peace, which has the potential to make us victims of professional paralysis, but rather

BOX TEXT 8.2 MIGRANT CEO GIVING BACK BY SUPPORTING REFUGEES AND IMMIGRANTS THROUGH BUSINESS

Hamdi Ulukaya is the founder and CEO of Chobani Greek yogurt. He grew up in a working-class background and immigrated to the United States from Turkey in his 20s. Frustrated with business owners who abandon communities reliant on their jobs, Ulukaya focused his business on partnering with the community, as well as investing in the lives and futures of his employees. He was the winner of the 2019 Global Citizen Business Leader Award, and, in his acceptance speech, he stated, "There is an idea out there that the sole purpose of business is to make money. Honestly, that's the dumbest idea I've ever come across . . . what matters most in business and in life is the difference you make for others, and in the end, the truest measure of the business is not return on the investment, but return on kindness . . . kindness and courage will triumph over poverty and hatred every time."

Ulukaya's values are demonstrated by his employees receiving pay above the minimum wage, paid parental leave, training for workers in the rural communities where his factories are located, and also the provision of full-time employees with company shares that are worth up to 10% of its value.

A focus of Ulukaya's social justice work is hiring refugees and immigrants. He has extended this mission and advocacy work through his nonprofit, Tent Partnership for Refugees. Tent encourages businesses to improve the lives of refugees through strategies such as hiring displaced individuals or investing in their businesses. Ulukaya shared this in his acceptance speech: "We as citizens must take a side on climate change, on income inequality, on gun violence . . . there are 25 million people who sleep tonight in muddy tents at refugee camps. The message for business is simple: Don't pity them, hire them!"

His impact extends to other injustices, such as school lunch debt. Ulukaya donated more than $100,000 to remove school lunch debt and raise awareness about food insecurity. He stated: "As a parent, this news breaks my heart. For every child, access to naturally nutritious and delicious food should be a right, not a privilege. When our children are strong, our families are stronger."

Ulukaya gave insight into his motivation by saying "Silence is criminal these days. Being silent is as bad as if you're doing the bad thing, especially when you are representing a company, representing a brand, representing a community. You have to get involved. You have to raise your voice, and you have to take a stand. We can't solve all the problems, but we have to make sure that we stand for something."

Sources: McCarthy, J. (2019, Dec 13). Meet Chobani CEO Hamdi Ulukaya, winner of the first-ever Global Citizen prize for business leader. Global Citizen. https://www.globalcitizen.org/en/content/hamdi-ulukaya-business-global-citizen-prize-2019/
Global Citizen. (2019, Dec 20). Hamdi Ulukaya, Global Citizen prize business leader winner [Video]. YouTube. https://www.youtube.com/watch?v=ZkJ2omMNyOk
Davidson, P. (2016, Apr 27). Chobani workers get ownership stake that could make them millionaires. USA Today. https://www.usatoday.com/story/money/2016/04/27/chobani-employees-get-surprise-ownership-stake/83585844/

to keep in mind that small acts of advocacy and activism are important in building toward greater change and a social justice agenda. As Martin Luther King Jr. said, "You don't have to see the whole staircase—just take the first step."

Given the urgency and the importance of eliminating social injustices, at times the need for action can be overwhelming, causing one to become a victim to personal apathy and professional paralysis. Questions may arise: Which social justice issue do I tackle first? Where do I start? How do I begin, given the complexity and multidimensionality of injustices? Which issue is more important? Which issue is more urgent? These questions, although valid, can lead to feeling overwhelmed so that no social action is taken. To address these questions, a former U.S. President and military leader, Dwight Eisenhower, developed the *Urgent/Important Principle* to sort out what activities are important and what are distractions (MindTools, 2021). His principle can be applied to social justice mental health since the work can be overwhelming and confusing when we try to prioritize issues as urgent versus important. Eisenhower clarified that urgent problems are not important and important problems are not urgent, underscoring the importance of not allowing urgent issues to dominate one's time and energy at the expense of tackling important issues that are more likely to ensure long-term success. We found this concept to be relevant to social justice–oriented mental health work, where the breadth of issues may become overwhelming and cause one to lose focus on one's goals. We believe this framework is a good way to prioritize the social justice issues facing clients. To avoid personal apathy and professional paralysis we suggest consulting and discussing with clients what they perceive as the most important issue for them at that moment and what they can delay working on while tackling more pressing issues.

UTILIZING FALSE SOCIAL JUSTICE GENEROSITY AS SOCIAL ACTION

As mentioned previously, social justice work does not simply include critical consciousness and emotional reactions, but also involves taking action and steps to promote justice. Too often, we have witnessed those who identify as social justice–oriented mental health professionals as individuals who talk about injustices and criticize others for not being aware of or addressing injustices, although they themselves do not do social justice or human rights work. They have the skills and opportunity to do so, but rather become what we call "armchair social justice mental health advocates." Awareness of and conversation about injustice does not equate to being a social justice–oriented psychologist or counselor. The act of "walking the talk" as opposed to just "talking the talk" is essential in promoting mental health-oriented justice work. We suggest that those who do not take action to dismantle unjust systems and barriers are not actually doing social justice work. We include in this group those who believe they are doing social justice work by only donating money (however small or large the amount) to specific charitable organizations. Paulo Freire (1970) calls this "false generosity" that "buys peace" and helps ease, soothe, and diminish our social justice conscience and guilt rather than directly "getting our hands dirty" by proactively challenging unjust situations, individuals, institutions, and systems.

Philanthropy is largely contributed by those with financial wealth and economic advantage and can result in minimal or no social change. In some situations, financial donations rarely impact those in need or simply provide only temporary relief. For social justice–oriented mental health professionals to only make monetary donations avoids the root causes of the injustice. Donations may give the patron immediate satisfaction and relief that something has been done, sometimes resulting in the belief that no further action is necessary. However, the question remains whether philanthropy really creates social change and whether monetary donations are social action. Cornel West (2016) responded to these questions by saying, "Now, I have nothing against philanthropy. I just don't confuse charity with justice." We share this view: we have nothing against charitable donations, yet we ask why a donor with the psychotherapy and counseling skills, abilities, capabilities, availability, and opportunity to do social justice–oriented work holds back. Why do you choose to make a donation rather than directly and proactively challenge unjust situations? Moving from being an armchair social justice mental health advocate and transforming false generosity into real social justice action and advocacy is an important consideration for social justice–oriented mental health professionals.

SUMMARY

When doing social justice work one will always face logistical and psychological barriers. Logistical barriers require developing strategies that generate systemic and institutional change, keeping in mind urgency versus importance, while psychological barriers necessitate more personal introspective work. Overcoming psychological barriers begins with understanding the origins of these blockages and why they exist. This information provides ideas about how to unpack the psychological barriers by confronting, challenging, maneuvering, overcoming, and eliminating them. After undergoing courageous, honest, in-depth self-examination and self-critique about our psychological barriers, it is helpful to ensure that our social justice support group is in place, surrounding ourselves with family, friends, and colleagues who have similar social justice beliefs and values. These are individuals who do not question our values and beliefs, those we do not need to constantly educate, people who do not negatively question our actions but rather constructively critique and assist in brainstorming effective social justice strategies and who are our social justice cheerleaders.

Again, we want to emphasize that social justice work does not need to be done alone; others are also doing similar work. Collaboration with stakeholders, allies, colleagues, and other social justice professionals is helpful. Partnerships with others help reduce social justice negative self-talk, providing clarity about what can be done given current circumstances and acceptance of reality, rather than agonizing over and dwelling on "if only I could" or "I should have" or "I wish I could have." This means focusing on, accepting, and embracing what you can do given your current situation. Dive into it, do your best, and celebrate both successes and attempts by proudly wearing the social justice attempts badge of honor. This helps reduce personal apathy and psychological paralysis in doing social justice work.

As we have mentioned, there is no place for social justice neutrality. As Pastor Martin Niemöller (1946) stated, "In Germany, they came first for the Communists, and I didn't speak up because I wasn't a Communist. Then they came for the Jews, and I didn't speak up because I wasn't a Jew. Then they came for the trade unionists, and I didn't speak up because I wasn't a trade unionist. Then they came for the Catholics, and I didn't speak up because I was a Protestant. Then they came for me, and by that time no one was left to speak up." Similarly, Albert Einstein said, "The world is too dangerous to live in—not because of the people who do evil, but because of the people who sit and let it happen."

Before we end this section, we would also like to comment about strength and resiliency in doing social justice work. Although we have focused on psychological barriers, this section is not meant to be taken negatively, but instead to encourage you to be honest, open, and courageous in challenging yourself. Social justice work comes with a price, and it is both highly rewarding and highly challenging. Through our ups and downs in social justice work, it is important to remember the strength and resiliency that we have as social justice advocates and ensure that we do intentional self-care. Building and nurturing our strength and resiliency helps build the foundation for our work (Chapter 26 will discuss self-care in more detail). We end this chapter with an adapted Cherokee tale: "A Cherokee elder sitting with his grandchildren told them: 'In every life there is a terrible fight—a fight between two wolves. One is evil: he or she is fear, anger, envy, greed, arrogance, oppression, self-pity, resentment, and deceit. The other is good: joy, serenity, humility, confidence, generosity, equality, truth, gentleness, and compassion.' A child asked: 'Grandfather, which wolf will win?' The elder looked her in the eye and softly responded, 'The one you feed.'"

DISCUSSION QUESTIONS

1. Describe the three major psychological components or the ABCs to social justice activism.
2. How many of you identify with the NCS or know someone who has NCS?
3. Which other psychological barriers do you identify with? How would you overcome this barrier?
4. What are some of the ethical barriers to doing social justice work, and do you imagine it might affect your work?
5. Discuss how the concept of urgency versus importance has affected or will affect your work life. Do you agree or disagree with this principle?
6. Describe false social justice generosity.

REFERENCES

Baumert, A., & Schmitt, M. (2016). Justice sensitivity. In C. Sabbagh & M. Schmitt (Eds.), *Handbook of social justice theory and research* (pp. 161–180). Springer.

BBC. (2016, Apr 25). Why feeling like a fraud can be a good thing. https://www.bbc.com/news/magazine-36082469

Bechtoldt, M. N. (2015). Wanted: Self-doubting employees—Managers scoring positively on impostorism favor insecure employees in task delegation. *Personality and Individual Differences, 86*, 482–486. doi:10.1016/j.paid.2015.07.002

Bellini, R., & Westmarland, N. (2021). A problem solved is a problem created: The opportunities and challenges associated with an online domestic violence perpetrator programme. *Journal of Gender-Based Violence, 1*–17. https://doi.org/10.1332/239868021X16171870951258

Bemak, F., & Chung, R. C-Y. (1998). Vietnamese Amerasians: Predictors of distress and self-destructive behavior. *Journal of Counseling and Development, 76*, 452–458. https://doi.org/10.1002/j.1556-6676.1998.tb02704.x

Bemak, F., & Chung, R. C-Y. (1999). Vietnamese Amerasians: The relationship between biological American father and psychological distress, and self-destructive behavior. *Journal of Community Psychology, 27*, 443–456. https://doi.org/10.1002/(SICI)1520-6629(199907)27:4<443::AID-JCOP6>3.0.CO;2-N

Bemak, F., & Chung, R. C-Y. (2008). New professional roles and advocacy strategies for school counselors: A multicultural social justice perspective to move beyond the nice counselor syndrome. *Journal of Counseling and Development, Multicultural and Diversity Issues in Counseling, 38*, 372–381. https://doi.org/10.1002/j.1556-678.2008.tb00522.x

Bennett, D. H. (1995). *The party of fear: The American far right from nativism to militia*. Vintage Books, Random House.

Bernard, D. L., Hoggard, L. S., & Neblett, E. W. (2018). Racial discrimination, racial identity, and imposter phenomenon: A profile approach. *Cultural Diversity and Ethnic Minority Psychology, 24*, 51–61. https://doi:10.1037/cdp0000161

Bravata, D. M., Watts, S. A., Keefer, A. L., Madhusudhan, D. K., Taylor, K. T., Clark, D. M., Nelson, R. S., Cokley, K. O., & Hagg, H. K. (2020). Prevalence, predictors, and treatment of impostor syndrome: A systematic review. *Journal of General Internal Medicine, 35*, 1252–1275. https://doi.org/10.1007/s11606-019-05364-1

Chung, R. C-Y., & Bemak, F. (in preparation). Courage in action: The call for psychology to social justice action. Counseling Department, George Mason University. https://education.gmu.edu/counseling/

Chung, R. C-Y., Bemak, F., Ortiz, D. P., & Sandoval-Perez, P. A. (2008). Promoting the mental health of migrants: A multicultural-social justice perspective. *Journal of Counseling and Development, Multicultural and Diversity Issues in Counseling, 38*, 310–317. https://doi.org/10.1002/j.1556-6678.2008.tb00514.x

Clance, P. R., & Imes, S. A. (1978). The imposter phenomenon in high achieving women: Dynamics and therapeutic intervention. *Psychotherapy: Theory, Research and Practice, 15*, 241–247. https://doi:10.1037/h0086006

CNN. (2008, Jun 26). Mandela in his own words. https://edition.cnn.com/2008/WORLD/africa/06/24/mandela.quotes/

Cokley, K. O., Awad, G., Smith, L., Jackson, S., Awosogba, O., Hurst, A., Stone, S., Blondeau, L., & Roberts, D. (2015). The role of gender stigma consciousness, impostor phenomenon and academic self-concept in the academic outcomes of women and men. *Sex Roles, 73*, 414–426. https://doi:10.1007/s11199-015-0516-7

Cokley, K., Smith, L., Bernard, D., Hurst, A., Jackson, S., Stone, S., Awosogba, O., Saucer, C., Bailey, M., & Roberts, D. (2017). Impostor feelings as a moderator and mediator of the relationship between perceived discrimination and mental health among racial/ethnic minority college students. *Journal of Counseling Psychology, 64*(2), 141–154. https://doi.org/10.1037/cou0000198

Cozzarelli, C., & Major, B. (1990). Exploring the validity of the impostor phenomenon. *Journal of Social and Clinical Psychology, 9*(4), 401–417. https://doi.org/10.1521/jscp.1990.9.4.401

Crawford, W. S., Shanine, K. K., Whitman, M. V., & Kacmar, K. M. (2016). Examining the impostor phenomenon and work-family conflict. *Journal of Managerial Psychology, 31*(2), 375–390. https://doi.org/10.1108/JMP-12-2013-0409

Curran, T., & Hill, A. P. (2019). Perfectionism is increasing over time: A meta-analysis of birth cohort differences from 1989 to 2016. *Psychological Bulletin, 145*, 410–429. https://doi:10.1037/bul0000138

Darcy, O. (2020, Jun 13). Fox News publishes digitally altered and misleading images of Seattle demonstrations. CNN. https://www.cnn.com/2020/06/13/media/seattle-fox-news-autonomous-zone-protest/index.html

Fang, M. (2020, Apr 20). Reports of Anti-Asian attacks in NYC have skyrocketed compared to this time last year. https://www.huffpost.com/entry/asian-americans-attacks-hate-crimes-coronavirus_n_5e9dbb23c5b6488571e8a24e?ncid=APPLENEWS00001

Ferrari, J. R., & Thompson, T. (2006). Impostor fears: Links with self-presentational concerns and self-handicapping behaviours. *Personality and Individual Differences, 40*(2), 341–352. https://doi.org/10.1016/j.paid.2005.07.012.

Freire, P. (1970). *Pedagogy of the oppressed.* Continuum.

Furedi, F. (2005). *Culture of fear: Risk-taking and the morality of low expectation* (revised ed.). Continnum.

Gallo, C. (2017, Oct 9). Steven Spielberg's first boss made this promise that unleashed the director's creativity. https://www.forbes.com/sites/carminegallo/2017/10/09/steven-spielbergs-first-boss-made-this-promise-that-unleashed-the-directors-creativity/#178d0e2946d7

Gallup. (2019). Global emotions. https://www.gallup.com/analytics/248906/gallup-global-emotions-report-2019.aspx?thank-you-report-form=1

Gallup. (2021). Global emotions. https://www.gallup.com/analytics/349280/gallup-global-emotions-report.aspx

Glassner, B. (2010). *The culture of fear.* Basic Books.

GoodTherapy. (2019, Oct 1). Malpractice insurance for counselors: What you need to know. https://www.goodtherapy.org/for-professionals/business-management/insurance/article/malpractice-insurance-for-counselors-what-you-need-to-know

Hailes, H. P., Ceccolini, C. J., Gutowski, E., & Liang, B. (2021). Ethical guidelines for social justice in psychology. *Professional Psychology: Research and Practice, 52*(1), 1–11. https://doi.org/10.1037/pro0000291

Hutchins, H. M., & Rainbolt, H. (2017). What triggers imposter phenomenon among academic faculty? A critical incident study exploring antecedents, coping, and development opportunities. *Human Resource Development International, 20*(3),194–214. https://doi.org/10.1080/13678868.2016.1248205

Lane, J. A. (2015). The imposter phenomenon among emerging adults transitioning into professional life: Developing a grounded theory. *Adultspan Journal, 14*, 114–128. https://doi:10.1002/adsp.12009

McAllum, K. (2016). Managing imposter syndrome among the "Trophy Kids": Creating teaching practices that develop independence in millennial students. *Communication Education, 65*, 363–365. https://doi:10.1080/03634523.2016.1177848

McClain, S., Beasley, S. T., Jones, B., Awosogba, O., Jackson, S., & Cokley, K. (2016). An examination of the impact of racial and ethnic identity, impostor feelings, and minority status stress on the mental health of black college students. *Journal of Multicultural Counseling and Development, 44*, 101–117. https://doi:10.1002/jmcd.12040

MindTools. (2021). Eisenhower's urgent/important principle. https://www.mindtools.com/pages/article/newHTE_91.htm

Mishra, P. (2017). *Age of anger: A history of the present.* Farrar, Straus and Giroux.

Niemöller, M. (1946). Holocaust Encyclopedia. https://encyclopedia.ushmm.org/content/en/article/martin-niemoeller-first-they-came-for-the-socialists#:~:text=Niem%C3%B6ller%20is%20perhaps%20best%20remembered,was%20not%20a%20trade%20unionist.

Pearson, D. A. S., & Ford, A. (2018). Design of the "Up2U" domestic abuse perpetrator programme. *Journal of Aggression, Conflict and Peace Research, 10*(3), 189–201. https://doi.org/10.1108/JACPR-04-2017-0280

Pyke, K. D. (2010). What is internalized racial oppression and why don't we study it? Acknowledging racism's hidden injuries. *Sociological Perspectives, 53*(4), 551–572. https://doi:10.1525/sop.2010.53.4.551

Risse, G. (2016). *Driven by fear: Epidemics and isolation in San Francisco's house of pestilence.* University of Illinois Press.

Roche, D. (Ed.). (2004). *Restorative justice: Ideals and realities.* Routledge. https://doi.org/10.4324/9781351 15012Rowley, W. J., & MacDonald, D. (2001). Counseling and the law: A cross-cultural perspective. *Journal of Counseling & Development, 79,* 422–429. https://doi.org/10.1002/j.1556-6676.2001.tb01989.x

Scibilia, J. P. (2020, Aug 1). Medical malpractice stress syndrome can affect physical, mental health. AAP News. https://www.aappublications.org/news/2020/08/01/wellness080120

Spencer, S. J., Steele, C. M., & Quinn, D. M. (1999). Stereotype threat and women's math performance. *Journal of Experimental Social Psychology, 35*(1), 4–28. https://doi.org/10.1006/jesp.1998.1373

Steele, C. M. (1997). A threat in the air: How stereotypes shape intellectual identity and performance. *American Psychologist, 52*(6), 613–629. https://doi.org/10.1037/0003-066X.52.6.613

Steele, C. M., & Aronson, J. (1995). Stereotype threat and the intellectual test performance of African Americans. *Journal of Personality and Social Psychology, 69*(5), 797–811. https://doi.org/10.1037/0022-3514.69.5.797

Stone, S., Saucer, C., Bailey, M., Garba, R., Hurst, A., Jackson, S. M., Krueger, N., & Cokley, K. (2018). Learning while Black: A culturally informed model of the impostor phenomenon for Black graduate students. *Journal of Black Psychology, 44*(6), 491–531. https://doi.org/10.1177/0095798418786648

Vergauwe, J., Wille, B., Feys, M., De Fruyt, F., & Anseel, F. (2015). Fear of being exposed: The trait-relatedness of the impostor phenomenon and its relevance in the work context. *Journal of Business and Psychology, 30*(3), 565–581. https://doi.org/10.1007/s10869-014-9382-5

West, C. (2016, Apr 6). Interview. https://www2.lehigh.edu/news/cornel-west-embrace-an-unapologetic-love-of-justice

CHAPTER 9

STUDENT CHAPTER

Embracing Myself

Tiffany Mitchell

am a 26-year-old African American female. I learned early in life that the color of my skin, tone of my voice, and physical appearance influenced the way others interacted to me. At the age of 6, I begin to feel isolated from my peers for having darker skin. I remember being told "these monkey bars are for White kids only" and that I had to use the old monkey bars (which were much further away and older). At the age of 10, I was teased for "talking White" by my peers. Other Black girls would approach me and insist that I wanted to be White. At the age of 14, I was ridiculed for the way I looked by my peers. I was constantly asked how my hair grew so long to have braids down my back or why my hair couldn't get wet in the pool. These experiences forced me to shut down and internalize my feelings. I taught myself to withhold certain emotions such as anger, frustration, and disappointment from my peers. I didn't want to be labeled as the mean Black girl. I was also taught that violence and aggression wouldn't be tolerated by my parents. Therefore, I learned to withhold what I perceived as negative emotions from my peers and teachers. Often, they would comment on my calm, respectful and non-confrontational demeanor. I maintained this demeanor throughout elementary and high school.

At the age of 18, I began college, and I met several people with whom I shared similar experiences, and, for the first time, I started to truly express my emotions with my peers. I was surprised that they also felt isolated and would suppress their feelings. It was with this group of peers that I began to express and explore my true feelings about race and the impact it had on me. The year I turned 20, I was accepted into the nursing program at Virginia Commonwealth University. I was excited because I had worked hard to get into this prestigious program. More than 300 students applied and only 60 were accepted: I was one of the 60. Being in the nursing program was challenging, the workload was rigorous and very competitive. I struggled with controlling my emotions during this time of my life. Although I had made progress since starting college, I did not feel supported by my peers or the faculty. My peers would hold study sessions and not invite me to participate. My teachers did not notice how hard the course work was for me, and, when I asked for help, they would tell me to study more or try harder. This brought strong feelings of isolation, confusion, sadness, and hopelessness.

Ultimately, I changed my major from nursing to psychology. Many people didn't understand my decision, but what mattered most was that my family and close friends supported me. It took me a year and half to come to terms with what had transpired in my life. I questioned my choices and what I really wanted to do. After much soul searching, I decided to enter the graduate counseling program at George Mason University. It was the first time in my adult life that I was challenged with opportunities to express how I genuinely felt without fear of being isolated. This was the first time I was not able to fly under the radar of my professors. They truly saw me as a person and valued my voice and ideas. I contributed to class discussions and actively listened to my peers, yet I knew I had more to offer. I would leave some classes wondering "why I didn't say more?" By the time I reached the social justice and multicultural counseling courses, my advisor and the professor for those courses, Dr. Chung, encouraged me to be more vocal and expressive of my opinions. Although I didn't know it at the time, I needed Dr. Chung's encouragement.

Once the courses began, I felt a natural desire to share and be open with my classmates. There were moments when we spoke about racial disparities during which I internally struggled with how hard to challenge myself and my classmates. This struggle came from fear of being isolated and unaccepted. The African American culture presentation (in class) brought out some powerful emotions and insights as they addressed the role of the Black church and the history of racial discrimination. I felt powerless, sad, and frustrated. I finally understood how some messages had been embedded in my culture and worldview. The challenge for me was adjusting to this and learning to be accepting of my own emotions. When I voiced my frustrations with the systems and took ownership for my experiences in class, I felt relief from within. The process of engaging in race dialogues allowed me to break through my wall. Some classes, I feared my classmates' perception of me would change; however, knowing myself and what I needed for my own healing was more powerful. As I continued to put my needs first, the fear of being too emotional disappeared. I felt empowered and at ease with the process of vulnerability. I learned to work with resistant classmates who were not as open to the process of being vulnerable yet. This did not hinder my ability to interact with them in or out of class: in fact, it fueled my desire to learn more from them. I have learned that shying away from the tough conversation is a disservice to all involved. When we experienced powerful moments in class, when we stopped fearing the what-if thoughts in our head around topics about oppression and systemic racism, we grew and developed more than we thought possible. For others in this field or similar fields, understanding that change comes with discomfort and vulnerability is transformative. Growth is a gradual process that requires one to have a growth mindset. This is not a field for instant gratification! Being agents of change and advocates starts from within, then transcends into the work. Advocacy work must start with yourself. Finding the courage to speak up comes from being an honest, humble, and vulnerable with yourself.

Without this experience I would not be prepared or ready to address the challenges that I will encounter as a professional school counselor. As I transition to becoming a licensed professional in the field, I feel a strong sense of excitement and humility after taking on multicultural and social justice issues. I am eager to meet and connect with my like-minded professional colleagues and those who share different views. To make strides in this field one must be willing and ready for the twists and turns. I feel confident that this program has adequately prepared me; now it's on me to continue my growth through professional development and personal ownership. I have developed a strong, authentic, and genuine approach toward building therapeutic relationships with individuals. This program has provided thought-provoking discussions and examples of why one must approach counseling from a culturally competent lens. I understand the importance of broaching race and other difficult topics and how they can help improve the therapeutic relationship with students, parents, teachers, and community members. I am excited and ready to start the next phase of my counseling training and development with a culturally conscious mindset.

CHAPTER 10

THE DEVELOPMENT OF THE MULTIPHASE MODEL OF PSYCHOTHERAPY, COUNSELING, HUMAN RIGHTS, AND SOCIAL JUSTICE

Frederic P. Bemak and Rita Chi-Ying Chung

Be the change that you want to see in the world.

—Mahatma Gandhi

Everybody can be great, because everybody can serve. You don't have to have a college degree to serve. You don't have to make your subject and your verb agree to serve. You don't have to know about Plato and Aristotle to serve. You don't have to know Einstein's theory of relativity to serve. You don't have to know the second theory of thermodynamics in physics to serve. You only need a heart full of grace, a soul generated by love, and you can be that servant.

—Martin Luther King, Jr.

Justice grows out of recognition of ourselves in each other—that my liberty depends on you being free, too.

—Barack Obama

REFLECTION QUESTIONS

1. Reflect on your own family experience growing up and today. How do you imagine this will affect you in working with families?

2. Have you ever been in a completely different culture than your own or known someone who described their experience of being in a culture different from your own? What are some of the first things you or others you knew had to do to adjust to or understand the cultural differences?

3. When someone is sharing pain or deep distress with you, how do you respond? How do you feel?

The Multiphase Model (MPM) of Psychotherapy, Counseling, Human Rights, and Social Justice is based on a number of principles that led to its development. In this chapter, we discuss the principles and the rationale for the development of the MPM. In developing the MPM, we believe it is important to apply the MPM within the ecological context of today's world, one that includes the social, historical, psychological, economic, political, environmental, and cultural aspects that influence everyday life (Bemak & Conyne, 2004). The very nature of these issues affects individuals and impacts the therapeutic relationship. Factors that are important to consider within an ecological framework include globalization; the worldwide movement and migration of people; changing ethnic and racial demographics; a growing diversity of lifestyles, religion, and religious and spiritual beliefs; increased intergroup and intragroup conflict; terrorism; escalating interpersonal and gender-based violence; the COVID pandemic; high rates of divorce; sexism and misogynistic behavior; growing rates of poverty; public health issues; mass shootings and gun violence; racial injustice; global warming and climate change; environmental racism; and a widening technological gap.

We believe that it is important for mental health professionals to consider these issues as we move into the future, that requires a reassessment of training, practice, skills, techniques, interventions, and supervision. The MPM was designed to address these issues and help mental health professionals more effectively include these matters as they work from a human rights and social justice perspective. Given the extent of injustices, there is a need for therapeutic models that integrate mental health with social justice and human rights within a relevant ecological framework. Our concern, as we discussed in previous chapters, relates to the lack of applicability of traditional models and pedagogy to contemporary issues that we face as psychologists and counselors. The patent absence of social justice and human rights within the traditional mental health interventions framework led us to design the MPM with these parameters in mind.

THE FOUR MPM PRINCIPLES

The MPM is based on four principles. The first premise, as stated previously, is that traditional professional mental health philosophies and practices are rooted in precepts of individualism that have origins in European and European American constructs and may not be applicable to increasingly diverse populations. The emphasis on individualistic society provides an underpinning for cultural values that permeate Western society and influence every aspect of life, including mental health and psychological well-being. The prominence of individualism in mental health theory and practice is juxtaposed with the fact that approximately 30%, or fewer than one-third, of the world's population come from individualistic societies (Triandis, 1994). More than two-thirds of the world's populations have origins in collectivistic societies that value interdependence and a social orientation that emphasizes family, community, and group traditions (Triandis, 1994). Differences between individualistic and collectivistic cultures can be seen in the United States, where 1 in 7 people are foreign-born (Batalova et al., 2020), while people of color represent 43% of the U.S. population (Boschma et al., 2021), with many of these groups coming from collectivistic cultures. Currently, the biracial/multiracial population is the fastest growing group in the United States, followed by Asian Americans, and Latinx (Batalova et al., 2020; Vespa et al., 2020).

According to the 2020 census, the United States is more diverse and more multiracial than ever before (Boschma et al., 2021), with projections that, by 2045, White Americans will be the minority group (Frey, 2018; Vespa et al., 2020). These demographics have the potential to make a significant impact on the mental health field, with projections that the United States will continue to be racially and ethnically diverse, and this will have a bearing on the makeup of future clientele. The importance of growing diversity is highly relevant for mental health practitioners given the protests and civil conflict around racial justice for people of color and indigenous populations in the United States and globally. To address the injustices and potential human rights violations impinging on society, it is important that social justice–oriented psychotherapy and counseling decolonize traditional Western theories and techniques while responding to shifting demographics and political and socioeconomic changes.

The second principle that led us to develop the MPM is based on the fact that individualistic constructs provide a foundation for Western colonial perspectives on mental health, as previously mentioned in Chapter 4 ("Social Justice Multicultural Psychology and Counseling"). Western psychology is firmly rooted in individualistic constructs based on precepts of European psychoanalysis, psychopathology, and mental illness. Thus, individuals who seek mental health treatment in the West often talk to psychologists and counselors irrespective of family and community engagement and awareness. They receive diagnoses that label their problems, and they work to resolve difficulties on their own rather than in conjunction with significant others in their lives. Modern manifestations of Western mental illness correlate with the medical disease model, which includes interpretations of biochemical and genetic disorders best treated with medication, despite concerns about cultural bias when working across cultures. A difficulty with the disease model is that it does not incorporate substantive sociopolitical and psychopolitical concepts such as justice, equity, and fairness, nor is it concerned with human rights. Nor does the disease model consider environmental factors, such as social support as a buffer for mental illness (Kessler et al., 2005; Pernice-Duca, 2010; Turner & Brown, 2010).

In fact, studies found that 40% of treatment outcomes were attributed to extratherapeutic factors, or factors outside of the actual therapy or counseling; these include social support networks (Lambert, 1992; Lambert & Bergin, 1994), correlating with the importance of social support in collectivistic cultures that value families and communities in helping and healing. It would be reasonable to believe that social supports in collectivistic cultures, where family and community are more highly valued than individuals, play a significant role in helping and healing. Research has found that social support has a direct relationship to positive mental health and psychological well-being (Harandi et al., 2017; Kessler et al., 2005; Pernice-Duca, 2010; Turner & Brown, 2010). Thus, the Western and colonial percepts that regard the individual as the foundation for mental health treatment present a formidable challenge when working with clients from diverse cultures. Subsequently, it would be important for psychologists and counselors to acknowledge the impact of culture on clients' conceptualization of their mental health problems, the manifestation and expression of symptoms, help-seeking behavior, treatment expectations, preferred treatment modalities, and factors that affect treatment outcomes outside of the actual therapy, all of which may not align with Western diagnoses and treatment protocols (Chung & Kagawa-Singer, 1995; Draguns, 2000; Hwang et al., 2008).

The third principle that led to the development of the MPM relates to findings that communities of color tend to underutilize mainstream Western mental health services (Hall et al., 2021; U.S. Office of the Surgeon General [U S. OSG] et al., 2001), either not accessing the services at all or dropping out early in the therapeutic process due to a lack of culturally appropriate responsiveness from mental health practitioners (Griner & Smith, 2006; Sue et al., 1991). Factors that may contribute to these findings include the tendency for psychologists and counselors to misdiagnose clients of color as a result of racial stereotyping, microaggressions (Gara et al., 2019; U.S. OSG et al., 2001; Sue et al., 2007, 2008; Williams & Cooper, 2019), and language barriers resulting in a number of psychologists and counselors unable to speak the native language of their clients or understand the nuances of effectively working with bicultural interpreters (Bemak & Chung, 2021a, 2021b; Bemak et al., 2003; Brisset et al., 2014; Ohtani et al., 2015; Resera et al., 2015). Furthermore, services may be difficult to access, with inaccessible locations and travel costs being barriers (Bemak & Chung, 2021a, 2021b). Finally, underutilization of mental health services may be due to the stigma attached within one's own racial/ethnic community to seeing a psychologist or counselor for support.

The fourth principle relates to the development of the MPM and is based on the reality that, historically, mental health has not considered issues of social justice or human rights. In our opinion, neglecting social justice and human rights in mental health work has been, until recently, a glaring deficit. The absence of considering social justice and human rights is evident when Arnett (2008, 2009) found that psychological research done in the United States focused on a narrow sample of only 5% of the world's population. Arnett (2008, 2009) argued that neglecting 95% of people in the world has broad implications about psychological findings, applications, and treatment related to such issues as collectivist versus individualistic cultures, socioeconomic status, gender roles, health, education, etc. More recently, Thalmayer et al. (2021) found parallel results and came to similar conclusions as Arnett, pointing out a slight improvement 13 years later, but still finding 89% of humanity discounted in U.S. psychological research. Thalmayer et al. (2021) pointed out that the narrow focus on 11% of the world's population in U.S. psychological studies was based on WEIRDs (i.e., an acronym coined by Henrich et al. [2010] that stands for "Western, educated, industrialized, rich, and democratic") that can't be presumed to be a representative sample of humanity. Given the almost 7 billion people who are not represented in the U.S. psychological research sampling we would concur with Arnett and Thalmayer, raising concerns about the lack of attention and findings regarding inequities, inequalities, injustices, and human rights violations.

Although it is fairly recent that social justice and human rights has been considered part of mental health treatment and that research studies have broadened the sampling pool, we believe that it is the psychologist's and counselor's moral and ethical obligation to firmly address and incorporate social justice and human rights in their training and practice. Statistics on injustices such as poverty, discrimination, gun violence and mass shootings, global warming/climate change, interpersonal, elderly, and gender-based violence, xenophobia, racial injustices, religious intolerance, environmental racism, inequities in education, justice and health care, etc. complement these four principles, pointing out the critical need to address social justice and human rights. We encourage readers to research statistics and data in your own region and country regarding social justice and human rights issues.

THE RATIONALE FOR THE DEVELOPMENT OF THE MPM

The absence of a more defined emphasis on social justice and human rights practice in psychology, counseling, and psychotherapy led us to develop the MPM (Bemak & Chung, 2008a; 2021a, 2021b; Bemak et al., 2003). Our goal was to develop a model that offers a framework to address today's rapidly changing society and effectively work with the myriad of historical and contemporary complex and interrelated issues that affect both human rights and mental health. The MPM was further aimed at assisting mental health professionals to be effective working with *all* groups and *all* clients from diverse racial, ethnic, and cultural backgrounds and the intersection of identities. Inherent in the model is the focus on proactive attention to social injustices and human rights violations that inhibit personal and social development and growth. The MPM is challenging in that it requires psychologists and counselors to move beyond their traditional roles and take a broader and more comprehensive view of mental health and psychological well-being that involves multiple levels of personal, social, and systemic change.

The MPM takes into account that clients may come into the counseling relationship affected by local, regional, national, and even international events and situations. The advancement of technology and social media provides information causing many clients to come to counseling and psychotherapy with a heightened awareness of the world around them and the impact of that world on their lives. Clients may enter therapy with strong reactions to injustices and human rights violations, wanting to take some type of action to address injustices they see in the media and in their lived experiences. We would suggest that this type of personal desire to take action is important to address in counseling and psychotherapy. This does not mean that one ignores deeper psychological issues and problems raised by individuals. Rather, it requires a careful assessment and consideration of when and how to address social and political responses within the therapeutic relationship and how to balance personal psychological concerns with a client's desire to proactively do something.

An example of balancing clients' personal concerns with action was seen in a school where a large number of students of color were placed in school detention, and the school counselor and school psychologist were working with a group of angry parents who were demanding some answers. Rather than help defend the school's practice, the counselor and psychologist raised questions about whether there was a disproportionate number of students of color receiving detention and, if this was in fact the case, what the counselor, psychologist, and parents could do to review this situation and change the practice. Generally, social justice issues such as this are broader issues that have social implications affecting larger groups of people, communities, and the society at large.

Inequities and injustices are often neither addressed nor attended to in mental health work. In fact, we would suggest that individual counseling and psychotherapy has taken a passive and often insidious role by focusing on changing the individual while neglecting the need to change the larger system. The danger with this approach is that there is a perpetuation of the status quo, which historically maintains unfair and unequal power and resource differentials that may in turn reinforce and contribute to injustices. Thus, the MPM is a holistic approach that views diverse clientele from ecological, macro, and micro viewpoints. The approach reconceptualizes traditional Western training within a universal social justice and human rights framework that incorporates and engenders cross-cultural applications that are based on the four therapeutically responsive principles noted above.

MPM APPLICATION

To effectively provide mental health interventions using the MPM requires a variety of skills, techniques, and experiences, as well as a clear sense of how social justice and human rights impact one's psychological well-being. Figure 10.1 depicts the skills, experiences, techniques, and critical consciousness that are essential when one employs the MPM.

CLIENTS' LIVED EXPERIENCES

Cultural humility and sensitivity are cornerstones of the MPM, with psychologists and counselors welcoming and working with clients' family and community worldviews, cultural values, beliefs, attitudes, customs, language, spiritual dimensions, identities, and intersectionality of identities. Concurrently, it is essential to consider the direct and indirect influential factors in the client's lived experiences, including the historical, sociopolitical, psychopolitical, psychosocial, ecological, and cultural experiences that constitute the foundation and worldview of a person's life. For example, when I (Fred) provided clinical consultation for 2½ years on an American Indian reservation for the mental health team, it was essential that I not only maintained a sense of cultural humility but also kept in mind historical genocide, current political oppression, injustices, and human rights violations facing the Nation, the Nation's interaction with the surrounding mainstream society, and the effect of my being a White male working with an American Indian group of professionals (which we discussed in depth). All of these issues had great impact on the mental health challenges facing the clientele and were important to keep in mind as we worked toward wellness, healing, and mental health.

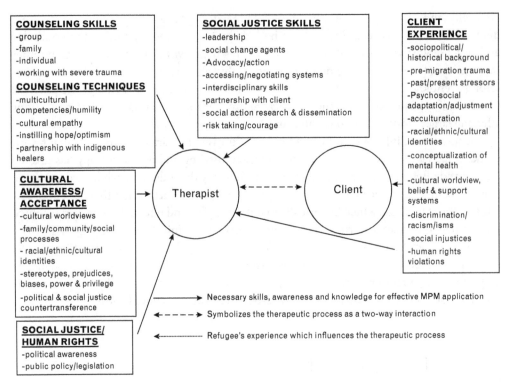

COUNSELING SKILLS
-group
-family
-individual
-working with severe trauma
COUNSELING TECHNIQUES
-multicultural
competencies/humility
-cultural empathy
-instilling hope/optimism
-partnership with indigenous
healers

**CULTURAL
AWARENESS/
ACCEPTANCE**
-cultural worldviews
-family/community/social
processes
- racial/ethnic/cultural
identities
-stereotypes, prejudices,
biases, power & privilege
-political & social justice
countertransference

**SOCIAL JUSTICE/
HUMAN RIGHTS**
-political awareness
-public policy/legislation

SOCIAL JUSTICE SKILLS
-leadership
-social change agents
-Advocacy/action
-accessing/negotiating systems
-interdisciplinary skills
-partnership with client
-social action research & dissemination
-risk taking/courage

**CLIENT
EXPERIENCE**
-sociopolitical/
historical background
-pre-migration trauma
-past/present stressors
-Psychosocial
adaptation/adjustment
-acculturation
-racial/ethnic/cultural
identities
-conceptualization of
mental health
-cultural worldview,
belief & support
systems
-discrimination/
racism/isms
-social injustices
-human rights
violations

Therapist

Client

⟶ Necessary skills, awareness and knowledge for effective MPM application

⟵ - - - ⟶ Symbolizes the therapeutic process as a two-way interaction

⟵·········· Refugee's experience which influences the therapeutic process

FIGURE 10.1 *Requirements for Effective MPM Application*

Other mediating factors that are important to consider include past and present stressors; traumatic experiences, including intergenerational trauma; psychosocial adaptation and adjustment; level of acculturation; racial, ethnic, and cultural identities and the intersectionality of identities; cultural support systems; spirituality; cultural beliefs in the conceptualization of mental health and resulting cultural manifestations or expressions of symptoms; cultural preferences in help-seeking behavior; expectations in treatment; experiences of discrimination, racism, and other "isms"; and potential social injustices and human rights violations. It is essential to reflect on and keep these parts of a client's lived experience in the forefront when applying the MPM.

PSYCHOTHERAPY AND COUNSELING SKILLS AND TECHNIQUES

To complement the awareness of the client's lived experiences in a broader sociopolitical context, there also must be a thorough knowledge and understanding of traditional Western psychotherapy and counseling within a multicultural social justice framework. Being culturally competent in the various skill areas of group, family, and individual counseling provides a basis for applying the MPM, while maintaining the ability to adapt, modify, alter, expand, and/or change traditional Western skills and techniques into practices that are effective from a cultural social justice/human rights perspective is equally essential. This is especially important when working with people from diverse backgrounds. As mentioned previously, "talk therapy" may be foreign to some groups, requiring mental health professionals to adapt accordingly and thus making it important that therapeutic and counseling relationships are viewed from cross-cultural and multicultural social justice viewpoints. For example, one of the ways I (Fred) have worked with refugee clients from Africa and Asia has been to discuss dreams and semi-guided imagery fantasies that are applicable to their problems and struggles.

Components of traditional Western psychotherapy and counseling such as empathy, boundaries, personal space, confidentiality, greeting of clients and their families, and clients' preferences to use indigenous healing methodologies need to be considered from a cross-cultural and multicultural perspective. For example, problems may arise if the psychologist or counselor is displaying Western traditional methods of empathy such as direct eye contact or physical touch. This type of nonverbal behavior may be highly offensive to some diverse clientele and may not be an appropriate way of engaging or connecting. Furthermore, eye contact between an older and a younger person, or between genders, may be considered a cultural taboo. Knowing about these issues beforehand, and being willing to learn about these cross-cultural differences while on the job, are crucial to creating a safe therapeutic environment. Cross-cultural empathy is important while understanding that traditional Western displays of empathy may be inappropriate and even discourteous for many clients (Chung & Bemak, 2002). Complementing culturally responsive empathy is the need for mental health professionals to understand how to work with trauma. This is especially significant given the traumatic life events many clients have experienced in dealing with human rights violations and injustices. Thus, we believe it is vital to understand working with posttraumatic stress disorder (PTSD) and related therapeutic issues such as loss, grief, and bereavement from a cross-cultural viewpoint.

CROSS-CULTURAL SKILLS IN WORKING WITH LANGUAGE TRANSLATORS AND CULTURAL INTERPRETERS

Another important consideration in successful implementation of the MPM is language. Speaking and understanding the different languages of clients seeking mental health services may present challenges when working with diverse clientele (Bemak & Chung, 2021a; Chung & Lin, 1994; Resera et al., 2015). A majority of U.S. psychologists (83.6%) identify as White and monolingual English speakers (Lin et al., 2018), which contrasts with cultural and language diversity within communities of color and migrant populations. The diversity in language and culture globally and within the United States makes it essential for mental health professionals to work in partnership with individuals who can not only provide language translation, but also provide cultural interpretation (Bemak & Chung, 2021a; Tribe & Lane, 2009). It is critical when working with bilingual interpreters in the mental health field that the translation of a client's response is not just verbatim. In our experience, literal language translation is inadequate to understand the cultural context of psychological problems. Verbatim language translation that ignores cultural intricacies and nuances such as facial expressions, changes in posture, pitch, tone, and speech cadence may miss deeper meanings derived from cultural perspectives. In addition, there may be some words that are not translatable, and, if literally translated, would make no sense (Bemak & Chung, 2021a; Chung et al., 1997; Resera et al., 2015), thus underscoring the importance for translators to also interpret the cultural context.

When working with interpreters it is important that psychologists and counselors define clear boundaries, roles, expectations, and relationships (Bemak & Chung, 2021a; Resera et al., 2015). Without this clarification interpreters may inappropriately answer for clients, feeling that they need to censor the translation because of embarrassment about what is being said by clients; think they already know what clients are about to say; want to modify, edit, or change clients' responses because they think it is an incorrect answer; want to be overly helpful to clients by providing them with additional information or clarity about what they think the psychologist or counselor means; or see clients as an ally (Bemak & Chung, 2021a; Resera et al., 2015). Other important factors to consider are (a) periodically checking in with interpreters since they may experience secondary trauma, transference, and countertransference (Tribe & Keefe, 2009); (b) striving to sustain long-term constancy with interpreters (Resera et al., 2015; Tribe & Lane, 2009); (c) ensuring that children and other family members are not used as interpreters since it dislodges traditional relationships, roles, and dynamics in the family (Bemak & Chung, 2021a); (d) realizing that sessions may run longer than usual given the inclusion of interpreters; and (e) maintaining a sensitivity to the presence of a third person in the room and its effects on the therapeutic dynamic. It is important to discuss the triadic relationship with the client and explain the presence and role of the interpreter to ensure they don't feel reliant on the interpreter to speak for them (Tribe & Keefe, 2009).

Language must never be seen as an impediment or detriment to therapy. Bilingualism and multilingualism should always be respected (Chung & Bemak, 2007) in the therapeutic setting. In fact, our experiences have been that language differences can easily be overcome. A great example of this occurred when I (Fred) was on a World Rehabilitation Fund research fellowship in India at the National Institute of Mental Health and Neuro Sciences (NIMHANS). NIMHANS was instituting a national pilot program that had a family residential component involving the full extended family residing on-site for three-week treatment periods. Families from all over India came; because India has a highly diverse language culture, most spoke different languages. In the intensive group therapy sessions, simultaneous translations were ongoing for the five different languages spoken, with these translations going back and forth between client or family member to client or family member and so on. Remarkably, going back and forth in five languages with multiple translations worked! A similar situation for Rita occurred when running a psychoeducational group for Southeast Asian refugees. The refugees sat together according to their native language for translation purposes. I (Rita) would speak first in English and then translate what I said in English into Chinese. While I was translating in Chinese, simultaneously four other interpreters translated what I said into four other Southeast Asian languages. The lesson in sharing these two examples is to show the importance of not to be daunted by language diversity and to respect and appreciate the richness and differences that language can bring and the importance of accommodating language and cultural interpretation.

BOX TEXT 10.1 GRASSROOT ADVOCACY IN INDIA

India has the highest rates of cancer and heart disease globally and increasing rates of childhood obesity. Priya Prakash (28 years old) founded the organization HealthSetGo, which uses technology to connect families, schools, and doctors to identify the health needs of children and provide any of the necessary interventions. It provides schools with reports on school-wide health so that communities can come together to address widespread issues in conjunction with individualized health needs. HealthSetGo also provides experiential curriculum, which educates students on health prevention (e.g., hygiene, nutrition, and physical and mental health). Prakash's organization has already been implemented in 77 cities across India and impacted more than 200,000 parents and children.

Prakash's motivation in creating HealthSetGo is based on her own experience of being bullied as a child for being overweight, which had a negative impact on both her physical and mental health. She was awarded the 2019 Cisco Youth Leadership Award, part of the Global Citizen Award, acknowledging and celebrating her work toward improving the physical and mental health of children in India. Prakash's focus on children is based on her belief that healthy habits start from a young age and impact the rest of children's lives. She believes that every child should have access to healthcare in order to end poverty and put a stop to the 60% of deaths that are considered preventable in India.

Sources: Rodriguez, L. (2019, Nov 22). Meet the Cisco Youth Leadership Award finalist who is ensuring schoolchildren in India stay healthy. Global Citizen. https://www.globalcitizen.org/en/content/priya-prakash-global-citizen-cisco-youth-leader/
Calderwood, I. (2019, Dec 21). Health activist Priya Prakash wins the Cisco Youth Leadership prize. Global Citizen. https://www.globalcitizen.org/en/content/priya-prakash-wins-the-cisco-youth-leadership-priz/

THE ELEMENTS OF HOPE AND OPTIMISM WITHIN THE MPM

When working with people whose human rights have been violated, the accumulation of negative and oppressive experiences may result in despair, helplessness, and hopelessness. It is our experience, when working with clients who are oppressed or have experienced different levels of trauma and personal and social violations, that hope is critical in the healing process. A study of therapeutic outcomes has shown that 15% of positive outcomes are attributed to the placebo effects of hope and expectations (Lambert & Bergin, 1994), while other studies have emphasized the importance of optimism (or hope) as it correlates with positive psychological well-being (Conversano et al., 2010; Gallagher & Lopez, 2009). Consequently, we believe it is important that psychologists and counselors are hopeful for their clients and project positivity in their work. A negatively inclined psychologist or counselor transmits messages of hopelessness, frustration, and despair. On the other hand, mental health professionals who feel positive and see the possibilities of influencing the future reflect a viewpoint that there is the possibility of change on personal, social, and community levels.

For example, when working with adolescents who want to stop taking drugs and are trying to take the difficult step to end long-standing friendships with other drug users, it is important for us, as a psychologists or counselors, to believe that these clients have the potential to take the steps to personally change as well as impact external circumstances, such as their social circle, that are psychologically harmful. Confidence in a positive outcome is essential in the therapeutic relationship, whereby the psychologist or counselor is a facilitator and partner, aspiring to different and healthier outcomes. This parallel process of hope becomes embedded in the therapeutic relationship so that our level of optimism and expectations for change may be mirrored by the clients' own beliefs and feelings.

CULTURAL SELF-AWARENESS: KNOW THYSELF

Mental health professionals and counselors working toward social justice and human rights must have more than the traditional requisite skills and go beyond using the usual techniques. Building on multicultural competencies to work with the complex issues of equity and justice, it is important to have a deeply rooted understanding of our own cultural heritage, values, and beliefs. Insight into our personal perspectives about social justice, social responsibility, and social activism and how these perspectives interplay with our biases, privilege, and power is vital to our work and identities. We believe that the impact of these multiple perspectives manifest in the therapeutic relationship and the therapeutic process. A more in-depth personal insight helps us understand the complexity of clients' multiple identities and lived experiences.

For example, instead of narrowly focusing on a single aspect of a client who identifies as a woman, it would be beneficial to explore the intersectionality of other identities, such as being a woman of color, or a transgender woman of color, or a transgender woman of color with a disability. Multiple identities may lead to some clients dealing with varied challenges and injustices on a daily basis. To understand this more clearly, consider a White mental health professional working with a client from a different racial or ethnic group. The White counselor or therapist would need not only to understand racial/ethnic identity theory (Cross & Vandiver, 2001; Helms, 1995) as it relates to the client, but also how White identity theory relates to the psychologist or counselor working across cultures (Helms, 1992). Embedded in this example is the importance of understanding the counselor's or therapist's and the client's responses to issues of power, privilege, bias, racism, xenophobia, discrimination, and oppression. Although initially White identity theory was established to assist White mental health professionals to assess their own power, racial biases, prejudices, stereotypes, and countertransference, we would expand upon this and suggest that it is critical for any mental health practitioner to have this level of awareness about their identity when working with clients from a racial, ethnic, or cultural group different from their own.

Another example would be, Vietnamese psychologists who must undergo a similar process if their clients are African American, Latinx, White, Muslim, American Indian, or from another Asian group. Issues of power, privilege, biases, prejudices, and countertransference are not limited to any one group but affect all psychologists and counselors regardless of race, ethnicity, gender, age, class, religion, sexual orientation, ability, and so on. For instance, a counselor who has strong religious beliefs may be negatively predisposed to LGTQI clients, or a Jewish therapist may have negative countertransference issues with a Palestinian client. Regardless of the situation, it is the mental health professional's ethical duty to ensure that they are aware of and acknowledge potential biases in their therapy and counseling and find ways to work toward eliminating such biases and prejudices. In summary, to be effective when working with inequities, the MPM requires mental health professionals to undergo a deep self-examination of their values, beliefs, and worldviews while coming to terms with their stereotypes, biases, prejudices, privileges, power, and political views that may interfere with providing effective treatment (U.S. DHHS, 2001; U.S. OSG et al., 2001).

THE RELATIONSHIP BETWEEN "ISMS" AND MENTAL HEALTH

Long-standing issues affecting clients are racism, sexism, classism, and numerous other "isms." Racism has been identified as a natural consequence of Westernized individualism (Pedersen, 2000), which may be extrapolated to other isms. Psychologists and counselors cannot ignore the impact of racism, sexism, and other forms of discrimination and oppression on their clients and their families and communities. Researchers point to how experiences of racism, prejudice, and discrimination correlate negatively to psychological well-being, having a damaging effect on people from ethnic, racial, cultural, and diverse backgrounds on their self-confidence, self-worth, self-image, interpersonal relationships, academic and work performance, and adaptation to the broader social environment (e.g., Carter, 2007; Franklin & Boyd-Franklin, 2000; McGee, 2016; Nadal et al., 2014; Pieterse & Carter, 2007; Smith et al., 2011; Steele et al., 2002; Sue, 2003). Racism and discrimination also contribute to substance abuse (Matsuzaka & Knapp, 2019), child abuse and neglect (Trent et al., 2019), suicide (Hollingsworth et al., 2017; Wong et al., 2011), and domestic violence (Brewer, 2006; Ho, 1990). Yet the traditional Western therapeutic interventions focus more on the presenting problems (such as suicide or substance abuse) rather than on ways to address the larger context of xenophobia, discrimination, and racism. This same phenomenon can be seen in relationship to the other isms and their consequent social inequities and inequalities.

Psychologists and counselors who presume that they are free of discrimination, prejudice, racism, and other biases underestimate the social impact of their own socialization and their inherited and, in some instances, subtly ingrained unintentional covert discrimination and racism. Taking racism once again as an example, we can see in many instances that racism emerges as an unintentional attitude among well-meaning, right-thinking, good-hearted, caring professionals who are probably no more or less free from cultural biases than other members of the general public (Pedersen, 2000). Research by Sue and his colleagues (e.g., Sue et al., 2007, 2008) on microaggressions demonstrates daily racist comments that in some cases are meant to be a compliment but instead portray derogatory racial slights and insults that negatively impacting people of color.

Examples of microaggressions would be telling an African American that she is "so articulate," conveying an underlying message that she can speak "proper" English; or telling an Asian that she speaks English very well, even though she is a fourth-generation American; or telling a Muslim American man that you're glad he is on "our" side, with the underlying assumption that Muslims are anti-American and terrorists. These are examples of microinsults, microassaults, and microinvalidations (Sue, 2010). To avoid acting on and internalizing "isms" consciously and unconsciously, and to be effective with all clients, it is important for psychologists and counselors to be aware of, understand, and respect clients' worldviews, beliefs, values, lived experiences, and cultural identities, all of which require continued cultural humility and self-reflection.

POLITICAL COUNTERTRANSFERENCE

When assuming a social justice and human rights perspective, one is not only working with clients to promote psychological health and wellness, but also working within the context of much broader political issues that influence clients' lives, as described earlier in this chapter. When considering these broader ecological and political issues, the outlook for a client's mental health interrelates with a wide range of associated issues that impact the client. Thus, it is important that mental health practitioners be aware not only of their personal response to clients, but also of their personal reactions at another level, reactions that we call *political countertransference* (PCT) (Bemak & Chung, 2021a; 2021b; Chung, 2005; Chung et al., 2008). PCT involves awareness of our personal reactions to the political context of clients' lives, which in turn effects the therapeutic relationship.

Two examples provide an illustration of PCT. The first example relates to ongoing terrorist attacks. The September 11, 2001 (9/11) attacks in the United States resulted in global heightened anxiety about future attacks. The anxiety was reinforced by ongoing terrorist actions throughout the United States and worldwide, such as attacks in London, New Zealand, Afghanistan, India, and Europe, to name only a few. Immediate media and social media coverage made situations more intense by providing minute-by-minute detailed accounts of the attacks, accompanied by constant updates about the numbers of injured and lives lost. Many psychologists and counselors witnessing these tragic and senseless acts of violence had strong feelings about the attacks, victims, survivors, and the losses experienced by the victims' families. These reactions contribute to intense feelings that are accompanied by political convictions and possibly even negative perceptions of Muslims or people of Islamic faith. Mental health practitioners working with clients from Islamic countries, or with clients who hold deeply rooted religious beliefs about Islam, may have strong reactions toward them, particularly in the face of ongoing terrorist attacks. These strong reactions on the part of the therapist or counselor are their PCT—that is, their reactions to the devastation and trauma caused by such attacks—and these have the potential to affect the therapeutic relationship.

SPREADING HOPE THROUGH SONG DURING THE COVID-19 PANDEMIC

Even though an annual choral festival in San Bernardino County, California, was canceled on March 2020 because of coronavirus concerns, a group of high school choir singers wanted their community to hear their voices anyway. Imee Perius, Director of communications for Chino Valley Unified School District, said that she saw videos flooding social media of Italian neighbors singing together to boost morale during COVID-19 lockdowns. She began thinking of a way to duplicate those moments in her community with students who were now forced to practice social distancing in their homes.

Nineteen Chino Hills High School chamber singers stepped up to record their individual parts to a song they'd practiced together for months: only this time, they had to sing alone and on camera. The students all sang their individual a cappella portion of "Over the Rainbow" in their separate homes and put them together to create this masterpiece (visit https://www.youtube.com/watch?v=ZSPG186HvMg).

Source: Ebrahimji, A. (2020, Mar 21). When their high school choir concert was canceled, technology helped them sing together anyway. CNN.
https://www.cnn.com/2020/03/21/us/school-virtual-choir-concert-trnd/index.html
https://www.npr.org/2020/03/22/819762794/with-concert-cancelled-california-students-perform-together-from-home

The second example relates to counseling a client who holds a firm religious belief against abortion. If you, as a psychologist or counselor, hold equally firm convictions that women should have the right to choose or that couples or partners should have the freedom to make choices about pregnancies, we suggest that the reaction is rooted not only in a response to the client, but also in response to a highly charged political issue. Again, we would call this PCT. It is essential that psychologists and counselors be aware of PCT as another dimension of countertransference that has an impact on the work they do with clients.

SOCIAL JUSTICE AND HUMAN RIGHTS AWARENESS

Employing the MPM requires that mental health professionals be aware of current global, national, governmental, state, and regional political issues that affect clients and their families and communities. Often clients do not talk about issues that seem somewhat removed from their everyday lives, such as policies that limit access to housing benefits and loans, immigration restrictions on family reunification, employment health benefits for same-sex partners, or repeated experiences of institutional discrimination against women, persons with disabilities, people of color, or LGBTQI individuals. Yet these are the underpinnings of clients' everyday lived experiences. An example can be seen in Flint, Michigan, where residents complained about contaminated water. Although access to clean water is a worldwide issue involving rights and justice, when raised as an issue in Flint, it was largely ignored by state and government officials despite records of major health problems. To discuss with Flint, Michigan, clients their frustration and anger over the lack of clean water is important, but it is not an endpoint when using the MPM. Rather, the therapist chould explore the basis for those feelings, the repercussions in their daily lives as residents in Flint, the family pressures and reactions to the situation, their interest or lack of interest in becoming involved in community action to address the concerns, and so forth. Employing the MPM, counselors and psychologists would also consider the psychological impact of these types of issues on clients as part of the therapeutic process.

SOCIAL JUSTICE ACTION SELF-ASSESSMENT

Building on Chapters 7 ("The Role of Social Justice Mental Health Professionals") and 8 ("Unpacking the Psychological Barriers that Prevent Social Justice Action"), when we discussed the importance of self-reflection on the motivations and barriers to doing social justice work, we feel it is important here to underscore the importance of self-assessment. To genuinely address social justice issues and effectively utilize the MPM, it is important that psychologists and counselors undergo a social justice action self-assessment, asking themselves: "To what degree am I willing to address social justice issues?" Some psychologists and counselors believe that they are actively addressing these issues by simply mentioning them, rather than challenging existing systems or individuals who support these injustices. In our opinion, using the MPM requires a close examination of the level of risk we are willing to take: "Am I willing to risk discomfort and possible ostracization by my colleagues, supervisors, family, and friends? Am I able to handle stronger feelings of discomfort and resistance? How far would I go in my job to challenge a violation of someone's rights?" and so on. We mentioned the nice counselor syndrome (NCS) in Chapter 8 and briefly mention it again to highlight the barriers that the NCS creates in using the MPM to do social justice work. You may recall that the NCS refers to counselors and psychologists who take a neutral stance to avoid conflict and upsetting the system or others in the system, attempting to maintain balance and harmony with coworkers, supervisors, and organizations. This involves giving positive reinforcement and feedback even when a situation warrants criticism, challenges, and confrontation (Bemak & Chung, 2008b). Challenging the status quo could result in being labeled a troublemaker and not a team player. We identify those who avoid social justice and human rights issues in order to sidestep tension and dissonance as having the NCS. To effectively employ the MPM, mental health professionals must carefully do a self-assessment regarding their having the NCS and reflect on how to move beyond this in doing effective social justice–oriented work.

REDEFINING TRADITIONAL WESTERN MENTAL HEALTH ROLES TO INCORPORATE SOCIAL JUSTICE SKILLS

Important in the application of the MPM is redefining our role to incorporate social justice–oriented work that requires a thorough knowledge and understanding of traditional Western psychotherapy and a familiarity with culturally responsive and decolonized theories, models, skills, techniques, strategies, and interventions. Consequently, well-established traditional roles must be reexamined, changed, and adapted to better suit cross-cultural human rights perspectives. Consideration in redefining the mental health professional's role involves knowledge of research findings, such as estimates that the therapeutic alliance accounts for 30% of successful outcomes (Lambert, 1992). This recharacterization of the role of the counselor and psychologist fosters an attention to and respect for social justice and human rights issues that are important to the client.

Therefore, it is essential to move beyond traditional training that incorporates a parallel understanding of our own power, privilege, worldview, attitudes, values, beliefs, biases, and prejudices to effectively work with a broader social and political context. This means moving beyond the traditional apolitical framework of psychotherapy and counseling to become politically knowledgeable in a way that transcends one's own political beliefs, rights, and choices. Taking on a newly defined role as social justice–oriented mental health practitioners, change agents, and advocates further involves incorporating mutually intertwined goals of social justice and mental health to support clients in also becoming their own human rights advocates.

Reconstructing roles creates different relationships with clients. Power, equity, access, and inequalities are viewed in a new light as clients are assisted in becoming self-determining empowered individuals within a broader social construct, ones who are able to be advocates for themselves and others. Inherent in this newly defined role is the need for counselors and psychologists to focus on prevention and intervention that creates broader changes in their clients' lives, going beyond individual adjustment and change. Instead, helping mental health professionals form collaborative partnerships with clients and stakeholders to achieve equity and justice within a larger family and community context and to challenge human rights violations that clients, their families, and their communities may encounter. As these newly constructed roles emerge, they add an element of partnering with clients to facilitate advocacy and social change (Bemak & Chung, 2005).

To achieve this goal, it is essential that helping professionals acquire skills to work across disciplines with anthropologists, social workers, public health professionals, politicians, journalists, educators, lawyers, economists, geographers, historians, other helping professionals, sociologists, and community leaders. It is helpful for counselors and psychologists to know about social change and garner organizational development skills, negotiation skills, group process skills, and systems skills. Skills of this nature are helpful when working with clients to figure out how to deal with the justice system, educational systems, health and mental health systems, juvenile justice services, social services, housing services, equal rights offices, children's services, etc. A further discussion on interdiscip-linary collaboration is presented in Chapter 21.

SUMMARY

In summary, this chapter discusses the rationale and principles involved in developing the MPM. Successfully utilizing the MPM requires mental health professionals to redefine and reconstruct their role and therapeutic approach to social justice and human rights advocacy and activism. Chapter 12 presents the MPM model and discusses its application in mental health work.

DISCUSSION QUESTIONS

1. What are four principles on which the premise of the MPM is based?
2. Can you think of a current issue where social justice and human rights concerns interrelate with mental health? Consider issues such as poverty, gender-based vio-lence, racial injustice, discrimination, mental health care access, and quality of mental health treatment.
3. Imagine yourself in 2050, when, according to the U.S. Census, 54% of the popula-tion will be composed of minority groups. Given your racial, ethnic, and cultural background, do you envision your professional life to be different from what it is today? If so, how?
4. Examine a current major newspaper or magazine. Count the number of news items referring to mass shootings, fear, civil conflict, and violence, and share this with colleagues.
5. Discuss your opinion of the "culture of fear." How do you think this will impact counseling relationships, and what approaches can you take to help your clients deal with this culture of fear?

REFERENCES

Arnett, J. J. (2008). The neglected 95%: Why American psychology needs to become less American. *American Psychologist*, 63(7), 602–614. https://doi.org/10.1037/0003-066X.63.7.602

Arnett, J. J. (2009). The neglected 95%, a challenge to psychology's philosophy of science. *American Psychologist*, 64(6), 571–574. https://doi.org/10.1037/a0016723

Batalova, J., Blizzard, B., & Bolter, J. (2020, Feb 14). Frequently requested statistics on immigrants and immigra-tion in the United States. https://www.migrationpolicy.org/article/frequently-requested-statistics-imm igrants-and-immigration-united-states#Immigrants%20Now%20and%20Historically

Bemak, F., & Chung, R. C.-Y. (2005). Advocacy as a critical role for school counselors: Working toward equity and social justice. *Professional School Counseling*, 8(3), 196–202. https://www.jstor.org/stable/42732 459?seq=1#page_scan_tab_contents

Bemak, F., & Chung, R. C.-Y. (2008a). Counseling refugees and migrants. In P. B. Pedersen, J. G. Draguns, W. J. Lonner, & J. E. Trimble (Eds.), *Counseling across cultures* (6th ed., pp. 325–340). Sage.

Bemak, F., & Chung, R. C.-Y. (2008b). New professional roles and advocacy strategies for school counselors: A multicultural/social justice perspective to move beyond the nice counselor syndrome. *Journal of Counseling & Development, 86*(3), 372–382. https://doi.org/10.1002/j.1556-6678.2008.tb00522.x

Bemak, F., & Chung, R. C-Y. (2021a). A culturally responsive intervention model for modern day refugee: A multiphase model of psychotherapy, social justice, and human rights. In J. D. Aten & J. Hwang (Eds.), *Refugee mental health* (pp. 103–136). American Psychological Association.

Bemak, F., & Chung, R. C-Y. (2021b). Contemporary refugees: Challenges and a culturally responsive intervention model for effective practice. *Counseling Psychologist (Special Issue), 49*(2), 305–324. https://doi.org/10.1177/0011000020972182

Bemak, F., Chung, R. C.-Y., & Pedersen, P. (2003). *Counseling refugees: A psychosocial cultural approach to innovative multicultural interventions.* Greenwood Press.

Bemak, F., & Conyne, R. K. (2004). Ecological group work. In R. K. Conyne & E. P. Cook (Eds.), *Ecological counseling: An innovative approach to conceptualizing person-environment interaction* (pp. 195–217). American Counseling Association.

Boschma, J., Wolfe, D., Krishnakumar, P., Hickey, C., Maharishi, M., Rigdon, R., Keefe, J., & Wright, D. (2021, Aug 13). Census release shows America is more diverse and more multiracial than ever. CNN. https://edition.cnn.com/2021/08/12/politics/us-census-2020-data/index.html

Brewer J. (2006). Public health responses to racism and domestic violence. Family Violence Prevention Fund. The National Health Resource Center on Domestic Violence. https://ja.cuyahogacounty.us/pdf_ja/en-US/DefendingChildhood/DH-PublicHealth-Responses-Racism-DomesticViolence.pdf

Brisset, C., Leanza, Y., Rosenberg, E., Vissandjée, B., Kirmayer, L. J., Muckle, G., Xenocostas, S., & Laforce, H. (2014). Language barriers in mental health care: A survey of primary care practitioners. *Journal of Immigrant and Minority Health, 16*(6), 1238–1246. https://doi.org/10.1007/s10903-013-9971-9

Carter, R. T. (2007). Racism and psychological and emotional injury: Recognizing and assessing race-based traumatic stress. *Counseling Psychologist, 35*(1), 13–105. https://doi.org/10.1177/0011000006292033

Chung, R. C.-Y. (2005). Women, human rights, and counseling: Crossing international boundaries. *Journal of Counseling & Development, 83*(3), 262–268. https://doi.org/10.1002/j.1556-6678.2005.tb00341.x

Chung, R. C.-Y., & Bemak, F. (2002). The relationship of culture and empathy in cross-cultural counseling. *Journal of Counseling and Development, 80*(2), 154–159. https://doi.org/10.1002/j.1556-6678.2002.tb00178.x

Chung, R. C-Y., & Bemak, F. (2007). Asian Immigrants and refugees. In F. Leong, A. G. Inman, A. Ebreo, L. Yang, L. M. Kinoshita, & M. Fu (Eds.), *Handbook of Asian American psychology* (2nd ed., pp. 227–244). Sage.

Chung, R. C-Y., Bemak, F., & Okazaki, S. (1997). Counseling Americans of Southeast Asian descent: The impact of the refugee experience. In C. Lee (Ed.), *Multicultural issues in counseling* (2nd ed., pp. 207–231). American Counseling Association.

Chung, R. C.-Y., Bemak, F., Ortiz, D., & Sandoval-Perez, P. (2008). Promoting the mental health of immigrants: A multicultural/social perspective. *Journal of Counseling & Development, 86*(3), 310–317. https://doi.org/10.1002/j.1556-6678.2008.tb00514.x

Chung, R. C.-Y., & Kagawa-Singer, M. (1995). Interpretation of symptom presentation and distress: A Southeast Asian refugee example. *Journal of Nervous and Mental Disease, 183*(10), 639–648. https://doi.org/10.1097/00005053-199510000-00005

Chung, R. C-Y., & Lin, K-M. (1994). Help seeking behavior among Southeast Asian refugees. *Journal of Community Psychology, 22*(2), 109–120. https://doi.org/10.1002/1520-6629(199404)22:2<109::AID-JCOP2290220207>3.0.CO;2-V

Conversano, C., Rotondo, A., Lensi, E., Della Vista, O., Arpone, F., & Reda, M. A. (2010). Optimism and its impact on mental and physical well-being. *Clinical Practice and Epidemiology in Mental Health, 6,* 25–29. https://doi.org/10.2174/1745017901006010025

Cross, W. E., Jr., & Vandiver, B. J. (2001). Nigrescence theory and measurement: Introducing the Cross Racial Identity Scale (CRIS). In J. G. Ponterotto, J. M. Casas, L. A. Suzuki, & C. M. Alexander (Eds.), *Handbook of multicultural counseling* (pp. 371–393). Sage.

Draguns, J. (2000). Psychopathology and ethnicity. In J. F. Aponte & J. Wohl (Eds.), *Psychological intervention and cultural diversity* (pp. 40–58). Allyn & Bacon.

Franklin, A. J., & Boyd-Franklin, N. (2000). Invisibility syndrome: A clinical model of the effects of racism on African-American males. *American Journal of Orthopsychiatry, 70*(1), 33–41. https://doi.org/10.1037/h0087691

Frey, W. H. (2018, Mar 14). The US will become "minority white" in 2045, Census projects youthful minorities are the engine of future growth. https://www.brookings.edu/blog/the-avenue/2018/03/14/the-us-will-become-minority-white-in-2045-census-projects/

Gallagher, M. W., & Lopez, S. J. (2009) Positive expectancies and mental health: Identifying the unique contributions of hope and optimism. *Journal of Positive Psychology, 4*(6), 548–556. doi:10.1080/17439760903157166

Gara, M. A., Minsky, S., Silverstein, S. M., Miskimen, T., & Strakowski, S. M. (2019). A naturalistic study of racial disparities in diagnoses at an outpatient behavioral health clinic. *Psychiatric Services, 70*(2), 130–134. doi:10.1176/appi.ps.201800223.

Griner, D., & Smith, T. B. (2006). Culturally adapted mental health intervention: A meta-analytic review. *Psychotherapy: Theory, Research, Practice, Training, 43*(4), 531–548. https://doi.org/10.1037/0033-3204.43.4.531

Hall, G. C. N., Berkman, E. T., Zane, N. W., Leong, F. T. L., Hwang, W.-C., Nezu, A. M., Nezu, C. M., Hong, J. J., Chu, J. P., & Huang, E. R. (2021). Reducing mental health disparities by increasing the personal relevance of interventions. *American Psychologist, 76*(1), 91–103. https://doi.org/10.1037/amp0000616

Harandi, T. F., Taghinasab, M. M., & Nayeri, T. D. (2017). The correlation of social support with mental health: A meta-analysis. *Electronic Physician, 9*(9), 5212–5222. https://doi.org/10.19082/5212

Helms, J. (1992). *A race is a nice thing to have.* Content Communication.

Helms, J. (1995). An update of Helms's White and people of color racial identity models. In J. G. Ponterotto, J. M. Casas, L. A. Suzuki, & C. M. Alexander (Eds.), *Handbook of multicultural counseling* (pp. 181–198). Sage.

Henrich, J., Heine, S., & Norenzayan, A. (2010). Most people are not WEIRD. *Nature 466*, 29. https://doi.org/10.1038/466029a

Ho, C. K. (1990). An analysis of domestic violence in Asian American communities: A multicultural approach to counseling. *Women & Therapy, 9*(1–2), 129–150. https://doi.org/10.1300/J015v09n01_08

Hollingsworth, D. W., Cole, A. B., O'Keefe, V. M., Tucker, R. P., Story, C. R., & Wingate, L. R. (2017). Experiencing racial microaggressions influences suicide ideation through perceived burdensomeness in African Americans. *Journal of Counseling Psychology, 64*(1), 104–111. https://doi.org/10.1037/cou0000177

Hwang, C., Myers, H. F., Abe-Kim, J., & Ting, J. Y. (2008). A conceptual paradigm for understanding culture's impact on mental health: The cultural influences on mental health (CIMH) model. *Clinical Psychology Review, 28*(2), 211–227. https://doi.org/10.1016/j.cpr.2007.05.001

Kessler, R. C., Chiu, W. T., Demler, O., & Walters, E. (2005). Prevalence, severity and comorbidity of 12-month DSM-IV disorders in the National Comorbidity Survey replication. *Archives of General Psychiatry, 62*(6), 617–627. https://doi.org/10.1001/archpsyc.62.6.617

Lambert, M. J. (1992). Psychotherapy outcome research: Implications for integrative and eclectical therapists. In J. C. Norcross & M. R. Goldfried (Eds.), *Handbook of psychotherapy integration* (pp. 94–129). Basic Books.

Lambert, M. J., & Bergin, A. E. (1994). The effectiveness of psychotherapy. In A. E. Bergin & S. L. Garfield (Eds.), *Handbook of psychotherapy and behavior change* (4th ed., pp. 143–189). Wiley.

Lin, L., Stamm, K., & Christidis, P. (2018). How diverse is the psychology workforce? *APA Monitor, 49*(2), 19. https://www.apa.org/monitor/2018/02/datapoint

Matsuzaka, S., & Knapp, M. (2019) Anti-racism and substance use treatment: Addiction does not discriminate, but do we? *Journal of Ethnicity in Substance Abuse, 14,* 1–27. doi:10.1080/15332640.2018.1548323

McGee, E. O. (2016). Devalued Black and Latino racial identities: A by product of STEM college culture? *American Educational Research Journal, 53*(6), 1626–1662. doi:10.3102/0002831216676572

Nadal, K. L., Wong, Y., Griffin, K. E., Davidoff, K., & Sriken, J. (2014). The adverse impact of racial microaggressions on college students' self-esteem. *Journal of College Student Development, 55*(5), 461–474. https://doi.org/10.1353/csd.2014.0051

Ohtani, A., Suzuki, T., Takeuchi, H., & Uchida, H. (2015). Language barriers and access to psychiatric care: A systematic review. *Psychiatric Services, 66*(8), 798–780.https://doi.org/10.1176/appi.ps.201400351

Pederson, P. B. (2000). *A handbook for developing multicultural awareness* (3rd ed.). American Counseling Association.

Pernice-Duca, F. (2010). Family network support and mental health recovery. *Journal of Marital Family Therapy, 36*(1), 3–27. https://doi.org/10.1111/j.1752-0606.2009.00182.x

Pieterse, A. L., & Carter, R. T. (2007). An examination of the relationship between general life stress, racism-related stress, and psychological health among black men. *Journal of Counseling Psychology, 54*(1), 101–109. https://doi.org/10.1037/0022-0167.54.1.101

Resera, E., Tribe, R., & Lane, P. (2015) Interpreting in mental health, roles and dynamics in practice. *International Journal of Culture and Mental Health, 8*(2), 192–206, doi:10.1080/17542863.2014.921207

Smith, W. A., Hung, M., & Franklin, J. D. (2011). Racial battle fatigue and the miseducation of Black men: Racial microaggressions, societal problems, and environmental stress. *Journal of Negro Education, 80*(1), 63–82. https://eric.ed.gov/?id=EJ942380

Steele, C. M., Spencer, S. J., & Aronson, J. (2002). Contending with group image: The psychology of stereotype and social identity threat. In M. Zanna (Ed.), *Advances in experimental social psychology* (vol. 23, pp. 379–440). Academic Press. https://doi.org/10.1016/S0065-2601(02)80009-0

Sue, D. W. (2003). *Overcoming our racism: The journey to liberation.* Jossey-Bass.

Sue, D. W. (2010). *Microaggressions in everyday life: Race, gender, and sex orientation.* Wiley.Sue, D. W., Capodilupo, C. M., Nadal, K. L., & Torino, G. C. (2008). Racial microaggressions and the power to define reality. *American Psychologist, 63*(4), 277–279. https://doi.org/10.1037/0003-066X.63.4.277

Sue, D. W., Capodilupo, C. M., Torino, G. C., Bucceri, J. M., Holder, A. M. B., Nadal, K. L., & Esquilin, M. (2007). Racial microaggressions in everyday life: Implications for clinical practice. *American Psychologist, 62*(4), 271–286. https://doi.org/10.1037/0003-066X.62.4.271

Sue, S., Fujino, D., Hu, L., Takeuchi, D., & Zane, N. (1991). Community mental health services for ethnic minority groups: A test of cultural responsiveness hypothesis. *Journal of Consulting and Clinical Psychology, 59*(4), 533–540. https://doi.org/10.1037/0022-006X.59.4.533

Thalmayer, A. G., Toscanelli, C., & Arnett, J. J. (2021). What American psychology needs most is the majority world: Reply to Webster et al. (2021). *American Psychologist, 76*(5), 806. https://doi.org/10.1037/amp0000795

Trent, M., Dooley, D. G., & Dougé, J. (2019). The impact of racism on child and adolescent health. *Pediatrics, 144*(2), 1–14. https://doi.org/10.1542/peds.2019-1765

Triandis, H. C. (1994). *Culture and social behavior.* McGraw-Hill.

Tribe, R., & Keefe, A. (2009). Issues in using interpreters in therapeutic work with refugees. What is not being expressed? *European Journal of Psychotherapy and Counselling, 11*(4):409–424. doi:10.1080/13642530903444795

Tribe, R., & Lane, P. (2009) Working with interpreters across language and culture in mental health. *Journal of Mental Health, 18*(3), 233–241. doi:10.1080/09638230701879102

Turner, J. R., & Brown, R. L. (2010). Social support and mental health. In T. L. Scheid & T. N. Brown (Eds.), *A handbook for the study of mental health: Social contexts, theories, and systems* (2nd ed., pp. 200–213). Cambridge University Press.

U.S. Department of Health and Human Services (DHHS). (2001). Mental health: Culture, race, and ethnicity - A supplement to mental health: A report of the Surgeon General. U.S. Department of Health and Human Services, Substance Abuse and Mental Health Services Administration, Center for Mental Health Services. https://www.ncbi.nlm.nih.gov/books/NBK44243/pdf/Bookshelf_NBK44243.pdf

U.S. Office of the Surgeon General (OSG); U.S. Center for Mental Health Services; U.S. National Institute of Mental Health (2001 Aug). Mental Health: Culture, Race, and Ethnicity: A Supplement to Mental Health: A Report of the Surgeon General. U.S. Substance Abuse and Mental Health Services Administration. https://www.ncbi.nlm.nih.gov/books/NBK44243/

Vespa, J., Medina, L., & Armstrong, D. M. (2020). Demographic turning points for the United States: Population projections for 2020 to 2060. *Current Population Reports*. https://www.census.gov/content/dam/Census/library/publications/2020/demo/p25-1144.pdf

William, D. R., & Cooper, L. A. (2019). Reducing racial inequities in health: Using what we already know to take action. *International Journal of Environmental Research Public Health, 16*(4), 1–26. doi:10.3390/ijerph16040606

Wong, Y. J., Koo, K., Tran, K. K., Chiu, Y.-C., & Mok, Y. (2011). Asian American college students' suicide ideation: A mixed-methods study. *Journal of Counseling Psychology, 58*(2), 197–209. https://doi.org/10.1037/a0023040

CHAPTER 11

STUDENT CHAPTER

Finding My Voice and Giving Voice to Others

Shirley C. Golub

At first, it began as innocent questions asked by curious children as I entered kindergarten. "Where are you from? Why are your eyes so small?" These innocent remarks became crueler and more intentional as I progressed through school, and it became clear to me that they were making fun of me simply because I looked different. Even as a young child, I could intuitively feel that I was categorized as "other," but it would take many more years for me to understand the implications of race and the experience of growing up as a Chinese immigrant in a predominantly White suburb of Washington DC. Back then, I was an extreme introvert with few friends, and I coped by running home every day after school and reading as many books as I could borrow from the library. I would spend hours reading and escaping into fantasy worlds, which helped to strengthen my language skills and develop my life-long love for reading. More importantly, these hours alone also developed my ability to empathize with characters of all ages, cultures, and walks of life from around the world.

In addition to the teasing, I faced a more serious form of discrimination at school. Although I had arrived in the United States at the age of three and had quickly picked up the English language, I was placed in English as a Second Language (ESL) classes for many years. I remained in ESL even after I succeeded in earning all A's in Language Arts and all other subject areas. At the time, I did not recognize this as institutionalized racism, but I now understand that I was being discriminated against by teachers and administrators who believed that I belonged in remedial classes simply because I was an Asian immigrant, or an "other."

As I grew older and became more of an extrovert, I began to speak out more in classes. A teacher finally recognized my academic abilities and advocated for me to join the more advanced English classes. I also began to "fit in" better with my peers after I joined the high school tennis team, obtained a part-time job, and started to form close friendships with peers from various races. At home, however, I paid a high price for my newfound social life. My traditional Chinese parents forbade me from attending any social events where boys or alcohol were possibly present, including football games and school dances. They even forbade me from attending all-girl slumber parties. They wanted me to focus strictly on academics and working hard at my part-time job. I became increasingly frustrated and fought constantly with my parents. I felt that they were overprotective and could not understand the importance of social events in the life of an American teenager. From their perspective, however, American culture was too permissive, and the last thing they wanted for their only daughter among six older sons, was to "fit in." At the time, I was unable and unwilling to understand their perspective and resorted to telling white lies about where I was going from time to time in order to attend an occasional football game or a party. I was able to justify my actions by telling myself that what I was doing was harmless and that I never drank, took drugs, or engaged in risky behavior while I was out with friends. I felt a great deal of anguish the first time that I told a white lie to my parents; however, my longing to finally be accepted by my peers overruled my desire to be the perfect daughter. Over time, I began to develop a thick skin to insulate myself not only from the earlier racism that I had experienced, but from the mixed emotions that resulted from being dishonest with my parents in order to fit in with my high school peers.

Only after graduating from college did I realize and appreciate that my parents had indeed instilled in me a strong set of values and an even stronger work ethic, as I started to build my career and my own family. Although I continued to experience what I later learned were racial microaggressions throughout the rest of my life, I thought that I had successfully navigated the earlier incidents of racism as well as the confusion and turmoil that came with assimilation during my teenage years. I even applied the lessons from my personal experiences to my professional career in human resources (HR) by advocating for qualified candidates of color who would have otherwise been overlooked by my peers in recruiting and management, just as my English teacher had advocated for me many years earlier.

After spending many years in HR and business, I decided to return to school to pursue a master's degree in counseling, which was my dream career that I had decided to put on hold in order to gain life experience. Fast forward to my graduate course in multicultural counseling. Prior to attending the class, I thought that I knew what the multicultural course would consist of. After all, I had lived my entire life as an Asian American and had many friends from different races. One evening after Dr. Chung had posed a question to the class about racial encounters, I raised my hand and recalled in detail a memory from one of my earlier experiences as a young girl in first or second grade, when several neighborhood children threw rocks at me and called me names. When I finished recounting the memory, Dr. Chung gently probed further by asking a follow-up question, and then, inexplicably, I started sobbing uncontrollably. Here I was, almost 40 years old, crying about a memory that I had shut out of my mind for most of my life. After that evening and after much reflection, I finally realized that in order to develop the thick skin that I thought had protected me all those years, I had repressed all of the emotions that accompanied my experiences. I had never processed any of those experiences or emotions, and it all came out in a torrent that evening as I cried in front of my entire class. I cried for myself as a little girl, as well as for my fellow classmates who had ever struggled with racism, discrimination, assimilation, and/or oppression.

I realized that evening that I could no longer ignore everything that I had experienced. I had always dismissed it by justifying to myself that it was part of life and that other groups had it much worse or that my behavior as a teenager was normal. The class taught me that both my experience and the pain that I had always carried with me were real and legitimate. The class also taught me that I would have to process these experiences and unlearn the defense mechanisms that I had utilized my entire life so that I could take action and be accountable from now on, both to myself and to my clients. From that day on, I opened up my mind and began to eagerly learn, process, and apply what I was learning in the multicultural and social justice counseling classes to both my personal and professional life. I learned how to find my voice again and how to speak out and take action when I witnessed social injustices. I learned how to give a voice to those who had been deemed voiceless in our society, through no fault of their own. For example, when it was made public that the past administration was separating young children from their parents as they sought asylum at the border in Mexico, I wrote a very personal and impassioned post, which I shared on social media. I tried to stay away from political attacks and instead focused on the feelings of confusion, fear, and panic that each one of us has felt as a young child when we temporarily lost sight our own parent for a few minutes and relate it back to the very real trauma that these children and their parents will face for many years as a result of these actions. I also learned how to advocate every day for my clients, many of whom have serious mental illness and rely on Medicaid, by helping them navigate a complicated system and, more importantly, by truly listening and meeting them where they are at, so that they, too, can gain the confidence to find their own voice and advocate for themselves.

At the same time, on a personal level, I experienced the loss of my mother and then, later, my father. During the grieving process, I finally began to accept and understand the challenges that my parents had faced as my brothers and I were growing up and the enormous sacrifices that they made for us. The counseling program, and the multicultural and social justice counseling classes in particular, took what I thought I knew about my life, threw it all upside down, and forced me to not only pick up the pieces, but to examine them carefully before putting them back together again. This journey, which is still ongoing, has been one of the hardest experiences of my life, but it has been well worth it to finally be honest with myself and my own experiences in order to become a better counselor, parent, wife, sister, neighbor, friend, and human being.

CHAPTER 12

MULTIPHASE MODEL OF PSYCHOTHERAPY, COUNSELING, HUMAN RIGHTS, AND SOCIAL JUSTICE

Frederic P. Bemak and Rita Chi-Ying Chung

All compromise is based on give and take, but there can be no give and take on fundamentals. Any compromise on mere fundamentals is a surrender. For it is all give and no take.

—Mahatma Gandhi

Believe and act as if it were impossible to fail.

—Charles F. Kettering

As you press on for justice, be sure to move with dignity and discipline, using only the weapon of love. Let no one pull you so low as to hate. Always avoid violence. If you succumb to the temptation of using violence in your struggle, unborn generations will be the recipients of a long and desolate night of bitterness, and your chief legacy to the future will be an endless reign of meaningless chaos.

—Martin Luther King

REFLECTION QUESTIONS

1. How do you feel about working with people who are culturally different from you? Which diverse groups would you imagine to be more difficult to work with for you?
2. Would you feel comfortable to include intervention techniques that go beyond talk therapy? Why or why not?

3. How would you feel about including human rights and social justice into your mental health work? Please explain your response.
4. What is your reaction to findings that 40% of positive mental health outcomes are due to extratherapeutic factors?

This chapter describes the Multiphase Model (MPM) of Psychotherapy, Counseling, Human Rights, and Social Justice, a model that emphasizes social justice and human rights, and a discussion on applying the MPM to everyday counseling and psychotherapy. The MPM is an intervention model that can be applied to groups facing oppression, disenfranchisement, and marginalization. It is a therapeutic model that incorporates affective, behavioral, and cognitive intervention and prevention strategies rooted in cultural foundations and related to social and community process and change. The MPM consists of five different phases (see Figure 12.1): Phase I: Mental Health Education; Phase II: Group, Family, and Individual Psychotherapy; Phase III: Cultural Empowerment via Social and Navigational Capital; Phase IV: Integration of Western and Indigenous Healing Methodologies; and Phase V: Social Justice and Human Rights. It is important to emphasize that there is no fixed sequence to implementing the MPM phases, so that they may be used concurrently or independently. Although there is an interrelationship among the five phases, each phase may be considered independent of the other phases, and each phase is essential for attaining the desired goals of psychotherapy and counseling. Psychologists or

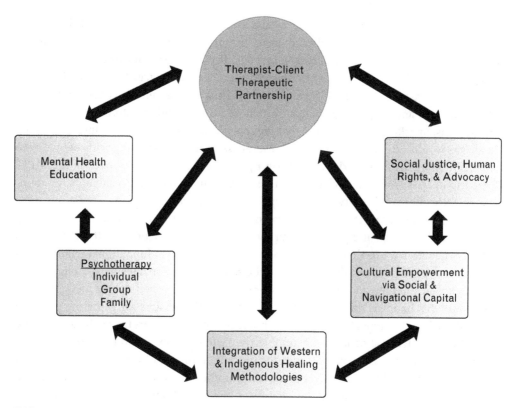

FIGURE 12.1 Multiphase model (MPM) of psychotherapy, counseling, social justice, and human rights

counselors may use any phase or elements of a phase at any point in the therapeutic process. For example, although it is important to discuss Phase I (Mental Health Education) at the beginning of the session, this could be revisited at any period during psychotherapy and counseling to ensure that the counselor or therapist's role is clear and that the goals for psychotherapy and counseling are unambiguous. The choice to use a particular phase or combination of MPM phases is determined by the psychologist's or counselor's assessment. Furthermore, it is important to note that the MPM is not a model that requires additional resources or funding.

PHASE I: MENTAL HEALTH EDUCATION

Phase I is focused on educating clients about the therapeutic encounter. Many clients are not familiar with mental health services and do not have a clear understanding of what happens in therapy and counseling. This may be especially true for clients who are seeking mental health counseling for the first time or are from non-Western cultures, where personal problems are not usually shared with people outside the family network or the spiritual or religious support system. An essential element during Phase I is to establish a therapeutic alliance, which has been identified as critical for effective psychotherapy and counseling (Wohl, 2000), accounting for 30% of therapeutic outcomes (Lambert & Bergin, 1994; Norcross & Lambert, 2018).

This may be particularly salient for racial and ethnic groups in the United States who have exhibited low utilization and premature dropout from Western mainstream mental health services due to the lack of cultural sensitivity displayed by mental health professionals (Green et al, 2020; U.S. Department of Health and Human Services [DHHS], 2001; U.S. Office of the Surgeon General [OSG] et al., 2001). Thus, a key element in Phase I is working to develop trust and rapport by being culturally responsive without stereotyping, making assumptions, or asking questions and making remarks that are hurtful and insulting to the client. We would extend this heightened awareness to include working with people who have been oppressed or experienced human rights violations. It is important in the MPM Phase I to discuss, define, and clarify the roles of the client and the psychologist or counselor and to explore and clarify culturally appropriate expectations.

An integral aspect of Phase I is a discussion of mental health basics (i.e., an introductory overview of the therapeutic process). During this discussion, mental health professionals offer an orientation to the therapeutic encounter; discuss expectations about meeting times and the concept of time, self-disclosure, and the sharing of personal feelings, thoughts, and events; explain the type and style of questioning that may be used during meetings; and talk about what happens during an intake session and the reasons for gathering personal information. It is also important for the psychologists and counselors to clearly describe the concept of confidentiality and to explain that they will have no communication regarding the client with anyone else except under the criteria outlined in their professional ethical standards. Clarity by helping professionals that community members will not be privy to any information discussed during the sessions is also important in ensuring a safe space, confidentiality, and boundaries, which may be particularly important for individuals who are beginning to develop trust after experiences of trauma, discrimination, oppression, and human rights violations.

For example, migrant populations who experienced physical or psychological abuse during their migration journey or faced political oppression in their countries of origin or citizens who were exposed to police violence may be hesitant or fearful to answer personal questions or share personal information. Migrants may have experiences of detainment; beatings; physical or sexual assault; or being robbed, tortured, and interrogated and may view intake questions and counseling with great distrust. Similarly, individuals who have had negative encounters with law enforcement may perceive questions by helping professionals as being similar to interrogation and may resist speaking openly about personal problems or issues. In discussing confidentiality, it is helpful for psychologists and counselors to share their view of what privacy means, making sure this is consistent with how the client defines confidentiality since clients' definitions may differ from those of professionals. For example, in some cultures, confidentiality may mean that family members and/or close friends have access to the client's personal information. If this is the case, the counselor or psycho-therapist must work with the client to establish an agreeable definition of confidentiality that is comfortable for the client. Given concerns about confidentiality, if interpreters are used in the therapeutic encounter, it is important to discuss their role and commitment to maintaining privacy, especially since the interpreter and the client may be connected to the same larger cultural community outside of the therapeutic milieu.

It is also important to discuss relationship boundaries while maintaining cross-cultural sensitivity, understanding that traditional Western professional boundaries may be in-appropriate for many clients who come from non-Western backgrounds (Bemak & Chung, 2015). For example, counselors and psychologists are taught to maintain clear profes-sional boundaries with clients and that the therapeutic relationship should not cross so-cial boundaries. However, for some cultures, professional and social boundaries are not so clearly defined and in fact are blended into relationships. The following example illustrates this point. A friend and colleague who is a well-known psychiatrist in Brazil described how he practiced: "My clients can call me anytime. If I decide they are having a serious problem I will go to their homes, sit in the living room, eat with them, and talk about the crisis. Sometimes I might even take off my shoes and sit with my feet up in their living room." For individuals from collectivistic cultures that emphasize family and community and do not distinguish social and professional relationships as narrowly as do Western countries, there may be confusion about the "distance" and "coolness" of the Western psychologist or coun-selor who refuses social invitations to dinner or a social community event that is significant to individuals, their families, or communities. This interpretation may cause mistrust of the helping professional and premature termination and dropout of the therapeutic session.

Medications also must be mentioned as part of Phase I. Educating clients about medi-cation use is important, especially as it relates to their choices and the rights they have taking prescribed drugs. Confusion may arise about the types, numbers, and colors of medications; when the medications need to be taken; the need to continue and complete the medication dosage even when they feel better; or their rights in deciding to take medica-tion. Furthermore, it is important to provide clear explanations about the dangers of sharing medications with family, friends, and community members who report similar symptoms. For example, I (Rita) discovered within the Chinese community that some of the older community members were sharing and exchanging medications, thinking that it was helpful and saving family and friends a visit to the doctor. In their daily interactions, they compared health symptoms and shared their medication with family members and friends whom they thought had symptoms or problems similar to their own. An important point related to discussing medications during Phase I is discussing the potential danger in taking a mixture of Western and traditional medications. A more detailed discussion on indigenous healing methodologies is presented in Phase IV ("Integration of Western and Indigenous Healing Methodologies").

It is also helpful to describe different psychotherapeutic techniques that may be used during therapy in terms that are understandable to the client. For example, the mental health professional may explain using genograms to better understand one's family, the use of drawings, artwork, and creative writing or journaling to depict deeper issues, or the use of therapeutic homework assignments to facilitate behavioral change. Reviewing these parameters of the therapeutic relationship helps clients engender expectations for what will happen during psychotherapy and counseling sessions. This is extremely important, particularly for individuals who experience little control over their lives and have felt powerless at different points in their lives. Defining mutual expectations for the helping relationship reduces clients' anxiety and confusion about how to act and what kind of behavior will be conducive to receiving the help they want through counseling. Thus, Phase I provides information as well as education and clarification for the individual, group, or family about the process of psychotherapy and the mental health encounter.

It is important to identify that Phase I involves two-way rather than one-way communication. Although psychologists and counselors are educating and outlining the parameters of the helping relationship, they are simultaneously hearing about clients' beliefs about healing, cultural perspectives on the origins and conceptualization of mental health problems, cultural preferences for help-seeking, treatment expectations, and comfort with therapeutic techniques that will be applicable during other MPM phases. In turn, the client is acquiring an understanding of what happens in psychotherapy and counseling and assists in defining the parameters of the therapeutic relationship in a culturally relevant manner. For example, clients may not realize that discussion of their family issues or intimate marriage problems is considered acceptable as a topic of conversation in counseling, while the psychotherapist or counselor may not realize that it is highly irregular in certain cultures to discuss interpersonal marital difficulties, such as sexuality, with someone outside the family or with someone from a different gender or age (Chung & Bemak, 2007a, 2007b). To present these topics as normative during the MPM Phase I assists the client in reframing what is acceptable within the therapeutic relationship, helping the psychotherapist or counselor understand the difficulty and taboo associated with discussions on such a personal level.

When employing Phase I it is helpful to keep in mind that clients with experiences of being underrepresented, undervalued, abused, marginalized, disfranchised, or oppressed may present as resistant, angry, anxious, and/or fearful. They may be distrustful of others, including the therapist. Consider the impact in the United States of slavery and medical experimentation on African Americans and Latinx populations, the genocide of Americans Indians, the internment of Japanese Americans, the killing fields in Cambodia, apartheid in South Africa, and the Nazi Holocaust in Germany as just a few examples that contribute to strong feelings and historical intergenerational trauma. Or, in more present-day situations, consider the African American male who is periodically stopped by police, the Latinx individual who is attacked after Mexicans were labeled by the 45th President of the United States (2017–2021) as "drug dealers, criminals, and rapists," or Asians who experience hate crimes as a result of being blamed for the COVID-19 pandemic by that same former president. On both systemic and personal levels, any of these examples require psychologists and counselors to be aware of and understand the experience of being a member of a group of people who felt violated, discriminated against, and oppressed and who carry the effects of intergenerational trauma and unfair treatment and injustice. During Phase I, at the beginning of the therapeutic encounter, awareness of the roots of clients' anger, fear, mistrust, and resistance is important. In fact, we would suggest that these characteristics may be construed as a survival strategy helping clients to maintain mental health in the face of human rights violations, inequities, and injustice, and this should be considered when planting the seeds of trust and establishing a safe environment. Awareness and sensitivity at the beginning of the therapeutic process may reduce deeply ingrained client fears, anxiety, and mistrust.

PHASE II: GROUP, FAMILY, AND INDIVIDUAL PSYCHOTHERAPY AND COUNSELING

Phase II is based on a combination of traditional Western individual, group, and family therapy and non-traditional Western techniques in a culturally responsive manner that focuses on and incorporates issues of social justice and human rights. As with any type of psychotherapy and counseling, the helping professional must first evaluate the presenting problem and client needs. This evaluation informs the theoretical basis for psychotherapy and helps identify related intervention strategies that will be most suitable for the client in *that* moment in *that* situation. Underlying the assessment and subsequent therapeutic intervention in this phase of the MPM is the integration with Phases III (Cultural Empowerment via Social and Navigational Capital), IV (Integration of Western and Indigenous Healing Methodologies), and V (Social Justice and Human Rights).

To employ culturally relevant techniques in Phase II that incorporate social justice and human rights, there must be an integration of theory, therapeutic processes, and models of prevention and intervention. Given the history and current conditions of oppression, injustices, discrimination, racism, sexism, and other isms that many clients encounter, it is essential to understand and consider clients' backgrounds as it impacts their psychological functioning. Ecological, historical, and sociopolitical factors may require vigilance about the contextual aspects of the person's lived experiences and a heightened awareness of how that affects the therapeutic relationship. For some clients, daily survival may require maintaining psychological defenses and not adopting an open, vulnerable posture. Daily microaggressions, such as invalidations, insults, or assaults, dramatically impact psychological well-being (Sue et al., 2019). For example, due to the daily, ongoing microaggressions and racial injustice, some African Americans may exhibit "healthy or cultural paranoia" as a defense mechanism in coping with potentially discriminatory situations (Jones, 1990; Parham et al., 2011; Ridley, 1995). This is part of the broader context that may be an aspect of an African American client's lived experiences. When a client who exhibits "healthy paranoia" as a coping strategy enters into counseling, the client may perceive a psychologist's highly personal questions as dangerous, threatening, and/or inappropriate. Since psychotherapy and counseling require openness and personal self-disclosure, trust and creating a safe space must be built carefully while keeping in mind the client's worldview based on historical, sociopolitical, and lived experiences.

SOCIAL JUSTICE–ORIENTED GROUP AND FAMILY PSYCHOTHERAPY AND COUNSELING

A criticism of traditional Western psychotherapy and counseling is that individual work perpetuates the status quo and emphasizes changing the individual at the expense of the family, social network, or community. Given that 70% of the world's cultures, and a majority of the ethnic and racial groups in the United States are from collectivist cultures, we suggest that group, family, and community mental health interventions are important to balance with individual interventions and provide a means to foster interdependence in social and family networks to promote social change (Chen et al., 2008; Hage et al., 2010; Hays et al., 2010; Smith & Chin, 2008). Combining individual counseling as part of a balanced systemic approach that is rooted in social networks is fundamental to the MPM and its focus on human rights. Within collectivistic cultures, the emphasis on the group and family is far more important than the emphasis on the individual. In many cultures that value interdependence, the contributions that an individual makes to meet the needs and benefit the family and community are far more important than individual needs and goals. For example, an individual's choice of a career may be contingent on how it fits into the constellation of the family in terms of being located close to where the family lives and/or the ability to generate income support for the extended and/or multigenerational family. Taking factors like this into consideration, the MPM emphasizes balancing group counseling, family therapy, and community interventions with individual interventions to more effectively attend to people from collectivistic cultures that are based on kinship with nuclear extended families and communities.

In providing group, family, or community interventions, it is essential that helping professionals have a clear understanding of and knowledge about the nature of social networks and systemic change within a cultural context that will help in determining who to include in broader socially based mental health interventions. The MPM includes an evaluation of the larger social network that incorporates grandparents, aunts, uncles, cousins, and others who are not biological family members yet are identified by the client as part of the family, such as religious and community leaders, neighbors, friends, or distant relatives (Bemak & Chung, 2021a, 2021b; Bemak et al., 2003). Individuals who are not in the biological family but are considered family members may influence the family system and relevant groups that the family belongs to, as well as the larger social community. Once psychologists or counselors have determined who is in the social network, whether it be family, friends, or associates, it is crucial that they are aware of hierarchy and social patterns of communication and that they appropriately acknowledge those who warrant greater respect by virtue of their role in the family or community. For example, if one enters a matriarchal culture where the woman elder of the community warrants greater authority or respect than the male head of the household, it is important and respectful for the psychologist or counselor to address the woman elder first. Group and family interventions that sensitively incorporate the larger social network while attending to social issues are excellent means of addressing injustices, rights, and inequities. Social justice–focused group and family psychotherapy therefore not only attends to the impact of social issues on the individual, but, in alignment with cultural values and worldviews, also focuses on how injustices affect the entire family and community.

CULTURALLY RESPONSIVE INTERVENTIONS

It is critical that helping professionals are culturally competent and have the skills and ability to adapt, modify, and change traditional Western techniques and interventions so that they are culturally responsive and effective for clients and families from diverse backgrounds. Intervention strategies are derived from an integration of cultural worldviews that incorporate cultural norms and practices into Western-based interventions. For some groups (e.g., Asians, Latinx, Muslims, etc.), talk therapy may not be the natural means of resolving problems. Therefore, it is essential that helping professionals understand the cultural values and worldviews of clients and creatively employ culturally responsive techniques while simultaneously practicing cultural humility. One example of an alternative to talk therapy could be using a genogram that maps out family history and relationships. This may be especially relevant to someone who comes from a culture that highly values family (such as Asian, African, Latinx, and American Indian cultures). With people from cultures (e.g., Africans, Asians, and American Indians) that believe that the spirit of those who have passed away remains present, another alternative to talk therapy may be to invite the presence of the spirit of the deceased. The perceptions and advice of the deceased ancestors may be discussed within the counseling session through metaphors and symbolism.

CULTURAL ADAPTATION OF TRADITIONAL WESTERN INTERVENTIONS

There have been a number of recommendations for traditional Western therapeutic techniques that have been adapted to working across cultures and have relevance for social justice. For example, cognitive-behavioral therapy (CBT) interventions that help clients reframe their experiences and learn adaptive behaviors have been found to be effective with individuals suffering from depression or trauma and survivors of sexual abuse and assault (Duffey & Haberstroh, 2020). Culturally adapted CBT has also been used successfully with refugees in assisting them to better acclimate by helping them move beyond painful memories and experiences, and reduce anxiety about the future (Bemak & Chung, 2021a, 2021b; Hinton et al., 2012). Ethnic and racial groups have also found the culturally adapted CBT and other solution-focused strategies effective. For instance, some Asian clients have found it helpful to incorporate Buddhism as a way to rethink psychological problems (Chen & Davenport, 2005; Lau et al., 2010, Sue et al., 2019). Others have found coherence between CBT and the African American, Latinx, and American Indian cultures (Aguilerea et al.,

2010; Sue et al., 2019), redefining problems and changing behavior within the framework of a cultural context. Another source of interventions that has been effective cross-culturally and is conducive to justice-oriented work is exposure techniques aimed at reducing anxiety disorders and trauma (Duffey & Haberstroh, 2020; Powers & Emmelkamp, 2008). Marriage and family therapy techniques have also been shown to facilitate improvement in clients (Ho, 1987; McGoldrick et al., 2005), while feminist therapies have been found to be helpful for women (Bowman et al., 2001; Diaz-Martinez et al., 2010).

NON-WESTERN TRADITIONAL INTERVENTIONS

Other therapeutic techniques are also incorporated into the MPM that move beyond traditional Western interventions and have a bearing on mental health and social justice. For example, dreamwork can play a central role in culturally sensitive therapy (Bemak, 1989; Bemak & Timm, 1994). I (Fred) worked with a refugee client who was resistant to traditional psychotherapy and used dreamwork as a means to resolve his posttraumatic stress (Bemak & Timm, 1994). Through the use of dreamwork, the client was able to discuss traumatic past events, eventually resolving his long-standing pain and fear about these events. Storytelling and projective drawing have also effectively assisted traumatized children to regain control over their lives (Bemak & Chung, 2021a; Fernández-Cao et al., 2020; Pynoos & Eth, 1984), facilitating the expression of unconscious feelings and thoughts. Narrative therapy, in which individuals are able to reconstruct their stories, has been useful in a variety of different settings (Ramirez & Monk, 2017). Play therapy has been used with many children and adolescents in numerous settings (Bratton et al., 2005; Bratton & Swan, 2017; Landreth, 2012), while interventions focusing on moral development and strongly valued cultural traits such as honesty were found to be an effective intervention with Haitian refugees (Charles, 1986).

Other techniques that may be employed in the MPM include *gestalt*, in which a counselor can have clients examine various parts of themselves as expressions of inner conflict; *mindfulness*, *meditation*, and *relaxation* techniques to reduce stress through deep breathing or systematic desensitization and muscle relaxation (Walsh & Shapiro, 2006); *role-playing*, in which clients can reenact past and anticipated situations, gaining new perspectives and insights; and *psychodrama* and *experiential reenactment*, which can be a helpful replaying of situations that have been highly traumatic, stressful, and anxiety-producing for a client. An example of experiential reenactment was when I (Fred) was working in Uganda with former child soldiers. I developed what I called "abduction therapy" for the most seriously traumatized clients, and, along with a colleague who was a Ugandan psychologist and with the agreement of the client, escorted former child soldiers back to the village where they had been abducted. This was their first return to the village after years of deep-rooted fears and anxiety about returning. Once in the village, escorted by my colleague on one side and me on the other, the client would walk through the village with us describing the details of the abduction. We would gently prompt the former child soldier with questions, probing feelings, tears, and deeply embedded pain as the client reenacted the experience. The experience was a breakthrough for clients who were deeply traumatized and unable to address their pain through traditional therapy. Of course, follow-up was important in supporting the clients after unleashing the pain of those disturbing experiences. A word of caution for those who are not experienced in working with severe trauma in employing experiential reenactment techniques. To ensure that clients are not retraumatized it is critical that mental health professionals first assess the clients' readiness to engage in this process, followed by regular and ongoing support and follow-up.

CULTURE AND DIAGNOSES

When using the MPM, we strongly advise caution when employing Western-based frameworks of diagnoses (e.g., the *Diagnostic and Statistical Manual of Mental Disorders* [DSM], the *International Classification of Disease* [ICD]). The Western assessment tools may not be appropriate or culturally responsive, especially when focusing on mental health and human rights. In fact, specific diagnoses may perpetuate stigmatization of clients and the loss of human rights, and, in many cases, may create labels that clients carry for life. We have previously discussed cultural influences on the conceptualization of mental health problems that result in cultural expression or symptom manifestations that frequently fall into patterns that are outside the discrete classifications of Western disorders. Even so, psychologists and counselors may try to force discrete categorizations that result in misdiagnoses and ineffective treatment (Chung & Kagawa-Singer, 1995; Ogundare, 2020; U.S. DHHS, 2001; U.S.

OSG et al., 2001). In fact, research has shown that misdiagnosis of mental health disorders of clients of color in the United States has resulted from psychotherapists' lack of understanding or knowledge of the clients' cultural and/or linguistic differences contributing to racial and ethnic stereotypes and misdiagnoses (Huertin-Roberts & Snowden, 1993; Liang et al., 2016; Ogundare, 2020; Payne, 2012; Suite et al., 2007; U.S. DHHS, 2001; U.S. OSG et al., 2001). To diagnose accurately, mental health professionals must be aware of how their clients conceptualize mental illness and express psychological distress. This requires an awareness of ethnocentric biases inherent in diagnostic categories (Chung & Kagawa-Singer, 1995; Council of National Psychological Associations for the Advancement of Ethnic Minority Interests [CNPAAEMI], 2003) as well as personal stereotypes, biases, and prejudicial views.

An example of potential misdiagnosis can be seen through my (Fred's) experience in working with an American Indian client living on a reservation. The client was struggling with a decision about leaving the reservation and shared an experience where he had a vision of meeting an elderly man who had been deceased for 20 years. The elderly man had spent his entire life on the reservation and had been recognized as an important elder who, because of his wisdom and experience, provided guidance to many people there. The client explained how he initially thought that his encounter with the elderly man was simply a dream. Although in the dream the elderly man was shrouded in a veil of clouds, the client could still identify him even though he was somewhat frightened by the encounter. As the client went to say hello, the elderly man leaped nearly six feet into the air to the top of a boulder and pointed to a large deer that was walking toward the reservation. The elderly man then told the client that he was not dreaming, and the encounter was real. The client woke up very frightened, believing the encounter was not a dream after all, but a true-life event. Given the authenticity of his encounter, he decided that he must follow the deer and remain at the reservation.

It would have been easy for me or other mental health professionals to think about this client as having delusions and therefore misdiagnose him, especially since the client did not believe that his experience was a dream, but rather considered it a real-life experience meeting a man who had died 20 years earlier. Instead, understanding the framework of his American Indian culture and supporting him in his beliefs and experience was instrumental in assisting this client with a major life decision. Hearing the client's story became a window into understanding his expectations, cultural values, worldview, and cultural ways of making decisions. Bridging the divide between his and my conceptualization of mental health was central to an effective diagnosis and subsequent interventions. This has been pointed out by Kleinman (1980) and requires psychologists and counselors to fully explore the totality of the situation, from etiology, causes, and the course of the problem to help-seeking behavior and treatment outcomes. This also incorporates understanding and acceptance of culturally unique manifestations and expressions of symptoms and beliefs, culturally preferred treatment, and cultural expectations that lead to cultural treatment outcomes.

Although progress has been made in incorporating cultural variables and more culturally sensitive and cross-culturally suitable categories in the diagnosis of psychiatric disorders (Alarcón, 2014; Sue et al., 2019), the question still remains regarding the cultural competencies of mental health professionals (Del Vecchio Good & Hannah, 2014; Sue et al., 2019). Furthermore, Western psychologists and counselors must be aware of any influence their own Eurocentric worldviews may have that interfere with culturally responsive diagnoses. For example, African Americans have been diagnosed with schizophrenia and major depression more often than individuals in other groups, while Asian Americans have been diagnosed more often as having personality disorders compared to other groups (Draguns, 2000; Gara et al., 2019; Rutgers University, 2019; Schwartz & Blankenship, 2014). In both cases, the increased incidence of the specific disorder may reflect misdiagnoses based on cultural worldviews, given racial injustice experienced by African Americans that may contribute to mistrust and paranoia, and the cultural viewpoint of many Asian Americans where family dependency is viewed as a healthy aspect of life. Again, these examples emphasize the importance for helping professionals to be multiculturally competent and exhibit cultural humility when working across cultures.

PHASE III: CULTURAL EMPOWERMENT VIA SOCIAL AND NAVIGATIONAL CAPITAL

The MPM's Phase III provides another important dimension in the healing of clients. Cultural empowerment is a critical element in the therapeutic process, assisting clients to acquire social and navigational capital that helps master their worlds. Clients entering therapy may have pressing issues related to basic survival needs, such as finding employment or housing, knowing how to access public health and medical services and support, or managing legal problems. For example, I (Rita) came across a refugee family who was living on a loaf of bread for two weeks while waiting for their Temporary Assistance for Needy Families (TANF) check. In fact, they had received their TANF check two weeks earlier, but didn't know about banks or how to cash a check. Their limited English led them to understand that the check could be directly exchanged in return for food at the local market. When their attempts to exchange the check for food failed, they were at a loss and thought the check was worthless. They didn't know what to do, so they just waited for the "real" check to arrive, rationing the bread among family members.

Clients may encounter multiple injustices and inequities, may be unable to access human service systems, may encounter discriminatory landlords and housing practices, or may be unfairly fired from a job. These and countless other injustices have far more immediacy for the client than delving into intrapsychic or interpersonal issues and require that clients become empowered and more knowledgeable about their rights and how to navigate their worlds. In fact, clients who experience high levels of anxiety, depression, anger, frustration, or stress that interfere with them being able to understand and resolve problems may benefit from working on developing cultural empowerment by acquiring social and navigational skills to master their environment rather than working on deeper psychological reactions (e.g., anxiety, depression, anger, frustration, or stress) to their situation. Psychologists and counselors can play a critical role in providing support, guidance, and information in enhancing cultural empowerment. The priority in working on cultural empowerment via social and navigational skills is not a substitute for psychotherapy and counseling, but instead is complementary and incorporated into psychotherapy and counseling sessions as an integral aspect of the work.

For example, with the client's permission, making phone calls or writing emails together to apply for jobs, writing letters to agencies, calling other professionals to determine the status of services and acquire information, and similar activities become a valuable use of time and an important component during the therapeutic encounter. Hence, the mental health professional is incorporating multiple tasks as part of the psychotherapy or counseling that contribute to the psychological well-being of the client. At the same time the psychologist or counselor is modeling successful navigation skills, demonstrating how to access and deal with systems while simultaneously assisting and teaching clients about how to integrate existing skills with newly learned skills by developing social and navigational capital. The aim of counseling during this phase is to eliminate stressors that inhibit clients' lives by empowering them to understand and respond to systems and organizational and interpersonal dynamics through the acquisition of requisite social and navigational skills and capital. Effective therapy will provide clients with a greater degree of control over their lives and may instill hope. In turn, obtaining skills to navigate and access systems will help alleviate some of the anxiety, frustration, depression, and feelings of helplessness and hopelessness. Establishing a basis for security and self-determination paves the way for further exploration of deeper psychological issues, reverting back to Phase II (Group, Family, and Individual Psychotherapy and Counseling).

INTERDISCIPLINARY COLLABORATION: WORKING WITH MULTIPLE AGENCIES

Since clients may become involved with multiple service systems, there may be a need for helping professionals to go beyond the constraints of traditional office walls to work with multiple agencies. Although we discuss in detail interdisciplinary collaboration in Chapter 21, we also provide a brief section in this chapter focusing on the importance of working across disciplines while utilizing the MPM. To obtain a holistic picture of clients' lives, it is essential to have a comprehensive understanding of the types of agencies and systems that clients are interacting with, as well as these agencies' respective impact on clients' lives. Agencies could include child protective services, social services, juvenile and adult correction services, housing, education, employment, health and public health, and/or medical services, to name a few. When the client is interacting with multiple agencies it is necessary for the helping professional, with the client's permission, to also be a part of this network and share information.

An example of this was encountered by me (Rita) regarding four immigrant women. Their English language skills were minimal, and one of them was having problems with her eyesight. To support each other, they decided that they would all go together for an appointment to the optometrist. Knowing the client could not see to recite the alphabet, her friends told her the answers in their native language during the exam so she could "pass." This lack of understanding that the eye exam was not a test that one needs to "pass" and that each of them needed to have their own exam and test results required me to educate them about how the medical eye exam works, explaining the diagnostic nature of the exam and that they didn't need to "pass." I also explored with the client healthy ways to gain support from her friends. This situation also warranted communication between the optometrist and me to inform him that the patients had memorized the eye chart to produce "good scores." This networking with the optometrist, with the permission of the client, was initiated by me and important for the clients. Helping the client understand the purpose of having an eye examination, the role that she had as a medical patient, and the part that her friends could play in supporting her were important in developing an understanding of and sense of mastery in her world.

Another example of linking with other agencies to help develop cultural empowerment and mastery and social and navigational capital was evident with an 18-year-old client who was having health problems and was diagnosed with hepatitis. He was told by the physician not to engage in "sexual activity" or have "physical contact" with anyone. The medical directive caused tremendous confusion and stress since the client was unsure about what "physical contact" meant, how long he needed to avoid it, what this meant for marriage, hopes of having children, and his future. Using the MPM, it would be important for mental health professionals to secure permission to access and discuss the medical information with the health provider, support and assist the client to gain social and navigational capital to acquire more information about his condition, and talk about ways to manage hepatitis in his life. This may involve supporting the client while he makes a phone call to the physician during counseling and role-playing conversations with his physician, his sexual partner, his employer, and so forth. Thus, the MPM necessitates that the psychologist or counselor be attuned and highly sensitive to the full scope of the client's life and become knowledgeable about institutional and systemic forces that impact the client. It requires a redefinition of their roles, one that expands beyond traditional "office-only talk therapy" practice and offers case management–type assistance, guidance, and resource information that will empower the client. It is important to note that this does not require additional time. Instead, cultural empowerment through enhancing social and navigational capital is an embedded core component of the therapeutic encounter that is included within regular meeting times and schedules.

CULTURAL SYSTEM INFORMATION GUIDE AND ADVOCATE

One way to think about cultural empowerment is for the mental health professional to assume responsibilities as a "cultural system information guide and advocate." In this capacity, the helping professional proactively assists clients in developing social and navigational skills to access relevant information about their rights, how systems work, how to resolve problems they encounter within those systems, and what subsequent new coping strategies are needed. Building clients' social and navigational capital will provide cultural empowerment and mastery over their environment. This requires rethinking how therapeutic time is spent, especially with the long-term goal of enabling the client to develop knowledge and skills to deal with systemic problems. The resultant mastery of these skills by the client leads to more successful experiences, cultural empowerment, and, ultimately, developing positive and healthy psychological well-being .

PHASE IV: INTEGRATION OF WESTERN AND INDIGENOUS HEALING METHODOLOGIES

The integration of indigenous healing methodologies and Western mental health practice constitutes MPM Phase IV. Generally, Western mental health has emphasized intrapsychic and behavioral processes, neglecting the importance of social and cultural factors and the relevance of spiritual and supernatural forces that contribute to psychological well-being (Bemak & Chung, 2021a; Gureje et al., 2015; Lefley, 1984; Yeh et al., 2004). Helms and Cook (1999) describe the difference, stating, "Sources of etiology for Western mental health systems include biogenetic, psychosocial, and interactional factors, in contrast to the supernatural, interpersonal, and interactional factors in non-Western healing systems" (p. 255). The World Health Organization (WHO, 2019) recognized that an integration of Western mental health practice and indigenous healing actually results in more effective outcomes. This is consistent with the widespread use of alternative healing methodologies throughout the world.

For example, it has been reported that approximately 36% of the U.S. population (Centers for Disease Control [CDC], 2004), an average of 26% of those in Europe (the percentage varies greatly from country to country, with Hungary at 10% and Germany at 40%) (Kemppainen, et al., 2018), and more than three-quarters of people worldwide regularly utilize some form of alternative or indigenous (non-Western) methods of healing (Micozzi, 1996; WHO, 2019) such as yoga, acupuncture, herbal medicine, aroma therapy, or prayer. Western and non-Western approaches to healing are becoming increasingly complementary as psychology gives more attention to this area (Beneduce, 2019; Pedersen, 2000). Even so, Western helping professionals are skeptical and routinely discount indigenous practices (Sue et al., 2019).

Including alternative healing practices requires an openness and acceptance of non-Western culturally bound forms of healing and an abandonment of beliefs that Western forms of healing are superior to any form of indigenous healing. Often, the rejection or inability to be open to other cultural healing practices is due to Eurocentric and ethnocentric perspectives that reinforce the idea that Western beliefs and practices are the only effective methods of healing. To broaden knowledge and acceptance of other cultural practices, some universities have begun to include courses in indigenous healing. For example, a course in indigenous healing is offered in some U.S. medical schools, including the prestigious Johns Hopkins University. Simultaneously, a small number of mental health training programs have begun to offer courses on indigenous healing, showing a movement to incorporate traditional healing practices into Western training. Furthermore, there has been an increase in the literature on cultural competence that emphasizes the integration of Western psychotherapy and traditional healing practices (e.g., Aponte & Wohl, 2000; Constantine, 2007; Constantine & Sue, 2005; Gielen et al., 2004; Hall et al., 2021; Ortega-Williams et al., 2021; Pedersen et al., 2002; Pham et al., 2021).

When working with clients who believed in spiritual practices rooted in their cultural traditions we (Fred and Rita) have collaborated with spiritual healers from local communities. One example was when I (Fred) was working with youth from Cambodia who had lost family members during the Pol Pot regime, which killed 1.5 to 2 million people (a quarter of the population) in Cambodia. The youth were grieving their losses and were deeply sad and regretful that the family members had not received a proper burial according to Buddhist tradition and custom. Psychotherapy could not heal this wound, so a partnership was formed with monks at a Buddhist temple who conducted ceremonies to respectfully honor and bury the deceased relatives. These rituals were combined with individual and family therapy, thus joining cultural practices and traditional Western psychotherapy. This method of an integrated intervention is in contrast with the sole use of traditional Western techniques that are rooted in psychodynamic and behavioral theories. The latter techniques are often rooted in psychopathological constructs that, we would suggest, are not grounded in addressing the human rights aspects of mental health.

When working with traditional healing, a word of caution is necessary. It is important to note that not all indigenous healers are legitimate, so Western practitioners must be mindful and determine authenticity before referring clients or collaborating with them. Establishing relationships with community, religious, and spiritual leaders will be helpful in exploring the type and method of preferred healing, as well as assessing the credibility of traditional healers. An example of this can be seen with a Somali client who had witnessed the murder of several of her family members by bandits before migrating to the United States. Not being able to get these events out of her mind, she was having increasing trouble sleeping, having nightmares, and losing concentration at work. Finally, in desperation, she went to see a counselor. The counselor had heard that within the Somali community there was an elderly man who practiced traditional medicine. With the permission of the client, the counselor contacted a local Somali community leader to discuss the legitimacy of the healer and explain the role and background of the counselor. After a lengthy discussion with the community leader, the healer's credibility was established and the counseling intervention was approved. The counselor and healer discussed the client's situation and determined that rituals to appease the spirits of the deceased family members would be very important in the client's treatment. Subsequently, the client participated in ceremonies with the healer, reading passages from the Koran, burning incense, and eating special foods while also continuing to see the counselor. The combination of healing practices helped this individual come to peace with the death of her family members.

TYPES OF TRADITIONAL HEALING METHODOLOGIES

A variety of culturally specific interventions have been found to be helpful to different communities of color, such as sweat lodges and Sun Dance ceremonies with American Indians (Schiff & Moore, 2006); pouring of libations and calling on ancestors and/or historical figures for assistance with healing for African Americans (Parham, 1989); cottage industry therapy groups for low-income East Indians; multiple-family therapy groups; the practice of *espiritismo* (spiritism), *santeria*, and *cuaranderismo* with Puerto Ricans, Cubans, and Mexican Americans (Comas-Diaz, 2012; Koss-Chioino, 2000); cleansing rituals by Buddhist monks (Chung & Bemak, 2007a); and shamanic healing, herbal remedies, physical/bodily manipulation or exercises (e.g., acupuncture, moxibustion, massage, coining, and breathing exercises such as tai chi or qigong) with some Asian cultures (Chung & Bemak, 2007b; Kleinman & Kleinman, 1985; Koss-Chioino, 2000; Muecke, 1983; So, 2005).

Presenting a groundbreaking concept in psychiatry, Jerome Frank (1974) originally wrote about a combination of psychotherapy and traditional healing being effective within diverse cultural groups. Partially stemming from his work, there has been a greater acceptance and appreciation in the mental health field of traditional healing, leading to the identification of four approaches by indigenous healers that provide a basis for understanding the formation of "treatment partnerships" with indigenous healers. Hiegel (1994) characterized the four approaches as physical treatments, magical healing methods, counseling, and medications. Within these approaches, religious and spiritual leaders may play an important part, particularly when working with families and communities that have strong roots in religious or spiritual practices.

Two examples of treatment partnerships are presented here to illustrate the efficacy of this work. First is the example of an Afghani family who had migrated to the United States. The mother had lost her two brothers and a cousin during the war. She had been a strong figure in the family but was growing increasingly lethargic and depressed, having nightmares about the "bombings and shooting." As problems in the family escalated, the family brought her to a mental health professional who had become reputable in the Afghani community. In the first counseling session, the psychotherapist learned that her client was very religious. From previous work, the psychotherapist already knew about religious and mental health practices in Afghanistan and about the importance of prayer, spiritual and religious leaders, and the practice of using specific verses of the Qur'an to cure certain illnesses. The psychotherapist also knew that certain rituals such as *ta'wiz* (writing down special verses and wearing the writings on a necklace), *shuist* (soaking the written verses in water and later drinking the water in a special ritual), and *dudi* (burning written verses with incense and inhaling the smoke) are healing practices based on the will of Allah. Of great concern to the Afghanis were *Jinns*, or supernatural beings, as well as *nazar*, or the evil eye, which may cause illness and is related to dreams. Acknowledging that this cultural belief system and these healing practices were beyond her training and ability as a mental health practitioner, the psychotherapist contacted the leader of a nearby mosque to form a treatment partnership. In this partnership, the therapist was able to ensure spiritual guidance and intervention for the family consistent with her ongoing work with the client.

A second example is an Asian woman who had been trafficked into the sex industry. I (Rita) learned that she was a devout Buddhist. With her permission I contacted the local Buddhist temple and asked about healing rituals for sexual assault and abuse. Although there was not a healing ritual developed specifically for sexual assault and abuse, I explained to the monks how a number of Asian women had been trafficked as sex workers, and I shared with them that I had worked in other countries with Buddhist monks on this issue. The monks then discussed the feasibility of developing a healing ritual for the cleansing of sexual assault and abuse, agreeing that this would be both possible and helpful. This treatment partnership facilitated the development of new practices by the monks that helped balance the mental health work.

These two examples illustrate being receptive to culture-bound practices and treatment partnerships with indigenous healers. Mental health professionals' receptivity and cooperation with healers and community elders during treatment can be very helpful in the healing process (Hiegel, 1994; Sue et al., 2019). Equally important is the realization that clients may prefer indigenous methods to Western-oriented psychotherapy, or a combination of Western with indigenous treatment techniques. In fact, a number of clients use both methods concurrently without the knowledge of the psychotherapist or counselor (Chung & Lin, 1994; Gureje et al., 2015). Ignoring cultural healing belief methodologies may result in intentional harm to the client (Wendt et al., 2015).

ACCESSING COMMUNITIES

Accessing communities may be challenging. Some communities that are not open to outsiders require counselors and psychologists to be creative about how to gain recognition and respect. A first and most important way of achieving credibility is to respect the cultural attitudes, values, beliefs, and practices of the community and individuals within that community. This necessitates an openness to and genuine valuing of the community and cultural humility. One may also attend religious and community events as a way of establishing contact, as many national figures in the United States did after the September 11, 2001, terrorist attacks by joining meetings and ceremonies at mosques and in Muslim communities. Similarly, after the 2019 terrorist attack at two mosques in Christchurch, New Zealand, Prime Minister Jacinda Arden (wearing a head scarf to show respect to the Muslim culture and community) attended mosques and Muslim community functions to participate in healing ceremonies.

Other ways to better engage with and make connections in communities may include something as simple as going to a community restaurant to try the food or even taking out food from a local restaurant on a regular basis and getting to know the owners and clientele of the establishment. It is also helpful for helping professionals to speak in local communities, explaining how therapy and counseling may contribute to healing. When I (Fred) was invited to as a consultant to a failing mental health program in an inner-city Latinx community it became clear why the program was unsuccessful. It was located in a traditional mental health clinic in a medical school and no clients were coming. I spoke with the local priest who agreed to house the program in his church. The priest also invited Latinx colleagues and me to speak to the congregation about mental health. Very quickly the mental health program filled with clients who were more comfortable in their home community setting rather than a medical school clinic. Regardless of how one reaches out, it is critical that it is done with respect, honesty, humility, and authenticity, with an aim to understanding and appreciating diverse cultures.

ESTABLISHING TRUE PARTNERSHIPS WITH TRADITIONAL HEALERS

The examples we have shared in describing Phase IV of the MPM demonstrate the importance of integrating Western and traditional healing practices through collaborative partnerships between mental health professionals and traditional healers. For more than 30 years, there has been a call by a number of psychologists and counselors for cooperation between traditional healers and Western helping professionals (e.g., Bemak et al., 2003; Bemak & Chung, 2008; Green & Colucci, 2020; LaFramboise, 1988; Moody & West, 2005; Ross, 2014; Wendt et al., 2015). Partnerships can be cultivated with community leaders, priests, monks, shamans, healers, elders, and other significant community members. Community members play an important role in assisting psychologists and counselors in learning about clients' cultural background, help-seeking behaviors, and perspectives on mental health and healing, and they can provide other related cultural perspectives on health and mental health issues. Significant community members also can assist mental health professionals in educating the community about mental health and counseling practices, while the helping professional can honor and support centuries of traditional healing practices and cultural beliefs.

Important to remember in working with indigenous healers is that, to be effective, the nature and quality of the relationship must be based on genuine mutual respect, trust, and understanding. This allows traditional healers to practice unencumbered by the Western practitioner's judgment while maintaining an open dialogue about their respective practices. It is important for Western-trained psychologists and counselors to remember that established traditional healers are respected and trusted within their communities, even though some psychologists and counselors may have concerns about collaborating (Kayombo et al., 2007). These concerns include feeling exploited by traditional healers to legitimize their credibility (Green & Colucci, 2020), concerns about too great a presence by traditional healers (Kahn & Kelly, 2001), traditional healers lacking professional or ethical standards (Ae-Ngibise et al, 2010; Kayombo et al., 2012); and concern about traditional healers bragging about their abilities to promote their reputations (Hiegel, 1994). In turn, mental health professionals' personal values should not get in the way in establishing partnerships with traditional healers. An example relates to eating or drinking certain foods, such as monkey brains, intestines, testicles, or snake or chicken blood. Although this may be repugnant to Western cultural practices, it may be considered valued in certain cultures as a means of healing. Supporting the client in eating these foods is valuing culturally responsive healing rituals.

A powerful example of honoring unfamiliar healing practices occurred when we (Fred and Rita) brought a Counselors Without Borders team to work in Haiti after the 2010 earthquake. We were told numerous times by local people that large numbers of Haitians privately believed in Voodoo practices. Although we don't hold those beliefs, it was important to accept the clients simultaneously visiting both Voodoo priests and our team of mental health practitioners for the good of the clients. This underscores the importance of accepting that forming partnerships with indigenous healers does not mean that Western mental health professionals need to believe or partake in the rituals, but rather they must maintain value-free and judgment-free openness to treatment partnerships and practices and a belief that both healing methodologies are beneficial. Another interesting example can be seen with my (Rita's) experience working collaboratively with Buddhist monks. The monks, being strict Buddhists, were not permitted to have direct interaction with women on certain days; on other days, they could interact with a woman only at certain hours of the day. Often, I would have to talk to a monk from behind a screen. At times it was frustrating, because the monks would make appointments to see me only at specific times that were allowed by their religion, sometimes inconvenient to my Western, fast-paced work schedule. In this situation, personal issues about not being treated as a professional and being insulted as a woman could easily emerge, clashing with my feminist views. If I had not accepted the monks practices it would have been detrimental to the treatment partnership and negatively impacted clients. Understanding, accepting, and being judgment-free and respectful of the Buddhist monks' practices was of utmost importance, allowing us to work together to help the client.

Even though the MPM highly recommends that psychologists and counselors work collaboratively and in partnership with indigenous healers, a word of caution is in order about stereotyping clients' treatment preferences. Psychologists and counselors should not assume that clients from diverse backgrounds prefer traditional healing as their treatment of choice. Using the MPM, we suggest an open exploration with clients and their social networks about incorporating any additional culturally applicable interventions. Thus, it is important for helping professionals to explore and investigate the efficacy of traditional healing as an effective intervention given specific circumstances, cultural belief systems, and ascertained credibility of the traditional healer.

PHASE V: SOCIAL JUSTICE AND HUMAN RIGHTS

As mentioned earlier, the MPM is based on the premise that counseling and psychotherapy are inextricably linked with social justice and human rights and provide a foundation for mental health interventions. We would suggest that the extratherapeutic factors accounting for 40% of positive therapeutic outcomes (Lambert & Bergin, 1994; Wampold, 2015) have a high correlation with social justice and human rights. More specifically, in the MPM, issues of equality, equity, and human rights violations that include oppression, racism, xenophobia, discrimination, gender-based violations, abuse, and physical and psychological danger, as well as a threat to one's safety, livelihood, hunger, poverty, or violence would be significant in this 40% category related to positive outcomes. We believe that the MPM is unique in addressing the social justice and human rights issues inherent in these extratherapeutic factors. The MPM shifts the view of mental health to emphasize social justice as a core component. This requires not only a philosophical change, but also a redefinition of one's role as a psychologist or counselor. Mental health professionals must therefore be courageous risk takers, take a proactive leadership role, and assume a social advocacy position with regard to the client's personal, social, political, economic, cultural, and ethical rights.

Phase V assumes that social justice and human rights are inherent in one's psychological well-being and an integral component of the therapeutic relationship. This perspective has been supported in the literature (e.g., Bemak & Chung, 2021a, 2021b; Burnes & Christensen, 2020; Ibrahim & Heuer, 2016; Johnson, 2021; Neville; 2015; Ratts & Pedersen, 2014; Ratts et al., 2016; Singh et al., 2020; Sue, 2015; Toporek et al., 2006), leading to our conviction that neglecting issues that violate clients' human rights is unconscionable and results in contributing to the perpetuation of those violations. Thus, mental health professionals must attend to more than psychodynamic, behavioral, and intrapsychic issues and expand their work to include concerns such as personal safety and security; adequate food and clothing; equal and equity access to appropriate and supportive social and legal services; access to quality education and health and mental health care; financial support as needed for heating, electricity, and clean water; housing benefits; individual and institutional strategies to deal with discrimination, racism, xenophobia, and unfair treatment;

and equal and equitable access to other resources and opportunities available in the community and society. Issues such as these contribute to mental health problems that paradoxically may be reduced or eliminated once adequate attention is paid to addressing human rights violations. Therefore, it is important that psychologists and counselors incorporate social advocacy that is derived from honoring human rights, social justice, and equity as an important value in mental health interventions.

SOCIAL JUSTICE ADVOCACY

Phase V, similar to the other phases of the MPM, is not a discrete linear step in the model. Rather, Phase V becomes infused throughout the MPM. Examples of integrating Phase V throughout the other four phases of the MPM includes educating clients about their rights; assisting clients, their families, and their communities to fight for equal treatment and access to resources and opportunities; and partnering with clients in writing to legislative government officials with the aim of changing and influencing policy and legislation; as well as participating in demonstrations and educating helping professionals about cultural differences in the manifestation of mental illness to avoid harmful misdiagnoses and poor treatment outcomes.

This requires that mental health professionals be courageous, proactive risk takers in assuming a social justice advocacy role by addressing violations of basic human rights that contribute to psychological problems for clients. In this paradigm, interventions are both proactive and active rather than only reactive. Given the degree of national and global injustices and unfair treatment and human rights violations, we believe that psychologists and counselors can no longer deny, avoid, or ignore their potential as proactive change agents. If the aim of the profession is to assist individuals, families, and communities toward healthy, positive well-being, then the profession *must* continue to move forward and not stay mired in past practices. To support social justice and human rights as integral to mental health and psychological well-being, it is important that psychologists and counselors also undertake continued research and writing to disseminate information about the efficacy of mental health and social justice interventions and the promotion of human rights issues.

DIFFERENCES BETWEEN THE MPM AND TRADITIONAL MODELS

To summarize this chapter, it is important to highlight the difference between the predominant models of Western-based individual psychotherapy and the MPM. Individual psychotherapy helps clients to more effectively deal with their problems, looking at issues from an individualistic viewpoint that speaks to changing oneself. Although variations on this technique have taken form with group, family, and community intervention models, individual psychotherapy remains the prevalent means of intervention. In contrast, the MPM encompasses the individual as part of a larger ecological system and aims to work in partnership with individuals for personal, social, family, community, and institutional change.

Put another way, rather than changing the individual to fit the system, the MPM advocates assisting individuals to change inequities in their lived experiences so that they have the same rights, opportunities, access, and treatment as others. Therefore, instead of changing the individual to fit the system, the MPM advocates changing the system so that there is universal equity, equality, and equal rights.

Fundamental in the MPM is the belief that social justice and human rights are driving forces in the psychological well-being of individuals, groups, families, and communities. For instance, take clients who face racial discrimination at the worksite. Traditional psychotherapy may assist these individuals in figuring out how to respond to racist comments, ignore the perpetrators, take time out to "collect themselves" rather than getting angry, become more assertive in responding to comments, reframe their thinking about their reactions, etc. These strategies do not address the ongoing racism directed at the clients and possibly their coworkers, nor does it attend to the larger problem that may be generalized to others at the worksite, even if the client personally comes to terms with how to handle the situation.

Using the MPM, psychologists and counselor's intervention strategies not only assist the individual's growth and mental health but also create larger institutional change. This may mean supporting clients through discussion and role-playing; speaking with the human resources department; helping clients figure out effective ways to discuss the problem with supervisors from a perspective that is broader than just their individual problems; talking with clients about designing a constructive course of action with peers experiencing similar problems at the worksite; helping clients construct means to educate management and workers about cultural diversity, inclusion, and tolerance; or assisting clients to develop strategies for approaching management to formulate anti-racist language, policies, and procedures to address racism and xenophobia in the organization. These interventions help clients to change discriminatory environments rather than narrowing the focus to the client's own personal problems that resulted from a racist work setting.

SUMMARY

In conclusion, many clients and their families have experienced or are experiencing social injustices and human rights violations. Although many clients are highly resilient, there are many others who have serious difficulties that are exacerbated by the violation of their human rights. Unfortunately, the mental health world continues to perpetuate Western traditions based on treatments that ignore more complex and psychologically destructive social injustices. In this chapter, we describe a model that combines mental health and social justice/human rights. The model is founded on the premise that the two cannot be separated and that a new paradigm of interventions must be developed to effectively work with both.

The MPM of Psychotherapy, Counseling, Human Rights, and Social Justice is a five-phase cross-cultural intervention approach that integrates traditional Western-based counseling with nontraditional approaches. It is a culturally responsive model incorporating traditional psychotherapy, indigenous healing methods, cultural empowerment, psychoeducational training, and social justice/human rights. The MPM takes into account historical perspectives, cultural belief systems, worldviews, social dynamics, family dynamics, community relationships, policies, politics, the economy, and experiences of social and racial injustice, xenophobia, discrimination, marginalization, and oppression to provide a holistic framework that conceptualizes a fluid and integrated strategy to meet the multifaceted needs of clients.

DISCUSSION QUESTIONS

1. Think of three different scenarios where the MPM model could be applied. Explain how you would use the MPM in each scenario.
2. Think of or imagine your first session with a client:
   a. How would you explain confidentiality to a recent Sudanese woman who immigrated to your country?
   b. How would you explain the same concept to a 10-year-old Latinx male who was referred to your office because of suspected domestic violence at home?
   c. How would you handle the privacy and confidentiality issues in a group of military veterans from the war in Afghanistan who are suffering from PTSD?
   d. Do you expect any particular reaction in each situation?
3. What has the MPM taught you about your strengths as a psychologist or counselor and about the areas in which you need further development?
4. Describe a way that you can show cultural sensitivity when working with a client whose worldview is different from yours.
5. Are there interventions and techniques for individual, group, and family psychotherapy that you have learned about in reading this chapter that go beyond talk therapy? Which of these interventions and techniques do you imagine you could use in your mental health work?

REFERENCES

Ae-Ngibise, K., Cooper, S., Adiibokah, E., Akpalu, B., Lund, C., Doke, V., & the MHAPP Research Programme Consortium. (2010). "Whether you like it or not people with mental problems are going to go to them": A qualitative exploration into the widespread use of traditional and faith healers in the provision of mental health care in Ghana. *International Review of Psychiatry, 22*(6), 558–567. doi:10.3109/09540261.2010.536149

Aguilera, A., Garza, M. J., & Munoz, R. F. (2010). Group cognitive-behavioral therapy for depression in Spanish: Culture-sensitive manualized treatment in practice. *American Journal of Clinical Psychology: In Session, 66,* 857–867. doi:10.1002/jclp.20706

Alarcón R. D. (2014). Cultural inroads in DSM-5. *World Psychiatry: Official journal of the World Psychiatric Association (WPA), 13*(3), 310–313. https://doi.org/10.1002/wps.20132

Aponte, J., & Wohl, J. (2000). *Psychological intervention and cultural diversity.* Allyn & Bacon.

Bemak, F. (1989). Cross-cultural family therapy with Southeast Asian refugees. *Journal of Strategic and Systemic Therapies, 8,* 22–27. https://doi.org/10.1521/jsst.1989.8.bonus.22

Bemak, F., & Chung, R. C.-Y. (2008). Counseling refugees and migrants. In P. B. Pedersen, J. G. Draguns, W. J. Lonner, & J. E. Trimble (Eds.), *Counseling across cultures* (6th ed., pp. 325–340). Sage.

Bemak, F., & Chung, R. C-Y. (2015). Cultural boundaries, cultural norms: Multicultural and social justice perspective. In B. Herlihy & G. Corey (Eds.), *Boundary issues in counseling: Multiple roles and responsibilities* (pp. 84–91, 3rd ed.). American Counseling Association.

Bemak, F., & Chung, R. C-Y. (2021a). A culturally responsive intervention model for modern day refugee: A multiphase model of psychotherapy, social justice, and human rights. In J. D. Aten & J. Hwang (Eds.), *Refugee mental health* (pp. 103–136). American Psychological Association.

Bemak, F., & Chung, R. C-Y. (2021b). Contemporary refugees: Challenges and a culturally responsive intervention model for effective practice. *Counseling Psychologist (Special Issue), 49*(2), 305–324. https://doi.org/10.1177/0011000020972182

Bemak, F., Chung, R. C.-Y., & Pedersen, P. B. (2003). *Counseling refugees: A psychological approach to innovative multicultural interventions.* Greenwood Press.

Bemak, F., & Timm, J. (1994). Case study of an adolescent Cambodian refugee: A clinical, developmental and cultural perspective. *International Journal of the Advancement of Counseling, 17*(1), 47–58. https://doi.org/10.1007/BF01407925

Beneduce, R. (2019). Madness and despair are a force: Global mental health, and how people and cultures challenge the hegemony of Western psychiatry. *Culture, Medicine, and Psychiatry 43*, 710–723. https://doi.org/10.1007/s11013-019-09658-1

Bowman, S. L., Rasheed, S., Ferris, J., Thompson, D. A., McRae, M., & Weitzman, L. (2001). Interface of feminism and multiculturalism: Where are the women of color? In J. G. Ponterotto, J. M. Casas, L. A. Suzuki, & C. M. Alexander (Eds.), *Handbook of multicultural counseling* (2nd ed., pp. 779–798). Sage.

Bratton, S. C., Ray, D., Rhine, T., & Jones, L. (2005). The efficacy of play therapy with children: A meta-analytic review of treatment outcomes. *Professional Psychology: Research and Practice, 36*(4), 376–390. https://doi.org/10.1037/0735-7028.36.4.376

Bratton, S. C., & Swan, A. (2017). Status of play therapy research. In R. L. Steen (Ed.), *Advances in psychology, mental health, and behavioral studies (APMHBS): Emerging research in play therapy, child counseling, and consultation* (pp. 1–19). Information Science Reference/IGI Global. https://doi.org/10.4018/978-1-5225-2224-9.ch001

Burnes, T. R., & Christensen, N. P. (2020). Still wanting change, still working for justice: An introduction to the special issue on social justice training in health service psychology. *Training and Education in Professional Psychology, 14*(2), 87–91. http://dx.doi.org/10.1037/tep0000323

Centers for Disease Control (CDC). (2004). More than one-third of U. S. adults use complementary and alternative medicine, according to new government survey. https://www.cdc.gov/nchs/pressroom/04news/adultsmedicine.htm

Charles, C. (1986). Mental health services for Haitians. In H. P. Lefley & P. B. Pedersen (Eds.), *Cross-cultural training for mental health professionals* (pp. 183–198). Charles C. Thomas.

Chen, E. C., Kakkad, D., & Balzano, J. (2008). Multicultural competence and evidence-based practice in group therapy. *Journal of Clinical Psychology, 64*, 1261–1278. doi:10.1002/jclp.20533

Chen, S. W. H., & Davenport, D. S. (2005). Cognitive-behavioral therapy with Chinese American clients: Cautions and modifications. *Psychotherapy: Theory, Research, Practice Training, 42*, 101–110. https://doi.org/10.1037/0033-3204.42.1.101

Chung, R. C-Y., & Bemak, F. (2007a). Asian Immigrants and refugees. In F. Leong, A. G. Inman, A. Ebreo, L. Yang, L. M. Kinoshita, & M. Fu (Eds.), *Handbook of Asian American psychology* (2nd ed., pp. 227–244). Sage.

Chung, R. C.-Y., & Bemak, F. (2007b). Immigrant and refugee populations. In M. G. Constantine (Ed.), *Clinical practice with people of color: A guide to becoming culturally competent* (pp. 125–142). Teachers College Press.

Chung, R. C.-Y., & Kagawa-Singer, M. (1995). Interpretation of symptom presentation and distress: A Southeast Asian refugee example. *Journal of Nervous and Mental Disease, 183*(10), 639–648. https://doi.org/10.1097/00005053-199510000-00005

Chung, R. C.-Y., & Lin, K. M. (1994). Help-seeking behavior among Southeast Asian refugees. *Journal of Community Psychology, 22*(2), 109–120. https://doi.org/10.1002/1520-6629(199404)22:2<109::AID-JCOP2290220207>3.0.CO;2-V

Comas-Diaz, L. (2012). *Multicultural care: A clinician's guide to cultural competence.* American Psychological Association.

Constantine, M. G. (Ed.). (2007). *Clinical practice with people of color: A guide to becoming culturally competent.* Teachers College Press.

Constantine, M. G., & Sue, D. W. (2005). *Strategies for building multicultural competence in mental health and educational settings.* Wiley.

Council of National Psychological Associations for the Advancement of Ethnic Minority Interests (CNPAAEMI). (2003). Psychological treatment of ethnic minority populations. American Psychological Association. https://www.apa.org/pi/oema/resources/brochures/treatment-minority.pdf

Del Vecchio Good, M-J., & Hannah, S. E. (2014). Shattering culture: Perspectives on cultural competence and evidence-based practice in mental health services. *Transcultural Psychiatry, 52*(2), 198–221. https://doi.org/10.1177/1363461514557348

Diaz-Martinez, A. M., Interian, A., & Waters, D. M. (2010). The integration of CBT, multicultural and feminist psychotherapies with Latinas. *Journal of Psychotherapy Integration, 20,* 313–326. doi:10.1037/a0020819

Draguns, J. (2000). Psychopathology and ethnicity. In J. Aponte & J. Wohl (Eds.), *Psychological intervention and cultural diversity* (pp. 40–58). Allyn & Bacon.

Duffey, T., & Haberstroh, S. (Eds.). (2020). *Introduction to crisis and trauma counseling.* American Counseling Association.

Fernández-Cao, M. L., Camilli-Trujillo, C., & Fernández-Escudero, L. (2020). PROJECTA: An art-based tool in trauma treatment. *Frontiers in Psychology, 11,* 568948. https://doi.org/10.3389/fpsyg.2020.568948

Frank, J. D. (1974). *Persuasion and healing: A comparative study of psychotherapy.* Schocken Books.

Gara, M. A., Minsky, S., Silverstein, S. M., Miskimen, T., & Strakowski, S. M. (2019). A naturalistic study of racial disparities in diagnoses at an outpatient behavioral health clinic. *Psychiatric Services, 70*(2), 130–134. doi:10.1176/appi.ps.201800223.

Gielen, U. P., Fish, J. M., & Draguns, J. G. (Eds.). (2004). *Handbook of culture, therapy, and healing.* Lawrence Erlbaum.

Green, B., & Colucci, E. (2020). Traditional healers' and biomedical practitioners' perceptions of collaborative mental healthcare in low- and middle-income countries: A systematic review. *Transcultural Psychiatry, 57*(1), 94–107. https://doi.org/10.1177/1363461519894396

Green, J. G., McLaughlin, K. A., Fillbrunn, M., Fukuda, M., Jackson, J. S., Kessler, R. C., ... Alegría, M. (2020). Barriers to mental health service use and predictors of treatment drop out: Racial/ethnic variation in a population-based study. *Administration and Policy in Mental Health and Mental Health Services Research, 47*(4), 606–616. doi:10.1007/s10488-020-01021-6

Gureje, O., Nortje, G., Makanjuola, V., Oladeji, B., Seedat, S., & Jenkins, R. (2015). The role of global traditional and complementary systems of medicine in the treatment of mental health disorders. *Lancet Psychiatry, 2*(2), 168–177. doi:10.1016/S2215-0366(15)00013-9

Hage, S. M., Mason, M., & Kim, J. (2010). A social justice approach to group counseling. In R. K. Conyne (Ed.), *The Oxford handbook of group counseling* (pp. 102–117). Oxford University Press.

Hall, G. C. N., Berkman, E. T., Zane, N. W., Leong, F. T. L., Hwang, W.-C., Nezu, A. M., Nezu, C. M., Hong, J. J., Chu, J. P., & Huang, E. R. (2021). Reducing mental health disparities by increasing the personal relevance of interventions. *American Psychologist, 76*(1), 91–103. https://doi.org/10.1037/amp0000616

Hays, D. G., Arredondo, P., Gladding, S. T., & Toporek, R. L. (2010). Integrating social justice in group work: The next decade. *Journal for Specialists in Group Work, 35*(2), 177–206. https://doi.org/10.1080/019339210037060 22

Helms, J. E., & Cook, D. (1999). *Using race and culture in counseling and psychotherapy: Theory and practice.* Allyn & Bacon.

Hiegel, J. P. (1994). Use of indigenous concepts and healers in the care of refugees: Some experiences from the Thai border camps. In A. J. Marsella, T. Bornemann, S. Ekblad, & J. Orley (Eds.), *Amidst peril and pain: The mental health and well-being of the world's refugees* (pp. 293–310). American Psychological Association. https://doi.org/10.1037/10147-015

Hinton, D. E., Rivera, E. I., Hofmann, S. G., Barlow, D. H., & Otto, M. W. (2012). Adapting CBT for traumatized refugees and ethnic minority patients: Examples from culturally adapted CBT (CA-CBT). *Transcultural Psychiatry, 49*(2), 340–365. doi:10.1177/1363461512441595

Ho, M. K. (1987). *Family therapy with ethnic minorities.* Sage.

Huertin-Roberts, S., & Snowden, L. (1993, Dec). *Comparison of ethnographic descriptors of depression and epidemiological catchment area data for African Americans* [Paper presentation]. American Anthropology Association 18th Annual Meeting, Washington, DC.

Ibrahim, F A., & Heuer, J. A. (Eds.). (2016). *Cultural and social justice counseling.* Springer International Publishing.

Johnson, K. F. (2021). Introduction to the special issue on social justice, liberation, and action. *Journal of Mental Health Counseling, 43*(3), 191–197. https://doi.org/10.17744/mehc.43.3.02

Jones, N. S. C. (1990). Black/White issues in psychotherapy: A framework for clinical practice. *Journal of Social Behavior and Personality, 5*(5), 305–322. https://search.proquest.com/openview/c95e11ae6cabb67d5 debf34fda145eda/1?pq-origsite=gscholar&cbl=1819046

Kahn, M. S., & Kelly, K. J. (2001). Cultural tensions in psychiatric nursing: Managing the interface between Western mental health care and Xhosa traditional healing in South Africa. *Transcultural Psychiatry, 38*(1), 35–50. https://doi.org/10.1177/136346150103800104

Kayombo, E., J., Uiso, F. C., & Mahunnah, R. L. (2012). Experience on healthcare utilisation in seven administrative regions of Tanzania. *Journal of Ethnobiology and Ethnomedicine, 8*(5), 1–8. http://www.ethnobio med.com/content/8/1/5

Kayombo, E. J., Uiso, F. C., Mbwambo, Z. H., Mahunnah, R. L., Moshi, M. J., & Mgonda, Y. H. (2007). Experience of initiating collaboration of traditional healers in managing HIV and AIDS in Tanzania. *Journal of Ethnobiology and Ethnomedicine, 3*(1), 1–9. https://doi.org/10.1186/1746-4269-8-5

Kemppainen, L. M., Kemppainen, T. T., Reippainen, J. A., Salmenniemi, S. T., & Vuolanto, P. H. (2018). Use of complementary and alternative medicine in Europe: Health-related and sociodemographic determinants. *Scandinavian Journal of Public Health, 46*(4), 448–455. https://doi.org/10.1177/1403494817733869

Kleinman, A. (1980). *Patients and healers in the context of culture.* University of California Press.

Kleinman, A., & Kleinman, J. (1985). Somatization: The interconnections in Chinese society among culture, depressive experiences, and the meaning of pain. In A. Kleinman & B. Good (Eds.), *Culture and depression: Studies in the anthropology and cross-cultural psychiatry of affect and disorder* (pp. 429–490). University of California Press.

Koss-Chioino, J. D. (2000). Traditional and folk approaches among ethnic minorities. In J. Aponte & J. Wohl (Eds.), *Psychological intervention and cultural diversity* (pp. 149–166). Allyn & Bacon.

LaFramboise, T. D. (1988). American Indian mental health policy. *American Psychologist, 43*(5), 388–397. https://doi.org/10.1037/0003-066X.43.5.388

Lambert, M. J., & Bergin, A (1994). The effectiveness of psychotherapy. In A. E. Bergin & S. L. Garfield (Eds.), *Handbook of psychotherapy and behavior change* (4th ed., pp. 143–189). Wiley.

Landreth, G. L. (2012). *Play therapy: The art of relationship* (3rd ed.). Routledge.

Lau, J. S., Chan, C. K.-Y., Li, J. C.-H., & Au, T. K. F. (2010). Effectiveness of group cognitive-behavioral treatment for childhood anxiety in community clinics. *Behavior Research and Therapy, 48,* 1067–1077. https://doi.org/10.1177/1049731516658351

Lefley, H. P. (1984). Delivering mental health services across cultures. In P. B. Pedersen, N. Sartorius, & A. J. Marsella (Eds.), *Mental health services: The cross-cultural context* (pp. 135–177). Sage.

Liang, J., Matheson, B. E., & Douglas, J. M. (2016). Mental health diagnostic considerations in racial/ethnic minority youth. *Journal of Child and Family Studies, 25*(6), 1926–1940. doi:10.1007/s10826-015-0351-z

McGoldrick, M., Giordano, J., & Garcia-Preto, N. (2005). *Ethnicity and family therapy.* Guilford Press.

Micozzi, M. S. (1996). *Fundamentals of complementary and alternative medicine.* Churchill Livingstone.

Moody, R., & West, W. (Eds.). (2005). *Integrating traditional healing practices into counseling and psychology.* Sage.

Muecke, M. A. (1983). In search of healers. Southeast Asian refugees in the American healthcare system. *Cross-Cultural Medicine, 139*(6), 835–840. https://www.ncbi.nlm.nih.gov/pmc/articles/PMC1011013/pdf/westjmed00196-0065.pdf

Neville, H. A. (2015). Social justice mentoring: Supporting the development of future leaders for struggles, resistance, and transformation. *Counseling Psychologist, 43,* 157–169. https://doi.org/10.1177/0011000014564252

Norcross, J. C., & Lambert, M. J. (2018). Psychotherapy relationships that work III. *Psychotherapy, 55*(4), 303–315. http://dx.doi.org/10.1037/pst0000193

Ogundare, T. (2020). Culture and mental health: Towards cultural competence in mental health delivery. *Journal of Health and Social Sciences, 5*(1), 023–034 https://doi.org/10.19204/2019/cltr6.

Ortega-Williams, A., Beltrán, R., Schultz, K., Ru-Glo Henderson, Z., Colón, L., & Teyra, C. (2021). An integrated historical trauma and posttraumatic growth framework: A cross-cultural exploration. *Journal of Trauma & Dissociation, 22*(2), 220–240. https://doi.org/10.1080/15299732.2020.1869106

Parham, T. (1989). Cycles of psychological nigrescence. *Counseling Psychologist, 17*(2), 187–226. https://doi.org/10.1177/0011000089172001

Parham, T. A., Ajamu, A., & White, J. L. (2011). *The psychology of Blacks: Centering our perspectives in the African consciousness.* Prentice Hall.

Payne, J. S. (2012). Influence of race and symptom expression on clinicians' depressive disorder identification in African American men. *Journal of the Society for Social Work and Research, 3*(3), 162–177. doi:10.5243/jsswr.2012.11

Pederson, P. B. (2000). *A handbook for developing multicultural awareness* (3rd ed.). American Counseling Association.

Pedersen, P. B., Draguns, J. G., Lonner, W. J., & Trimble, J. E. (Eds.). (2002). *Counseling across cultures* (6th ed.). Sage.

Pham, T. V., Koirala, R., Wainberg, M. L., & Kohrt, B. (2021). Reassessing the mental health treatment gap: What happens if we include the impact of traditional healing on mental illness? *Community Mental Health Journal, 57,* 777–791. https://doi.org/10.1007/s10597-020-00705-5

Powers, M. B., & Emmelkamp, M. G. (2008). Virtual reality exposure therapy for anxiety disorders: A meta-analysis. *Journal of Anxiety Disorders, 22*(3), 561–569. https://doi.org/10.1016/j.janxdis.2007.04.006

Pynoos, R., & Eth, S. (1984). Children traumatized by witnessing acts of personal violence: Homicide, rape or suicide behavior. In S. Eth & R. Pynoos (Eds.), *Post-traumatic stress disorder in children* (pp. 17–44). American Psychiatric Press.

Ramirez, N., & Monk, G. (2017). Crossing borders: Narrative therapy with undocumented Mexican women on a journey beyond abuse and violence. *Journal of Systemic Therapies, 36*(2) 27–38. doi:10.1521/JSYT.2017.36.2.27

Ratts, M. J., & Pedersen, P. B. (2014). *Counseling for multiculturalism and social justice: Integration, theory, and application* (4th ed.). American Counseling Association.

Ratts, M. J., Singh, A. A., Nassar-McMillan, S., Butler, S. K., & McCullough, J. R. (2016). Multicultural and social justice counseling competencies: Guidelines for the counseling profession. *Journal of Multicultural Counseling and Development, 44*(1), 28–48. https://doi.org/10.1002/jmcd.12035

Ridley, C. R. (1995). *Overcoming unintentional racism in counseling and therapy: A practitioner's guide to intentional intervention.* Sage.

Ross, R. (2014). *Indigenous healing: Exploring traditional paths.* Penguin Group Canada.

Rutgers University. (2019, Mar 21). African-Americans more likely to be misdiagnosed with schizophrenia, study finds: The study suggests a bias in misdiagnosing blacks with major depression and schizophrenia. *ScienceDaily.* www.sciencedaily.com/releases/2019/03/190321130300.htm

Schiff, J. W., & Moore, K. (2006). The impact of the sweat lodge ceremony on dimensions of well-being. *American Indian and Alaska Native Mental Health Research (Online), 13*(3), 48–69. https://doi.org/10.5820/aian.1303.2006.48

Schwartz, R. C., & Blankenship, D. M. (2014). Racial disparities in psychotic disorder diagnosis: A review of empirical literature. *World Journal of Psychiatry, 4*(4), 133–140. https://doi.org/10.5498/wjp.v4.i4.133

Singh, A. A., Nassar, S. C., Arredondo, P., & Toporek, R. (2020). The past guides the future: Implementing the multicultural and social justice counseling competencies. *Journal of Counseling & Development, 98*(3), 238–252. https://doi.org/10.1002/jcad.12319

Smith, L. C., & Chin, R. Q. (2008). Social privilege, social justice, and group counseling: An inquiry. *Journal for Specialists in Group Work, 33*(4), 351–366. doi.10.1080/01933920802424415

So, J. K. (2005). Traditional and cultural healing among the Chinese. In R. Moodley & W. West (Eds.), *Integrating traditional healing practices into counseling and* psychotherapy (pp. 100–111). Sage.

Sue, D. W. (2015). Therapeutic harm and cultural oppression. *Counseling Psychologists, 43*(3), 359–369. https://doi.org/10.1177/0011000014565713

Sue D. W., Sue, D., Neville, H. A., & Smith L. (2019). *Counseling the culturally diverse* (8th ed.). Wiley.

Suite, D. H., La Bril, R., Primm, A., & Harrison-Ross, P. (2007). Beyond misdiagnosis, misunderstanding and mistrust: Relevance of the historical perspective in the medical and mental health treatment of people of color. *Journal of the National Medical Association, 99*(8), 879–885. https://www.ncbi.nlm.nih.gov/pmc/articles/PMC2574307/

Toporek, R. L., Gerstein, L. H., Fouad, N. A., Roysircar, G., & Israel, T. (2006). *Handbook for social justice in counseling psychology.* Sage.

U.S. Department of Health and Human Services (DHSS). (2001). *Mental health: Culture, race, and ethnicity - A supplement to mental health: A report of the Surgeon General.* U.S. Department of Health and Human Services, Substance Abuse and Mental Health Services Administration, Center for Mental Health Services. https://www.ncbi.nlm.nih.gov/books/NBK44243/pdf/Bookshelf_NBK44243.pdf

U.S. Office of the Surgeon General (OSG); U. S. Center for Mental Health Services; U.S. National Institute of Mental Health (2001, Aug). *Mental Health: Culture, Race, and Ethnicity: A Supplement to Mental Health: A Report of the Surgeon General.* U.S. Substance Abuse and Mental Health Services Administration. https://www.ncbi.nlm.nih.gov/books/NBK44243/

Walsh, R., & Shapiro, S. L. (2006). The meeting of meditative disciplines and western psychology: A mutually enriching dialogue. *American Psychologist, 61*(3), 227–239. https://doi.org/10.1037/0003-066X.61.3.227

Wampold B. E. (2015). How important are the common factors in psychotherapy? An update. *World Psychiatry, 14*(3), 270–277. https://doi.org/10.1002/wps.20238

Wendt, D. C., Gone, J. P., & Nagata, D. K. (2015). Potentially harmful therapy and multicultural counseling: Bridging two disciplinary discourses. *Counseling Psychologist, 43*(3), 334–358. https://doi.org/10.1177/0011000014548280

Wohl, J. (2000). Psychotherapy and cultural diversity. In J. Aponte & J. Wohl (Eds.), *Psychological intervention and cultural diversity* (pp. 75–91). Allyn & Bacon.

World Health Organization. (2019). Global report on traditional and complementary medicine 2019. https://www.who.int/traditional-complementary-integrative-medicine/WhoGlobalReportOnTraditionalAndComplementaryMedicine2019.pdf?ua=1

Yeh, C. J., Hunter, C., Madan-Bahel, A., & Arora, A. K. (2004). Indigenous and interdependent perspectives of healing: Implications for counseling and research. *Journal of Counseling & Development, 82*(4), 410–419. doi:10.1002/j.1556-6678.2004.tb00328.x

CHAPTER 13

STUDENT CHAPTER

I Am a Work in Progress: Riding the Multicultural Social
Justice Rollercoaster

Courtney Pearce

I am a 25-years-old White female and I grew up on the east coast of the
United States. I have lived in a rural area of southern Virginia for most of my life, where almost everyone knows everyone and, if you do not know them, it is more than likely they
know someone you know or have heard of you. I did not grow up in an area that consisted of
a diverse population; for many years I was surrounded only by a majority of individuals who
looked similar to myself—that was until I decided to transfer to Virginia Commonwealth
University to finish my bachelor's degree. I lived in the city, and, even though I hate admitting
this, that was honestly my first time being exposed to multicultural diversity. Then, I decided to get my master's degree at George Mason University and moved up north; that is
when culture shock made itself known for the first time and I found myself in a place where
my comfort zone was completely put into disarray.

Before enrolling in the multicultural counseling and social justice counseling courses,
I honestly thought I understood what each class would encompass. Now, looking back,
I can see how naïve that seems and even how narrowminded I was actually being, even
though at that time I thought differently. See, at that time, I believed that I was so fortunate
to be in my program because I was learning so much, and I felt that I was moving in the right
direction because I had found a new sense of self-awareness for myself and had started to develop a more culturally aware lens. Now I know that, even though I had made some strides
in my journey at that time, I had really only cracked open the door on my possibilities for
personal and professional growth, understanding, and knowledge, not only in being an effective counselor, but also a functioning individual in today's society. It has taken me two
years to get to the place I am currently at, and honestly, I plan to continue to build onto what
I have begun and grow each day, week, month, year, and so on because I refuse to accept and
believe that this, my current place, is my peak or end-all.

It is still hard for me to admit that for almost my whole life, I never, not once, stopped and took a moment to think about the tribulations of other individuals, not even my own classmates or friends, and what they experienced and how it could have affected them. That changed when I took the multicultural counseling class and learned more in the social justice counseling class. Every time I think about my journey, I see it in phases. I see it in phases where each phase pushed me to confront, understand, and process a lot of my life and who I wanted to be moving forward. For me, my journey felt like a rollercoaster. It was a rollercoaster of a variety of components that kept me moving along . . . well, sometimes moving. Honestly, my journey consisted of ups, downs, and standstills, but I worked through it and, whether at the time I liked it or not, I can say that I was impacted in a very influential way, which in return I know makes it all worth it. I am a work in progress, and I know I have come a long way from where I started, not only before enrolling in multicultural counseling and social justice counseling courses, but also before I even started my master's program.

At times I found myself feeling like a sponge taking in water, while at other times it felt like I was so full that, at any moment, I had the potential to burst. I am part to blame for this feeling because one thing I have learned thus far is that self-care is so important. But, as soon as I balance my life, a curve ball gets thrown into the mix; I guess that is life, and one day— hopefully soon—I will master that. The other part of this feeling comes from the amount of information I consumed, personal experiences that were shared with me, and vital feedback that I was given; I know it was necessary for my development and I am grateful to have received it, but honestly at times I felt like I was on overload, not sure if I could take anything else in . . . yet I found room. Then I had times where I had this feeling like I was on fire; I would become so amped up and feel so empowered that it would feel like I had a flame burning inside, pushing me to take action in some form or way. These feelings first started in multicultural counseling and grew as I entered social justice counseling.

After the process of being vulnerable and open when confronting parts of my life and who I was, I was down and without support—and not just check-in-on-someone-every-now-and-then support, but continuous I-am-here-with-you support that lifts you up and gives you the empowerment that you are strong and capable of change. It was when I found my support network and allies in my classmates and professors that this began to change, that led to me being able to see the differences in myself and my environment. That is why I love empowerment. I feel that it plays such a role in life that, once it is seen, strength and inspiration can begin to be built off it.

I know it seems like I did all this work—like having deep discussions with my classmates and professors and putting myself in situations where I was taking risks and having the courage to undergo in-depth self-examination from the first day of class—but, honestly, it took a few classes at first because when I was growing up "it" was never really talked about, and I was taught by my family to either be careful or stay away from talking about race, culture, ethnicity, and many other sociodemographic characteristics. At first, I was afraid to speak up because I was fearful that I would say the wrong thing, that I would offend someone when that was not my intention, or worse be labeled a racist. I learned that my apprehension and the easiness of being able to turn a blind eye was because of my White privilege. Acknowledging White privilege was difficult, and that is extremely embarrassing to admit: it was hard because I had formed this internalized definition of it and had to work even harder to change and understand what it actually encompassed. When I truly came to understand it though, it opened up my eyes: it did not have to be a bad thing, and I could use my privilege to help remove barriers and stand alongside others to create victories. One thing that brought me to the field of counseling was that I was passionate about helping others: these courses provided me the means to have a solid and buildable foundation of multiculturalism and social justice. Which just goes to show the power and influence of one's voice, intention, mentality, and experiences.

It was in multicultural counseling when I was first challenged. I was challenged about areas I thought I understood: areas like privilege, forgiveness, and tolerance. I was challenged not once but multiple times throughout the class, and, during those instances, I would find myself getting defensive, shutting down, or making up stories or circumstances about myself: kind of selfish some would say, and I would completely agree with them. See, *that* person—the previous version of myself—held one perspective tight and would deny over and over again, saying no, I was not being selfish. But now, *this* version of myself would say yes. I would say yes now because I was in fact being selfish. But getting to this place of being able to be admit it and be honest about it with others and myself took having to be okay with being uncomfortable when challenged; confronting and finding a form of resolution for areas of my life that I had tucked away so I did not have to deal with them, like my family structure or traumatic experiences; and pushing myself to want to be more and even stronger. See, that previous version of me was so caught up in being a wounded individual, someone who truly believed that their experiences and hardships accounted for more and were worse than anyone else's. I had such a small lens and a wicked tunnel vision for myself; I just needed to grasp that the world did not revolve around my problems and hardships because, even though I had hard times, I still had many good times as well in my life. So, yes, at first all the challenging was hard to face, and I did in fact struggle, but it ended up being a positive struggle because it led me to rewrite areas of my life, redevelop my perspective and lens, and foster a new level of compassion and empathy that was stronger than before.

CHAPTER 14

THE CRITICAL INTERSECTION OF SOCIAL CHANGE AND SOCIAL JUSTICE

Rita Chi-Ying Chung and Frederic P. Bemak

Change is the law of life and those who look only to the past or present are certain to miss the future.

—John F. Kennedy

Change will not come if we wait for some other person or some other time. We are the ones we've been waiting for. We are the change that we seek.

—Barack Obama

If you want to make enemies, try to change something.

—Woodrow Wilson

If not us, then who? If not now, then when?

—John E. Lewis

It's been a long, a long time coming, but I know a change gonna come, oh, yes it will.

—Sam Cooke

REFLECTION QUESTIONS

1. Try to recall a time when you personally changed. What prompted you to decide to change?
2. What were the barriers that you faced in making the change happen?
3. Did the change occur as you hoped, or were there difficulties along the way?
4. What are some of the things that you want to change now? What is holding you back?

FIGURE 14.1 Five components of social justice action and mental health

5. Have you observed or heard about people who are not able to express their personal rights? If so, what have you seen these individuals or groups try to do to transform that situation and gain their rights? What happened?
6. Consider what process means and all that goes into the saying, "Change is a process."

Working on social justice and human rights issues involves a variety of components: social change, leadership, advocacy, empowerment, and interdisciplinarity collaboration. Figure 14.1 illustrates these key elements that are critical in creating a just, fair, and equitable world for all. To be an effective change agent, it is necessary to possess leadership and advocacy skills, understand authentic empowerment, collaborate across disciplines, and have an awareness of the process and intricacies of social change. Each of these components is discussed in respective chapters. This chapter focuses on social change and its relationship to social justice and human rights. Since social change is at the very essence of social justice work, it is necessary to understand the theories and models of change. The chapter will help you understand the multidimensionality of social change; gain an understanding about the relationships among social change, social justice, and human rights; and offer insights about how to be an effective change agent in the mental health field.

THE RELATIONSHIP BETWEEN SOCIAL JUSTICE AND SOCIAL CHANGE

All of us working in the field of psychology and counseling are change agents. The goal of our work, whether it is with one client, groups, families, larger communities, or entire systems, is to promote healthy positive change. Historically the emphasis of psychotherapy was on changing the individual. Incorporating social justice and human rights into counseling and psychotherapy broadens the dimensions and scope of change to include groups, families, and systems. The inclusion of systemic change is the understanding and acceptance that mental health work is broader than individual psychopathology. For example, it is clear that global movements such as the 2020 racial justice protests, the #MeToo movement, and the climate movement are social issues that are embedded in systems and organizations and not rooted in individual psychopathology. The perspective of examining individuals and communities in the context of historical, social, political, economic, cultural, and environmental issues implies that the larger system must change, and, along with that change there must be attention to social justice and human rights.

The emphasis on human rights as it relates to empowerment, equity, fairness, and justice focuses on external factors that may be beyond an individual's circumstances or control. Given the presumption that individual problems are largely influenced by social, community, and societal issues, interventions are needed that address this context of the individual's problems. For example, I (Fred) was once asked to consult in a public school to address mental health issues after numerous seventh-graders complained about being bullied, discriminated against, and harassed by the ninth-graders. Rather than attend to seventh-grade students individually, in collaboration with school administration, I decided to generate an intervention with the entire ninth grade to work on broader issues of safety, bullying, and fairness that would affect the entire middle school. This is an example of moving away from only offering psychotherapy that would emphasize individual counseling with more than 30 seventh-graders who were experiencing mental health issues due to the actions of the ninth-graders. Instead, the focus was on changing the larger system that was steeped in discrimination, intolerance, and bullying.

Thus, social justice and human rights work are closely intertwined with social change. This is in contrast to general change models (i.e., individuals changing personal behaviors, such as drinking or smoking). We define social change as it relates to social justice to include the changing or altering of systems (such as institutions and organizations) and structures (such as laws, policies, regulations, procedures, social roles, and functions) that hinder, obstruct, block, impede, and interfere with positive and optimal growth, development, opportunities, physical safety and security, and economic and psychological well-being for *all* individuals, families, groups, and communities. Although, social change can occur with individuals, organizations, communities, and the society at large, we suggest that, regardless of the level at which the change occurs, when counseling toward social justice, the impact of the change ultimately affects multiple levels (i.e., individuals, families, groups, and communities). Mental health social justice work is therefore how we, as helping professionals, proactively, consciously, and intentionally contribute to social change. The aim of our psychotherapy and counseling in social justice work is to propel social change that will intervene in and eliminate, reduce, and prevent existing and potential inequities, inequalities, "isms," and unfair treatment, as well as disproportionate distribution of and access to power, wealth, resources, and opportunities. Therefore, understanding social change and the components of change, its process, effects, and impact is essential for counselors and psychologists.

CHANGE IS NOT EASY

> We would rather be ruined than changed; we would rather die in our dread than climb the cross of the moment and let our illusions die.
>
> —W. H. Auden

Those who expect moments of change to be comfortable and free of conflict have not learned their history.

—Joan Wallach Scott

Change is everywhere. As counselors and psychologists, we live, breathe, and support change. Our world is filled with constant bombardment of change, even more accelerated by technological advancement. We continually have access, through our technological devices and wherever we are located, to communicate 24/7 with others and view any news events (wars, conflicts, disasters, protests/demonstrations, human tragedies, music concerts, etc.), nationally and globally, in real time. With the swift change of technology, we witness technological advances of yesterday become old today and experience the rapid obsolescence of what were our state-of-the-art smart phones, tablets, and computers. For us, as mental health professionals, these issues come into play both through the world we live and work in and in our clients' lived experiences and worldviews. Despite the fact that change is everywhere and mental health professions aim to promote positive transformations, change remains difficult for many people. Personal and social modifications present a dilemma: Do we stay the same course or modify the course?

The translation of "crisis" in Chinese clearly depicts the predicament of change (see Figure 14.2). The two characters that make up the Chinese word for "crisis" literally translate to mean *danger* and *opportunity*. Change can be an opportunity, a chance to transform, grow, and develop. Simultaneously, change can be dangerous, scary, and fearful since it alters how one is and how one does things. Consequently, change is both exciting and anxiety-producing. It should be noted that the mixed reaction to change happens with both major changes, such as stopping a personal addiction, and with more minor changes, such as modifying a pattern of interaction with a loved one or losing a small amount of weight. Depending on the degree of change, there is an accompanying gradation of discomfort, anxiety, frustration, and distress, which may provoke fear, uncertainty, tension, and insecurity. To fully understand personal and social change and its relationship to social justice, the next section discusses psychological change and principles of social change, including a brief summary of community social change models. To help illuminate these concepts, we will examine how to infuse issues of change into social justice work, discussing the role

FIGURE 14.2 Chinese character for crisis

of systems in social change and how power and resistance play a part in promoting social change. Recommendations about social change will conclude the chapter.

THE PSYCHOLOGY OF CHANGE

Research has shown that counselors and psychologists do in fact create change (Lambert et al., 1986; Smith et al., 1980). Interestingly, it has also been found that the kind of growth that comes from psychotherapy and counseling can also result from other mechanisms outside of therapy (Hubble et al., 1999; Wampold, 2015). Prochaska and his colleagues (Prochaska, 1999; Prochaska & DiClemente, 1982; Prochaska et al., 1992, 1994) found that individuals use the same change strategies in therapy that they use in solving other life problems. For example, if I am trying to exercise more, I would apply the same tactics in my personal efforts to exercise as I would as a client in psychotherapy where I am attempting to change the interaction patterns I have with my sibling. This presents interesting findings, illustrating that individuals have the potential to independently change without the assistance of psychotherapy (Norcross & Prochaska, 1986a, 1986b).

In an attempt to explain how people change, regardless of whether or not it is with professional help, Prochaska and DiClemente (1992) developed the *transtheoretical model* (TTM) of change. The TTM is one of the more comprehensive models of change in the field of psychotherapy and counseling, and it provides an explanation about the various stages of change. Research about the TTM has revealed that it is a viable model in settings ranging from outpatient therapy to self-change (e.g., DiClemente & Hughes, 1990; DiClemente & Prochaska, 1985; DiClemente et al., 1985; Lam et al., 1988; McConnaughy et al., 1989; Prochaska & DiClemente, 1992). The TTM consists of five stages of change: precontemplation, contemplation, preparation, action, and maintenance (see Figure 14.3). We believe it is a critical basis for psychologists and counselors to understand and use the TTM as a springboard to social justice and human rights work, so we will describe the stages in depth. The first stage, *precontemplation*, has been described as one of the most difficult (Brogan et al., 1999). Individuals in this stage have no intention of changing. Many are unaware of their problem or even the need to change. Clients in this stage are typically in therapy because there is pressure by others (such as a partner, spouse, or family members) that may cause limited change because of external pressure. So, if my family wants me to stop eating fried food because of my high cholesterol, then I may cut back when family members are around. When I am alone, however, I may continue to eat fried food since I really don't believe this change is necessary. Thus, once the pressure is diminished, people quickly return to their old ways. During this stage, change is cursory and not sustained.

The *contemplation* stage finds individuals a little further along, with an awareness of and a commitment to overcome existing problems. Thus, the person eating fried food now realizes that their cholesterol level is high and that it could lead to a heart attack. Despite this awareness and a promise to change, there is still not a commitment to take action (Krebs et al., 2018). The person knows what needs to be done but is thinking about it, rather than doing something. For example, we know that exercise is good for us, and we may seriously think about doing some type of physical exercise. We can contemplate doing exercise for

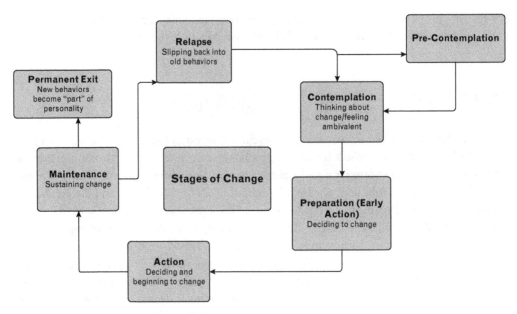

FIGURE 14.3 Stages of change: The transtheoretical model

Adapted from Prochaska & DiClemente, 1982.

many months or even years, but not take the steps to actually exercise. A danger in this stage is that individuals may become stuck.

In the third stage, the *preparation* stage, there is a combination of intention and behavior. Individuals in this stage intend to take action soon and often have unsuccessfully tried to change in the past. Such a person may think, "I want to stop eating fried food," or "I want to exercise," but has not yet actually stopped eating fried food or started exercising. In this stage, there may be small behavioral changes, but an effective overall change has not yet taken root. When one is in the preparation stage, there is the intention to take action in the near future. So, in this stage, I may have purchased a steamer to cook my food as an alternative to fried food or purchased workout clothes in preparation for exercise that I will begin at some point. Prochaska et al. (1992) call this the "early action stage."

The fourth stage, *action*, differs from the preparation stage since individuals actually take steps to address their problems. I am now cooking with my steamer and going to the gym three times a week. This stage is characterized by overt behavioral changes and requires considerable commitment of time and energy. Individuals in this stage talk about "working hard to change" and "actually doing something." This stage should not be confused with the actual change, which requires movement to the last stage to be considered complete change in this model. According to Krebs et al. (2018), the hallmarks of the action stage are the modification of the target behavior to an acceptable criterion and significant overt efforts to change. Finally, one is actually "doing it."

Maintenance is the final stage, in which individuals work to sustain the gains attained during the action stage. This stage may be viewed as static; however, this phase is just as important as the action stage because it is a continuation and maintenance of change. Not only have I begun working out at the gym and not eating fried foods, but I am continuing to do so. Preserving changes can be lifelong work and can be seen in the efforts of individuals dealing with addictive behaviors. The hallmark of this stage is stabilizing and maintaining behavioral change that avoids and prevents relapse. Individuals who reach the final stage and then relapse will wind up at the beginning stage once again, necessitating repeating the change process through all of the five stages. So, if I revert back to eating French fries and fried dough after cooking with my steamer for six months and completely avoiding any fried foods, when I try again in my eighth month to go back to the steamer, I will begin back again at the precontemplation and contemplation stages, considering again whether or not it makes sense to change. Thus, the process of change once again begins from the start. These five stages are important to keep in mind as we move into a discussion about the principles of social change in the next section.

PRINCIPLES OF SOCIAL CHANGE

Now that we have discussed how people change, we would like to expand this change model to include the broader sphere of social change. Moving from individual to social change provides important building blocks and a foundation for social justice work. In the next section, we examine some of the basic principles of social change that we have adapted from Homan (2008, 2018). It is important to note that the list of principles is not exhaustive, but highlights fundamental beliefs that we think are essential for counselors and psychologists doing social justice and human rights psychotherapy and counseling (see Box Text 14.1). In addition, although there are ideas that overlap in some of the principles, we feel it is important to address each principle separately to present the full scope.

1. *The critical link – healthy environments lead to psychologically heathy people.* Our environments shape us. A healthy and safe environment correlates with psychological well-being and mental health. In contrast, an unsafe, depressed, or distressed community is more likely to create distress (Homan, 2018). It is important that counselors and psychologists doing social justice work understand this correlation and how it impacts counseling interventions. Clearly addressing and promoting community change, either with the client's own exploration of advocacy or directly with the surrounding community and stakeholders, has significant implications for fostering healthy and safe communities that value individuals, families, and the community as a whole. As social justice–oriented counselors and psychologists, we can proactively and collaboratively work with clients and stakeholders to challenge circumstances that do not promote equity, fairness, and equality.
2. *Social change involves an ecological systems perspective.* Since individuals do not live in total isolation, it is critical that we examine issues from an ecological perspective. An example is gun violence. A situation where one family member mistakenly shoots another family member can affect the entire neighborhood, the town, the state, or the country. This situation, similar to the mass shootings we have witnessed in public places such as schools, nightclubs, religious places of worship, outdoor

BOX TEXT 14.1 PRINCIPLES OF CHANGE

Description

1. Critical link—healthy environments lead to psychologically healthy people
2. Social change involves an ecological systems perspective
3. To constructively change the social environment mental health professionals must plan and be intentional
4. Social justice is not arbitrary
5. Social change demands having the courage to take risks to use new behavior and go in new directions
6. Critical to social justice work is the issue of power
7. Even when empowerment starts with the individual, it has the potential to expand to others
8. Authentic empowerment means partnerships, not therapeutic imperialism
9. Build on existing individual and community resiliency, strengths, and assets
10. Identify and respect cultural diversity and inclusion
11. Change requires awareness, understanding, acceptance, and appreciation of the sociopolitical, historical, psychological, cultural and ecological perspectives
12. Change is a process, not a quick fix
13. Change can come in small or large quantities
14. There is a difference between planning and implementing change and action
15. Promoting social justice through social change is not about ego, it is about working toward a larger cause
16. Effective social change agents combine learning and teaching

---

concerts, shopping malls, and movie theaters may generate discussion about gun violence and legislation not only within those particular communities and states, but also at the federal and even global levels. With globalization and global interconnectedness, addressing issues on multiple levels is critical. What is happening in the United States today impacts other parts of the world. For example, it is striking to us, as we write this book while in New Zealand, how the impact of and conversation regarding 693 mass shootings in 2021, in the United States, contributing to 44,861 gun violence deaths there (Gun Violence Archive, 2022), is affecting NZ gun policies and practices. Other examples are the racial justice protests and the #Metoo movement throughout the United States that sparked similar demonstrations and movements worldwide.

An ecological approach (Clauss-Ehlers et al., 2019; Homan, 2018) involves looking at problems from a larger systemic perspective. There is an inherent relationship between various subsystems and the larger system. Changing any level or part of the larger system will therefore affect the entire ecosystem. For example, if an individual is experiencing bullying at work, this will impact her mental and physical health. Her work productivity may diminish, and her personal relationships may suffer. In fact, when looking further into the problem, one might find a number of others at the same work site experiencing the same problem. To adequately address this problem, counselors or psychologists doing social justice work not only discuss with the individual how to better cope with their situation, but also respond to the bullying behavior in their environment. Looking at the situation from an ecological macro standpoint, one would need to strategize with the client(s) about how to advocate within the system. If the mental health professional was employed at the work site, it would be important to address the larger scope of the bullying issue that is inherently a part of the workplace and affects numbers of employees. Therefore, it is critical that the issue be examined from a holistic perspective.

3. *To constructively change the social environment, mental health professionals must plan and be intentional.* Social justice work is intentionally changing the unjust status quo. When we aim to transform and improve on current conditions, we must be deliberate and intentional. The result of such intentionality is to interrupt the status quo that reinforces and maintains social inequities and unfair treatment. As we anticipate resistance and understand process, we develop plans of action to address expected hesitation. For example, if a mental health center is trying to shift to incorporate more group therapy, it could be predicted that the center's professionals who are more comfortable doing individual therapy will resist the change. Planning ahead to diminish resistance and to have staff agree with the proposed change could involve the center's mental health professionals self-select how much increase or decrease there would be in their case load for group therapy rather than have a mandated administrative clinical requirement. Taking small steps toward change may be more effective in this situation. (Also see Point 13 below [change can come in small or large quantities]).

4. *Social justice is not arbitrary.* It is important that social-oriented psychologists and counselors focus on issues that clearly violate human rights. The actual violation of human rights must be visible to all parties involved. Clarity about particular injustices helps unify those involved and solidifies direction and goals. Educating clients and stakeholders about social injustices is an important aspect of our mental health work.

5. *Social change demands having the courage to take risks to use new behaviors and go in new directions.* Social change requires that one move away from old ways of thinking and doing things. New directions and new behaviors are integral to facilitating social justice action. Counselors and psychologists must aid individuals, families, groups, and communities in developing new approaches as they tackle problems. Contemplating new behaviors is linked to the TTM for change discussed earlier in the chapter and requires the individual to go through its respective stages. Finding new ways involves the ability, courage, and vision to be a risk taker as well as the capability to openly explore new directions with clients and others.

6. *Critical to social justice work is the issue of power.* It has long been understood that some who hold power and consciously and unconsciously define the structure, norms, and dynamics within the social, political, and economic context are reluctant to let this power go. To confront or contest the status quo means to challenge an existing power base. This reality is often juxtaposed with negative connotations

about the meaning of "power" in counseling and psychology, where power may be associated with the negative elements of authority, domination, force, and coercion. Yet power is a critical tool in social change and social justice, and, within the framework of social justice work, it has a positive subtext. Considering power as a means toward social justice is to proactively and positively challenge power blocks and structures that inhibit or suppress equity, fairness, and justice. In fact, power is an essential ingredient for social change and a tool that mental health professionals must become comfortable using as they challenge and advocate for social justice. A clinician named Stephen provides an example. Stephen is working in a youth residential treatment program. Although he is liked by staff, Stephen ignores and excuses problem behaviors exhibited by the adolescents, such as drinking or using marijuana, despite being warned to report anyone caught with illicit drugs or alcohol. Rather than confronting his young clients about the behavior, Stephen continues to make private "deals" that he would not report them if they were well-behaved when he was around. In preparing to confront and possibly dismiss Stephen given his interactions with clients, it is important to anticipate a strong reaction by staff, ascertain his power base, and determine which of his friends would "back" him regardless of the concerns and who on staff would value the goals of treatment over a well-liked colleague. It was determined that the associate director, who was well-respected in the organization and known to be highly supportive of treatment integrity, had an excellent power base and would be a good first point of contact in eventually having Stephen removed from his position. Assessing the power structure of the organization was important in removing a problematic employee.

7. *Even when authentic empowerment starts with the individual, it has the potential to expand to others.* Authentic empowerment does not happen in isolation, separate and detached from others. We believe that when we work with a client we are impacting not only the client, but also the client's world. As we help clients become authentically empowered and gain the confidence, skills, and courage to take action and challenge inequities, we are impacting the family, social, and vocational networks of the client's life. As empowerment takes hold there is change in a client's surrounding environment. Thus, if one person speaks out and questions inequities and discrimination in the community, there is potential that others will join. Social psychology research on conformity has illustrated this process (Bond & Smith, 1996; Cialdini & Goldstein, 2004).

8. *Authentic empowerment means partnerships, not therapeutic imperialism.* When we are working with clients, we are creating equal partnerships as we do social justice counseling and psychotherapy. We are not the experts telling clients what to do; we are not controlling therapeutic sessions and setting up co-dependent relationships; we do not assume roles of therapeutic imperialists. Rather we are fostering a therapeutic partnership that aims for advocacy and social change.

9. *Build on existing individual and community resiliency, strengths, and assets.* Change agents must be able to identify what resiliency, strengths, and resources already exist within both the individual and the community. Capitalizing and building on these resources provides a good starting point for promoting social change.

Knowing that a client has leadership qualities and experiences or community organizing skills helps counselors and psychologists acknowledge and build on those skills to promote positive social change. Acknowledging existing strengths is instrumental in helping individuals and communities recognize their skill sets as well as the strategies that can be useful in addressing social inequities. Utilizing existing skills and abilities provides and reinforces authentic empowerment in clients and communities.

10. *Identify and respect cultural diversity and inclusion.* Effective social change requires a clear and solid understanding of social justice multicultural competencies. Our communities are composed of people from different racial, ethnic, and cultural backgrounds. The diversity within our communities and societies calls for us to be multiculturally competent as counselors and psychologists. We must be aware of, understand, accept, appreciate, and honor different cultural perspectives and worldviews, as well as culturally dissimilar values, means of resolving problems, perspectives of time, negotiation and communication styles, and so on. We know that multiculturalism has the potential to generate a tremendous richness and openness and is conducive to social justice work.

   An example is our experience when we were invited to bring a Counselors Without Borders (CWB) mental health team to work on an American Indian reservation in California after wildfires that caused tremendous destruction. Having previously worked on reservations, we respectfully approached the Tribal Council to ask for permission to work on the reservation. The meeting with the Tribal Council consisted of a few hours of discussion, getting to know one another, seeing if our goals were in line, and an unspoken testing by the Tribal Council to see if we were truly respectful and culturally responsive to their cultural beliefs, values, attitudes, and worldviews and whether or not the mental health support we were proposing would fit into that cultural framework.

11. *Change requires awareness, understanding, acceptance, and appreciation of the sociopolitical, historical, psychological, cultural, and ecological perspectives.* A critical element of being multiculturally competent is to be aware of, acknowledge, accept, understand, and appreciate the sociopolitical, psychopolitical, and historical perspectives of social justice issues within the individuals' and communities' cultural background. Specific groups continue to experience racial injustice, discrimination, xenophobia, and oppression on individual, community, and societal levels. For counselors and psychologists to truly understand the social injustices experienced by clients, we need to incorporate not only the cultural, but also the sociopolitical, psychopolitical, historical, and ecological perspectives. Similarly, it is also important to understand and acknowledge past, current, and transgenerational trauma.

12. *Change is a process, not a quick fix.* In a society where we value quick solutions and sound bites, we are often too impatient to allow the process of change to unfold. As mental health professionals working toward social justice, it is essential that we become comfortable with allowing the process to run its course and to "trust the process." Social justice work, action, and activism cannot be superficial: it must take

root and grow over time. Homan (2018) identified seven phases in the community change process, which are as follows:

a. *Introduction phase* begins when the problem is recognized.

b. *Initial action phase* is a time when information is gathered and allies are identified.

c. *Emergence of leadership and structure phase* involves a leader emerging while the group simultaneously begins to take shape.

d. *Letdown phase* occurs when there is some deflation; there is a clear demarcation of those who are committed to change and those who are not as interested in the "real" work that needs to take place.

e. *Recommitment, new task, and new members phase* constitutes a time when the group reconfigures; the direction is further defined as leaders become more solidified in their roles and remotivate the group.

f. *Sustained action phase* involves a deepening of the group's work and expansion to take on new challenges.

g. *Growth, decline, or termination phase* is the final phase, when the group is either going through the first six phases more expediently as it moves to fulfill the goal for social change, or it is beginning to end based on meeting or not meeting its goals.

13. *Change can come in small or large quantities.* Doing social justice work and creating social change does not always have to imply major changes. Sometimes there are small changes that are part of the fabric of a longer-term change process. Regardless of whether the changes are small or large, there is a disruption of the equilibrium and status quo, with impact on individuals as well as in the larger community. It is important to not underestimate small changes. Taking "baby steps" to initiate and contribute to the process of change leads to changing more complex and larger issues. For example, having an informal talk with colleagues, friends, or family members challenging their homophobic attitudes or attitudes toward the homeless may begin a longer-term process of changing their values and behavior and result in them questioning others' values. This is the planting of "social justice seeds" and may have ramifications that are not always immediately evident. We suggest that it is not necessary to witness immediate results of our social justice work (which may tie more into our own need for immediate results), but instead to accept that social justice is a process that often requires small steps. Clearly, the civil rights, feminist, or gay rights movements did not happen overnight. It is critical that psychologists and counselors recognize and acknowledge that small changes contribute and lead to larger transformations. We encourage celebrations of a wide range of successful social justice changes, both small and big accomplishments.

14. *There is a difference between planning and implementing change and action.* There are significant differences between planning change and actually implementing change, with each requiring different skills. It is important that counselors and psychologists recognize the distinctive skills needed by each. Although it can be motivating and exciting to plan how to promote social change, it is also important to identify, recognize, and acknowledge potential barriers and challenges in preparation to taking steps to implement the plan. Similarly, it is vital that we, as social justice–oriented

psychologists and counselors, are able to conceptualize the overall action plan that will help determine the skills needed to develop strategies to overcome the barriers to implementation.

15. *Promoting social justice through social change is not about ego, it is about working toward a larger cause.* When we are working to promote social justice, it is important to keep in mind that we are working toward a larger goal. In some ways, promoters of social justice change can be seen as servants to a larger cause, working in partnership *with* people and *not* for people. This means, that during each phase of change, the input, suggestions, and ideas of clients, stakeholders, and community members are important, as is creating a safe space and place where everyone has equal input. As discussed in Chapter 7 ("The Role of Social Justice Mental Health Professionals") we, as social justice counselors and psychologists are not working to serve our own needs, but rather are working with others as social justice collaborative partners.

16. *Effective change agents combine learning and teaching.* A number of years ago, I (Fred) was working with street children in Brazil. The children were under the threat of violent attacks and murder from vigilante groups who were trying to "clean up the cities." My experience of doing research with these children, and in part attempting to address the violence and murder of innocent children, was profound since at times our roles were reversed. I became the student, and the street children were the teachers, educating me about their lived experiences. In fact, this experience led me to publish an article describing how professionals working with street children transformed into what I called *street researchers*, becoming students of the street children who taught them about the world of the streets (Bemak, 1996). It is our belief that this concept carries over to the social justice work we do as mental health professionals. Our roles are transformed, we are no longer *only* the healer or helper or teacher: we are also students. It is important that we learn from the individuals and communities with whom we work and be ready and willing to abandon an unwavering role as the authority or expert. After all, those who are living with social injustice are the experts. Our experience has taught us that the lack of social justice humility combined with an inability to let go of control promotes the expert role, one that we have labeled the "psychological imperialist."

In summary, social justice work, action, and activism are about change, whether it is with an individual, in the community, or at a societal level. Social justice change is critical to ensure that *all* individuals, their families, their communities, and stakeholders have the opportunity for optimal psychological and physical safety, growth, development, and well-being. To be effective change agents, we must embrace an ecological perspective of our clients' situations by acknowledging and understanding both the complex multidimensionality of multiple systems and how issues on a systematic level can trickle down and impact individuals and their families. Social justice work involves intentionally and proactively disrupting systems and the status quo that have been built on and maintained unfair treatment and unequal access, resources, and opportunities. While systems affect people, people can also affect systems (Cowan & Egan, 1979). We as psychologists and counselors are part of a system and therefore have the ability to change systems.

THE MEANING OF POWER IN SOCIAL CHANGE

Social change and power go hand in hand. Although power was noted as a principle of change, we would like to further examine the relationship between power and social justice. In social justice and human rights work, counselors and psychologists are constantly faced with issues of power. Who has the power? How does one handle one's power? What constitutes the constructive use of power to achieve social justice? How do we change the power base so that all people, regardless of socioeconomic status, gender, sexual orientation, religion, abilities, ethnic, racial, or cultural background, and so on gain equal access, resources, wealth, and opportunity?

When considering power in relationship to social change, the aim is to help people move toward constructive outcomes (Homan, 2019). The use of power in social justice work is positive, intentional, and proactive. A primary aim in using one's power is to eliminate barriers that prohibit equity, equality, and fair treatment. An example of this occurred when I (Fred) had a senior-level state position in the department of mental health as the executive director of a regional treatment program for adolescents, and I could use this position of power to advocate for and change some of the policies that were inhibiting the rights of youth. Similarly, I (Rita) as a faculty member organized a meeting with students of color in a university graduate program and used this as a platform to recommend changes to university administration on the recruitment and retention of students, faculty, and staff of color.

The various definitions of power in social justice suggest that, even though it may be to differing degrees, all individuals possess power (e.g., Robinson & Hannah, 1994; Rubin & Rubin, 1986; Wrong, 1995) and that power is purposeful and intentional. There are clear expectations in social justice psychology and counseling that when one uses one's power, it is for the benefit of clients, stakeholders, and the larger social network and community. Often there is a collaborative use and sharing of power by stakeholders (clients, families, and communities) working toward mutual solutions for the development of new or improved conditions. For example, mental health professionals in the United States may encourage different racial and ethnic groups (such as African Americans, Asian Americans, American Indians, Latinx, Arab Americans, etc.), the LGBTQI community, and various religious organizations to join together to lobby against hate crimes, with an aim to pass tougher laws on hate crimes and hate crime prevention.

The use of power in social justice work *never* involves manipulation or coercion. Power in social justice work is conducive to sharing and cooperation. For example, you and a group of colleagues have concerns that an administrator has been inadequately addressing racial tension in the work environment. When the issue has been raised in the past, it has been ignored and brushed aside. As a collective group of concerned employees, you approach the administrator and suggest strategies to address these issues. This is a constructive and positive step, one using a collective sense of power to address a brewing issue within your work site. No one was forced to join the group of concerned colleagues, and the aim was for a positive result through collectively approaching the organization with a concern about racial justice. I (Fred) personally experienced a similar situation as a new assistant professor; I was constantly hearing complaints and dissatisfaction from the majority of my peers who were untenured assistant professors in the college. Rather than join in with the destructive undertone of displeasure, I approached the Dean to explain the dissatisfaction and its impact on the college climate, and I offered to convene meetings to generate recommendations from this group of untenured professors. The Dean welcomed the suggestion and later positively responded to many of the recommendations proposed by this group.

Although everyone has power, some people, by virtue of their race/ethnicity, gender, age, positions, or personality, have more power than others. The degree of power depends on the situation and the interplay among those involved. For instance, as a group therapist, you have power over the group members, establishing when to meet, for how long, who enters the group, parameters for psychological and physical safety within the group, etc. Or, as a senior faculty member or higher-ranking supervisor in your workplace, you may have more authority by virtue of seniority. Thus, power involves relationships among people, and these can be either positive or negative. One's impact on others through the use of power relates to the degree of control one has over resources, finances, information, etc., and the dependency that other individuals have on those resources. For example, if your income from a job supports your family; pays the bills, buys the food; and pays for transportation, clothing, and so on, the influence that your job supervisor has over you may be greater than if you did not need that income to support your family and pay expenses.

Social change requires a degree of power to move individuals or groups in new healthy and positive directions. Sometimes our power is used to motivate or mobilize action steps conducive to change. Power in this situation is viewed as positive since it can influence and impact change from an undesirable to a desirable situation. When we are encouraging and activating people to promote social change, it is important that we respectfully use power. This requires respecting others while keeping a clear picture of the goals and avoiding using power for personal gain or interests. Finally, working toward social change and justice does not entail that we, as mental health professionals, do it alone. Working collaboratively with our clients, stakeholders, and allies has the potential to strengthen our power and increase the chances of meeting our goals. Chapter 21, on interdisciplinary collaboration, further addresses this issue.

RESISTANCE TO CHANGE

> People don't resist change. They resist being changed!
>
> —Peter Senge

> Faced with the choice between changing one's mind and proving that there is no need to do so, almost everyone gets busy on the proof.
>
> —John Kenneth Galbraith

As we have discussed, inherent in change are uncertainties and unpredictability. Not surprisingly, given the lack of clarity that may accompany change and shifts in power, some people are resistant to change. Change disrupts what we know, how we do things, and our ability to predict the future. Interestingly, even if individuals are aware that their situation is unhealthy, negative, or undesirable, they may still resist change, preferring to have order and certainty rather than the unexpected. It is striking that we often hear people talk about their dissatisfaction about their job or work, yet they do little or nothing to improve their work environment or look for another job. Two old proverbs illustrate the ambivalence regarding change: one is

"The devil you know is better than the devil you don't know," and the other, "Jumping from the frying pan to the fire." Both depict the caution involved in considering change.

Resistance is a natural part of change. Knowing the world we live in may be far easier than recreating a new world that we don't know. Homan (2018) pointed out the difficulties people have in letting go of the time and energy they have invested in their worlds; they often find that all the skills they developed to handle particular situations are no longer pertinent. As mentioned previously, resistance may manifest when individuals in positions of privilege, power, and leadership are reluctant to share or give up their status or circumstances. Unpredictability and fear of disruption further contribute to resistant behaviors. The uncertainty about outcome is a natural response since social change may involve many twists and turns along the way. Even though change may be the most beneficial result, there are inevitably pros and cons to changing, as well as recuperations, such as the loss of a job, status, or relationships with colleagues, friends, and family. The lack of clarity may create self-doubt about the direction of change, one's ability, and one's future position. In fact, there may be grieving for the loss of one's status and the way things used to be, which may appear strange when one grieves about an unsatisfactory situation in one's life.

To better understand this, we might consider people who experience oppression and yet have basic needs of food, shelter, and clothing taken care of at a minimal level. Gaining independence and freedom from their burdensome circumstances may cause a loss of security and the predictability of having basic needs met while neglecting to consider other elements of the experience, such as the freedom to make their own choices and live their lives freely. The freedom and uncertainty may come with fear, or what has been called the "fear of freedom" (Fromm, 1942). This concept describes how those who are oppressed may desire freedom, but, when freedom is granted to them, there is hesitation, doubts, uncertainties, anxiety, and fear. Furthermore, when individuals who have been told what to do and how to think and act are then given freedom, it may be very difficult because they may psychologically believe they are not equipped with the abilities and skills to handle a life of independence and self-determination.

IDENTIFYING RESISTANCE

In counseling and psychotherapy, "resistance" refers to client behavior that has the potential to obstruct the therapeutic process and sabotage growth and positive change. Mental health professionals and counselors promoting social change will encounter similar types of resistance that inhibit the facilitation of human rights and equity. This happens both externally, from outside sources, and internally. Resistance that has been identified in multicultural training (i.e., Ridley, 2005; Singh et al., 2020) is similar to the type of resistance found in doing social justice–oriented work. When doing multicultural and social justice–oriented work, it is essential to be cognizant of and identify resistant behavior and not be misled by what may appear to be agreement to social change but is, in reality, resistance. Overt resistance is easy to identify when individuals clearly voice their opposition or their unwillingness to change. Covert and passive resistance may be less easily identified since reactions may not be so apparent. Resistance in accepting or following through on assignments, avoidance, changing topics, deflecting questions, or agreement to ideas followed by "but" statements may be more difficult to detect. An example was the graduate student who refused to take my (Rita) seminar in cross-cultural psychology, appealing to the Dean that the content was threatening. Upon further exploration it was determined that the student was negatively predisposed to issues of diversity and inclusion and being challenged about White privilege, which manifested in an attempt to waive the class. Resistance is heightened for individuals who have high needs for psychological safety and security driven by personal vulnerability, which oftentimes results in them controlling as much of their lives as possible. It is helpful for psychologists and counselors to maintain an awareness that behavior driven by the need to control may be at times underlying resistance and can thwart change.

UNDERSTANDING THE SOURCE OF RESISTANCE

Dealing with resistance is part of the work of social change. Rather than trying to avoid resistant clients or groups, the question for us as psychologists and counselors is how to align and find areas of agreement with those who are opposing change. Given our mental health training we are in an advantageous position to understand unwillingness, aversion, and reluctance. Are those who are resistant feeling vulnerable, are they misinformed, are they hostile, are they scared? Our training in exploring and interpreting the actual source of resistance, fear of change, and associated anxieties is very helpful in promoting social change.

STRATEGIES FOR DEALING WITH RESISTANCE

Using our insights regarding the psychological roots of resistance, we can develop strategies that are person-specific and system-specific to address the motivation behind the actual resistance and defensiveness to social change and social justice. Homan (2008) suggests that the most profound source of resistance to change is simply what we tell ourselves. Given this supposition, one way to minimize resistance is to clearly inform people about the reasons and goals for change. For example, "We are carefully examining the policies about suspension in this secondary school because 78% of the students suspended are students of color, even though they compose only 41% of the student body." This would be a clear and transparent sharing with staff, teachers, parents, and students about why there is an examination of the policy, why a change of policy and practice are being considered, and how it could impact students' mental health and school climate. Open and transparent communication has great potential for helping people understand the issue at hand and assists with considering how to develop equitable and just solutions.

Based on our psychological and counseling training, teaching, and professional experiences, we have developed 11 strategies (see Box Text 14.2) that we found to be effective in dealing with resistance to social change (Bemak & Chung, 2018; Chung et al., 2018). The first strategy is to create a safe space, an environment that is nonthreatening, a place where there is open, transparent communication and where respectful discussion can take place. Second, in forming this safe environment, it is important to ensure that all stakeholders have a seat and voice at the table. Third, the reason, rationale, and objectives for the social action and change must be presented in a clear manner, as mentioned above, without any ambiguity or a hidden agenda. Everyone involved should have a full understanding of the goals. Fourth, the discussion must be presented as a "win-win" scenario in that everyone has the right to speak and share their viewpoint and that blaming is not part of the encounter. Fifth, it is important to identify, point out, call out, and address overt and covert resistant behavior rather than avoid these behaviors. Instead of being fearful of accepting and hearing strong feelings and emotions, it is critical that we understand and discuss the source of these reactions. Sixth, avoid being side-tracked by resistant behavior since it is a barrier that distracts from the social justice goal. This involves staying focused on the purpose and aim of the social justice work. Seventh, when resistant behavior appears as a personal attack, it is important to not become defensive. In such moments, it is important to remember what our training taught us, understanding the source of the resistance and defensiveness, keeping in mind process rather than content. Eighth, when appropriate, incorporate exercises that help individuals identify the source of their resistance. Ninth, establish small steps toward social activism that are achievable, rather than propose goals that will require multiple steps to achieve and may be overwhelming. Tenth, find ways to reward or celebrate small social justice action steps. This is important to incorporate throughout the process of change, acknowledging progress along the way. And, finally, eleventh, always exercise patience, persistence, and tenacity.

SUMMARY

To successfully work with clients, families, stakeholders, and communities in promoting social action, social justice–oriented counselors and psychologists must have awareness and understanding about the principles, theories, and models of social change. With this knowledge mental health professionals are adequately prepared to identify and deal with hesitancy and resistance to change. Movement toward growth, development, and justice may be difficult, even when there is acknowledgment that circumstances are unhealthy or oppressive. This chapter discusses the complexities and stages of the change process along with an examination of the relationship between the positive use and abuse of power and social change and social justice. The chapter also outlines 16 principles of social change along with strategies for dealing with resistance.

DISCUSSION QUESTIONS

1. After reading the chapter, please interpret in your own words the following passage: "Social justice and human rights work are closely intertwined with social change. This is in contrast to general change models (i.e., individuals changing personal behaviors). . . . We would define social change to include the changing or altering of systems . . . and structures . . . that hinder, obstruct, block, impede, and interfere with positive and optimal growth, development, opportunities, and physical and psychological well-being for all individuals, families, groups, and communities."
2. How do you think global communications has impacted the idea of change in different parts of the world? What are some of the strengths? What are some of the obstacles?
3. Consider Prochaska and DiClemente's (1982) transtheoretical model of change:
   a. Identify one of your personal challenges to change (you can use the one you used in the reflection question). Identify each of the stages you progressed through in making this change and your struggles, decisions, and outcomes.
   b. Examine a community issue that you believe needs to change. Identify each of the stages in changing it, as well as your struggles and decisions and their outcomes.
4. This chapter discusses different meanings of power and the importance of using power in a proactive way.
   a. What type of power do you have as a student or in your work setting?
   b. How would you be able to use proactively your power in these settings?
   c. Can you identify others in your university or work site who have significant power? Are they using their power in positive ways or not? What would you do to change the situation?
5. The chapter mentions one of the social change principles as "effective change agents combine learning and teaching" and discussed the problems of personal ego getting in the way of change.
   a. Identify your challenges with regards to these two statements.
   b. How can you help others understand the importance of these two concepts?

REFERENCES

Bemak, F. (1996). Street researchers: A new paradigm redefining future research with street children. *Childhood*, 3(2), 147–156. https://doi.org/10.1177/0907568296003002002

Bemak, F., & Chung, R. C-Y. (2018). Race dialogues in group psychotherapy: Key issues in training and practice. *International Journal of Group Psychotherapy, 69*(2), 172–191. https://doi.org/10.1080/00207 284.2018.1498743

Bond, R., & Smith, P. B. (1996). Culture and conformity: A meta-analysis of studies using Asch's (1952b, 1956) line judgment task. *Psychological Bulletin, 119*(1), 111–137. https://doi.org/10.1037/ 0033-2909.119.1.111

Brogan, M. M., Prochaska, J. O., & Prochaska, J. M. (1999). Predicting termination and continuation status in psychotherapy using the transtheoretical model. *Psychotherapy: Theory, Research, Practice, Training, 36*(2), 105–113. https://doi.org/10.1037/h0087773

Chung, R. C-Y., Bemak, F., Talleyrand, R. M., & Williams, J. (2018). Challenges in promoting race dialogues in psychology training: Race and gender perspectives. *Counseling Psychologist, 1*–28. https://doi.org/ 10.1177/0011000018758262

Cialdini, R. B., & Goldstein, N. J. (2004). Social influence: Compliance and conformity. *Annual Review of Psychology, 55*(1), 591–621. https://doi.org/10.1146/annurev.psych.55.090902.142015

Clauss-Ehlers, C. S., Chiriboga, D. A., Hunter, S. J., Roysircar, G., & Tummala-Narra, P. (2019). APA Multicultural Guidelines executive summary: Ecological approach to context, identity, and intersectionality. *American Psychologist, 74*(2), 232–244. https://doi.org/10.1037/amp0000382

Cowan, G., & Egan, M. (1979). *People in systems: A model for development in the human-service professions and education.* Brooks/Cole.

DiClemente, C. C., & Hughes, S. L. (1990). Stages of change profiles in outpatient alcoholism treatment. *Journal of Substance Abuse, 2*(2), 217–235. https://doi.org/10.1016/S0899-3289(05)80057-4

DiClemente, C. C., & Prochaska, J. O. (1985). Processes and stages of change: Coping and competence in smoking behavior change. In S. Shiffman & T. A. Wills (Eds.), *Coping and substance abuse* (pp. 319–343). Academic Press.

DiClemente, C. C., Prochaska, J. O., & Gillbertini, M. (1985). Self-efficacy and the stages of self-change of smoking. *Cognitive Therapy and Research, 9*(2), 181–200. https://doi.org/10.1007/BF01204849

Fromm, E. (1942). *The fear of freedom.* Routledge.

Gun Violence Archive. (2022, Jan 17). Gun violence archive 2021. https://www.gunviolencearchive.org/ past-tolls

Homan, M. S. (2008). *Promoting community change: Making it happen in the real world* (4th ed.). Brooks/Cole.

Homan, M. S. (2018). *Rules of the game: Lessons from the field of community change* (2nd ed.). Routledge.

Hubble, M. A., Duncan, B. L., & Miller, S. D. (1999). *The heart & soul of change: What works in therapy.* American Psychological Association. https://doi.org/10.1037/11132-000

Krebs, P., Norcross, J. C., Nicholson, J. M., & Prochaska, J. O. (2018). Stages of change and psychotherapy outcomes: A review and meta-analysis. *Journal of Clinical Psychology, 74*(11), 1964–1979. https://doi.org/ 10.1002/jclp.22683

Lam, C. S., McMahon, B. T., Priddy, D. A., & Gehred-Schultz, A. (1988). Deficit awareness and treatment performance among traumatic head injury adults. *Brain Injury, 2*(3), 235–242. https://doi.org/10.3109/ 02699058809150947

Lambert, M. J., Shapiro, D. A., & Bergin, A. E. (1986). The effectiveness of psychotherapy. In S. L. Garfield & A. E. Bergin (Eds.), *Handbook of psychotherapy and behavior change* (3rd ed., pp. 157–212). Wiley.

McConnaughy, E. A., DiClemente, C. C., Prochaska, J. O., & Velicer, W. F. (1989). Stages of change in psycho-therapy: A follow-up report. *Psychotherapy, 26*(4), 494–503. https://doi.org/10.1037/h0085468

Norcross, J. C., & Prochaska, J. O. (1986a). Psychotherapist heal thyself: I. The psychological distress and self-change of psychologists, counselors, and laypersons. *Psychotherapy: Theory, Research, Practice, Training, 23*(1), 102–114. https://doi.org/10.1037/h0085577

Norcross, J. C., & Prochaska, J. O. (1986b). Psychotherapist heal thyself: II. The self-initiated and therapy-facilitated change of psychological distress. *Psychotherapy: Theory, Research, Practice, Training, 23*(3), 345–356. https://doi.org/10.1037/h0085622

Prochaska, J. O. (1999). How do people change, and how do we change to help people? In M. A. Hubble, B. L. Duncan, & S. D. Miller (Eds.), *The heart & soul of change: What works in therapy* (pp. 227–258). American Psychological Association. https://doi.org/10.1037/11132-007

Prochaska, J. O., & DiClemente, C. C. (1982). Transtheoretical therapy: Toward a more integrative model of change. *Psychotherapy: Theory, Research & Practice, 19*(3), 276–288. https://doi.org/10.1037/h0088437

Prochaska, J. O., & DiClemente, C. C. (1992). Stages of change in the modification of problem behaviors. In M. Hersen, R. M. Eisler, & P. M. Miller (Eds.), *Progress in behavior modification* (pp. 184–214). Sycamore Press.

Prochaska, J. O., DiClemente, C. C., & Norcross, J. C. (1992). In search of how people change: Applications to the addictive behaviors. *American Psychologist, 47*(9), 1102–1114. https://doi.org/10.1037/0003-066X.47.9.1102

Prochaska, J. O., Norcross, J. C., & DiClemente, C. C. (1994). *Changing for good.* William Morrow.

Ridley, C. R. (2005). *Overcoming unintentional racism in counseling and therapy: A practitioner's guide to intentional intervention* (2nd ed.). Sage.

Robinson, B., & Hanna, M. G. (1994). Lessons for academics from grassroots community organizing: A case study—the industrial areas foundation. *Journal of Community Practice, 1*(4), 63–94. https://doi.org/10.1300/J125v01n04_05

Rubin, H., & Rubin, I. (1986). *Community organizing and development.* Merrill.

Singh, A., Nassar, S. C., Arredondo, P., & Toporek, R. (2020). The past guides the future: Implementing the new Multicultural and Social Justice Competencies. *Journal of Counseling & Development, 98*(3), 238–252. https://doi.org/10.1002/jcad.12319

Smith, M. L., Glass, G. V., & Miller, T. I. (1980). *The benefits of psychotherapy.* Johns Hopkins University Press.

Wampold, B. E. (2015). How important are the common factors in psychotherapy? An update. *World Psychiatry, 14*(3), 270–277. https://doi.org/10.1002/wps.20238

Wrong, D. (1995). *Power: Its forms, bases and uses.* Transaction Publishers.

CHAPTER 15

STUDENT CHAPTER

Proud and Comfortable with My Identity: Deconstructing
Internalized Racism, Colonialism, Sexism, and
Religious Intolerance

Sara Fodil-Cherif

I have always been drawn to a career in counseling which is rooted in social justice. Since human beings are innately social beings, they will continuously affect and be affected by their surrounding environment. Therefore, from a counseling lens, I needed to find an approach which recognized that presenting psychological issues may not always be attributed to the psyche but can rather be symptomatic of external, more pervasive issues tied to the individual's environment. For many marginalized individuals, these issues can stem from exposure to daily social injustices such as racism, economic inequity, discrimination on the basis of identity, and all other forms of oppression. These stressors can be chronic and part of everyday life. Social justice counseling, as outlined by Drs. Chung and Bemak (2012), actively addresses these issues within the therapeutic process and collectively with clients and communities to help change unjust systems from the ground up. Social justice counseling also emphasizes the need for counselors to engage in intense, self-reflective dialogue which can bring into awareness counselor bias and assumptions with regards to social issues. It is not until these biases are identified and addressed that counselors can truly begin to do social justice work. The self-reflective component can also bring into awareness the counselor's own experiences with social justice and how these events have shaped their worldview and values over time. Personally, my own experiences with social justice have motivated me to enter this field and seek out work with various underprivileged groups in society and in the world.

To share some of my experiences, here is a little background about me. I am a 28-year-old female immigrant who is originally from Algeria. I moved here with my parents and two siblings when I was nine. Although I have made America my home, I still have childhood memories of growing up in a different part of the world, and I still feel connected to my country of origin. I feel fortunate to have had the opportunity to connect with and identify with two very distinct cultures because I believe cross-cultural identities develop open-mindedness and wider perspectives. I also sometimes feel torn because, like many other immigrants, I do not feel a complete sense of belonging in either culture. In fact, I have grown up feeling very different because of my race, ethnicity, and religion. A feeling that would quickly subside once I would set foot in my native country. As a woman, I also experienced and continue to experience gender discrimination, an issue that seems to remain with me no matter where I am in the world. I do not know a world that does not take issue with *any* aspects of my identity. I have come to accept that this is my reality, but also that this is a problematic reality which needs to change.

I have experienced harassment, double standards, mansplaining, and blatant disrespect from men who felt threatened and inhibited by my mere existence. I have been told I was "overqualified" for a job and have been discouraged from higher education by professors who said graduate school would "intimidate" a person like me. I have had my hair yanked, chopped, and fried by hairdressers who said I did not have "good hair." I am almost always selected for "random" checks at airports.

These are just a few injustices which impact a large number of people like me. Having also endured intergenerational trauma byway of European/White colonialism, this added a certain complexity to my self-reflection which I was not expecting. Prior to entering this graduate program, I had not quite taken the time to process the effects of colonialism on myself and other individuals in my life. This program allowed for that. In fact, when one of my classmates asked: "What does it mean to have a White identity? And have any of the people of color in the class experienced letting go of their cultural identity in order to fit in with White identity?" This question took me straight back to memories of my childhood growing up in an emerging, post-colonial society. I remembered dinner table stories with my beloved grandfather, an Algerian independence war veteran. His stories were recollections of the torture he endured from French soldiers who captured him during the war. He recalled massacres and other merciless acts of terror done to people on the basis of their race and the perceived inferiority of their race. He also recalled the heroism and resilience of people who refused to define themselves within the confines of oppression and collectively stood up for justice. I was not the only child who grew up listening to stories of trauma. Many Algerians today could attest to the generational transmission of trauma within their own families and the effect this had on their racial identity.

So, regarding the question about letting go of cultural identity in order to fit in with White identity: as a child and teenager growing up in Western society, though my developmental need was to belong, my historical context of trauma with White supremacist identity could not allow me to forget my culture of origin for the sake of belonging to the dominant group. This, combined with the ongoing racism and discrimination I was experiencing in my new culture, further outcast me as "the other."

I continued to struggle with this internal conflict of the desire to fit in while fearing the loss of an identity that my ancestors fought so hard to preserve. I always questioned myself: "If I fully let go of my Algerian identity, would I *really* gain the acceptance I was looking for?" and "Why did I really need to be accepted by White people?" I did not get the answers to these questions until I entered adulthood and realized that my contemplation of White identity had always been from a colonial frame of mind, whether conscious or unconscious.

This is evidence of the pervasiveness and long-term effects of racial oppression on the human psyche. Today, I am proud and comfortable with my identity in its many shades and layers. My parents and grandparents have modeled the strength, courage, and resilience I needed to build to stand up against oppression in all forms. They have taught me to recognize my hardships, but to then learn from my experiences and move forward in transforming my world and the world of others. This has helped me choose a career which facilitates positive change not just in individuals but also in the greater society. My professors continue to give me the courage to speak up against oppression and develop a critical eye in examining my own internalizations of these issues. The more I know about myself, the more I will be able to address my biases and assumptions and be there for my clients.

The experiences I have had with social justice have also pushed me to stay informed about today's socioeconomic-political challenges and to continue to develop a sense of awareness about the issues faced by various marginalized groups today. If I were privileged in my racial, gender, and religious identity, I would probably have to endure a longer, more tedious journey in developing interest in the lives of the underprivileged and empathizing with their struggles. Through the various readings and discussions I have done in this program, I have also learned that one must first develop an awareness about one's own privilege (on the basis of race, gender, socioeconomic status, etc.) before engaging in social justice discourse. My reasoning for this is that being someone who has experienced injustice gives you a predisposed motivation or *hunger* to seek justice for yourself or others. Coming from a place of privilege means that you would not have had much contact with the effects and consequences of social injustice. Therefore, not being touched directly by injustice, not knowing it, means that you might have to access some kind of "precursor" of motivation, which might allow you to develop a reason to confront injustice. I find that this is a harder task that not everyone who is simply "passionate" about social justice work can accomplish.

A key lesson I have learned from the social justice class has been that the most effective way of working through the egoic detachments of privilege is to fully immerse one's self in the world of the underprivileged and to engage in open, honest dialogue. I have learned that only then can one begin to understand issues of social justice. After having taken the course, it seems impossible that the work of a social justice counselor can be achieved from afar. As Dr. Chung always emphasized, true social justice counseling involves working in connection, in partnership, in alliance, and in advocacy with and for others.

My plan moving forward with developing my social justice skills is to step out of my comfort zone and meet and bond with others who are "unlike" me. I might find more similarities than differences between us simply through dialogue. I also want to nurture my cross-cultural identity, visit my country of origin whenever I can, and welcome the diversity in knowledge, contact, and history that this country can give me. I also want to build and maintain a support network with other social justice counselors to exchange ideas and information about the field. Last, I want to continue to educate myself about social justice, not just through research and literature, but also through direct contact with people faced by these hardships. *They* are the experts in this field.

REFERENCE

Chung, R. C-Y., & Bemak, F. (2012). *Social justice counseling: The next steps beyond multiculturalism.* Sage.

CHAPTER 16

LEADERSHIP AND SOCIAL JUSTICE

Rita Chi-Ying Chung and Frederic P. Bemak

One of the criticisms I've faced over the years is that I'm not aggressive enough or
assertive enough or maybe somehow, because I'm empathetic, it means I'm weak.
I totally rebel against that. I refuse to believe that you cannot be both compassionate
and strong.

—Jacinda Ardern, Prime Minister of New Zealand

The ultimate measure of a man is not where he stands in moments of comfort and
convenience, but where he stands at times of challenge and controversy.

—Martin Luther King, Jr.

A leader is a dealer in hope.

—Napoleon Bonaparte

A leader is best when people barely know he exists, not so good when people obey
and acclaim him, worse when they despise him. But of a good leader who talks little,
when his work is done, his aim fulfilled, they will say: We did it ourselves.

—Lao-Tzu

Leadership and learning are indispensable to each other.

—John F. Kennedy

REFLECTION QUESTIONS

1. Where did you learn about leadership?
2. Recall when you have had an experience as a leader. What was it like?
3. What strengths do you have that would be helpful as a leader?
4. When you have assumed leadership positions or watched others as leaders, what
   qualities did they exhibit that worked? What did they do that didn't work?

5. Who are leaders that you admire? Why do you admire them?
6. What kind of leader do you want to be?
7. What are the things that are holding you back from being a leader on social justice issues?

To eliminate, prevent, and intervene in social injustice and human rights violations it is important that we as psychologists and counselors are equipped with multiple skills, abilities, and capabilities. Chapter 14, on social change, discussed being a change agent as a core element of social justice and human rights work and the importance of understanding and acknowledging that change can be challenging for individuals and systems. With this knowledge we are prepared to deal with resistance to social change. Also mentioned in Chapter 14, to do effective social justice work that promotes change, it is important to acquire leadership skills. This chapter focuses on social justice leadership, beginning with a discussion about the importance of leadership as it relates to social justice and human rights. To provide a foundation for understanding the significance of leadership in social justice work, the chapter provides a brief overview of leadership types and styles, followed by an examination of culture and gender in leadership along with a discussion of social justice leadership in psychotherapy and counseling. Finally, a discussion about leadership characteristics of a social justice and human rights mental health professional is presented.

THE IMPORTANCE OF LEADERSHIP SKILLS IN SOCIAL JUSTICE WORK

With the social injustices that have been accompanying rapid changes in society, there is an increasing need for helping professionals to develop leadership skills. In recognizing this need, major psychology and counseling professional organizations (e.g., American Psychological Association and American Counseling Association) have held national conferences with leadership as a theme, offering numerous workshops, presentations, and seminars on leadership. Even so, leadership skills and qualities have not been emphasized in traditional training or licensure for psychologists and counselors. Although elements of leadership may be found in some of the courses at the doctoral level, there are rarely specific courses or sections of courses on leadership or the infusion of leadership skills at the master's level. Most often, psychologists and counselors who assume leadership positions acquire leadership skills on the job after their graduate training.

For mental health professionals working with social justice and human rights issues, it is important to have leadership skills. To advocate for and with clients and to authentically empower clients, psychologists and counselors must know how to motivate clients and communities to take action and know how to work collaboratively with a wide variety of stakeholders that include clients, their families, communities, agencies, service providers, institutions, and/or organizations (see Chapter 21 on interdisciplinary collaboration). This requires a distinct kind of leadership that is unique to mental health professionals working toward social justice and human rights. To fully understand the uniqueness of leadership in social justice and human rights, the following is a brief overview of traditional leadership models.

LEADERSHIP MODELS

Merriam-Webster (n.d.) defines a leader as someone who is a "guide or conductor." Leadership is defined as "the act or instance of leading" (Merriam-Webster, n.d.). Much of the literature on leadership and leadership styles in the field of psychology and counseling relates to organizations or agencies.

HISTORICAL OVERVIEW
GREAT MAN STUDIES

The earliest studies on leadership were called the "great man studies" (Short & Greer, 2002) that focused on men in leadership positions. The methodology used in this approach was to identify universal personality traits of great military, political, and industrial male leaders, with the assumption that the qualities and skills of great men were genetic traits that were identifiable and could not be acquired through training or experience.

TRAIT APPROACH

It was hoped that by using the trait approach (Mann, 1959; Stogdill, 1948) there could be a more precise measure of leadership characteristics. This approach assumed that leadership was a one-way process, so that only leaders could possess special leadership qualities. Leadership traits were identified through interviews, observations, tests, checklists, and rating scales. The identified leadership traits were grouped into five categories: (1) capacity (e.g., intelligence, alertness, verbal facility, originality, and judgment), (2) achievement (e.g., scholarship, knowledge, and athletic achievement), (3) responsibility (e.g., dependability, initiative, persistence, aggressiveness, self-confidence, and desire to excel), (4) participation (e.g., activity, sociability, cooperation, adaptability, and humor), and (5) status (socioeconomic, position, and popularity) (Mann, 1959; Stogdill, 1948). There were two major criticisms to the trait approach. The first questioned the universality of traits and their transferability to different circumstances. Could a leader in one situation who possessed one or a combination of these traits actually emerge as a leader in different circumstances? The second criticism was the reliability and validity of the methodologies used given the lack of consistency among the measures employed to identify the leadership traits. Despite the concerns, the approach did identify certain personality traits thought to be critical for leadership, such as intelligence, responsibility, and participation (Short & Greer, 2002). We add a third criticism in that the leadership traits were identified exclusively among men, discounting the long history of women who have exhibited exceptional leadership capabilities.

SITUATIONAL LEADERSHIP

The situational leadership approach emerged given that the trait approach was unable to predict efficacy as a leader across different settings (Hersey & Blanchard, 1969). This approach viewed leadership as a response to group characteristics, such as size, homogeneity, stability, satisfaction, and cohesion. Group characteristics were measured through interviews with leaders and group members, observations using sociometric instruments, ratings of group members' performance on simulation exercises, and analyses of group procedures. Interestingly, situational leadership faced criticisms similar to those leveled against the trait approach.

BEHAVIORAL APPROACH

The behavioral approach focused on leadership behaviors observed by group members (Short & Greer, 2002). A variety of settings were investigated, ranging from airliners to schools. The Leadership Behavior Description Questionnaire (LBDQ) was developed to observe leaders; it consisted of two factors: consideration and initiating structure (Schriesheim & Stogdill, 1975). The consideration factor is the human relations dimension, referring to the leader's relationships and ability to relate to group members. Thus, if Kris was in a leadership position, then the consideration factor would examine Kris's relationship to others, if there was a difference in relationships to women versus men, older versus younger colleagues, those who are physically challenged, those identified as LGBTQI, and those from different racial or ethnic backgrounds? In comparison, the initiating structure factor refers to the task dimension or the leader's organizational abilities, seeing how effective Kris is when working at the job itself and getting the work done.

CONTINGENCY THEORY

Contingency theory evolved from a combination of behavioral approaches, situational leadership, and personality traits. This theory builds on the belief that leadership characteristics depend on a multitude of factors, such as specific tasks, the presenting situation, leader and member relationships, leader personality, and group characteristics (Fiedler, 1978; Hersey et al., 1979; House & Mitchell, 1974; Tannenbaum & Schmidt, 1973). Therefore, when considering "What constitutes a leader?" contingency theorists would respond, "It depends" (Short & Greer, 2002). Even so, there are different opinions held by contingency theorists with regard to whether it is possible for leaders to change their administrative and personal style in different situations. Some argued that it is not possible for leaders to change their style, and therefore it is better to place leaders in situations that match their personal leadership style and the demands of the situations (Fiedler, 1978). Others (e.g., Hersey & Blanchard, 1969) postulate that leadership qualities and styles are adaptable and can change to fit the task and needs of the group in different situations.

DIVERSITY IN LEADERSHIP

As mentioned previously, leadership skills are a key component to doing effective social justice–oriented work. However, the majority of the mainstream literature on leadership skills has concentrated on leaders of organizations and companies, emphasizing a Western, heterosexual, male perspective. Leaders of color and women leaders, along with civil rights, social justice, and human rights leaders, have been overlooked in this discussion. With increasing global interconnectedness resulting in multinational organizations that reflect diverse national and global populations, it is important that leadership positions also mirror this diversity. The dominant White, heterosexual, male leader paradigm has inhibited the unique leadership approaches, perspectives, and experiences of individuals coming from backgrounds outside the dominant leadership paradigm. Diverse individuals not only bring with them an expanded representation, but also the ability to navigate both majority and minority cultures that translates to an overall better approach to solving problems (Eagly & Chin, 2010).

BOX TEXT 16.1 SIXTEEN-YEAR-OLD CLIMATE ACTIVIST BECAME *TIME*'S 2019 PERSON OF THE YEAR

Sixteen-year-old Swedish climate activist Greta Thunberg created the "Fridays for Future" movement in 2018. She began by skipping school and simply sitting outside of the Swedish parliament building every Friday to protest the lack of commitment by world leaders in combatting climate change. Otherwise known as School Strike for Climate, the movement spread worldwide as students all over the globe began protesting by walking out of schools to gain national and international attention and demand those in power to take immediate and actual steps to curb climate change. As the movement gained prominence, Greta met with students and leaders around the world, even speaking at the UN Climate Action Summit, reprimanding world leaders for not taking action to protect children's futures, urging the UN to look to children for hope. On September 20, 2019, Greta led approximately 4 million people, spanning 161 countries, in the largest climate strike in history. When asked why she began the strike, Greta responded that she has been thinking about the lack of action reducing the impact of climate change since she was eight years old and didn't understand why adults were not acting. Greta has autism, which she explains as a source of her strength as an activist. In December 2019, *Time Magazine* named Greta Thunberg "Person of the Year."

Source: Woodward, A. (2019, Dec 11). How 16-year-old Greta Thunberg —Time's 2019 person of the year — became the face of climate activism in just one year. Business Insider. https://www.businessinsider.com/greta-thunberg-bio-climate-change-activist-2019-9

With growing national and global diversity there is a need to go beyond studying interactions between gender, race, and leadership and include an array of identities, such as religion, age, sexual orientation, and ability status, as well as to focus on the intersectionality of identities. Embracing diverse leadership styles expands the definition of leadership to be more inclusive by challenging traditionally held views and biases of who can be a leader. Eagly and Chin (2010) present examples of diverse leadership perspectives, noting that, in general, people of color are more concerned about integrity and justice; African American women's style is generally self-confident and assertive; Asian Americans often adopt collectivistic-oriented leadership styles, emphasizing harmony among group members; and sexual minority leaders are generally found to be more adaptable and embrace change. These qualities are important to keep in mind, given growing national and global diversity and the need for leaders to reflect this diverse population. In addition, carrying leadership attributes specific to one's diverse background may enhance performance, a greater openness to cultural differences, and possible openness to social justice issues. Applegate et al. (2009) noted the extensive discourse on the issue of visibility and invisibility in leadership, highlighting the importance of incorporating diversity in the practice of and research about leadership.

GENDER DIFFERENCES IN LEADERSHIP

Women are more prominent in the helping professions as compared with their male counterparts, yet leadership in the professional organizations does not reflect its membership. Take for example psychology, where, in 2018, 71% of active U.S. psychologists were women (American Psychological Association [APA], 2020), however, within the APA's history of 129 years, only 19 APA presidents have been women (APA, 2021). Similarly, approximately 49.6% of the world's population are women, and, although women are increasingly involved in high-level politics globally, they remain underrepresented in state and governmental leadership positions (Vogelstein & Bro, 2020). For example, as of July 2020, less than 10%, or 19 out of 193 countries, have women as heads of state or government (Vogelstein & Bro, 2021). In the United States, Kamala Harris is the first woman and first woman of color to be a vice president, and she was the third woman in U.S. history to be chosen as a VP candidate. We encourage you to research statistics about women in leadership positions in your professional organizations, workplaces, communities, state, and government.

Research comparing leadership styles of women and men shows similarities and differences, finding gender-influenced or gender-related styles but not gender-specific leadership styles (Tarule et al., 2009). A meta-analysis found a tendency for women to lead in a more democratic and participative ways, while men tended to be more autocratic and directive (Eagly & Johnson, 1990). Women are associated with communal or more relational approaches to leadership (Braun et al., 2018), more concerned with human aspects, interpersonal factors, and the morale and welfare of the organization. In contrast, men are associated with embodying agentic or more dominant forms of leadership, emphasizing a more rational, task-oriented focus and the performance and accomplishment of activities (Chin et al., 2018; Eagly & Johnson, 1990; Tarule et al., 2009).

This may be attributed to multiple variables rather than gender stereotypes or biological differences, including such issues as the underrepresentation of women in executive, administrative, and managerial positions and subsequent lack of female role models; the inequalities and inequities in the treatment of men and women in organizations; salary differences; status differences in organizations; and gender role stereotypes that depict women leaders as caring and nurturing rather than having stereotypical masculine leadership characteristics. All of these factors not only can influence how one leads, but also limit opportunities for women to emerge as leaders (Bordas, 2007; Chin et al., 2018; Eagly & Chin, 2010; Tarule et al., 2009). With restricted opportunities and underrepresentation of women in leadership positions, women may be viewed as a minority group with token status (Kanter, 1977), raising questions about how they became leaders. As a result, many women in leadership positions have advanced by conforming to and meeting the expectations of the dominant stereotypical masculine role (Ayman & Korabik, 2010).

In addition to structural challenges, women leaders also encounter gender stereotyping and misogynistic perspectives. For example, being physically attractive is viewed as a more helpful characteristic for women than men, while displaying emotions is viewed as harmful to women leaders in both politics and business as compared to male colleagues (Menasce Horowitz et al., 2018). Being ambitious and assertive for men is viewed as an advantage and a strength, yet for women it is regarded as a detriment (Menasce Horowitz et al., 2018; Sanbonmatsu, 2020). An example could be seen in Hillary Clinton, the first woman to ever be nominated to run for the U.S. presidency in 2016. She was a highly qualified U.S. presidential candidate given her previous role as the U.S. Secretary of State, and yet she was subjected to a continual bombardment of public misogynistic questioning, and attacks undermining her leadership abilities (Sanbonmatsu, 2020). Such misogynistic attitudes, values, and behavior may be a reason why fewer women attain leadership positions. Even though, in 2020, there were more women (23.7%) in the U.S. Congress (127 out of 535 members) (Center for American Women and Politics, 2020), gender-based discrimination is, unfortunately, still operating (Sanbonmatsu, 2020). This is evident in the covert, subtle, and unintentional forms of discrimination women experience despite the U.S. Civil Rights Act (1964) that prohibits employment discrimination. Eagly and Chin (2010) suggest that the pretense of selecting the "best candidate for the job" disguises microaggressions and implicit biases toward women.

Thus, women leaders are often viewed as incongruent with both societal gender roles and successful leadership stereotypes. Women's leadership abilities are evaluated by gender stereotypes (e.g., subordination, family, group and community orientation, kind, warm, and gentle) that don't fit into the masculine traits and stereotypes of leaders being dominant, competent, confident, ambitious, and self-sufficient. This stereotypical mismatch creates confusion, prejudice, and discrimination against women pursuing or in leadership positions, causing them to be perceived as deficient in leadership skills. Consequently, women leaders are caught in a double bind. To succeed in leadership positions that are Western male dominated, they must conform, operate, act, and behave similarly to male colleagues while simultaneously displaying female traits, such as being warm and friendly. This places women leaders in a challenging situation since they may be assessed as being either overly masculine or feminine (Eagly & Chin, 2010). Therefore, by altering leadership styles to fit into

BOX TEXT 16.2 PAKISTANI ACTIVIST FOR FEMALE EDUCATION IS YOUNGEST NOBEL PRIZE LAUREATE

Malala Yousafzai is a Pakistani activist for girls' education and is the youngest Nobel Prize laureate. In 2007, the Taliban began to control northwestern Pakistan where Malala lived. Cultural activities such as dancing and watching TV were prohibited. The Taliban strongly opposed girls being educated and banned girls from attending schools, destroying approximately 400 schools. Malala, alongside her father, criticized the Taliban. She advocated for girls' right to education by using media and public campaigns. For example, on Pakistani TV she said: "How dare the Taliban take away my basic right to education?" and started to anonymously blog on the British Broadcasting Corporation website. Her voice grew louder, and, over three years, she and her father became known throughout Pakistan for advocating for girls' right and access to a free, quality education. In 2011, she was awarded Pakistan's National Youth Peace Prize.

On October 9, 2012, at 15 years old, while on a bus going home from school, Malala was shot three times in the head by two Taliban members. After recovering from multiple surgeries in 2013, Malala spoke on her 16th birthday at the United Nations in New York about girls' right to be educated. She co-founded with her father the Malala Fund and traveled to Jordan to meet Syrian refugees, to Kenya to meet young female students, and to northern Nigeria where she spoke out in support of the abducted girls who were kidnapped by Boko Haram, a terrorist group which, like the Taliban, tries to stop girls from going to school.

In October 2014, Malala, along with Indian children's rights activist Kailash Satyarthi, was named a Nobel Peace Prize winner. At age 17, she became the youngest person to receive this prize. Accepting the award, Malala reaffirmed that "This award is not just for me. It is for those forgotten children who want education. It is for those frightened children who want peace. It is for those voiceless children who want change."

Sources: Malala Fund. https://malala.org/
Malala Yousafzai. Nobel Prize 2014. https://www.nobelprize.org/prizes/peace/2014/yousafzai/biogr aphical/

the stereotypical masculine definitions of leadership, women are forced to adopt an androgynous leadership style despite the research demonstrating women leaders as being more democratic and participative (Eagly & Chin, 2010). In summary, it is clear that the underrepresentation of women in leadership roles is not because of a lack of qualifications or skills but related to barriers and challenges that put women at a disadvantage when compared to White males, who have a preferential access to leadership opportunities and roles that are reinforced by gender role stereotypes (Eagly & Chin, 2010).

Unlike White women who experience gender disparities, women of color experience discrimination based on gender and racial biases. Given very limited research on the intersection of race, gender, and leadership (Chin, 2010), and leadership theories and models being historically based on White males, women of color leaders experience greater scrutiny and pressure to live up those standards (Chin, 2010; Sanchez-Hucles & Davis, 2010). This intersectionality of racial and gender stereotypes may lead to perceiving women of color leaders as lacking essential leadership qualities. Examples of this can be seen in racial biases and stereotypes of African American women as being antagonistic and lacking competence, Latinx being uneducated and unambitious, and Asian Americans as quiet and unassertive. These biases can result in self-fulfilling prophecies that undermine women of color from seeking out leadership opportunities (Eagly & Chin, 2010). Stereotype threat research reinforces these findings (Steele, 1997). The interaction of gender and racial stereotypes and societal norms about gender and leadership can create more pressure for women of color, causing them to doubt their leadership abilities and feel anxious about perceived racial stereotypes. This situation becomes more complex if we broaden the examination of leadership abilities from a race and gender interaction to include the intersectionality of numerous identities—for example, the leadership style of a transgender person of color who is physically challenged.

LEADERSHIP STYLES RELATED TO SOCIAL JUSTICE WORK

As we reflected on the need for psychologists and counselors to be social justice–oriented leaders and examined the leadership literature, it was clear that there is a paucity of information about diverse leadership styles and their relationship to social justice and human rights work. As we discussed earlier, leadership is typically associated with organizational development and business rather than with mental health, psychology, and counseling. An organizational leader must be able to employ a vision that moves an organization forward while also dealing effectively with individuals in the system. Thus, leadership includes systemic, interpersonal, instructional, and imagination skills, all of which are related to social justice–oriented work. Six different leadership styles that have relevance to social justice work are discussed next (see Box Text 16.3).

AUTOCRATIC LEADERSHIP

An autocratic leader is often viewed by followers as one who is distant and unapproachable, makes independent decisions, and has full control (Burke et al., 2007). These leaders typically have difficulties in delegating tasks and activities since by doing so they diminish their control. I (Fred) encountered an example of such a leader when I was in Colombia, consulting for a large social service agency. The director of the agency was highly authoritarian and unapproachable. Staff were afraid to approach him or discuss with him problems they were having. These traits were in direct contrast to those of the deputy director, who combined effective leadership with laughing, joking, and personal engagement with staff. Autocratic leadership style was exemplified by the director of the Colombian agency, dictating that employees were followers, docile, obedient, passive, and expected to obey orders. Autocratic leadership is difficult to employ doing social justice-oriented work.

BENEVOLENT LEADERSHIP

A benevolent leader is frequently viewed as having a parental style (Burke et al., 2007). The leader will listen to subordinates before making decisions, but with an expectation that laws, rules, and decisions will be followed to maintain an orderly environment. I (Rita) consulted for Asian social service agencies where the leaders were actually addressed as "Mum" or "Dad." Similar to an ideal relationship between parents and their children, the relationship between the leader and the followers incorporates munificent qualities. The benevolent leader is seen as caring and approachable but is still recognized to have the final say. This style is effective if the leader is highly skilled and the followers depend on those skills for direction and guidance. Although benevolent leadership depends on the leader to provide direction, a very well-accomplished benevolent leader has the potential to be effective doing social justice work.

BUREAUCRATIC LEADERSHIP

In contrast, a bureaucratic leader emphasizes managerial efficiency, focusing on order, clear policies, and rules (Uhl-Bien et al., 2007). This leader will delegate only to those who are skilled and loyal, and they harbor expectations that followers are loyal to the organization. Bureaucratic leaders generally have good interpersonal and social skills, making them approachable and good listeners. Tasks and expectations are clearly defined, and individuals know which tasks and activities will be delegated. Bureaucratic leaders may be able to engage in social justice work, although there could be challenges in encouraging vision and the creativity of staff.

EMPOWERING LEADERSHIP

The empowering leader is usually more democratic and has a participatory and collaborative approach (Burke et al., 2006). This leader is an active listener and clarifier. One potential dilemma for this type of leadership style is finding a balance between institutional demands, personal values, and human needs. The empowering leader is stylistically democratic, committed to making the organization more humane, and willing to modify rules according to personal conscience. Followers expect to be able to participate in some of the decision-making. This type of leadership is more consistent with social justice–oriented work, where one is balancing multiple factors while trying to empower others.

SERVANT LEADERSHIP

Servant leadership is concerned with the quality of interaction within the organization as well as the impact of the organization on society (Avolio et al., 2009). Servant leaders will seek maximum development for employees, foster interdependent governance by peer teams, and encourage group decision-making along with mutual responsibility and collegiality. Followers typically assume greater responsibility and work at high levels of trust and collegiality. Similar to empowering leadership, servant leadership is more aligned with social justice, cultivating autonomy, cooperation, and self-determined directions and decisions.

TRANSFORMATIVE LEADERSHIP

Finally, the sixth leadership style represents the highest level of consciousness (Montuori & Donnelly, 2017) and is rarely found. At this phase, leadership and followership are merged. All activity is interdependent in nature and global in concern. Leaders emphasize improving the balance between the world of material goods and the needs of each human being. The work is focused on issues related to ecology, human rights, reconciliation of conflicting groups, and the creative and humane use of technology. On a continuum of leadership for social justice and human rights–oriented mental health workers, the sixth leadership style is the ideal goal, surpassing even empowerment and servant leadership and is characterized by its values, which are based on equity, fairness, and human rights with regard to clients and organizations.

SOCIAL JUSTICE–ORIENTED LEADERSHIP

The six leadership styles just described (see also Box Text 16.3) have relevance to social justice leadership in mental health in public and private agencies, institutions, and schools.

Lewis et al. (2003) stated that an effective leader in community agencies and organizations has the ability to assist people to realize their potential and contribute to the goals and purpose of an organization. This means that effective leadership can be viewed in part by how leaders facilitate the personal and professional development of the people whom they supervise. This must be combined with vision, which is a core characteristic in leadership. Adding vision to this mix brings in elements of potential and growth, strategic planning skills, implementation strategies, and the ability to envision the future of the organization as a whole (Hasbi, 2012; Senge, 1990). As Senator Robert Kennedy said, adapting from Irish-British playwriter and political activist, George Bernard Shaw, "Some men see things as they are and say, why: I dream things that never were and say, why not" (New York Times, 1968).

Although we believe that some of the perspectives of leadership qualities (such as intelligence, vision, organization, and good interpersonal skills) fit in with mental health social justice work, we acknowledge that the traditional definitions of leadership are based on Western individualistic notions that do not adequately account for differences in culture, gender, and the intersectionality of identities. These differences are especially important when working on issues of social justice and human rights, which may require additional leadership qualities and skills, and they are particularly relevant when working within the framework of cultures that do not adhere to Western notions of individualism, independence, self-responsibility, self-reliance, self-importance, self-development, and so forth.

It is important to note that, as we discuss social justice leadership, we are intentionally avoiding imperialist leadership qualities such as dominance, manipulation, a take-control attitude, "leading the way," "showing people how to," "having all the ideas," etc. Instead we are considering leadership from a more egalitarian, collaborative perspective to promote social change, power balances, and equity. These attributes are similar to some of the qualities of the empowering, servant, and transformative leadership styles. In the following section, we discuss courage as an essential quality for social justice–oriented leadership in mental health, followed by sharing our ideas about leadership, leadership qualities, and leadership skills as they relate to social justice and human rights.

COURAGE AS A DIMENSION OF SOCIAL JUSTICE LEADERSHIP

As leaders working with social justice and human rights issues it is important that we lead by example, by "walking the talk," which involves actually doing social justice work rather than only talking about injustices. Effective human rights leadership requires a degree of courage since the work challenges unjust practices, rules, regulations, policies, and systems. Having the courage to act also involves taking risks since challenging the status quo may result in resistance and negative and hostile responses. We have witnessed individuals who are aware of social injustices, passionate about these issues, and motivated to want to do something, yet they do not take actually take steps to promote social change. As I (Rita) reflected on this, I thought about Saint Augustine's comment in the 4th century: "Hope has two beautiful daughters; their names are Anger and Courage—Anger at the way things are, and Courage to see that they do not remain as they are." Considering Saint Augustine's comment made me think about intense social justice discussions in my graduate classes and why strongly held social justice beliefs and values often did not translate to action. Based on the class discussions there appear to be two sides of the social action leadership coin: fear as a major barrier, and courage as the vital component for social justice–oriented work. This prompted us (Rita and Fred), to investigate how individuals attain social justice courage and take risks that lead to social action (Chung & Bemak, 2023).

Our study found two barriers to social justice action. Not surprisingly, fear was reported as the major barrier to social justice work. Fear was comprised of multiple components including internalized fear, fear of professional and career repercussions, and fear of social justice work having a backlash on clients and stakeholders. The second barrier involved logistical obstacles such as time, supervisory support, and funding. The study also found several factors involved in moving from the cognitive and affective aspects of social justice to social action. Having social justice critical consciousness, principles, conviction, passion, and the willingness to take a risk that leads to action were found to be prerequisites for attaining courage and risk-taking behavior. Adding to the above factors, four other variables were found to lead to social justice courage and risk-taking: (a) participants reported achieving a strong sense of self through the graduate training program due to having a safe and brave space for undergoing in-depth, genuine self-reflection of personal biases, prejudice, privilege, power, and positionality; (b) having positive social support; (c) having role models, such as faculty or peers, who took leadership roles in tackling social justice issues; and (d) having awareness, understanding, and acceptance of potential barriers in doing social action.

Interestingly, recognizing and identifying the source of the barriers to social action are important components for gaining the courage that leads to social justice action (Chung & Bemak, 2023). The findings of the study suggest to us that having courage to do social justice work does not mean an absence of fear; instead, social justice courage is to have the foresight and ability to recognize and critically assess barriers, weighing the pros and cons of one's actions, and psychologically and strategically prepare to deal with the outcome and consequences. This study illuminated some of the skills important in social justice–oriented leadership and complements the vision and ability necessary to identify and acknowledge the barriers, challenges, and fears associated with social activism. The study suggests that the essence of understanding challenges is a critical aspect when preparing to do social justice work, rather than naïvely and blindly jumping into the work.

CHARACTERISTICS OF SOCIAL JUSTICE AND HUMAN RIGHTS LEADERS

The concept of authentic leadership, which has relevance to our work in social justice, challenges traditional principles of leadership that focus on notions of power, dominance, and manipulation (Duignan & Bhindi, 1997). Braun et al. (2018) identified four characteristics that authentic leaders possess: (1) self-awareness, (2) relational transparency, (3) internalized moral perspective, and (4) balanced processing (or willingness to consider different perspectives). Authentic leadership examines empowerment through culture and community-building, decision-making, and the ability to build trusting environments (Block, 1993). Social justice leaders are unique in that they build on these qualities as the foundation for social justice leadership. Therefore, qualities of social justice leaders differ from traditional leadership given the responsiveness to social injustices that support a process built on respect, care, recognition, and empathy (Theoharis, 2007). Furthermore, social justice leaders advocate and speak out, intentionally emphasizing and challenging historical, sociopolitical, and current social injustices (Theoharis, 2007).

The intent of social justice leaders is to alter, change, and dismantle institutions and organizations that uphold inequities and injustices by proactively addressing, (re)claiming, sustaining, and advancing human rights, equity, equality, and fairness in social, economic, political, educational, legal, and medical institutions, organizations, and systems (Goldfarb & Grinberg, 2002). Fine (1994) describes social justice leaders as intentionally *unearthing, disrupting,* and *transforming* existing ideology, policies, institutions, and systems that are socially unjust. She further explains that social justice leaders must break the silence about social injustices and give voice to those who have been silenced (i.e., the oppressed, the disenfranchised, and the marginalized), thus providing hope and vision for the future, emphasizing "what could be" rather than accepting "what is." Finally, Fine (1994) talks about social justice leadership involving the development of reflective consciousness that involves four main competencies: (a) learning to believe the dream is possible, (b) identifying models of equity and justice, (c) deepening administrators' knowledge of self, and (d) fostering a rebellious, oppositional imaginations in others.

As psychologists and counselors, our training taught us about human relations, group dynamics, and communication and interpersonal skills, all of which are essential for social justice leaders. For example, active listening skills enable us to more effectively listen to the ideas, needs, challenges, and concerns of clients, families, colleagues, and supervisees. We know how to create a safe and brave space and environment, one in which others can share their dissatisfaction, discontentment, frustrations, dreams, hopes, recommendations, and suggestions. A clear and insightful understanding of personal and organizational concerns and short- and long-range goals places psychologists and counselors in a unique position to help individuals and groups resolve issues and move forward to achieve personal and organizational goals. Similarly, the combination of verbal and nonverbal communication skills enables social justice–oriented mental health leaders to understand communication at multiple levels and helps forge alliances and partnerships. We are in a distinctive position to facilitate the articulation of a clear vision that includes a commitment by all stakeholders.

Counselors and psychologists are also knowledgeable about group dynamics and group process. We are trained to be cognizant of interpersonal dynamics and to facilitate groups, both skills that are essential in facilitating and promoting social change and human rights. Thus, sitting with a group of people considering a change in programming for homeless children, psychologists and counselors are at an advantage because they not only understand the issues at hand, but they also are skilled in group process and human relations. This type of training is essential for helping professionals, providing an excellent foundation for social justice and human rights work. An example is an article we wrote on race dialogues in group therapy where we discussed the importance of including and facilitating race dialogues within the group setting as a means of attending to group members' experiences of microaggressions, racism, and racial injustices (Bemak & Chung, 2018). Yet it is not only counseling and psychotherapy skills that one needs to be an effective social justice leader. Other skills and qualities are also necessary. We discuss here 14 social justice leadership qualities and characteristics that we see as essential to being an effective social justice leader (see Box Text 16.4).

FOURTEEN CHARACTERISTICS OF A SOCIAL JUSTICE LEADER

1. *Genuineness.* We suggest that authenticity is critical for social justice leaders and has the potential to generate deep-rooted respect, trust, and support. Genuineness is especially important as we forge relationships with clients, families, and communities, creating a safe and brave space for them to discuss challenging issues and engage in difficult, courageous dialogues (Bemak & Chung, 2018; Chung et al., 2018) that promote social change and human rights. Two ways of creating genuineness and authenticity are to demonstrate cultural empathy (Chung & Bemak, 2002) and practice cultural humility (Hook et al., 2013) and social justice humility.

2. *Authentic collaborator.* We, as social justice mental health professionals, must let go of the need to maintain control and power over our clientele. True partnerships mean sharing the vision, ideas, power, and decision-making authority with all

stakeholders (i.e., clients, their families, and their communities). True collaboration, therefore, means social justice leaders are able to give as well as receive directions and instructions from stakeholders, thereby creating a shared collaborative leadership. An example of this was when we (Fred and Rita) developed parent groups to support their children who were failing academically. In those groups, it was essential that everyone—rather than just us as the group leaders—had an equal say over the agenda for group discussions, the content of the discussions, and the decisions of the group.

3. *Courageous risk taker.* Social change, improvements in human rights, and fighting for equity have never taken place without individuals taking risks. As discussed above, there is always a degree of courageous risk-taking involved when trying to create change. Therefore, social justice–oriented leaders must learn how to be courageous in challenging inequities, inequalities, and unfair policies, practices, treatment, and decisions. If we don't take the risk to speak out and take action, we are maintaining the status quo and adding to, perpetuating, reinforcing, and supporting the injustices (Chung & Bemak, 2023). Staying in one's comfort zone means maintaining and reinforcing the status quo.

4. *Challenges systems.* To achieve social justice and human rights requires leaders to have the courage to challenge existing policies, rules, and regulations. Although the expected way of doing things may be what everyone assumes and knows, it is essential for leaders to challenge any status quo that is unjust, unfair, and unequal in the treatment of individuals or groups of people. Challenging systems requires having knowledge about how the system works and its history and sociopolitical viewpoints. With this knowledge social justice leaders can be savvy and creative in finding the most effective approach to create change.

5. *Creativity.* To be a leader in social justice work means thinking beyond what is presented to us. We must explore ideas that extend past typical ways of addressing issues, think outside the box, and remain flexible as we engage in the process of change. Being creative also means having the courage and vision to do things differently and try different strategies and approaches to social change. Chapter 23 discusses creativity and social justice work more in depth.

6. *Motivator.* A leader must have the ability to motivate and energize people. As social justice leaders we are indeed standing on the shoulders of giants who were able to motivate national and international audiences, such as Benazir Bhutto, Nelson Mandela, Stephen Bantu Biko, Frederick Douglass, Golda Meir, Mahatma Gandhi, Indira Gandhi, Phillis Wheatley, the Dalai Lama, Caesar Chavez, Yuri Kochiyama, Harriet Tubman, Abraham Lincoln, Malcolm X, John F. Kennedy, Robert Kennedy, Martin Luther King, Jr., W. E. B. Du Bois, Ida B. Wells, and John Lewis, to name a few. Most of us will be working on a much smaller scale as we focus on individuals and our local, regional, and state communities. We do not have to move a nation or world, yet we still need to know how to motivate people to embrace social justice and human rights. This quality is similar to that described in Jerome Frank's work on persuasion and healing (Frank & Frank, 1991). Frank discussed how mental health professionals must be convincing and persuade clients that psychotherapy, as the selected means of treatment, is helpful. We extend this to say that mental

health professionals must be capable of persuasion and motivation that includes a human rights agenda. Part of being a motivator is instilling hope and belief in a promising and hopeful vision, helping stakeholders move from accepting "what is" to believing in "what could be."

7. *Humility, lacking ego.* In our work, to help others become empowered we must learn to step aside and not interfere with client growth and development. A desired outcome in social justice mental health work is for the client and stakeholders to become self-reliant and no longer need us. This requires that we, as helping professionals, not let our own issues of being needed get in the way and that we allow clients to move on. Part of this process of stepping out of the way involves having the humility to step aside, recognizing that we are not always the ones who have all the answers or understand our clients' problems better than the clients themselves. Rather, we are partners in the process of change. Therefore, we must accept and recognize our own limitations while truly acknowledging others' strengths and growth, while letting go of our egos.

8. *Taking and accepting responsibility.* We live in a world where it is easier to blame others than to take responsibility for our behavior and actions. We hear endless stories from the media of instances where others are blamed, such as an individual suing McDonald's because the coffee was too hot and caused a burn. True leadership is the ability to own up to mistakes, errors, and ideas and plans that did not work, instead of blaming someone else or the system. We must also model taking ownership of our behaviors and actions for our clients and stakeholders. In the same way that counselors and psychologists encourage clients to learn from their mistakes and failures, we also can utilize our errors as opportunities to grow and lead more effectively in the future.

9. *A guide, not an expert.* A social justice leader must assume the role of guide rather than expert. An authentic partnership and redistribution of power requires a guide to facilitate a process of justice and change, not an expert who is always in charge and makes decisions. An aspect of assuming a guiding role stems from Carl Rogers's (1957) work that emphasized trust as a core element in the therapeutic relationship. Therefore, social justice leaders must acknowledge that their clients and stakeholders have something to contribute, and hence they must utilize community and clients' skills, expertise, and resources.

10. *Generates empowerment.* Leaders in social justice are empowerment enhancers. It is essential in striving for social justice and human rights that leaders work toward empowerment for each person and all people, not just for some or a selected few. See Chapter 19 for details about authentic empowerment.

11. *Understands self.* To be effective social justice leaders, we must first understand our own historical, sociopolitical, and cultural values, beliefs, attitudes, worldviews, power, privileges, and positionality. This understanding is similar to our process of acquiring multicultural competencies, when an understanding of how and what we believe helps us to be clear about ways to best help others and prevents our own biases and prejudices from obstructing this process. For example, if a psychologist has negative feelings about immigrants because of embarrassment about their own immigrant parents, they may have difficulty working with a migrant who needs help

adjusting to U.S. culture. Therefore, as a helping professional, one must "know thyself" to be an effective social justice–oriented leader.

12. *Understands, appreciates, and celebrates diversity and inclusion.* As leaders in the field of social transformation, we must not only understand ourselves, but also have a deep appreciation and respect for our clients, their families, and the communities with whom they work. Thus, it is important to know, understand, and accept others' history, the influence of history and contemporary psychopolitical issues on their lives today, the sociopolitical and sociocultural issues that impact their daily lives, and the psychological and ecological factors that have bearing on them as people and groups of people. One aspect of knowing ourselves and our biases and prejudices, is that it helps ensure there are no barriers to respecting and celebrating rather than simply tolerating diversity and inclusion. I (Fred) was very much opposed to the "Teach Tolerance" car bumper stickers that were popular in the United States years ago. When one traces the Latin derivative of the word tolerance, *tolerantia,* it means to "bear" or "endure." This, in my opinion, falls far short of honoring and embracing differences and diversity.

13. *Able to use and understand research and data.* It is essential that social justice leaders use data and research to drive their work. Leadership regarding social change should not be based only on personal opinion, but also be supported by science and data. For example, if mental health professionals are aware of the research about the destructiveness of lead paint on intellectual functioning, they can educate their clients who live in housing that is at risk of lead paint about the research findings to help them better advocate for themselves.

14. *Model for others.* It is essential that leaders for social change become models for others to emulate. In many respects, leaders working toward social justice are paving the way and have many eyes watching them. Being a role model for others is an important step in cultivating the next generation. In other words, we must "walk the talk" not just "talk the talk."

These 14 leadership qualities for social justice leaders provide a challenge for any of us in the mental health field who are trying to facilitate social transformation. Each quality by itself is a challenge, yet, given our training as counselors and psychologists, we are in an ideal position to already be well-grounded in these skills.

SUMMARY

For mental health professionals to incorporate social justice and human rights into their work they must understand social change and be equipped with leadership skills to promote social transformation. This chapter discusses the interface between social justice and leadership, examining six leadership styles, the impact of culture and gender on leadership capabilities, and the importance of having courage as a leader. Fourteen leadership qualities for social justice mental health leaders are described that are key to effectively promoting justice, equity, human rights, and equality.

DISCUSSION QUESTIONS

1. What qualities must a leader have?
2. What are some of the qualities that social justice counselors and psychologists must have?
3. What characteristics do you already have that enable you to be an active counselor/psychologist social justice leader?
4. How do you think your role as a leader will affect (positively or negatively) your clients?
5. How do you think your graduate program has helped you shape your role as a leader? Be specific.
    a. Take a look at the university program mission statement.
    b. What classes have you taken?
    c. Is leadership infused in classes and your graduate program?
    d. Have you been able to put into practice some of these concepts in the community and schools?
6. Think of a social justice and multicultural leader in the mental health profession.
    a. What makes this leader distinctive from other mental health professionals?
    b. What skills does this person have?
    c. How has this person impacted the community and the profession?
7. What are some of your fears or concerns about becoming a leader and advocate?
8. Looking at Box Text 16.3, the six social justice leadership styles, which leadership style is closest to your current style? What leadership style do you aspire to have? How and what do you need to reach your goal of being an effective social justice leader?

REFERENCES

American Psychological Association (APA). (2020). CWS data tool: Demographics of the U.S. psychology workforce. https://www.apa.org/workforce/data-tools/demographics

American Psychological Association (APA). (2021). Former APA presidents. https://www.apa.org/about/governance/president/former-presidents

Applegate, J. H., Earley, P. M., & Tarule, J. M. (2009). Support for women leaders: the visible and invisible. In C. A. Mullen (Ed.), *Leadership and building professional learning communities* (pp. 151–160). Palgrave Macmillan.

Avolio, B. J., Walumbwa, F. O., & Weber, T. J. (2009). Leadership: Current theories, research, and future directions. *Annual Review of Psychology, 60,* 421–449. https://doi.org/10.1146/annurev.psych.60.110707.163621

Ayman, R., & Korabik, K. (2010). Leadership: Why gender and culture matter. *American Psychologist, 65*(3), 157–170. https://doi.org/10.1037/a0018806

Bemak, F., & Chung, R. C-Y. (2018). Race dialogues in group psychotherapy: Key issues in training and practice. *International Journal of Group Psychotherapy, 69*(2), 172–191. https://doi.org/10.1080/00207284.2018.1498743

Block, P. (1993). *Stewardship: Choosing service over self-interest.* Berrett-Koehler.

Bordas, J. (2007, Fall). How salsa, soul, and spirit strengthen leadership. *Leader to Leader, 2007*(46), 35–41. https://doi.org/10.1002/ltl.255

Braun, S., Peus, C., & Frey, D. (2018). Connectionism in action: Exploring the links between leader prototypes, leader gender, and perceptions of authentic leadership. *Organizational Behavior and Human Decision Processes, 149*, 129–144. https://doi.org/10.1016/j.obhdp.2018.10.003

Burke, C. S., Sims, D. E., Lazzara, E. H., & Salas, E. (2007). Trust in leadership: A multi-level review and integration. *Leadership Quarterly, 18*(6), 606–632. http://doi.org/10.1016/j.leaqua.2007.09.006

Burke, C. S., Stagl, K. C., Klein, C., Goodwin, G. F., Salas, E., & Halpin, S. M. (2006). What type of leadership behaviors are functional in teams? A meta-analysis. *Leadership Quarterly, 17*(3), 288–307. http://doi.org/10.1016/j.leaqua.2006.02.007

Center for American Women and Politics. (2020). Women in the U. S. Congress 2020. https://cawp.rutgers.edu/women-us-congress-2020

Chin, J. L. (2010). Introduction to the special issue on diversity and leadership. *American Psychologist, 65*(3), 150–156. https://doi.org/10.1037/a0018716

Chin, J. L., Ladha, A., & Li, V. (2018). Women's leadership within a global perspective. In S. L. Cook, A. Rutherford, C. B. Travis, J. W. White, W. S. Williams, & K. F. Wyche (Eds.), *APA handbook of the psychology of women: Perspectives on women's private and public lives* (pp. 565–581). American Psychological Association. doi:10.1037/0000060-030

Chung, R. C-Y., & Bemak, F. (2002). The relationship between culture and empathy in cross-cultural counseling. *Journal of Counseling and Development, 80*, 154–159. https://doi.org/10.1002/j.1556-6678.2002.tb00178.x

Chung, R. C-Y., & Bemak, F. (2023). Courage in action: The call for psychology to social justice action. Counseling Department, George Mason University. https://education.gmu.edu/counseling/

Chung, R. C-Y., Bemak, F., Talleyrand, R. M., & Williams, J. (2018). Challenges in promoting race dialogues in psychology training: Race and gender perspectives. *Counseling Psychologist,* 1–28. https://doi.org/10.1177/0011000018758262

Duignan, P. A., & Bhindi, N. (1997). Authenticity in leadership: An emerging perspective. *Journal of Educational Administration, 35*(3), 195–209. https://doi.org/10.1108/09578239710170119

Eagly, A. H., & Chin, J. L. (2010). Diversity and leadership in a changing world. *American Psychologist, 65*(3), 216–224. https://doi.org/10.1037/a0018957

Eagly, A. H., & Johnson, B. T. (1990). Gender and leadership style: A meta-analysis. *Psychological Bulletin, 108*(2), 233–256. https://doi.org/10.1037/0033-2909.108.2.233

Fiedler, F. E. (1978). The contingency model and the dynamics of the leadership process. *Advances in Experimental Social Psychology, 11*, 59–112. https://doi.org/10.1016/S0065-2601(08)60005-2

Fine, M. (1994). Dis-stance and other stances: Negotiations of power inside feminist research. In A. Gitlin (Ed.), *Power and method: Political activism and educational research* (pp. 13–35). Routledge.

Frank, J. D., & Frank, J. B. (1991). *Persuasion and healing: A comparative study of psychotherapy* (3rd ed.). Johns Hopkins University Press.

Goldfarb, K. P., & Grinberg, J. (2002). Leadership for social justice: Authentic participation in the case of a community center in Caracas, Venezuela. *Journal of School Leadership, 12*(2), 157–173. https://doi.org/10.1177/105268460201200204

Hasbi, H. (2012). Leader vision for effective leadership. *Journal Polingua Scientific Journal of Linguistics Literature and Education, 1*(1), 16–20. doi:10.30630/polingua.v1i1.46

Hersey, P., & Blanchard, K. H. (1969). Life-cycle theory of leadership. *Training and Development Journal, 23*(5), 26–34. https://psycnet.apa.org/record/1970-19661-001

Hersey, P., Blanchard, K. H., & Natemeyer, W. E. (1979). Situational leadership, perception, and the impact of power. *Group & Organization Studies, 4*(4), 418–428. DOI:10.1177/105960117900400404

Hook, J. N., Davis, D. E., Owen, J., Worthington Jr., E. L., & Utsey, S. O. (2013). Cultural humility: Measuring openness to culturally diverse clients. *Journal of Counseling Psychology, 60*(3), 353–366. doi:10.1037/a0032595

House, R. J., & Mitchell, T. R. (1974). Path-goal theory of leadership. *Journal of Contemporary Business, 10*(3), 81–97. https://doi.org/10.1016/S1048-9843(96)90024-7

Kanter, R. M. (1977). Some effects of proportions in group life: Skewed sex ratios and responses to token women. *American Journal of Sociology, 82*(5), 965–990. https://doi.org/10.1086/226425

Lewis, J. A., Lewis, M. D., Daniels, J. A., & D'Andrea, M. J. (2003). *Community counseling: Empowerment strategies for a diverse society.* Brooks/Cole.

Mann, R. D. (1959). A review of the relationships between personality and performance in small groups. *Psychological Bulletin, 56*(4), 241–270. https://doi.org/10.1037/h0044587

Menasce Horowitz, J. Igielnik, & Parker, K. (2018, Sep 20). Women and leadership 2018. https://www.pewsocialtrends.org/2018/09/20/women-and-leadership-2018/

Merriam-Webster. (n. d.). Leadership. Merriam-Webster.com dictionary. https://www.merriam-webster.com/dictionary/leadership

Montuori, A., & Donnelly, G. (2017). Transformative leadership. In J. Neal (Ed.), *Handbook of personal and organizational transformation* (pp. 1–33). Springer. doi:10.1007/978-3-319-29587-9_59-1

New York Times. (1968, Jun 9). Text of Edward Kennedy's tribute to his brother in cathedral. https://www.nytimes.com/1968/06/09/archives/text-of-edward-kennedys-tribute-to-his-brother-in-cathedral.html

Rogers, C. R. (1957). The necessary and sufficient conditions of therapeutic personality change. *Journal of Consulting Psychology, 21*(2), 95–103. https://doi.org/10.1037/h0045357

Sanbonmatsu, K. (2020). Women's underrepresentation in the U. S. congress. https://www.amacad.org/publication/womens-underrepresentation-us-congress

Sanchez-Hucles, J. V., & Davis, D. D. (2010). Women and women of color in leadership. *American Psychologist, 65*(3), 171–181. https://doi.org/10.1037/a0017459

Schriesheim, C. A., & Stogdill R. M. (1975). Differences in factor structure across three versions of the Ohio State leadership scales. *Personnel Psychology, 28*(2), 189–206. https://doi.org/10.1111/j.1744-6570.1975.tb01380.x

Senge, P. M. (1990). *The fifth discipline: The art and practice of the learning organization.* Doubleday.

Short, P. M., & Greer J. T. (2002). *Leadership in empowered schools: Themes from innovative efforts* (2nd ed.). Merrill Prentice-Hall.

Steele, C. M. (1997). A threat in the air: How stereotypes shape intellectual identity and performance. *American Psychologist, 52*(6), 613–629. https://doi.org/10.1037/0003-066X.52.6.613

Stogdill, R. M. (1948). Personal factors associated with leadership: A survey of the literature. *Journal of Psychology, 25*(1), 35–71. https://doi.org/10.1080/00223980.1948.9917362

Tannenbaum, R., & Schmidt, W. H. (1973). How to choose a leadership pattern. *Harvard Business Review, 51*(3), 162–180. https://hbr.org/1973/05/how-to-choose-a-leadership-pattern

Tarule, J. M., Applegate, J. H., Earley, P. M., & Blackwell, P. J. (2009). Narrating gendered leadership. In D. R. Dean, S. Bracken, & J. Allen (Eds.), *Women in academic leadership: Professional strategies, personal choices* (pp. 31–49). Stylus.

Theoharis, G. (2007). Social justice educational leaders and resistance: Toward a theory of social justice leadership. *Educational Administration Quarterly, 43*(2), 221–258. https://doi.org/10.1177/0013161X06293717

Uhl-Bien, M., Marion, R., & McKelvey, B. (2007). Complexity leadership theory: Shifting leadership from the industrial age to the knowledge era. *Leadership Quarterly, 18*(4), 298–318. https://doi.org/10.1016/j.leaqua.2007.04.002

US Civil Rights Act. (1964). https://www.ourdocuments.gov/doc.php?flash=false&doc=97

Vogelstein, R. B., & Bro, A. (2021, Mar 29). Find out where women around the world wield political power—and why it matters. Council on Foreign Relations. https://www.cfr.org/article/womens-power-index

CHAPTER 17

STUDENT CHAPTER

Trusting the Process: Overcoming Being Scared to
Challenge Myself and Others

Ashley Weiser

Growing up I was always the kid making racist jokes and not thinking twice about it. I was this type of person because I was not educated on the realities of our society. I was not educated on the harsh truths about how people of color are still treated as less. I was not educated because I did not care to be, because I did not need to be, because I am White. I never really thought about my race until I took a multicultural counseling class and was forced to. I was forced to look in a mirror I had never before known existed and to open up parts of myself that I wasn't even sure were there.

I wanted to become a counselor in part because I have always preferred focusing on others rather than myself. I think that is why it took me until graduate school to face this journey. I had always considered myself a strong and independent woman who hated showing weakness and vulnerability. At the time I thought that was just who I was, but now, looking back on myself, I realize that I built up that tough exterior because I was afraid of realizing I needed to change. On the first day of class I dreaded knowing we were going to be talking about race, religion, culture, and politics. Coming from a conservative family and being that "strong and independent" person, these were not things I often talked about. These topics make people vulnerable and emotional, two things I already knew I did not like being. I will be honest: I was scared. I was scared to learn more about myself for fear of what I would find and for fear that this class would try to change me. I was scared that the things I grew up believing in for my entire life would be challenged and that I would be alone in it. However, mostly I think I was scared that if I became educated on these topics and my views changed, the people I loved the most would not change with me, would not accept who I was becoming, would not support me, and, mainly, would not love me anymore.

Coming from a very conservative family meant no one in my family would agree with what I was learning about in terms of focusing on social justice and multicultural counseling.

My family is very set in their ways, and I inherited my reluctance to change from them. Both of my grandfathers were strict, driven, hardheaded, career military men in an age when they were not fond of "coloreds." My grandmothers got married in a time when women kept to the home and agreed with the opinions of their husbands. My maternal grandfather told me once that he thinks my cousin likes Black men and that "he sure hoped not." My paternal grandmother once said that she did not agree with interracial marriage. My uncle once kicked my cousin out of the house because she was seeing a Black man. I thought a lot about how I would write this section, and I kept telling myself to include a part about how I don't think my family is racist but rather simply unaware of the impact of their words, but then I felt like I was just making excuses because I was scared to face the realities of who my family was. Then I told myself that other people don't have the choice but to face harsh realities every day, so I could not avoid it any longer.

After the first few classes in graduate school all I could do was think about race. I was overcome with emotion surrounding the stories my classmates told regarding their experiences with racism. This was all so new to me that I did not know how to react. I felt like I needed time to process what had been shared, but how could I process it when all I was doing was thinking about how terrible I felt about the person I was? The entire time in class I felt like my jaw was dropped to the floor. I was in shock that things like this still occurred because, growing up, I was so blinded to it all. During the car ride home every week I was fighting back tears thinking about everything. From the moment the class started having dialogues about race, there was a shift in me. I went from not being accepting of others to not being accepting of myself. There was so much work I felt I needed to do in myself and so many wrongs that I needed to right.

Even with all the work I was doing on myself, there was still something holding me back: my family. I wanted to speak out on my newfound beliefs and speak up for those who couldn't, but I was still afraid of what my family would say. It was a constant struggle to find the balance between advocating for what I believed in while not stepping on the toes of the people who have given me everything I could have ever asked for. I felt it was not my place to challenge my family yet because it was all so new to me. This feeling of being stuck, along with being overwhelmed with what I was learning in class, led to feelings of numbness. I wanted to shut out all the thoughts about race and my White guilt, and I wanted to separate myself from it all. Other students in class echoed these feelings of numbness and being stuck, and I came to realize through them that this was because I was trying to do too much without knowing where to go. I went from not thinking about race to being flooded with these topics, and that made me feel like I was behind in my efforts to combat racism. These thoughts had me working overtime, and I was wearing myself out. Social justice and multicultural counseling work is exhausting, and I was really feeling that.

Not only was I struggling with how much to do, but I was also struggling with how to do it. Seeing as racial dialogues were still new to me, this meant I had never challenged anyone on their views of race until a few months ago, and it all still made me emotional. Every time I heard a racist comment I could play thousands of different ways to challenge them in my head but I could not to find a way to vocalize it. I didn't want to speak because I did not want to get angry or sad. Those were the only two reactions I was experiencing when discussing race, and I knew if I tried to broach the subject that way then no one would listen to me, and, if they did, they would think I was irrational. I needed to find a way to get over these feelings and move on to a place of acceptance and progress. The only answer I could find for this was time. It took time to understand my feelings, time to process the drastic change my world-view had undertaken, and time to realize what my purpose was in this journey. The more time I spent thinking about my life and my environment, and the more time I spent engaging in race dialogues, no matter how small, was beneficial in getting me to a place where I felt that I could really do this. There was not a day when a lightbulb went off above my head and signaled that I was finally ready for this kind of work but rather a growing confidence in myself. There was a confidence in my beliefs and my abilities to challenge the beliefs of others. There was a confidence in knowing I would be able to handle whatever someone said, not take it personally, not get emotional, and be able to give a level-headed response that could really get a message across.

Through everything, I learned that I needed to balance my efforts. I needed to find the line between who I was trying to become and who I still was. I was never going to be able to turn off my family, my thoughts, my guilt, or the racism in this country. I needed to remind myself that my efforts did not have to be heroic to make a difference. We always talk about planting the seed, and this is truly how it has to work. To this day, my family still gets angry when I bring up race, but they precede that anger with "I knew you were going to say that." While they still may get angry, at least I know they are listening, and at least I know I am making them think about what they were going to say. Yes, they still said it, but they went from not even thinking about it to thinking about it beforehand. And one day they may go to not even saying it. In the end, no matter how painful and exhausting this journey was, it changed my life for the better. Looking back on who I was when I started this journey and thinking about who I am now, I know that I am in a better place to make a difference in the lives of others because I am now aware of this part of myself. Sometimes I am still scared to confront people and to dig deeper, but I am less scared than I was when I started and that helps me to never forget to trust the process.

CHAPTER 18

SOCIAL JUSTICE AND HUMAN RIGHTS ADVOCACY IN MENTAL HEALTH

Rita Chi-Ying Chung and Frederic P. Bemak

Never be afraid to raise your voice for honesty and truth and compassion against injustice and lying and greed. If people all over the world ... would do this, it would change the earth.

—William Faulkner

It took a long time to develop a voice, and now that I have it, I'm not going to be silent.

—Madeleine Albright

Vision without action is a daydream. Action without vision is a nightmare.

—Japanese Proverb

It only takes a single idea, a single action to move the world.

—Author Unknown

Human progress is neither automatic nor inevitable.... Every step toward the goal of justice requires sacrifice, suffering, and struggle; the tireless exertions and passionate concern of dedicated individuals.

—Martin Luther King, Jr.

REFLECTION QUESTIONS

1. Draw a horizontal line on a piece of paper. On the line, mark the dates and events when you advocated for an issue. This is your *Advocacy Line.*

2. Draw a horizontal line under your *Advocacy Line*. Make a mark on the line every event that you wished you had advocated for but didn't. This is your *Advocacy Wish Line*.

3. Below the *Advocacy Wish Line* list the issues that you would hope to advocate for in the future. This is your *Advocacy Vision List*.

Social justice advocacy can be defined as: "the belief that individual and collective actions are necessary to fight injustices that lead towards improving conditions for the benefit of both individuals and groups" (House & Martin, 1998). Advocating for clients can be viewed as speaking up or taking action that leads to environmental changes on behalf of clients (Ratts & Hutchins, 2009). The role of a multicultural social justice advocate in the mental health profession is to work on behalf of and/or with their clients who are encountering systemic challenges and barriers (Toporek & Daniels, 2018). This concept, along with multicultural social justice leadership and empowerment, helps to frame social justice and human rights for psychologists and counselors. To effectively combat and dismantle social injustices and human right violations, advocacy is an essential component of the work.

U.S. mental health professional organizations, such as the American Psychological Association (APA) and the American Counseling Association (ACA), have made public announcements condemning unjust and unfair U.S. policies and legislation that have adverse psychological effects with a goal to influence, shape, and change government policies, programs, and initiatives. Fundamentally, the aim is for a just and fair quality of life and psychological well-being for all. Some social issues addressed by the APA and ACA include the U.S. administration's forced separation of migrant parents/caretakers and their children; xenophobia; racial injustice; inequities in healthcare and education; marriage equality; criminal justice; LGBTQI rights; gender equity; global warming; gun and gender-based violence; and public safety (Garrison et al., 2017). Since our professional organizations are active in advocacy work, it would make sense that we as multicultural social justice–oriented psychologists and counselors also follow suit. This chapter discusses advocacy as it relates to multicultural social justice–oriented psychology and counseling. We begin with a brief overview of the history of advocacy in psychology and counseling, followed by a discussion of advocacy strategies, skills, and applications to social justice–oriented psychological and counseling work.

BRIEF HISTORICAL OVERVIEW OF ADVOCACY IN PSYCHOLOGY AND COUNSELING

In the past decade, "advocacy" has become a buzzword in the helping professions and a growing trend in psychology and counseling. Hence the resurgence of literature on the topic (e.g., Bemak, 2000; Bemak & Chung, 2005, 2007, 2008; Goodman et al., 2018; Kiselica & Robinson, 2001; Kozan & Blustein, 2018; Pearrow & Fallon, 2019; Ramirez Stege et al., 2017; Toporek et al., 2006; Toporek & Ahluwalia, 2021). Responding to the renewed interest in advocacy and social justice, the APA and ACA have established committees, published special journal issues, and developed website resources on advocacy tools and competencies. We refer readers to their respective professional associations for these resources.

Despite the more recent attention to advocacy in psychology and counseling, it is not a new concept in the field. Mental health advocacy began in the 1700s, when there was a public movement to improve treatment of the mentally ill (Brooks & Weikel, 1996). In 1908, Clifford Beers advocated for the mentally ill (Kiselica & Robinson, 2001), while, at the same time, Frank Parsons (1909) introduced vocational counseling as a means to address unemployment for youth who dropped out of school. A half-century later, social activism took root (e.g., civil rights, women's rights, opposition to the Vietnam War, and the gay rights movements) in the United States, causing debate in the helping professions about the role of advocacy for therapists and counselors. Garrison et al. (2017) documented the APA's history of advocacy and clients' rights. As a result of oppression, racism, xenophobia, and discrimination multicultural counseling (e.g., Arredondo et al., 1996; Atkinson et al., 1993; Leung, 1995), feminist therapy (e.g., Comas-Díaz, 1987; Ennis, 1993), and community psychology (e.g., Lewis et al., 2002; Lewis & Lewis, 1983; Lewis et al., 1998; Prilleltensky, 1997) emphasized the importance of incorporating advocacy as a critical role for mental health professionals.

During the 1970s, community mental health advocacy gained recognition as a component of counseling. This changed in the late 1980s and 1990s, when advocacy and social change diminished in importance and the counseling field strove to establish credibility and public acceptance by increasing the focus on accreditation and credentialing (McClure & Russo, 1996). While some mental health professionals continue to support the role of advocacy in the profession, many others are adamantly against it. The opposition's position is rooted in traditional beliefs, arguing that the focus of mental health interventions is to help individuals with personal, behavioral, social, and intrapsychic problems. Should there be injustice or patterns of unfairness or inequities in the client's world, the traditional position of counselors and psychologists has been to explore the internal processes of the client, change behavior to more effectively adapt or adjust, solve short-term and immediate problems, and assist with a shift in cognition so that the client's reactions change. Thus, critics claimed that incorporating advocacy into the counseling profession was unrealistic and inappropriate (Weinrach & Thomas, 1998), creating professional boundary issues, dual roles (Toporek, 2000), and authoritarianism (Sollod, 1998).

Based on these criticisms many work settings neither supported advocacy nor viewed it as part of client services, seeing it instead as a potential threat since empowered clients may challenge the politics, procedures, and structure of organizations, agencies, and institutions (Bemak & Chung, 2005). Other concerns were raised about incorporating advocacy into work with clients, such as clients' dependency (Pinderhughes, 1983), clients' powerlessness (McWhirter, 1994), and condescending and disempowering attitudes toward clients (Toporek, 2000). While the inclusion of advocacy was being debated there was growing acknowledgment about the need to address social injustices in the mental health field (Bemak & Chung, 2005; Myers et al., 2002). Thus, in 2003, the ACA endorsed the advocacy competencies (Lewis et al., 2002), later updated in 2018, further confirming the importance of advocacy work in counseling (Toporek & Daniels, 2018). Similarly, the 2012 APA competency guidelines noted the importance of advocacy work for psychologists, recommending that psychologists be trained to safeguard clients' welfare and address and promote change in unfair and unjust systems that impact the psychological well-being of clients, their families, and communities (Pearrow & Fallon, 2019). This is consistent with our beliefs that advocacy is not only part of our work, but also an ethical and moral obligation for psychologists and counselors, and is part and parcel of being an effective mental health professional.

SOCIAL JUSTICE PSYCHOLOGY AND COUNSELING AND HUMAN RIGHTS ADVOCACY

As noted previously, one argument against incorporating advocacy in mental health work is that the profession is a science, and, as scientific disciplines, psychology and counseling should not take political positions. We argue that helping people psychologically heal includes helping them receive just and fair treatment, equivalent opportunities, and equal access to resources, which is not just a science, but involves humanitarian values and beliefs and a moral obligation. In the 21st century, we are living in an increasingly complex environment where psychological make-up is interwoven with historical, social, political, and cultural issues. This is evident in such areas as the research that documents the relationship between race-related stressors, racism, and racial injustice with mental health and psychological well-being (e.g., Hernández &Villodas, 2020; Paradies et al., 2015; Priest et al., 2013; Steele et al., 2002; Sue, 2003; Williams, 2018). Furthermore, findings (e.g., Lake & Turner, 2017; Moreno et al., 2020; Prilleltensky, 1997; Sue et al., 2019) show that due to the rapid changes in our society, traditional methods of clinical interventions that once worked are no longer effective, given the external factors that play a vital part in clients' growth and development. Politics and policies that impact people's lives, such as funding priorities for social service programs, legal decisions, unemployment, unequal access to job promotion, voting laws, continued xenophobia, racism and discrimination, racial injustice, inequitable salaries, gender discrimination, unequal treatment of those who are physically challenged, migration, COVID-19, responses to natural disasters and global warming, and failing to provide healthcare benefits for LGBTQI partners all play a major role in clients' psychological well-being.

Acknowledging the impact and interrelationship of environmental factors on our clients is important. Overlooking the toll that social, political, economic, and historical factors take on clients is to ignore a large and powerful aspect of clients' lives. Incorporating social justice perspectives into our work requires helping clients figure out how to address the injustices they face through authentic empowerment, self-advocacy, and the promotion of human rights. At the same time, we can actively encourage change within our professional associations and through political channels when we experience unjust policies and practices. One example I (Fred) experienced that illustrates the connection between individuals and environment was during a consultation for the Ministry of Health in Northern Ireland. Sadly, Northern Ireland has a very high rate of youth suicide. The government has been valiantly attempting to develop and introduce new intervention programs, yet the high rates of suicide remain constant. A colleague and I were invited by Northern

Ireland's Ministry of Health to conduct an assessment and develop an intervention plan. We visited numerous programs in the Catholic and Protestant sectors of Belfast and Derry (or Londonderry, depending on one's political affiliations), visited community centers under the protection of local community members, met with top Northern Ireland health and mental health officials, and made recommendations to the government. It was clear to us that the government's plan for designing suicide prevention programs and interventions had been based on individual psychotherapy, without regarding the impact of the "troubles" (the term used to denote the Irish sectarian conflict) on individuals, families, and communities.

We were clear in our recommendations to the Ministry of Health officials that the "troubles" were pervasive in every meeting we held and a central topic in every discussion about suicide, whether it was with local citizens, Catholic or Protestant, or mental health workers. Based on our assessment, we recommended holding community and group meetings to discuss the loss, grieving, suicide, and feelings of despair that were so dominant in the Northern Ireland communities we visited. We suggested beginning with intrasectarian groups and gradually move to intersectarian groups (facilitated by neutral parties), maintaining a clear focus on youth suicide. This was flatly rejected by the health administrators and viewed as being potentially volatile and not within the purview of a health department. Interestingly, as time passed and other intervention attempts failed, two years later our recommendations were being touted as the next step in mental health treatment, with substantive regional discussions about how to design and implement community interventions to address this very difficult and frightening problem facing youth across sectarian groups within the Northern Ireland community. We use this example as an illustration of the interaction between the environment and individuals and the importance of taking a serious psychological problem and linking it back to relevant factors within the larger community.

No different from Northern Ireland, individuals, regardless of where they live or their sociodemographic background, cannot avoid the influence of society on their mental health and psychological well-being. As counselors and psychologists, we do not work in a vacuum that isolates individuals from their surrounding world. It is essential in our work that we understand, acknowledge, recognize, and act on factors that have bearing on the psychological well-being and quality of life of our clients, their families, and their communities. Sometimes this involves assuming an advocacy role, which is consistent with Lerner's (1972) earlier contentions that the helping profession creates a false dichotomy between social action and psychotherapy. According to Lerner, the aim and outcome of psychotherapy and social action is the same, with the difference being that psychotherapy is aligned with having intrapsychic obstacles, while social action is aligned with external obstacles. Lerner outlined the dichotomy between those who work on their clients and those who work for their clients.

Working for and with clients, mental health professionals are in a unique position to incorporate advocacy as part of their work. Given the fact that being a counselor or psychologist means having status and credibility rooted in institutional power and privilege, one can influence practices, procedures, and policies. Added to mental health professionals' understanding of intrapsychic complexities of human suffering and pain, interpersonal dynamics, and organizational structures is access to resources, organizations, policymakers, and avenues for change that are frequently not accessible to clients. Understandably, not all counselors or psychologists will have the time or energy to effect major institutional or policy changes, yet all have the capability to facilitate some type of social change and human rights work, such as simply educating clients about their situation and their rights or teaching them advocacy skills (Ratts & Hutchins, 2009). Adopting advocacy as part of psychotherapy has the potential to make a difference and create a better world that goes beyond an individual client.

An example occurred when I (Fred) was consulting in a high school by conducting weekly group therapy sessions for two groups of 10th-graders identified as being at the highest risk of failing. The group therapy was in its seventh week and students had already demonstrated significantly improved grades, better attendance, and less disciplinary referrals. As statewide testing was approaching the school principal ordered all non-academic activities to be cancelled and replaced with study halls. The students in the groups were enraged, believing that the group therapy was essential support for them that helped to improve their academic performance. Their anger led to a strong desire to do something to try to continue the groups. After brainstorming about what they could do, they decided to write letters to the principal, advocating that the group therapy continue, and explaining why. Much to their amazement their request was approved, so that the therapy groups were the only non-academic activities allowed to continue in the school. My role as group therapist included helping students advocate for themselves, which was instrumental in promoting their psychological well-being.

Similar to this example, we suggest that mental health professionals incorporate advocacy in their direct work with clients. This is not meant to discount the importance of advocating for policy change or funding that affects clients' lives and mental health. Yet, in our experience, it is of equal importance to include advocacy in the therapeutic work as a tool to eliminate institutional and societal barriers that impede clients' psychological growth, development, and well-being. This type of advocacy approach has a more direct and immediate effect on the clients, their families, and communities. When doing this more direct type of advocacy work it is important that counselors and psychologists are clear about the reasons and intentions for employing advocacy and aware of the impact on clients.

An example of this was a White colleague, a professor at a major university, who was very verbal about her tremendous support and advocacy for African American graduate students. Although the African American students' work and level of responsibility was similar to all other students in the graduate program, it was well known by students and faculty alike that the White faculty member was excessively supportive of African American students. When African American students handed in their papers late, deadlines were relaxed, or when African American students missed class without an excusable reason, grading standards for attendance were relaxed. The same policies did not hold true for other students. The result of this was to not hold African American students equally accountable for their behaviors and actions and to the same standards as other students.

When we probed this issue with the faculty member it became clear that she had grown up in a home where her father was blatantly racist toward African Americans. "I will never do what my father did, never!" Her awareness of why and how she was advocating for African American students, and the ramifications of having different standards for African Americans compared to other students, presented an interesting challenge for the professor. We suggest that, in this situation, the impact of lesser standards for one group than another is a disservice rather than helpful and may have long-range implications. This professor, who unwittingly set up different standards for African American students, created a situation with serious implications for all students in the department. Thus, if psychologists and counselors do advocacy work because of personal unresolved issues or guilt about family members, or their own power, privilege, or prejudices, then the use of advocacy may be inappropriate and at times even detrimental to clients and families. It is important to be aware of our own issues and countertransference that may be disguised as advocacy when we work toward social justice.

Although there is an increase in literature about best training and practice in incorporating advocacy in graduate training program curricula (e.g., Goodman et al., 2018; Koch & Juntunen, 2014a, 2014b, 2014c; Kozan & Blustein, 2018; Ramirez Stege et al., 2017), there is still a scarcity of research about the effectiveness and outcome of social justice advocacy in psychology and counseling training. To address this issue, we (Rita and Fred) conducted a pilot study with 99 alumni who graduated from a counseling graduate training program that emphasized social justice and multiculturalism. The study consisted of an online questionnaire assessing whether their training, one that emphasized values and commitment to action in multicultural social justice (MSJ) psychology and counseling, had longevity, maintenance, and sustainability post-graduation (Chung & Bemak, 2016). The participants (86% women and 13% men) had graduated from the program ranging from 2 to 13 years ago, with a median of 5 years in the workforce after graduation. They were employed in mental health agencies (45%) and schools (55%), with 54% of the participants identifying as White, 16% African Americans, 11% Latinx, 9% Asian, 2% Arab or Muslim or from a Middle Eastern background, and 4% biracial/multiracial. The findings showed that almost all (98%) of the participants reported that, as a result of the MSJ training, there was reinforcement and promotion of strong or stronger MSJ values, they attained cultural competence to work with diverse clientele, they acquired MSJ counseling and advocacy skills that provided a foundation for their professional work, and they were prepared to be social justice advocates. Most participants (90%) indicated that they still held strong MSJ values, while 73% reported that they are currently incorporating MSJ into their work as a therapists and counselors. Participants also reported that approximately 47% of their supervisors/administrators and 45% of their colleagues/peers understand the MSJ work they do, and approximately 55% of supervisors/administrators and 45% of their colleagues/peers support their MSJ work.

Examples of the social justice advocacy work they were doing included educating clients about their rights; educating colleagues, administrators, and community regarding social injustice, unfair and inequitable policies, initiatives, and programs; advocating for federal, state, and regional legislation and policies; advocating for and establishing programs for vulnerable and disenfranchised populations; providing MSJ training for colleagues and staff; and collaborating with human rights and advocacy organizations. In summary, the pilot study provides evidence that positive and sustainable MSJ values and actions are maintained after graduation and supports the inclusion of MSJ advocacy training in mental health professional training program curricula. The next section discusses the various advocacy strategies, techniques, and activities that can be employed by mental health professionals; the characteristics necessary for effective social justice advocacy; and the challenges and realities of actually being a social justice–oriented advocate in the mental health field.

SOCIAL JUSTICE ADVOCACY STRATEGIES, TECHNIQUES, AND ACTIVITIES

Toporek and Liu's (2001) advocacy model incorporates both empowerment and social action as dimensions of advocacy. The model presents a continuum, with empowerment on one end and social action on the other. Both empowerment and social action consider the sociopolitical context of individuals and the involvement of families and/or communities. When working with empowerment, and understanding that many clients may not have the skills or knowledge to generate social change, the model describes the role of the counselor and psychologist to initially assist clients in achieving their goals, leading to greater independence and becoming truly empowered. (Social justice empowerment is discussed in more detail in the next chapter.) Their model also describes the mental health professional's social activist role as one who actively participates to remove barriers encountered by clients, their families, and their communities. They describe social action as different from empowerment in that social action is conducted at a macro social level, targeting issues affecting clients, such as legislation or policies.

Keeping Toporek and Liu's model in mind it is important to note that social justice work in mental health involves individual advocacy and intervention advocacy. *Individual advocacy* consists of three types: (a) educating and empowering clients by teaching them skills so they can advocate for themselves, (b) partnering with clients as advocates, and (c) advocating on behalf of clients. *Intervention advocacy* addresses unjust and inequitable systems, such as organizations, work sites, communities, and schools that have oppressive and harmful policies, programs, and initiatives that impact clients' quality of life and psychological well-being (Toporek & Daniels, 2018). Illustrations of individual advocacy can be seen when counselors and psychologists provide clients with the skills or partner with clients to advocate or co-advocate on their behalf against injustices (e.g., Astramovich & Harris, 2007; Chen-Hayes, 2000; D'Andrea & Daniels, 2000; Goodman & Waters, 2000; Goodman et al., 2018; Herring, 2000; Sanders, 2000). Individual advocacy focuses on empowering clients, while the intervention advocacy focuses on broader societal and political institutions. The two are not mutually exclusive and may intersect and be implemented simultaneously (Myers et al., 2002).

We (Rita and Fred) both have worked on both levels of advocacy to create social change. For example, I (Fred) directed the Massachusetts Department of Mental Health Region I adolescent treatment program for what at the time was labeled "untreatable" adolescents. I had morning meetings with the state commissioners of mental health, youth services, social services, and education to discuss funding, policies, and changes across the state. Then, in the evening, I went to the program's residential facility to eat dinner with the residents and staff and speak with residents about their lived experiences, their families, and how they were doing in school. Sitting with a 16-year-old emotionally troubled adolescent requires a different set of skills than negotiating budgets with the state commissioner of mental health. Similarly, I (Rita) would have morning meetings with community groups of refugees to talk about their psychosocial adjustment and adaptation to a new country and then attend afternoon meetings with policy makers, English as second language teachers, and directors of social services and community agencies to share the refugee community's concerns and challenges. The goal of the afternoon meetings was to set the stage for refugees to have direct dialogue with service providers and policymakers to ensure that programs and policies for new migrants were culturally responsive. Talking to the refugees themselves required one set of skills, whereas discussions with service providers, policymakers, and administrators required an entirely different set of skills and political savvy.

Complementing individual and intervention advocacy is social justice–oriented mental health work with a focus on prevention and intervention. Lewis and Lewis (1983) looked at advocacy from this perspective, citing three tiers of advocacy: (a) *here and now advocacy*, which is an instant response to an immediate situation; (b) *preventive advocacy*, which is an action taken to prevent injustices against a group of individuals; and (c) *citizen advocacy*, which is the movement to encourage others to take on social issues. Ezell (2001) identified and provided a comprehensive review of 13 different types of human services advocacy activities that can be incorporated into any of the social justice advocacy levels and tiers. The 13 types of advocacy are wide-ranging, from case advocacy that concentrates on advocacy for individuals, to class advocacy that focuses on groups of individuals who share the same problem, to policy advocacy that involves attempts to influence legal, social, economic, and governmental programs and policies.

To provide mental health professionals with additional ideas on the type of advocacy work that can be done, Kiselica and Robinson (2001) presented a list of advocacy initiatives compiled from various sources (e.g., Baker, 1981, 2000; Kiselica, 1995, 2000; Kiselica & Ramsey, 2000) that ranged from ambitious to modest types of advocacy initiatives. Each different type of advocacy activity has its own impact. Their examples ranged from talking to newspaper reporters and making television appearances, challenging cultural biases in standardized testing, and publishing articles and books on justice and rights related issues.

BOX TEXT 18.2 TYPES OF SOCIAL JUSTICE ADVOCACY

1. Arguing for better services
2. Pushing for increased clients' rights in the agency
3. Negotiating with agencies
4. Giving testimony to decision makers
5. Lobbying individual policymakers
6. Litigating or seeking legal remedies
7. Representing a client in an administrative hearing
8. Influencing administrative rule-making in other agencies
9. Teaching advocacy skills to clients to solve a problem
10. Educating clients on their rights
11. Educating the public on an issue
12. Monitoring other agencies' performance
13. Conducting issue research
14. Organizing coalitions
15. Influencing media coverage of an issue
16. Mobilizing constituent support
17. Political campaigning
18. Facilitating client access to information provided by institutions
19. Mediating between clients and institutions
20. Negotiating with outside agencies and institutions to provide better services for clients
21. Influencing policy makers through educational lobbying efforts
22. Directing complaints regarding inadequate services or oppressive policies to funding agencies
23. Using the internet/social media to:
    - Market counseling services and raising awareness of mental health concerns and issues
    - Access social media forum and platforms for social advocacy, activism and action
    - Deliver multimedia-based assessment and information resources that match the ethnicity/race, age, gender, sexual orientation, religion, abilities, etc. of the user
    - Reach clients who have transportation difficulties or live in geographically remote areas
    - Improve client access to self-help groups
    - Supplement traditional face-to-face supervision with long-distance, online supervision
    - Expand opportunities for communication among psychologists/counselors

Source: Adapted from Ezell, M. (2001). *Advocacy in the human services*. Brooks/Cole.
Kiselica, M. S., & Robinson, M. (2001). Bringing advocacy counseling to life: The history, issues, and human dramas of social justice work in counseling. *Journal of Counseling & Development, 79*(4), 387–397.

Their suggested activities are important to underscore that advocacy does not necessarily mean holding demonstrations, lobbying, political campaigning, or mobilizing constituent support, but also involves many other strategies. For example, I (Rita) contacted a journalist at a major newspaper and talked to him about the psychosocial adjustment challenges of refugees. The goal and outcome of speaking with the journalist was for him to educate the public and bring awareness to policymakers by writing a series of articles about the challenges facing refugees. This led to better social services for this population. Box Text 18.2 provides a list of different types of advocacy initiatives.

DISSEMINATION OF SOCIAL JUSTICE WORK AS AN ADVOCACY STRATEGY

We would like to underscore Kiselica and Robinson's (2001) assertion about the importance for mental health professionals to publish and disseminate their social justice work in professional journals, books, videos, community newsletters, websites, and social media, as well as present their findings at professional conferences and community venues that include such places as nonprofit organizations, churches, schools, and policy hearings. It is vital that the work we do is shared with our colleagues, communities, government officials, policymakers, other professionals, and the public. Part of doing social justice and human rights work is to educate through local, state, government, national and globally venues. Living in the Age of Technology, our work can be disseminated through a variety of sources. We (Rita and Fred) both have had the opportunity to give numerous local, national, and international presentations in both governmental and nongovernmental settings, as well as publish and present about our work in different outlets.

For example, I (Rita) along with a co-author, conducted a study that examined cultural influences on the conceptualization, manifestation, and expression of mental illness of four different Southeast Asian refugee groups (Chung & Kagawa-Singer, 1995). The study found that these groups did not express mental illness in the same way as the *Diagnostic and Statistical Manual of Mental Disorders* (DSM) and *International Classification of Diseases* (ICD) defined expressions of mental illness for Western populations. The results had significant implications for diagnosis and subsequent treatment interventions for this group. When we generalize and do not acknowledge that Western diagnostic classifications have cultural limitations, we are potentially harming diverse groups by forcing them to fit into discrete Western diagnostic categories that could prove to be ineffective and even harmful. With this knowledge of cultural misdiagnosis, combined with the findings of our study, my co-author and I felt compelled to educate mental health professionals about the cultural biases of Western diagnostic measures and subsequent treatment. We intentionally chose to publish the study in one of the oldest and most highly reputable U.S. psychiatric journals, knowing that the primary readers of the journal were psychiatrists and psychologists. The choice was two-fold: first to educate about cultural considerations of diagnoses and treatment and, second, in knowing that some of the journal readers were the main collaborators on designing and updating the DSM and ICD, the study provided evidence of the critical need to address cultural considerations in mental health diagnosis and treatment.

There are other examples. Through my (Rita) academic scholarship I have received numerous invitations to do presentations at various events such as at the United Nations in New York on my work on trafficking of Asian girls into the commercial sex trade (Chung, 2008), participate in the APA Expert Summit on Immigration, and do APA training videos on working with clients of color, immigrants, refugees, and social justice training. In turn, I (Fred) have been invited to present several times to the Association for State Legislatures

National Conference regarding immigrant mental health and have also made APA and ACA videos related to working with clients of color, immigrant mental health, and social justice training. Furthermore, due to my scholarship I have been invited by other governments (i.e., Nicaragua, El Salvador, Taiwan, Ireland) to assist in developing governmental mental health prevention and intervention programs. This "snowballing" of social justice action work frequently happens when we are engaged in social justice projects. We believe that part of human rights and social justice work involves not only direct action with individuals, stakeholders, communities, and policymakers, but also sharing and disseminating our research and practice to a broader audience.

QUALITIES NECESSARY FOR EFFECTIVE SOCIAL JUSTICE ADVOCACY

In addition to knowing the types and models of advocacy, it is important to know how to proceed as an advocate. Possessing solid clinical and counseling skills is not the only prerequisite for helping professionals who want to become effective advocates. As one of my (Rita) students in a multicultural counseling class told me, "I used to think that the most important information that I would gain from the graduate counseling program was solid counseling skills, but I learned that the skills are not relevant if I also do not have solid multicultural awareness, knowledge, and competencies." An extension of this is to add social justice skills, which many of our students spoke about as being as important as multicultural competencies. Being a social justice and human rights advocate requires the core clinical skills and multicultural competencies, along with energy, commitment, motivation, passion, persistence, tenacity, flexibility, patience, assertiveness, organization, resourcefulness, creativity, a multidisciplinary perspective, the ability to negotiate and access systems, and the courage to deal with conflict and confrontation. We add to this long list of characteristics the need for cultural and social justice humility coupled with a profound dignity and respect for others.

Underscoring the characteristics mentioned above it is important to have an organizational perspective that helps envision the larger systemic picture of the goals we are trying to promote. Since social change can be challenging, it is important to maintain a perspective on the larger context of our advocacy work, assessing who one's potential allies are and who will be partners to help gather momentum and create social change. For example, when I (Fred) was trying to make significant changes in a large complex organization, rather than the state mental health commissioner, who would be the logical person to be associated with, I found and linked with the state deputy mental health commissioner who became an ally helping to promote policy changes. This type of organizational savvy and assessment is important in understanding the systems in which we are working.

Doing advocacy work necessitates that psychologists and counselors collaborate and partner with clients and stakeholders to test sometimes long-standing and undisputed traditions, policies, procedures, and notions that create and reinforce unfair treatment and inequities. Advocating requires both organizational and communication skills. As advocates,

BOX TEXT 18.3 WHY ARE GENDER PRONOUNS IMPORTANT?

In 2019, Merriam-Webster announced that the singular "they" was added to the dictionary. In the same year, the American Psychological Association (APA) encouraged using the singular "they" in the place of "he or she" to be more inclusive of non-binary individuals who do not identify as solely male or female. These actions followed years of interest for desired pronouns to be "they/their" such as singer/songwriter Sam Smith or actress/singer Demi Lovato. While many still argue that the singular "they" is grammatically incorrect, history shows that this use of the word has occurred in the English language since at least the 16th century. Furthermore, gender-neutral pronouns have existed in other cultures and languages for centuries. There are a number of other pronouns used by non-binary individuals, but the singular "they" is currently the most commonly used.

Non-binary individuals, also known as *gender nonconforming*, experience invalidation of their gender expression on a daily basis through microaggressions, rigid identity documentation, and regular misgendering. Cisgender individuals (those whose identified gender [male or female] matches that of their sex at birth) experience considerable privilege in being addressed with correct pronouns every day and often take for granted how their gender identity is affirmed in these exchanges. In comparison, non-binary or gender nonconforming individuals have their identity under constant attack or misjudged. When both gender nonconforming and cisgender individuals begin disclosing their preferred pronouns and honoring the pronouns of others, the diversity of gender identities is both celebrated and normalized in a society that has historically denied their existence. By using preferred pronouns, one is acknowledging, accepting, and affirming different gender expressions and showing support as an ally.

Sources: Merriam-Webster. (2019, Dec 9). "They" is Merriam-Webster's word of the year 2019. https://www.merriam-webster.com/words-at-play/woty2019-top-looked-up-words-they
Knutson, D., Koch, J. M., & Goldbach, C. (2019). Recommended terminology, pronouns, and documentation for work with transgender and non-binary populations. *Practice Innovations, 4*(4), 214–224. https://doi.org/10.1037/pri0000098

we must take it upon ourselves and have courage to dispute and challenge the status quo and the traditional models of changing the individual to fit the system and instead assert and act to change the larger environment and surrounding socioecological systems. Within the advocacy framework, both the helping professional and the client are instrumental in promoting this change. Lewis et al. (1998) purport that advocacy serves two primary purposes: (a) increasing clients' sense of personal power and (b) fostering environmental change that reflects greater responsiveness to their personal needs (p. 172). Balancing these two principal purposes requires skills to work directly with clientele, changing social policy through scholarship and research and meetings with supervisors, administrators, and policymakers.

CHALLENGES AND REALITIES OF SOCIAL JUSTICE ADVOCACY

Being an advocate is not easy. One can experience burnout, become emotionally drained (see Chapter 26 on self-care), or be seen as a troublemaker and be alienated. Doing social justice advocacy can put one's job at risk, and you may become the target for backlash or harassment from colleagues, family members, and friends (e.g., Bemak & Chung, 2005, 2007, 2008; Kiselica & Robinson, 2001; Kozan & Blustein, 2018). Even so, there is a great degree of personal satisfaction (Toporek & Ahluwalia, 2021; Kiselica, 1998, 1999) in being an advocate, coupled with a critical need to act in this capacity (Bemak & Chung, 2005, 2007, 2008). It is inevitable that advocacy will create problems. Challenging the status quo and pushing for change has the potential to produce personal and professional difficulties. Taking on a system by becoming an advocate for social equity requires assuming a very different position from that of the traditionally defined counselor or psychologist. In our experience, there is typically resistance and resentment toward advocates for "rocking the boat."

The story of a new counselor in a community agency recently came to our attention. As a new employee in a substance abuse treatment facility, she was assigned to work with a senior group co-therapist. In the group therapy sessions, members were accustomed to being lectured at by the therapists and told how to behave in public and in group therapy. It was clear to the new counselor that group members had little say about what happened in the group and no authority or power to change the dynamics. The clients felt powerless and disinterested in the group, often dozing through the sessions. In an attempt to empower the members, the counselor set out to try to change these dynamics, asking group members what they felt was important to discuss in the group therapy sessions related to their substance abuse. Her advocacy for their empowerment led to dissension with the co-therapist, meetings with the agency director who talked about "how things are done here," and resentment from peers who had serious concerns about the upstart new employee. The aim of the counselor was certainly not to create friction and animosity from colleagues, but rather to fit in as a team player and help clients. Instead of being obstinate or refusing to recognize historical practices as "given practices," she questioned current practices in an attempt to improve services and advocate for fairness and equity that could empower and more fully benefit the clients (Bemak & Chung, 2005).

As in this case, it is risky to advocate, challenge, and confront supervisors and organizations to move toward social equity and authentic client empowerment. Challenging the politics, procedures, and practices in the place where we work may lead to negative repercussions (Bemak & Chung, 2005). Yet our question is, "How can we not do this work?" Consequently, an important aspect of being a successful advocate is figuring out how to sustain good professional relationships while challenging supervisors and organizations to adopt goals that benefit all clients, including those who are marginalized or disenfranchised.

MOVING BEYOND NICE COUNSELOR SYNDROME TO BECOME SOCIAL JUSTICE ADVOCATES

Although we discussed the nice counselor syndrome (NCS) in Chapter 8 ("Unpacking Psychological Barriers That Prevent Social Justice Action") we feel that it warrants further discussion as we continue to talk about advocacy as a primary task of social justice–oriented psychologists and counselors. In Chapter 8, we mentioned that the NCS (Bemak & Chung, 2008) is typically seen with many good-hearted, well-intentional mental health professionals who are commonly viewed as being the overly pleasant and the congenial "nice" person at their work places, those who avoid interpersonal conflict with others that may be needed when advocating for the best interests of clients. They may strive to promote harmony with others to sidestep disagreements and tensions that may accompany differences of opinion when promoting client rights and fair treatment (Bemak & Chung, 2008). We developed the NCS considering the personal and professional ramifications of social advocacy and how, at times, the lack of social advocacy had a detrimental impact on clients and their families. An example of NCS is the fear of being disliked, subjected to personal or negative peer pressure, or being targeted for professional ostracism, all of which may be personal obstacles. This may happen when we do not conform to the traditional role of helping in a nice, noncontroversial, supportive, and friendly manner, which may lead to being labeled as a troublemaker (Bemak & Chung, 2008) and could result in professional character assassination. Colleagues or administrators may discredit the reputation and character of counselors or psychologists who practice advocacy, which could lead to their jobs being jeopardized (Bemak & Chung, 2008).

To simply adopt advocacy as part of one's role without any preparation or advanced consideration is similar to walking into a lion's den. Psychologists and counselors who are advocates must walk a fine line, trying to support causes of equity, justice, and fairness while keeping their jobs. It is essential that mental health professionals and counselors acquire skills to balance the institutional realities of working within systems where they may have minimal power to respond to or act on issues for which they have ethical and moral responsibility to do social justice advocacy for their clients. Critically important is to figure out strategies to deal with institutional and individual barriers. To assist in this process, we (Bemak & Chung, 2005, 2008) provide 13 recommendations on the types of skills needed for counselors to be effective advocates within educational settings (see Box Text 18.4). These skills can also be adapted to and used in community settings.

SOCIAL JUSTICE ADVOCACY EXAMPLE

A psychologist, Terry, took a new job and began providing counseling in a mental health clinic. After six months, she noticed an increasing number of clients coming to the mental health clinic concerned about various issues, but all of them complained about headaches, skin rashes, and stomachaches. At first, Terry helped clients specifically with issues such as

BOX TEXT 18.4 THIRTEEN RECOMMENDATIONS FOR PSYCHOLOGISTS/COUNSELORS AS ADVOCATES

1. *Define role:* Includes responsibilities and tasks of psychologists/counselor that contribute to success

2. *Emphasize equity and equal opportunity:* Even distribution of support, time allocation, resources

3. *Restructure intervention strategies:* Intervention strategies should reach out to the larger community

4. *Teach clients their rights:* Provide tools that promote constructive change for clients that lead toward social justice, equal opportunities, and parity

5. *Formulate partnerships with clients:* Formulate partnerships with clients who may lack the skills and knowledge to self-advocate

6. *Align with clients to gain access to existing resources within their environments:* Requires knowledge about organizational systems that are helpful in promoting positive change toward equity

7. *Form alliances with others in clients' environment:* Work with individuals who will provide assistance for social change and decreasing inequities

8. *Utilize data to change one's role and incorporate advocacy:* Gather data and factual information that supports the changing role and advocate for that change

9. *Encourage trainings in leadership and advocacy skills:* Encourage training within organizations and in graduate programs; requires knowledge about organizational structure and change

10. *Collaborate with other mental health professionals:* Collaboration with professionals in the mental health field to compile data which advocate for change

11. *Participate in reform efforts:* Advocate to become a participant who contributes to these important efforts

12. *Promote social action within a sociopolitical context:* Requires an understanding of how to promote social action within the sociopolitical domain

13. *Collaborate with community agencies that provide other services:* Generate team support by utilizing additional resources

Source: Bemak, F., & Chung, R. C-Y. (2005). Advocacy as a critical role for urban school counselors: Working toward equity and social justice. *Professional School Counseling, 8*(3), 196–202.

trouble concentrating, marital conflict, a growing anxiety about driving after witnessing a pedestrian being hit by a car, and behavioral problems in school. This was done without considering their physical complaints. Yet Terry noticed that everyone who came to see her also mentioned their physical ailments. As more clients came for counseling Terry continued to hear about the headaches, skin rashes, and stomachaches. She grew concerned about the frequency of bodily ailments and decided to investigate whether there might be a reason for the physical problems. She soon learned that all her clients lived near a chemical waste plant that had been taken over by a new owner one year earlier. Terry began to gather information about the plant, the new owner, and the environmental effects of the kind of toxic waste that was being processed at the plant. It soon became clear from media reports and public health officials that there was a potential for serious mental and physical reactions to how the plant disposed of waste and that the new owner had a track record of fines and citations for not following safety guidelines.

At this point, Terry took on a role as an advocate on two levels. First, on a systemic level, she began to question the practices of the chemical plant through letters to the editor of the local newspaper, calls to elected officials, meetings at the state level, and contacts with the public health department. Second, rather than discount the information gathered from her investigations, she decided to share it whenever a client complained about headaches, skin rashes, or stomachaches. She told clients about the potential dangers of the chemicals being processed locally and provided information about the track record of the plant owner. If, in therapy, clients indicated that they wanted to do something about the situation, Terry would help them explore avenues for action and advocacy. In this way, she herself became an advocate for her clients while simultaneously helping them advocate for themselves if they chose to take action. As increasing numbers of her clients became interested in taking action Terry helped facilitate a meeting with clients and other interested stakeholders to discuss their common concerns and how to address the problem. In time, Terry's clients, along with other stakeholders, became less dependent on her as they took responsibility for their social activism.

SUMMARY

In summary, part of our role as psychologists and counselors is to advocate to create a just and fair society in which all people have equal opportunities and access to resources to pursue their potential; to ensure that programs, services, procedures, and policies are accessible and efficient for all people; to establish and protect balanced, equal, and equitable rights and entitlements; and to eliminate the negative and unethical impacts of social, economic, and political influences. We must move forward and beyond the traditional approach of focusing solely on intrapsychic and behavioral issues to accept and recognize the impact of sociopolitical factors on our clients, their families, and communities and determine how our advocacy can effectively address those issues. As we take on this work, it is important that we attempt to understand our own issues and processes and that we are clear about why we are becoming advocates and how we are incorporating advocacy into our job responsibilities. As promoters of social change and justice it is important to work cooperatively with other professionals, clients, and stakeholders, exercising courage, patience, persistence, tenacity, flexibility, and creativity since advocacy, similar to psychotherapy and counseling, is a process.

Acknowledging that advocacy is one of many roles we play as mental health professionals is important. Since not every activity and action with clients falls under the umbrella of advocacy, it is important to have a clear working definition of advocacy that guides our actions and interventions. A framework for advocacy that is helpful to keep in mind is that it is a goal-seeking endeavor and that advocacy involves obtaining, modifying, and promoting change to accomplish the targeted goal(s). Advocacy perpetuates changing the status quo (Ezell, 2001) so that being an advocate requires intentionality, a plan, and targeted efforts to generate change on social, economic, legal, cultural, and policy levels.

DISCUSSION QUESTIONS

1. Take a look at the advocacy competencies endorsed or the position on advocacy taken by your professional organization or university.
   a. What are some of things you are already doing as an advocate, either at your place of work or study, or personally?
   b. If your professional organization does not have advocacy competencies, create advocacy competencies you believe should be part of your profession.
   - What are your strengths as an advocate?
   c. What are some competencies endorsed or the position taken by your professional organization that you lack?
   d. What are some competencies or skills that you are willing to work on to improve?
2. Analyze the following statement from this chapter: "our beliefs is that advocacy is not only part of our work, but also an ethical and moral obligation for psychologists and counselors and is part and parcel of being an effective mental health professional."
   a. How would you argue this position in front of other mental health professionals who take the position that counseling and psychotherapy does not involve advocacy work and argue that advocacy is not the role of mental health professionals?
3. The chapter describes some characteristics of social justice–oriented work. Three of the characteristics are cultural and social justice humility, profound dignity, and respect for others.
   a. How would you identify each of these characteristics in your own work and personality if you were faced with a situation where two teenage gang members were sent to your office because both girls were found drawing graffiti on a wall in their middle school?
   b. How would you show respect?
   c. How would you display humility?
   d. What would be a personal challenge for you in this situation?
4. According to Lewis and Lewis (1983), the three tiers of advocacy actions are here and now, preventive advocacy, and citizen advocacy. Identify what your preferred level is, and identify some actions you could take at each level.
5. Advocacy involves challenging the status quo and has the potential to cause personal and professional difficulties. Reflect on your own fears and concerns about being an advocate and risk-taker that might cause interpersonal and organizational tension.

REFERENCES

Arredondo, P., Toporek, R., Brown, S. P., Jones, J., Locke, D. C., Sanchez, J., & Stadler, H. (1996). Operationalization of the multicultural counseling competencies. *Journal of Multicultural Counseling & Development, 24*(1), 42–78. https://doi.org/10.1002/j.2161-1912.1996.tb00288.x

Astramovich, R. L., & Harris, K. R. (2007). Promoting self-advocacy among minority students in school counseling. *Journal of Counseling and Development, 85*(3), 269–276. https://doi.org/10.1002/j.1556-6678.2007.tb00474.x

Atkinson, D. R., Thompson, C. E., & Grant, S. K. (1993). A three-dimensional model for counseling racial/ethnic minorities. *Counseling Psychologist, 21*(2), 257–277. https://doi.org/10.1177/0011000093212010

Baker, S. B. (1981). *The school counselor's handbook.* Allyn & Bacon.

Baker, S. B. (2000). *School counseling for the twenty-first century* (3rd ed.). Merrill.

Bemak, F. (2000). Transforming the role of the counselor to provide leadership in educational reform through collaboration. *Professional School Counseling, 3*(5), 323–331. https://search.proquest.com/openview/27e9062d242819f4e00434ecb41cf29b/1?pq-origsite=gscholar&cbl=11185

Bemak, F., & Chung, R. C.-Y. (2005). Advocacy as a critical role for urban school counselors: Working toward equity and social justice. *Professional School Counseling, 8*(3), 196–202. https://www.jstor.org/stable/42732459?seq=1#page_scan_tab_contents

Bemak, F., & Chung, R. C.-Y. (2007). Training counselors as social justice counselors. In C. C. Lee (Ed.), *Counseling for social justice* (2nd ed., pp. 239–258). American Counseling Association.

Bemak, F., & Chung, R. C.-Y. (2008). New professional roles and advocacy strategies for school counselors: A multicultural/social justice perspective to move beyond the nice counselor syndrome. *Journal of Counseling and Development, 86*(3), 372–381. https://doi.org/10.1002/j.1556-6678.2008.tb00522.x

Brooks, D. K., & Weikel, W. J. (1996). Mental health counseling: The first twenty years. In W. J. Weikel & A. J. Palmo (Eds.), *Foundations of mental health counseling* (pp. 5–29). Charles C Thomas.

Chen-Hayes, S. F. (2000). Social justice advocacy with lesbian, bisexual, gay, and transgendered persons. In J. Lewis & L. Bradley (Eds.), *Advocacy in counseling: Counselors, clients and community* (pp. 89–98). ERIC Counseling and Student Services Clearinghouse.

Chung, R. C-Y. (presentation) (2008, November). *Cultural perspectives on child trafficking, human rights and social justice.* United Nations Psychology Day. United Nations, New York.

Chung, R. C-Y., & Bemak, F. (2016, Mar 31–Apr 3). *How effective is social justice counseling training?* Paper presentation. American Counseling Association and Canadian Counselling and Psychotherapy Association International Conference, Montreal, Canada.

Chung, R. C-Y., & Kagawa-Singer, M. (1995). An interpretation of symptom presentation and distress: A Southeast Asian refugee example. *Journal of Nervous and Mental Disease, 183*(10), 639–648. https://doi.org/10.1097/00005053-199510000-00005

Comas-Díaz, L. (1987). Feminist therapy with Hispanic/Latina women: Myth or reality? *Women & Therapy, 6*(4), 39–61. https://doi.org/10.1300/J015V06N04_06

D'Andrea, M., & Daniels, J. (2000). Youth advocacy. In J. Lewis & L. Bradley (Eds.), *Advocacy in counseling: Counselors, clients and community* (pp. 71–78). ERIC Counseling and Student Services Clearinghouse.

Ennis, C. Z. (1993). Twenty years of feminist counseling and therapy: From naming biases to implementing multifaceted practice. *Counseling Psychologist, 21*(1), 3–87. https://doi.org/10.1177/0011000093211001

Ezell, M. (2001). *Advocacy in the human services.* Brooks/Cole.

Garrison, E. G., DeLeon, P. H., & Smedley, B. D. (2017). Psychology, public policy, and advocacy: Past, present, and future. *American Psychologist, 72*(8), 737–752. https://doi.org/10.1037/amp0000209

Goodman, J., & Waters, E. (2000). Advocating on behalf of older adults. In J. Lewis & L. Bradley (Eds.), *Advocacy in counseling: Counselors, clients and community* (pp. 79–88). ERIC Counseling and Student Services Clearinghouse.

Goodman, L. A., Wilson, J. M., Helms, J. E., Greenstein, N., & Medzhitova, J. (2018). Becoming an advocate: Processes and outcomes of a relationship-centered advocacy training model. *Counseling Psychologist, 46*(2), 122–153. https://doi.org/10.1177/0011000018757168

Hernández, R. J., & Villodas, M. T. (2020). Overcoming racial battle fatigue: The associations between racial microaggressions, coping, and mental health among Chicana/o and Latina/o college students. *Cultural Diversity and Ethnic Minority Psychology, 26*(3), 399–411. https://doi.org/10.1037/cdp0000306

Herring, R. (2000). Advocacy for Native American Indian and Alaska Native clients and counselees. In J. Lewis & L. Bradley (Eds.), *Advocacy in counseling: Counselors, clients and community* (pp. 37–44). ERIC Counseling and Student Services Clearinghouse.

House, R., & Martin, P. (1998). Advocating for better futures for all students: A new vision for school counselors. *Education, 119*(2), 284. https://www.questia.com/library/journal/1G1-53985384/advocating-for-better-futures-for-all-students-a

Kiselica, M. S. (1995). *Multicultural counseling with teenage fathers: A practical guide.* Sage.

Kiselica, M. S. (1998). Preparing Anglos for the challenges and joys of multiculturalism. *Counseling Psychologist, 26*(1), 5–21. https://doi.org/10.1177/0011000098261001

Kiselica, M. S. (1999). Confronting my own ethnocentrism and racism: A process of pain and growth. *Journal of Counseling and Development, 77*(1), 14–17. https://doi.org/10.1002/j.1556-6676.1999.tb02405.x

Kiselica, M. S. (2000, April). *The mental health professional as advocate: Matters of the heart, matters of the mind.* Keynote address. Great Lakes Regional Conference of Division 17 of the American Psychological Association, Muncie, IN, United States.

Kiselica, M. S., & Ramsey, M. L. (2000). Multicultural counselor education: Historical perspectives and future direction. In D. C. Locke, J. E. Myers, & E. L. Herr (Eds.), *The handbook of counseling* (pp. 433–452). Sage.

Kiselica, M. S., & Robinson, M. (2001). Bringing advocacy counseling to life: The history, issues, and human dramas of social justice work in counseling. *Journal of Counseling and Development, 79*(4), 387–398. https://doi.org/10.1002/j.1556-6676.2001.tb01985.x

Koch, J. M., & Juntunen, C. L. (Eds.). (2014a). Non-traditional teaching methods that promote social justice. *Special issue, Part 1, Counseling Psychologist, 42*(7). https://doi.org/10.1177/0011000014551772

Koch, J. M., & Juntunen, C. L. (Eds.). (2014b). Non-traditional teaching methods for social justice *Special issue, Part 2, Counseling Psychologist, 42*(8). https://doi.org/10.1177/0011000014551772

Koch, J. M., & Juntunen, C. L. (2014c). Non-traditional teaching methods that promote social justice: Introduction to the special issue. *Counseling Psychologist, 42*, 894–900. doi:10.1177/0011000014551772

Kozan, S., & Blustein, D. L. (2018). Implementing social change: A qualitative analysis of counseling psychologists' engagement in advocacy. *Counseling Psychologist, 46*(2), 154–189. https://doi.org/10.1177/0011000018756882

Lake, J., & Turner, M. S. (2017). Urgent need for improved mental health care and a more collaborative model of care. *Permanente Journal, 21*, 17–024. https://doi.org/10.7812/TPP/17-024

Lerner, B. (1972). *Therapy in the ghetto: Political impotence and personal disintegration.* Johns Hopkins University Press.

Leung, S. A. (1995). Career development and counseling: A multicultural perspective. In J. G. Ponterotto, J. M. Casas, L. A. Suzuki, & C. M. Alexander (Eds.), *Handbook of multicultural counseling* (pp. 549–566). Sage.

Lewis, J., Arnold, M., House, R., & Toporek, R. (2002). *ACA advocacy competencies.* https://www.counseling.org/docs/default-source/competencies/aca-advocacy-competencies-may-2020.pdf?sfvrsn=85b242c_6

Lewis, J. A., & Lewis, M. D. (1983). *Community counseling: A human services approach.* Wiley.

Lewis, J. A., Lewis, M. D., Daniels, J. A., & D'Andrea, M.J. (1998). *Community counseling: Empowerment strategies for a diverse society* (2nd ed.). Brooks/Cole.

McClure, B. A., & Russo, T. R. (1996). The politics of counseling: Looking back and forward. *Counseling and Values, 40*(3), 162–174. https://doi.org/10.1002/j.2161-007X.1996.tb00849.x

McWhirter, E. H. (1994). *Counseling for empowerment.* American Counseling Association.

Moreno, C., Wykes, T., Galderisi, S., Nordentoft, M., Crossley, N., Jones, N., Cannon, M., Correll, C. U., Byrne, L., Carr, S., Chen, E., Gorwood, P., Johnson, S., Kärkkäinen, H., Krystal, J. H., Lee, J., Lieberman, J., López-Jaramillo, C., Männikkö, M., Phillips, M. R., ... Arango, C. (2020). How mental health care should change as a consequence of the COVID-19 pandemic. *Lancet Psychiatry, 7*(9), 813–824. https://doi.org/10.1016/S2215-0366(20)30307-2

Myers, J. E., Sweeney, T. J., & White, V. E. (2002). Advocacy for counseling and counselors: A professional imperative. *Journal of Counseling and Development, 80*(4), 394–402. https://doi.org/10.1002/j.1556-6678.2002.tb00205.x

Paradies, Y., Ben, J., Denson, N., Elias, A., Priest, N., Pieterse, A., Gupta, A., Kelaher, M., & Gee, G. (2015). Racism as a determinant of health: A systematic review and meta-analysis. *PLOS ONE, 10*(9), e0138511. https://doi.org/10.1371/journal.pone.0138511

Parsons, F. (1909). *Choosing a vocation.* Houghton Mifflin.

Pearrow, M. M., & Fallon, L. (2019, Aug 29). Integrating social justice and advocacy into training psychologists: A practical demonstration. *Psychological Services, 17*(S1), 30–36. http://dx.doi.org/10.1037/ser0000384.

Pinderhughes, E. B. (1983). Empowerment for our clients and for ourselves. *Social Casework, 64*(4), 331–338. https://doi.org/10.1177/104438948306400602

Priest, N., Paradies, Y., Trenerry, B., Truung, M. Karlsen, S., & Kelly, Y. (2013). A systematic review of studies examining the relationship between reported racism and health and wellbeing for children and young people. *Social Science & Medicine, 95*, 115–127. https://doi.org/10.1016/j.socscimed.2012.11.031

Prilleltensky, I. (1997). Values, assumptions, and practices: Assessing the moral implications of psychological discourse and action. *American Psychologist, 52*(5), 517–535. https://doi.org/10.1037/0003-066X.52.5.517

Ramírez Stege, A. M., Brockberg, D., & Hoyt, W. T. (2017). Advocating for advocacy: An exploratory survey on student advocacy skills and training in counseling psychology. *Training and Education in Professional Psychology, 11*(3), 190–197. https://doi.org/10.1037/tep0000158

Ratts, M. J., & Hutchins, A. M. (2009). ACA advocacy competencies: Social justice advocacy at the client/student level. *Journal of Counseling & Development, 87*(3), 269–275. https://doi.org/10.1002/j.1556-6678.2009.tb00106.x

Sanders, J. L. (2000). Advocacy on behalf of African-American clients. In J. Lewis & L. Bradley (Eds.), *Advocacy in counseling: Counselors, clients and community* (pp. 15–24). ERIC Counseling and Student Services Clearinghouse.

Sollod, R. N. (1998). Unexamined religious assumptions. *American Psychologist, 53*(3), 324–325. https://doi.org/10.1037/0003-066X.53.3.324

Steele, C. M., Spencer, S. J., & Aronson, J. (2002). Contending with group image: The psychology of stereotype and social identity threat. In M. Zanna (Ed.), *Advances in experimental social psychology* (pp. 379–440). Academic Press. https://doi.org/10.1016/S0065-2601(02)80009-0

Sue, D. W. (2003). *Overcoming our racism: The journey to liberation.* Jossey-Bass.

Sue, D. W., Sue, D., Neville, H. A., & Smith, L. (2019*). Counseling the culturally diverse: Theory and practice.* (8 ed.) Wiley.Toporek, R. L. (2000). Developing a common language and framework for understanding advocacy in counseling. In J. Lewis & L. Bradley (Eds.), *Advocacy in counseling: Counselors, clients and community* (pp. 5–14). ERIC Counseling and Student Services Clearinghouse.

Toporek, R. L., & Ahluwalia, M. K. (2021). *Taking action: Creating social change through strength, solidarity, strategy & sustainability.* Cognella.

Toporek, R. L., & Daniels, J. (2018). American Counseling Association advocacy competencies. American Counseling Association. https://www.counseling.org/docs/default-source/competencies/aca-2018-advocacy-competencies.pdf?sfvrsn=1dca552c_6

Toporek, R. L., Gerstein, L. H., Fouad, N. A., Roysircar, & Israel, T. (Eds.). (2006). *Handbook for social justice in counseling psychology: Leadership, vision, and action* (pp. 1–16). Sage. https://doi.org/10.4135/9781412976220.n1

Toporek, R. L., & Liu, W. M. (2001). Advocacy in counseling. In D. B. Pope-Davis & H. L. K. Coleman (Eds.), *The intersection of race, class, and gender in multicultural counseling* (pp. 385–413). Sage.

Weinrach, S. G., & Thomas, K. R. (1998). Diversity-sensitive counseling today: A postmodern clash of values. *Journal of Counseling & Development, 76*(2), 115–122. https://doi.org/10.1002/j.1556-6676.1998.tb02384.x

Williams, D. R. (2018). Stress and the mental health of populations of color: Advancing our understanding of race-related stressors. *Journal of Health and Social Behavior, 59*(4), 466–485. https://doi.org/10.1177/0022146518814251

CHAPTER 19

THE MYTHS AND REALITIES OF EMPOWERMENT

Frederic P. Bemak and Rita Chi-Ying Chung

You may never know what results come of your actions, but if you do nothing there will be no result.

—Mahatma Gandhi

We become successful by helping others become successful.

—Author Unknown

You may not control all the events that happen to you, but you can decide not to be reduced by them.

—Maya Angelou

You can, you should, and if you're brave enough to start, you will.

—Stephen King

REFLECTION QUESTIONS

1. Consider a therapeutic relationship where the aim of the therapy or counseling is to authentically empower the client. How would you describe the power dynamics between the therapist and client?
2. Do you believe there are any risks in working toward the authentic empowerment of clients? If so, what are the risks?
3. How would you describe the connection between authentic empowerment and advocacy?

Social justice, social change, and empowerment cannot be separated. Ironically, we have noticed that there is a great deal of discussion and agreement about empowering clients while the mental health professional makes all the decisions regarding the problem, diagnosis, treatment, and follow-up. Authentic therapeutic partnerships are an integral part of justice-oriented mental health work and empowerment, rather than therapeutic relationships in which mental health professionals dictate the process of treatment. An outcome of social justice and human rights mental health work is a shift of power, with clients and stakeholders gaining more say and influence over their lives and the lives of others. To be effective in empowering people, we must recognize the way power influences social justice and the human rights of individuals, families, and communities. We must also recognize and understand that powerlessness creates obstacles to personal, social, and community growth and development as well as creating other ongoing disadvantages, such as lack of access to opportunities and resources and equal rights. Rappaport (1987) stated that empowerment is personal mastery and control over one's life, caring about others, and the ability to exert political and social influence.

At the root of empowerment is the concept of power, as discussed in Chapter 14 ("The Critical Intersection of Social Change and Social Justice"). Power can be viewed through the lens of the character of the relationship, incorporating five types of power with both destructive and constructive elements (May, 1972). Destructive aspects of power include exploitation and manipulation. Other types of power, depending on how they are used, are either constructive or destructive. Competitiveness could be used either positively or negatively, while nutritive power, or having power for others, and integrative power, or power with others, could also be used in helpful or unhelpful ways.

In psychology and counseling, an aim is to support and foster client outcomes that assist with personal empowerment. When we do clinical work from a social justice framework, the outcome and goals expand to include not only *personal* empowerment, but also *social, systemic,* and *political* empowerment. Thus, when we counsel and advocate with and for clients' rights, we are aiming to support clients in gaining a say over their own lives as well as affecting the world around them. A way to think about this is to consider a Latinx in-home program supervisor who came for counseling because of experiencing unfair treatment and discrimination by staff from other agencies. The mental health clinician could have simply focused on feelings of despair and frustration and successfully aided the client in coping with the situation. To address the social aspects of the situation meant exploring and supporting the client's interest in challenging the discriminating individual(s) at work and trying to work things out. This would be empowerment on a social level.

The clinician may also want to emphasize systemic empowerment by exploring what the client wants to do with the awareness that other Latinxs in the agency were also facing unfair treatment and feeling upset and angry. If the client wanted to advocate and challenge the discrimination beyond their personal experience, to improve the interagency relationships and address the broader issue within the larger human services programs, this would constitute systemic empowerment. Systemic empowerment is reinforced when the supervisor supports advocating for organizational change. The clinician could assist and buttress the supervisor's interest in advocating for Latinxs to be represented on various interagency committees that could address this issue and introduce new actions and policies, thus enhancing political empowerment.

As we discussed in previous chapters, historically, helping professionals have not been involved in their clients' worlds outside of the personal processes and behaviors that are explored in psychotherapy and counseling sessions. Working toward social justice and human rights involves a significantly broader awareness and emphasis on the intersecting factors that impact a client's life and attention to the rights of others, requiring client empowerment that goes beyond intrapsychic processes. To achieve authentic social justice empowerment requires going further than individual social empowerment to include systematic and political empowerment (Cattaneo et al., 2014).

Social justice empowerment therefore involves the helping professional working with the clients' everyday lived experiences and injustices. The socioeconomic, sociocultural, sociohistorical, sociopolitical, and ecological contexts of a client's life are essential elements to incorporate into counseling and psychotherapy (Bemak & Conyne, 2004; Ramirez Stege et al., 2017; Toporek & Liu, 2001). Researchers (i.e., Koggel, 2010) underscored this, emphasizing that empowerment must consider perspectives within which clients live. In moving toward social equity and equal rights it is important that clients can influence these dimensions that affect their lives.

Consequently, empowerment acknowledges the central role of power dynamics at societal, community, cultural, familial, and individual levels (Pinderhughes, 1983). To ignore the importance of power in a broader context and how political, institutional, structural, and systemic power disempowers clients is to ignore a crucial element in empowerment. Simply recognizing oppression, marginalization, discrimination, xenophobia, poverty, racism, etc., and how clients manage these issues is not enough. Instead, counselors and psychologists must act on social injustices by expanding their traditional roles and developing awareness of and taking action on social, political, economic, and ecological barriers encountered by marginalized, oppressed, and disenfranchised clients (Bemak & Chung, 2008; Toporek et al., 2006; Vera & Speight, 2003).

AUTHENTIC EMPOWERMENT IN SOCIAL JUSTICE AND HUMAN RIGHTS WORK

Nowadays, "empowerment" is a commonly used term in psychology. Counselors and psychologists regularly talk about empowering individuals, families, and communities, and they agree that empowerment is important in psychological work. The concept and term are used regularly in discussions about clients and psychological interventions. No one is opposed to empowerment, and everyone supports empowering others as a goal. Yet the casual and everyday inclusion of empowerment as part of counseling and psychotherapy has, in our opinion, diminished its potency and meaning. By focusing purely on empowering individuals to enhance agency without acknowledging and attending to the historical, political, social, economic, cultural, institutional, and structural issues that disempower them is creating a relational, interdependent, "pseudo-empowerment" (Koggel, 2010). Without addressing justice as a part of client empowerment perpetuates the status quo of disempowerment and oppression (Cattaneo et al., 2014). Social justice empowerment stresses the importance of connecting individual and social power and understanding the intersection between the two. We believe this is instrumental in authentically empowering individuals and communities.

In addition, it is important that client empowerment also considers the cultural aspects, definitions, and interpretations of empowerment. The English term "empowerment" and the process of achieving empowerment may have different meanings in different cultures (Chamberlin, 1997; Erzinger, 1994). For example, in Chinese culture, the term "empowerment" may include various types of empowerment such as pragmatic, autocratic, hidden, lonely romantic, or fashionable empowerment (Yip, 2004). Furthermore, we have been struck by how some proponents of empowerment have difficulty letting go of control, giving up elements of their own power in therapeutic encounters or actually supporting clients to "run with" their newfound power. At times, well-intentioned therapeutic encounters have fallen short of meeting the goal of empowerment. Thus, when we consider empowerment, we have used the term "authentic empowerment," to take into account cultural dimensions.

To successfully achieve authentic empowerment, mental health professionals must have the courage to take uncomfortable risks and adjust to disruptions in the status quo and changes in social connections and power. This in turn, may become part of changing dynamics in the therapeutic relationship. As clients grow and begin to experience authentic empowerment, there may be an accompanying assertiveness or challenging of the therapist, which may initially present difficulties for the mental health professional. This may involve forfeiting our own power, risking losses of our individual and social power as clinicians. Although the goal of psychological interventions is decreased dependence and eventual termination, the reality that we are less needed and depended on and that our clients have attained true autonomy and self-mastery may raise strong countertransference reactions that precipitate conscious or unconscious resistance to the client's empowerment.

AUTHENTIC EMPOWERMENT AND ADVOCACY

Authentic empowerment is seen as a dimension of advocacy in which helping professionals assist clients in achieving goals and eliminating barriers that prevent clients and families from attaining fair treatment and an equitable quality of life. Initially, counselors and psychologists may educate clients about their circumstances, teach them advocacy skills, and collaborate with them in an effort to enhance social justice, with an objective that clients master the skills to advocate for themselves. Authentic empowerment occurs when counselors and psychologists are genuinely supporting clients in developing personal authority and their ability to positively influence the world around them. Clients begin to have a more profound sense of self, with a deeper understanding about what this means for improving themselves and their environments, resulting in advocacy activities. The advocacy that comes along with social justice and human rights begins with the resolution of personal issues that allows clients to gain a sense of self that provides a base from which to help and care for others.

FACTORS IN AUTHENTIC EMPOWERMENT

Becoming an advocate for empowerment to promote social justice is not an automatic process. It takes time, commitment, and certain attributes. Here, we describe 10 factors that we consider key in fostering authentic empowerment (see Box Text 19.1).

1. *Personal commitment.* To facilitate authentic empowerment, one must have a personal investment in the issue at hand. Being personally involved and dedicated to the social justice issue leads to self-empowerment and the empowerment of others. The commitment to change has a direct relationship with empowerment. Therefore, if people are committed to equal same-sex marriage rights, it is more likely that they will become empowered in pursuit of this goal.

2. *Hope.* When we have hope, or the belief that there will be a positive outcome as a result of our actions, then there will be a greater potential for authentic empowerment (Chamberlain, 1997; Chamodraka et al., 2017). In contrast, the absence of viable success or progress toward creating change and justice has the potential to deflate and disempower. Thus, even small successes at reaching social justice goals generate faith that actions will result in positive outcomes. For example, if a person is being discriminated against at their workplace due to having a disability, they may go to a psychologist to work on feelings of anger and frustration. If, in counseling, they realize that others with disabilities are experiencing similar issues, they may decide to take action with supervisors to address the broader issue of workplace discrimination. If action is taken at the work site and the discrimination decreases, the likelihood is that the individual will feel empowered by seeing that things, in fact, can change.

3. *Social support.* When one knows that there are others who will join in and act to promote human rights and social justice, it facilitates authentic empowerment. This is also true if individuals have a social support network to join them. This means that if I recognize that my peers and colleagues encounter similar problems and I know that they will join in the effort to create change, I feel empowered.

4. *Common goals.* Shared goals are a factor that contributes to authentic empowerment. When one shares the same vision for social justice with others, there is a sense of mutuality and empowerment. Knowing that there are others who feel upset over the treatment of LGBTQI youth in a particular community helps those involved know there is support and feel empowered to take action.

5. *Knowledge of rights and information leading to available action.* When one is knowledgeable about individual rights and informed about options for advocacy, there is optimism that empowerment and change can happen (Chamberlin, 1997). For example, when several high school students were caught with alcohol, the assistant principal gave harsher penalties to the African American students involved than to the White students. A number of African American parents were upset and received support from the school psychologist, resulting in the group approaching the principal. Having available information and knowing their rights and the mechanism by which to take steps to address this problem helped the parents feel empowered.

6. *Not being afraid of conflict or tension.* Tackling social justice and human rights issues and challenging existing structures and the status quo creates dissonance. Having the courage and ability to handle tension and conflict is critical in facilitating authentic empowerment. Avoiding interpersonal tension may cause disempowerment.

7. *Comfort with discomfort.* Challenging existing structures to promote equity, access, opportunities, and fairness has the potential to generate confusion and chaos. Having the capacity to adapt and accept a disorderly world while change is happening is an important factor in feeling empowered.

8. *Understanding process.* Authentic empowerment requires us to understand both how change happens and how process works. Progression and change take time, so one must be patient and accept that process is a "movement toward" rather than more immediate "results and gratification" to feel empowered.

9. *Historical successes.* We base our experiences of empowerment on the past. If we have had small successes in creating change in the past or observed others having successes, then we are much more likely to feel empowered and cultivate authentic empowerment.

10. *Having a role model who was empowered.* Having someone who stood for social justice and human rights and who is a role model is important. An exemplary figure who has tackled the issues of change to improve society helps to foster authentic empowerment. Role models could be family members, neighbors, or national or international figures such as Martin Luther King Jr., Albert Einstein, Harriet Tubman, John F. Kennedy, Nelson Mandela, Amelia Earhart, the Dalai Lama, Mahatma Gandhi, Mohammed Ali, Cesar Chavez, Frederick Douglass, Sitting Bull, Shirin Ebadi, Rosa Parks, Jackie Robinson, or Harvey Milk.

CASE STUDY EXAMPLE OF SOCIAL JUSTICE AND AUTHENTIC EMPOWERMENT

To illustrate social justice, advocacy, and authentic empowerment, the following is a real-life case study example of how mental health professionals can utilize advocacy to assist their clients in becoming empowered. We (Fred and Rita) received funding from a foundation to conduct a project aimed at improving academic performance with high-risk failing students through family involvement. The project was based in a school in a low-income urban area with high numbers of students with very low school performance who qualified for free and reduced-price meal programs. The project goal was to improve academic achievement and performance for students at the highest level of risk for academic failure in the school.

This project specifically targeted families who were disengaged from the school by generating a counseling intervention support group for student caretakers which included parents and guardians. The project was based on research showing that family involvement helps improve students' academic performance (Jeynes, 2007). The longer-term goal for the group was for families to assume ownership and responsibility for the project and re-engage in the students' education. "Disengaged families" were defined as those who were not actively involved with their children's school lives and had little or no contact with school personnel. All the families, in fact, had long-standing records of not responding to repeated attempts by school administrators, counselors, psychologists, and teachers to reach them and discuss their children's school performance and behavior (Bemak & Cornely, 2002).

Initially, the school principal was extremely hesitant about the project, worried that parents would mobilize and challenge her leadership and authority. After several meetings where we advocated for the potential positive outcomes of the project, the principal relented and gave permission to implement it. Students involved in the project were selected based on the criteria of poor academic performance, behavioral problems, and little or no family contact with school personnel. Working with the school counselors, 10 students were identified who were failing seventh grade and whose families were not involved with the school. Our next step was contacting their parents and guardians. Contacting the parents was a major challenge since one of the criteria for selection was that parents or guardians had a history of ignoring any attempts by the school to reach them. After numerous telephone calls and follow-up visits to homes, we were able to persuade eight parents/guardians to attend a meeting to discuss their children's school performance.

At the first meeting, we discussed the goals for the project. Participants were initially suspicious, hesitant to speak, and distrustful of attending another meeting where they were talked "at." Rather than tell the parents and guardians what we were going to do at the meetings, we encouraged them to help us define what would be most helpful to support their children in school. In effect, they defined the project rather than the project defining them. They were intrigued with the idea that they could and would set the agenda and the goals for our meetings. The experience of being valued participants was quite unique for these parents and guardians, and, as the first meeting progressed, the participants became animated and excited as they defined the agenda and goals for the meeting. After a highly productive discussion and unanimous agreement that "this meeting was very different from any other school meeting they had ever been to," the question was posed to the group about how often to meet. The group itself decided that they *wanted* to meet on a regular basis every two weeks.

In the parents/guardians' group, there was no regular set agenda; instead, there was an open forum in which the members set the agenda for each meeting within the framework of improved academic performance of the children. Meetings were facilitated by us (Fred and Rita). At first, parents and guardians kept asking us to "tell them what to do" since they were accustomed to participating in that manner. Aiming toward *authentic empowerment* and equity, we continually asked them as a group to set the agenda, group rules, and norms. Members agreed that they were all concerned about their children and began discussions about how to improve their school performance. As the participants talked about their children, discussions evolved into sessions of sharing about their personal lives and challenges, fears, difficulties, and challenges they faced as parents and guardians. Relationships within the families were discussed, as were personal issues that had been unresolved, such as prior incarceration, homelessness, prostitution, and drug abuse. These sessions led to self-healing, greater awareness, and skill-building in providing support for their children's education.

One day, one of the mothers expressed frustration about not having time, energy, or knowledge to help her child in school, stating, "I work many jobs and long hours, so when I get home I am exhausted. My kids, they all come running up to me yelling and carrying on, so I just run to my bedroom, lock the door, and turn on loud music. They just bang away at my door, but I ignore it." Through the meetings and group support, the mother established healthier relationships with her family, learning how to come home and balance time with her three children while finding a moment for her to catch her breath.

The meetings were held regularly on a bimonthly basis for the entire school year. Each meeting involved working out transportation for those members without transport or gas money. University student volunteers provided tutoring to the students and childcare for younger children. Dinner was provided for all participants at each meeting through foundation funding. During the entire academic year, not one of the parents or guardians, students, or volunteers dropped out of the project. In fact, as the year progressed, a second parent or guardian for some of the participating children started to regularly attend the meetings, and other parents and guardians of other eligible children joined the group. After a few months, there was a waiting list to join, generated by interested students and parents/guardians. The group of parents and guardians decided that everyone had to make a commitment to attend the meetings and that anyone who missed two meetings in a row without a good reason would not be permitted to remain in the group.

Meetings were held in the school gym. Several activities were conducted simultaneously. In one corner of the gym, we (Fred and Rita) met with parents and guardians to discuss parenting as well as associated personal, family, and work-related problems, all of which impacted their children's academic performance. These sessions were most often deeply personal, with tears, hugs, and a tremendously supportive environment. In another section of the gym, the children, divided according to age level and/or school subject, worked on their homework and studies with volunteer tutors. Yet another area of the gym was designated for younger siblings who required childcare and were looked after by other university student volunteers. The set-up in the gym resembled a living room, where all family members were present and visible to each other, and there were multiple ongoing activities. At times, everyone joined together for a large community meeting that allowed parents and guardians, children, and volunteers to speak together about issues, common goals, and the program.

As the project progressed, the students began to improve their performance in school, and the parents and guardians began to feel empowered. The groups' stories of life challenges and community meetings affected family relationships and changed interactions with children, resulting in the group becoming a safe and supportive haven in a trying world. Mothers, fathers, and grandparents collectively brainstormed about how to overcome each other's problems, gave helpful advice to each other, and encouraged one another to make significant changes. Members talked about the group as a life-changing experience. One mother shared how joining the group was a turning point in her life. The phrase took root, and the members named the group and the project "Turning Point."

Upon hearing the name for their caretakers' group, the children also wanted an identity, so we had a community meeting to decide about the name for their portion of the project. They decided collectively to use the term "TP" since it was a "cooler" term than "Turning Point," demonstrating that not only the parents/guardians but also the children took ownership and gained a say in their lives. As word got around, students would wait outside the school building to request to be part of the TP. The Turning Point parents/guardians decided that any student could be involved in the project, with the only criterion being that a parent or guardian must also attend.

At the end of the school year an event occurred that included other parents not involved in the project, one that mobilized the Turning Point group. On the last day of school, administrators sent letters to parents and guardians of students who needed to repeat a grade (no one in Turning Point received a letter), informing them that their children would be held back for another year. Many of the parents and guardians were in total shock since they had no idea that their children were doing so poorly academically. Because the letters were sent on the last day of school, it was impossible for parents to discuss the matter with teachers or the school principal since the school was closed. The Turning Point group was outraged and irate over how school administrators had handled the situation, leading them to brainstorm how to tackle the problem.

As a group, they decided to contact other parents in their neighborhood and circulate a petition about the principal's decision, demanding a meeting with parents and the principal. They also decided that, rather than stage a demonstration, a small group of parents would contact the State Department of Education to talk to the state superintendent. Before the beginning of the new academic year, the parents were informed that a new principal had been assigned to the school. Although it was unclear whether this was a direct outcome of the work of the Turning Point group, it reinforced the parents' conviction that they had some influence and were empowered to advocate and create change, not only for themselves but for others.

Results of the project were significant. Parents and guardians became more positive and provided care, attention, and appropriate discipline to their children; children communicated more openly and positively with parents and guardians; disruptive behaviors both in school and at home significantly decreased; and grades and attendance dramatically improved. Utilizing four academic criteria—attendance, grades, disciplinary referrals, and suspension (Bemak et al., 2014)—it was clear that the students had improved their academic performance. Furthermore, the parents and guardians of the Turning Point group became involved and invested in their children's education as they became empowered by having knowledge about their rights and possible ways to advocate. Their social actions empowered others to also stand up for their rights.

This case example illustrates social justice advocacy, leadership, and authentic empowerment, where individuals truly defined strategies, goals, and directions for their own positive healthy growth and development. The group was a disenfranchised and impoverished population that historically had no say about their children's education or their own lives. The system had silenced them. Given the opportunity to take leadership roles and have a voice to advocate for each other, and eventually with the school system, led to authentic empowerment where they excelled.

SUMMARY

Social justice, social change, and empowerment are interconnected. This chapter presents an in-depth examination of the myths and realities of culturally responsive social justice-oriented empowerment and the transformation of empowerment to authentic empowerment. The authors describe 10 key factors necessary for promoting authentic empowerment and explicate the constructive and destructive use of power as a means of achieving authentic empowerment. There is a description of the importance of psychologists and counselors expanding their traditional roles by attending to cultural, institutional, social, political, and historical issues to facilitate authentic empowerment including a case example.

DISCUSSION QUESTIONS

1. Can you identify one or two myths of empowerment?
2. Discuss the definition of authentic empowerment presented in the chapter.
3. What are some of the components of authentic empowerment that will be important in your work as a mental health professional?
4. Analyze the following statement: "Simply recognizing oppression, discrimination, poverty, racism, etc., and how clients manage these issues in their lives is not enough."
   a. Identify a current issue that is affecting your local area.
   b. Design some strategies that you could employ as a mental health professional to address those injustices.
   c. What elements of empowerment would you use?
5. Choose one of the 10 key factors in fostering authentic empowerment and reflect on how this is important in the process of empowering yourself and others.
6. Using the example of Turning Point presented in the chapter, identify the factors that were important to fostering authentic empowerment in the group members.
7. The chapter describes the importance of resolving personal issues in order to help others. List two or three personal social justice resolutions that you could include in your daily practice to make sure you are working toward authentic empowerment with your clients.

REFERENCES

Bemak, F., & Chung, R. C-Y. (2008). New professional roles and advocacy strategies for school counselors: A multicultural social justice perspective to move beyond the nice counselor syndrome. *Journal of Counseling and Development, Multicultural and Diversity Issues in Counseling Special Issue, 38*, 372–381. https://doi.org/10.1002/j.1556-6678.2008.tb00522.x

Bemak, F., & Conyne, R. (2004). Ecological group work. In R. K. Conyne & E. P. Cook (Eds.), *Ecological counseling: An innovative approach to conceptualizing person-environment interaction* (pp. 195–217). American Counseling Association.

Bemak, F., & Cornely, L. (2002). The SAFI model as a critical link between marginalized families and schools: A literature review and strategies for school counselors. *Journal of Counseling and Development, 80*(3), 322–331. https://doi.org/10.1002/j.1556-6678.2002.tb00197.x

Bemak, F., Williams, J., & Chung, R. C-Y. (2014). Four critical domains of accountability for school counselors. *Professional School Counseling, 18*(1), 100–110. https://doi.org/10.1177/2156759X0001800101

Cattaneo, L. B., Calton, J. M., & Brodsky, A. E. (2014). Status quo versus status quake: Putting the power back in empowerment. *Journal of Community Psychology, 42*(4), 433–446. https://doi.org/10.1002/jcop.21619

Chamberlin, J. (1997). A working definition of empowerment. *Psychiatric Rehabilitation Journal, 20*(4), 43–46. http://polkcountypbsn.org/wp-content/uploads/2012/10/Working-definition-of-empowerment.pdf

Chamodraka, M., Fitzpatrick, M. R., & Janzen, J. I. (2017). Hope as empowerment model: A client-based perspective on the process of hope development. *Journal of Positive Psychology, 12*(3), 232–245. doi:10.1080/17439760.2016.1225115

Erzinger, S. (1994). Empowerment in Spanish: Words can get in the way. *Health Education Quarterly, 21*(3), 417–419. https://doi.org/10.1177/109019819402100312

Jeynes, W. H. (2007). The relationship between parental involvement and urban secondary school student academic achievement: A meta-analysis. *Urban Education, 42*(1), 82–110. https://doi.org/10.1177/0042085906293818

Koggel, C. (2010). The ethics of empowerment. *Development, 52*(2), 175–178. https://doi.org/10.1057/dev.2010.7

May, R. (1972). *Power and innocence.* Norton.

Pinderhughes, E. B. (1983). Empowerment for our clients and for ourselves. *Social Casework, 64*(4), 331–338. https://doi.org/10.1177/104438948306400602

Ramírez Stege, A. M., Brockberg, D., & Hoyt, W. T. (2017). Advocating for advocacy: An exploratory survey on student advocacy skills and training in counseling psychology. *Training and Education in Professional Psychology, 11*(3), 190–197. https://doi.org/10.1037/tep0000158

Rappaport, J. (1987). Terms of empowerment/exemplars of prevention: Toward a theory for community psychology. *American Journal of Community Psychology, 15*(2), 121–148. https://doi.org/10.1007/BF00919275

Toporek, R. L., Gerstein, L. H., Fouad, N. A., Roysircar, G., & Israel, T. (Eds.). (2006). *Handbook for social justice in counseling psychology: Leadership, vision, and Action* (pp. 1–16). Sage. https://doi.org/10.4135/9781412976220.n1

Toporek, R. L., & Liu, W. M. (2001). Advocacy in counseling. In D. B. Pope-Davis & H. L. K. Coleman (Eds.), *The intersection of race, class, and gender in multicultural counseling* (pp. 385–413). Sage.

Vera, E. M., & Speight, S. L. (2003). Multicultural competence, social justice, and counseling psychology: Expanding our roles. *Counseling Psychologist, 31*(3), 253–272. https://doi.org/10.1177/0011000003031003001

Yip, K-S. (2004). The empowerment model: A critical reflection of empowerment in Chinese culture. *Social Work, 49*(3), 479–487. doi:10.1093/sw/49.3.479

CHAPTER 20

STUDENT CHAPTER

I Cannot Let Fear and Intimidation Prevent Me from Being
an Advocate

Dajah Nolan

As an African American woman in graduate training, while reading and hearing about the social justice reflections from both faculty and other graduate students, I was quickly given a sense of inspiration. Reading about the hardships Dr. Chung had to endure as an immigrant and the perseverance Dr. Bemak displayed even at a young age at his high school made me evaluate my own social justice journey. Prior to this graduate program I would always envision social justice and one's decision to be involved in this work as a grand gesture in which you are appointed and follow the works of those like Nelson Mandela and Dr. Martin Luther King. However, reading and hearing from fellow students about their journeys made me realize that a social justice perception and way of life had been implanted in my life very early on. Although many of these experiences were hurtful, discriminatory, and confusing, they all played a huge role in the passion I have for advocating for those who look like me and experience similar pain. Reading the chapters and attending classes I realized that many times this social justice journey is marked by mishaps and altered plans. No one started their lives envisioning themselves as powerful leaders and advocates, however, each of their unique journeys built the foundations for who they are now, whether the experience was positive or negative.

With this, I could quickly recollect the experiences I had that led me to become interested in becoming a social justice counselor. In kindergarten, being the only African American girl in a private Christian school, I was quickly reminded of my differences and perceived inferiority. After an experience in which I was called out for being the only Black person, I confided in my mother to explain the confusion, hurt, and anger I was feeling. I can vividly remember her explaining to a 5-year-old me, with tears in her eyes, how this society and life is not fair many times for people who look like us, and, unfortunately, it is something we have all experienced and probably will continue to experience. I remember feeling both shocked and helpless. The world I looked at so innocently was quickly changed into a brutal reality. I wanted to do something about this injustice, this injustice that made my mother and everyone I care about sad. Little did I know that I would get the opportunity now, 20 years later, to fight against that hopelessness I felt so long ago.

Although I continued to experience incidences of discrimination and racism growing up as an African American girl, I always found myself very aware of the differences and privileges even within my own school and community. When attending a middle school in a predominately middle-class African American area, I noticed how several middle schools within the same county with predominately White residents were thriving with new buildings, supplies, and sports programs. Meanwhile, the middle school I attended would at times barely have enough textbooks to distribute to students. This angered and saddened me even as middle schooler, and, although I understood the basis of systemic racism, I just couldn't understand how it could happen so blatantly. In hindsight, even though I did not think of a grand plan to alleviate discrimination within school systems, it was something that always interested me. Through my parents always providing information and engaging us in important dialogue, I began to do research and watch documentaries about the systemic racism within school systems and the troubles those less fortunate faced, eventually leading to my passion for school counseling. The ability to have an inside look and provide insight to improve a broken system that I was a product of is something I wanted and where I could see myself making a difference.

With this passion, I hope to inspire little Black girls like myself, with the passion and fire inside themselves, to recognize injustice and envision something better. I hope to engage in important dialogues with my students, colleagues, and other stakeholders about the importance of equity in all aspects within a school and the impact it has on students of color when these important implications are ignored. Although I continue to have an overwhelming passion for social justice within schools, especially for African American students, I would be naïve to believe that because I am now educated these concerns and issues that I present will be accepted with open arms. However, I am still an African American woman in a society that places our value at less than others. Because of this, I sometimes am apprehensive about becoming the face of certain issues and fighting back against injustice because of the stigma surrounding Black women in this country and the narrative of the "angry Black woman." As much as I would like to become vigilant and ignore consequences, I know that the price to pay for these actions is far steeper for those who look like me.

Even so, as much as this is a chilling reality, I cannot let fear and intimidation prevent me from fighting and creating awareness around issues that my people and other people of color face. Anytime that I feel scared or intimidated, I must remind myself of that little girl who, when learning of this horrifying truth of injustice, found the passion she felt to make it right for herself, her community, and her family.

CHAPTER 21

INTERDISCIPLINARY COLLABORATION AS A MEANS OF ACHIEVING SOCIAL JUSTICE

Frederic P. Bemak and Rita Chi-Ying Chung

I offer you peace. I offer you love. I offer you friendship. I see your beauty. I hear your needs. I feel your feelings. My wisdom flows from the Highest Source. I salute that Source in you. Let us work together for unity and love.

—Mahatma Gandhi

Justice consists not in being neutral between right and wrong, but in finding out the right and upholding it, wherever found, against the wrong.

—Theodore Roosevelt

It's a drop of water in the sea. But after this drop, the sea will never be the same.

—Mother Teresa

REFLECTION QUESTIONS

1. What professional disciplines do you think are linked to counseling and psychology?
2. Describe how each of the professional disciplines you listed in Question 1 links with counseling and psychology.
3. What would counselors and psychologists learn from collaborating with professionals from the disciplines you listed in Question 1?
4. How would you reach out and collaborate with someone from another discipline? Discuss strategies you might use to do this.
5. Describe a project that you might propose with colleagues from another discipline.

In moving toward social justice–oriented work, it is helpful for mental health professionals to embrace perspectives from other professional disciplines. The mental health field, with roots in European American individual psychotherapy, has been isolated, promoting a narrow perspective that traditionally excludes other professional disciplines. This is especially true given a constricted emphasis on individual interventions rooted in traditions of psychopathology and a disease model and resulting in little reason to find benefit from perspectives outside of mental health. Moving beyond this restricted view to include socio-ecological, community, sociohistorical, sociopolitical, psychosocial, and family contexts related to counseling and psychotherapy, one can find a natural connection with other disciplines. Social work, sociology, psychology/counseling, public health, education, medicine, psychiatry, anthropology, geography, ethnic studies, women's studies, nursing, law, economics, and political science intersect with mental health in ways that can contribute to holistically alleviating problems and combine human rights and social justice frameworks.

Working with individuals, families, groups, and communities on human rights violations and social injustices is a complex and multifaceted issue. Other disciplines offer different and unique perspectives. In our (Rita and Fred) careers, we collaborated closely with sociologists, cultural anthropologists, public health officials, geographers, economists, and lawyers to better understand the problems faced by urban children and families, refugees and immigrants, survivors of human trafficking, disaster survivors, and other disenfranchised and marginalized groups. Their training and work provide new and different ways to examine research and develop prevention and intervention programming, offering us understanding that goes beyond our psychological training. The same could be said working with a homeless family where a mental health professional might collaborate with the housing office, employment programs, the local school, social services, juvenile services, and public health officials.

Interdisciplinary collaboration requires the counselor or psychologist to reconceptualize strategies to engage individuals, groups, communities, institutions, and societies and partner with others to address social issues and inequities from holistic and ecological perspectives. We would suggest that contemporary counseling and psychology has been markedly deficient in linking to the larger society and world in embodying the principles of social action and advocacy to address the social, political, historical, cultural, and economic problems faced by hundreds of millions of people globally, making it essential to redefine our role as partners in achieving social justice. Building on Bronfenbrenner's (1996) description of the association between social, psychological, and educational needs, a core belief of ours is that there is a relationship between human rights and social, cultural, psychological, educational, political, health, historical, and economic problems. Similarly, others have argued for the need to link with community resources (Heath & McLaughlin, 1987; Herman et al., 2019), while Bemak (1998) argued that interdisciplinary collaboration is a means to work for human rights and social change. Models have been developed to address multidimensional problems (Herman et al., 2019). Major foundations such as the Ford Foundation, Annie E. Casey Foundation, Russell Sage Foundation, and W. K. Kellogg Foundation have funded projects aimed at interagency and interdisciplinary cooperation that leads to new collaborative directions for mental health professionals and necessitates a careful examination of reforms that incorporate interdisciplinary interventions and research.

THE NEED FOR AND IMPORTANCE OF SOCIAL JUSTICE INTERDISCIPLINARY COLLABORATION

There has been a growing emphasis on the sociopolitical, historical, economic, cultural, and political context in psychology. This is evident is shifting paradigms in graduate training programs that incorporate the larger ecological context in preparing future mental health professionals. Although training curricula generally does not include issues such as teamwork, leadership, social action, poverty, public health, sociology, anthropology, policy, and advocacy, there is more discussion about these issues and disciplines than previously (Bemak & Chung, 2007). For example, the American Psychological Association (APA), since 2016, has a prize for interdisciplinary team research (Palmer, 2017). The American Counseling Association (ACA) included in their 2014 ACA Code of Ethics an emphasis on the importance of counselors working with interdisciplinary teams (Atieno & Geroski, 2015; see Box Text 21.1).

Maintaining the status quo of traditional psychological and counseling training is what we believe is a flawed assumption that counseling/psychology, as a profession, can effectively stand alone with theories and strategies that remain encapsulated in a limited professional framework. University curricula and practitioners narrowly explore solutions to psychological problems without acknowledging the value of interdisciplinary perspectives.

BOX TEXT 21.1 CASE STUDY OF INTERPROFESSIONAL COLLABORATION

In one family, members are involved with multiple human services agencies. The 16-year-old son is missing school and has been referred to the Department of Youth Services (DYS) for stealing a car; his 14-year-old sister receives individual counseling from a local mental health clinic; another sister sees the school counselor weekly; and the parents are enrolled in a Department of Social Services (DSS) job training program and counseling to become financially self-sufficient and not dependent on welfare. The fact that DYS, DSS, the local school, and a mental health clinic are all working with different members of this family provides an opportunity for a collaborative intervention that would provide consistency in addressing the broad scope of family problems. As the system is now organized, each of these distinct organizations will develop strategies and provide interventions that do not take into account the other ongoing interventions with the larger family system. We suggest that the problems are interrelated and require an interdisciplinary approach, one addressing causal factors rather than symptoms, that could be attended to through cross-agency cooperation and trust.

Simultaneously, the depth and complexity of modern society's problems are growing for many of our clients, students, families, schools, institutions, agencies, and communities and cannot be viewed through the lens of only one discipline. Viewing societal problems through only one discipline creates an erroneously egocentric viewpoint that can ultimately result in providing substandard services and treatment while at the same time reinforcing social injustices. To change the status quo and establish interdisciplinary efforts that enhance social justice and human rights, we suggest four areas of consideration.

REALIGNMENT AND SHARING OF POWER

We believe that to adapt to rapidly changing, globalized, technological social dynamics in society, psychologists and counselors must partner with other professional disciplines to focus on planned social change. This requires collaborative, systematic interventions that address basic social structures and impact individual and social values, attitudes, behaviors, and policies. For example, collaboration among the mental health disciplines (psychology, counseling, psychiatry, social work, and psychiatric nursing), with an aim to change mental health public policy, may be far stronger than each discipline advocating independently. Another example might be counselors and psychologists forging alliances with public policy officials, public health officials, sociologists, nurses, and housing officials to discuss building healthy and safe communities in low-income housing areas. This would require a shift in traditional power bases that fosters equitable input from the respective disciplines working toward a greater shared goal. The idea of proactively redefining role and position is a particularly sensitive issue since social change and action involve a realignment and sharing of power, authority, and decision-making. Furthermore, acknowledging the expertise of other professional disciplines requires relinquishing power and control to meet the greater goals. To illustrate, consider the traditional relationship between counseling/psychology and the field of psychiatry. Both of us (Fred and Rita) have headed mental health interdisciplinary teams that included psychiatrists, who traditionally lead teams by virtue of their professional degrees rather than their skill or knowledge. Our leadership on these teams shifted traditional power roles; the psychiatrists were no longer the final authority, but rather contributing members of the teams sharing their expertise in psychiatry. This is a dramatic shift from existing structures that are steeped in hierarchical models of authority and expertise, one that more effectively utilizes the respective areas of expertise of team members.

HOPE: A KEY INGREDIENT

Another important aspect of creating change through interdisciplinary collaboration is to foster hope and a vision for change. Hope has been identified as significant for enduring action (Greenaway et al., 2016). In fact, hope has been found to contribute to between 15% to 27% of positive treatment outcomes (Asay & Lambert, 2002; Lambert & Bergin, 1994; Thomas, 2006). It may be stated that, without aspirations, hope, and vision, the momentum for change is lost. When I (Fred) designed a program in Anne Arundel County,

Maryland, U.S. that focused on reducing violence in an inner-city low-income community, it required fortitude, patience, and skills as well as a belief in the possibility of change. Without the hope and belief that violence could in fact be reduced in this county, the school staff, parents, and human services agency personnel would have been disillusioned, and, in our opinion, the project wouldn't have worked. Penn and Kiesel (1994) described the role of the African American psychologist as one who defines hope and can discern a future that supports a commitment to unity and solidarity. We suggest that this definition is applicable to all counselors and psychologists in their roles as social change agents.

THE ECOLOGICAL CONTEXT

As a result of the multitude of challenges facing society, counselors and psychologists are presented with individuals, families, groups, and communities who face numerous obstacles to fulfilled lives due to the pressures, life circumstances, and sociopolitical, economic, legal, educational, and health policies. The historical, social, economic, political, and cultural forces that influence our clients' lived experiences have significant bearing on them, necessitating mental health professionals to consider client challenges from an ecological perspective (Bemak & Conyne, 2004; Cook, 2015; Williams & Greenleaf, 2012). The complexity of social issues raises further concerns about utilizing individual counseling without considering a broader holistic ecological viewpoint that may be enhanced by cross-disciplinary work. For example, when we (Rita and Fred) worked in the area of refugee mental health, we regularly found it important to collaborate with attorneys, immigration lawyers, healthcare officials, probation officers, social service providers, school personnel, economists, geographers, and political scientists. They have been helpful in understanding policies, community planning, rights, demographics, and planned programming, all of which consider different aspects of the refugees' lived experiences that impact their mental health. Reconceptualizing presenting problems within an ecological context, as with the refugee work, will accompany a redefinition of the traditional therapeutic role that includes working across disciplines.

ONE STEP BEHIND

Mental health may be regarded as one of the professional areas that has the most potential to promote psychosocial change. Yet we would suggest that, as a profession, we have been slow in keeping pace with the relevant shifts in social, economic, cultural, political, and technological developments that critically impact society. We propose that one reason the mental health profession is not considered a major force in social transformation relates to not giving more systematic attention to interdisciplinary collaboration as a means to address complex modern problems. This relates to a characterization of psychology and counseling within a Western framework of individual counseling, intrapsychic issues, and psychopathology, without acknowledging the impact of the ecological context of community and external variables. For example, when we both (Rita and Fred) work on issues of child trafficking, it is not surprising that we are the only psychologists on the interdisciplinary teams. Similarly, it is not surprising that there is a danger of school counselors being relegated to "clerk work" and becoming obsolete (Bemak, 2000) and of psychologists and counselors not being regularly consulted about social concerns such as xenophobia, discrimination, sexism, racism, poverty, terrorism, and global warming. To keep pace with rapidly changing times, the profession must reexamine the basic tenets of counseling and psychotherapy and support a greater emphasis on interdisciplinary collaboration as a means to create social and political change (see Box Text 21.2).

RECOMMENDED ACTIONS AND STRATEGIES

To change one's outlook and incorporate interdisciplinary perspectives requires a different way of thinking and a shift in traditional theory and practice. It also entails rethinking territoriality, which has implications for authority, funding, and responsibility. Breaking down these well-established boundaries is a significant task, yet one that is necessary and essential for the advancement of social justice–oriented mental health work. To shift in this direction, psychologists and counselors must move beyond thinking that their narrowly prescribed viewpoint is the only perspective that provides answers for understanding human behavior and larger societal issues. Acknowledging that a mental health viewpoint is only one of many perspectives requires not only a shift in one's belief system, but also humility, acceptance, acknowledgment, and respect for other ways of perceiving the world and its problems. We believe that psychologists and counselors are well positioned to assume leadership roles when forming positive collaborative interdisciplinary partnerships given their training and skills in human relations, human behavior, and group leadership.

GUIDING PRINCIPLES FOR SOCIAL JUSTICE INTERDISCIPLINARY COLLABORATION

To promote interdisciplinary collaboration as an essential component for social change, we suggest 12 guiding principles, described below (see Table 21.1). Although there is overlap in some of the guiding principles, we believe that each area is significant enough to warrant an independent categorization.

1. *Reduce interprofessional conflict, hostility, and mistrust.* Various disciplines remain skeptical and distrustful about the value of contributions by other disciplines. Territory has been well defined by different disciplines, including psychology and counseling, as have approaches to social, economic, cultural, and political issues. The differences in approach coupled with the lack of appreciation for other

---

TABLE 21.1 **Twelve guiding principles for interdisciplinary collaboration**

1. Reduce interprofessional, conflict, hostility, and mistrust
2. Provide broader solutions beyond those narrowly defined mental health work
3. Plan and implement mutually defined projects and goals that support and facilitate cooperative partnerships
4. Reconstruct professional roles
5. Shared power and decision-making
6. Reconstituted rewards and incentives
7. Relocate offices to foster teamwork
8. Rethink and reallocate funding schemata
9. Provide cross-agency and cross-disciplinary training
10. Develop interdisciplinary university training at the graduate level
11. Develop an understanding of change theory and its application to counseling and psychotherapy
12. Collaborate on cross-disciplinary publications and presentations

---

perspectives provides a basis for conflict between various professional groups and agencies. Procter and Vu (2019) noted that we need to be mindful when doing multidisciplinary collaboration, remembering not to imply that everyone's work is done in the same way and risk a loss of professional identity. Rather, they note, working together involves using professionals' respective expertise to provide a broader perspective of the issues.

2. *Provide broader solutions beyond those narrowly defined in mental health work.* Utilizing multidisciplinary approaches requires mutual understanding, openness, and respect about differences and similarities in value systems, perceptions, and theoretical bases. For example, when I (Fred) collaborated with a good friend who is a European sociologist working with urban youth at risk, he talked about space within urban areas as being a key in defining and promoting at-risk behaviors, a viewpoint that greatly expanded my conceptualization of the problem. It is important to embody different perspectives such as this and consider that the most effective solutions may not rest solely within the traditional mental health domain.

3. *Plan and implement mutually defined projects and goals that support and facilitate cooperative partnerships.* Engaging parties from different professional areas to develop outcomes and objectives helps to promote cooperation. Collective responsibility engenders shared goals as well as co-ownership. For example, in developing a school-community-family partnership program in an urban school area, we (Fred and Rita) brought in school personnel, parents, agencies, and community members who all contributed to developing and implementing the plan. As we proceeded with the project, it was clear that the entire group, rather than us, owned the project. The project overcame traditional professional boundaries and was vital in cultivating a robust and vigorous collaborative work environment.

4. *Reconstruct professional roles.* Within the mental health field, as in all professional disciplines, there is a set of values, beliefs, and explicit and implicit norms about the profession. The culture of counseling and psychology has been passed on for generations and is very well established. To work collaboratively we have found that it is important to deconstruct historical and current assumptions about our professional function and role and recreate a new role definition that is effective across disciplines. A byproduct of this redefinition is the need to manage the discomfort and uncertainty of reconstructed professional roles within a cross-disciplinary context.

5. *Share power and decision-making.* An important element of interdisciplinary collaboration is ensuring that all parties have equal opportunities for contribution and participation. In contrast, when a hierarchical multidisciplinary group is formed, there is disparity in influence, input, and acceptance of various professional perspectives. We would agree with Friend and Cook (1996), who identified parity and shared decision-making as the distinguishing features of collaborative teams. In the mental health field, psychiatry is well-known to assume the role as the dominant authority, despite having less training in direct psychotherapy and counseling. A more equal power distribution would consider psychiatric training as one voice in the discussion, rather than as the authoritative notion of what constitutes a problem and how to treat it. In the same vein, it has been our experience that designating a facilitator,

rather than a "leader" who is chosen by virtue of their profession, has proved to be the most formidable way to harness the wealth of knowledge and perspectives in multidisciplinary teams (Procter & Vu, 2019).

6. *Reconstitute rewards and incentives.* Typically, scholarly professional performance or merit rewards are based on accomplishments within one's own discipline. A guiding principal for better interdisciplinary collaboration is to develop a system of rewards and incentives that support interdisciplinary partnerships aimed at social change. For example, similar to the APA prize mentioned earlier, there could be more awards given by professional associations at the county, regional, state, or national and international levels honoring the best interdisciplinary social action project; an award for best innovative interdisciplinary project, paper, or presentation to create societal change; or university or agency awards that promote social action through multidisciplinary work. To further standardize cross-disciplinary rewards and incentives, funding could be shared across organizations.

7. *Relocate offices to foster teamwork.* Prior to the COVID-19 pandemic we had suggested that physical space is an important dimension in promoting effective social justice interdisciplinary teams. Multidisciplinary teams housed in the same area allow office space to be reassigned to facilitate cooperation and a team approach to problems. Reallocation of office space could be assigned so that staff, some of the time, would be housed in another organization's office. We (Rita and Fred) have actually done this by locating mental health clinics within health and social services offices, as well as in schools. Given the age of technology, compounded by the reliance on technology during the COVID-19 pandemic that resulted in lockdown and social distancing, individuals were forced to work from home, utilizing virtual meetings for work and social events. In an effort to create camaraderie and better teamwork virtual social hours could be enhanced to foster multidisciplinary cooperation, especially when access to physical space is not an option.

8. *Rethink and reallocate funding schemata.* Funding is almost always awarded directly and solely to one agency, school, or organization, which has the ultimate responsibility for and authority to use the money in ways that their organization best sees fit. It is far less usual to develop alternative funding methods that enhance the development of interdisciplinary work. Two possibilities come to mind to illustrate this point. First, funding could be used within agencies, organizations, or schools to fund individual staff to designate a portion of their time to participate in collaborative interdisciplinary social action projects. Thus, the work site becomes the motivator and supporter of interdisciplinary work. The second possibility is illustrated in an example from an urban school district school-community-family project that I (Fred) developed and administrated. I was based at a university and received funding to develop an interagency project focused on programming for vulnerable youth. I designed funding to be allocated for the team, rather than a specific agency, thus requiring cooperative programming, shifting job responsibilities, and resource commitment by respective organizations to support the collaborative structure. Other similar projects have the potential to develop new paradigm shifts in resource allocation and more effective service delivery.

9. *Provide cross-agency and cross-disciplinary training.* Traditionally, training rarely includes staff from outside one's organization. To have participants from different disciplines join and participate in training aimed at specific problem areas, rather than training aimed at specific professional discipline areas, creates the potential for cross-disciplinary fertilization and exchange of ideas. For example, I (Fred) implemented a three-day start-up training for a multidisciplinary team working with low-income at-risk inner-city families. Training began with redefining the roles and relationships of the team members, followed by breaking down institutional barriers and establishing mutual project goals. The training utilized activities described by Johnson and Johnson (1997) for building effective teams, including activities to develop collaborative skills, group processing, positive healthy interdependence, personal accountability, and direct communication. Interestingly, discussion about the barriers that inhibited collaboration resulted in those obstacles being dissolved.

10. *Develop interdisciplinary university training at the graduate level.* To have mental health practice incorporate interdisciplinary work, it is helpful to have exposure to cooperative partnerships at the university level. We suggest that interdisciplinary collaboration and cross-disciplinary training models be established as prototypes that can be developed and embedded as part of the training. This would challenge current graduate-level training that is discipline-specific and return to graduate study coursework and applied practica that years ago were multidisciplinary, all with an aim of facilitating cooperation (Golightly, 1987; Humes & Hohenshil, 1987). Proctor and Vu (2019) argue that multidisciplinary collaboration requires an application of skills that go beyond that of a single discipline, requiring an integrative approach to graduate training. An excellent example of cross-departmental training is the doctoral program in the College of Education and Human Development at George Mason University, where all the PhD students are admitted to the graduate school and have a specialization in their area of concentration (e.g., counseling, special education, educational leadership, etc.). Before beginning their specialization courses, all students take six courses as a cohort group, studying topics such as leadership, ways of knowing, organizational development, research, and so forth.

11. *Develop an understanding of change theory and its application to counseling and psychotherapy.* For mental health professionals to work effectively in promoting social change across disciplines with colleagues, there must be an understanding of organizational and systemic change. Frequently, psychologists and counselors talk about changing communities and promoting equity and human rights, but their efforts often fall short due to a lack of skills in social change. We suggest that to try to do social justice work within the mental health field without the tools that come from training, supervision, and experience will produce failure and frustration. Therefore, counselors and psychologists must understand theories about social change and mental health. Readings to better understand how to facilitate change could include the following: Alinsky (1971), Bemak and Chung (2005), de la Sablonnière (2017), and Prilleltensky and Prilleltensky (2003). See also Box Text 21.3.

BOX TEXT 21.3 CHILD ALONE CONFERENCE: AN EXAMPLE OF CROSS-DISCIPLINARY WORK

I (Fred), along with the United States Deputy Assistant Secretary of State, co-organized a global conference entitled Child Alone that focused on the protection of unaccompanied and separated children worldwide from an interdisciplinarity perspective. The conference funded participants from 47 countries to attend the U.S.-based conference that included leading international and national government and nongovernmental officials and leaders. The sponsoring and participating organizations included the U.S. Department of State, U.S. Department of Homeland Security, U.S. Department of Health and Human Services, and United Nations High Commission for Refugees. I was one of the only mental health professionals at the conference and gave a featured presentation. The exchange of information with professionals from other disciplines provided a rich forum for cross-disciplinary collaboration that resulted in impacting multiple areas, such as national and international policy about migration and programming, family reunification, security and safety issues, and health and mental health prevention and intervention.

12. *Collaborate on cross-disciplinary publications and presentations.* Professional publications and presentations are generally discipline-specific. We suggest that this perpetuates professional isolation. In our experience, even with cross-disciplinary projects, there is little cross-fertilization of scholarly publications or professional presentations. Therefore, another guiding principle we recommend is publishing and presenting across professional disciplines. By disseminating the team's work to other disciplines broadens the impact of the work (Procter & Vu, 2019) and facilitates rewards and incentives for working across disciplines. For example, we have presented at conferences for psychiatrists, school boards and school administrators, politicians, social workers, public health officials, physicians, international security personnel, international nongovernmental organizations (INGOs), and other international organizations. Similarly, we have published research journal articles and book chapters outside of the mental health field. Correspondingly, at an APA annual convention, I (Fred) invited members of a project (i.e., school district administrators, business leaders, and a judge) focused on decreasing school violence and aggression in a major urban school district to co-present with me. The result was to not only work together, but to present our work at a major national forum that fostered even greater collegial relationships and greatly enhanced the impact of the project.

SUMMARY

The 21st century presents an opportunity for and urgency in attending to social injustices to improve our world. Given ongoing global, national, and local crises that precipitate social injustices, human rights violations, and subsequent mental health problems, this century offers the mental health field a unique opportunity to reexamine itself and review the parameters and scope of how various professional disciplines can more effectively contribute to a better world. Historically, there was a call in the mental health field for social action as a core professional responsibility, which was evident with earlier projects in impoverished inner cities, advocating for the rights of mental health clients, or working with youth facing family and school problems. Over time the ecological context from these earlier days has changed. Even so, some things have remained consistent in that the cultural, sociopolitical, psychopolitical, and economic domains continue to influence peoples' lives, and psychologists and counselors have an opportunity to impact these situations in a broader context than one individual at a time.

It is only logical, considering the changing contemporary landscape, that the role, structure, and function of the mental health profession transform and adapt to better address the complexities of the 21st century and keep up with the times. Joining with other professions and collaborating with other departments, agencies, organizations, and institutions that go beyond the all-important but limited scope of counseling and psychotherapy will be crucial to the mental health profession's ability to keep pace and make a significant contribution to social change and a better world.

DISCUSSION QUESTIONS

1. Your supervisor just chose you to be in charge of creating a prevention program for vulnerable culturally and linguistically diverse adolescents. Be creative and describe what your program would consist of, using the following guidelines.
   a. You have the chance to choose five professionals from different professional disciplines to start with you on this initiative. Which professionals would you like to have in your team? List at five in order of preference. Discuss.
   b. What are some of the preconceptions you may have about each profession? Explain.
   c. How would you present your case to your supervisor that those are the professionals your program needs?
   d. What are some of the challenges you may encounter?
2. What does it mean to "take off the blinders" and assume a leadership role in proactively forming positive partnerships with other disciplines?
   a. What are some of your own blinders? List four blinders you might have.
   b. List at least three actions you will be implementing in your daily work to be proactive in collaborating with other disciplines.

3. Analyze your graduate program curriculum. What are some of the components that you would recommend adding to your program to better incorporate knowledge and experience in interdisciplinary work?

REFERENCES

Alinsky, S. D. (1971). *Rules for radicals*. Random House.

Asay, T. P., & Lambert, M. J. (2002). Therapist relational variables. In D. J. Cain (Ed.), *Humanistic psychotherapies: Handbook of research and practice* (pp. 531–557). American Psychological Association. https://doi.org/10.1037/10439-017

Atieno Okech, J. E., & Geroski, A. M. (2015). Interdisciplinary training: Preparing counselors for collaborative practice. *Professional Counselor, 5*(4), 458–472. doi:10.15241/jeo.5.4.458

Bemak, F. (1998). Interdisciplinary collaboration for social change: Redefining the counseling profession. In C. C. Lee (Ed.), *Counselors and social action: New directions* (pp. 279–293). American Counseling Association.

Bemak, F. (2000). Transforming the role of the counselor to provide leadership in educational reform through collaboration. *Professional School Counseling, 3*(5), 323–331. https://search.proquest.com/openview/27e9062d242819f4e00434ecb41cf29b/1?pq-origsite=gscholar&cbl=11185

Bemak F., & Chung, R. C-Y. (2005). Advocacy as a critical role for urban school counselors: Working toward equity and social justice. *Professional School Counseling, 8*(3),196–202. https://www.jstor.org/stable/42732459?seq=1

Bemak, F., & Chung, R. C-Y. (2007). Training social justice counselors. In C. Lee (Ed.), *Counseling for social justice* (pp. 239–258). American Counseling Association.

Bemak, F., & Conyne, R. (2004). Ecological group counseling: Context and Application. In R. K. Conyne & E. P. Cook (Eds.), *Ecological counseling: An innovative approach to conceptualizing person-environment interaction* (pp. 219–242). American Counseling Association.

Bronfenbrenner, U. (1996). *The ecology of human development: Experiments by nature and design*. Harvard University Press

Cook, E. P. (2015). *Understanding people in context: The ecological perspective in counseling*. John Wiley.

de la Sablonnière R. (2017). Toward a psychology of social change: A typology of social change. *Frontiers in Psychology, 8*, 397. https://doi.org/10.3389/fpsyg.2017.00397

Friend, M., & Cook, L. (1996). *Interactions: Collaboration skills for school counselors* (2nd ed.). Longman.

Golightly, C. J. (1987). Transdisciplinary training: A step forward in special education teacher preparation. *Teacher Education and Special Education, 10*(3), 126–130. https://doi.org/10.1177/088840648701000305

Greenaway, K. H., Cichocka, A., van Veelen, R., Likki, T., & Branscombe, N. R. (2016). Feeling hopeful inspires support for social change. *Political Psychology, 37*(1), 89–107. https://doi.org/10.1111/pops.12225

Heath, S. B., & McLaughlin, M. W. (1987). A child resource policy: Moving beyond dependence on school and family. *Phi Delta Kappan, 68*(8), 576–580. https://www.jstor.org/stable/i20403433

Herman, K. C., Reinke, W. M., Thompson, A. M., & Hawley, K. M. (2019). The Missouri Prevention Center: A multidisciplinary approach to reducing the societal prevalence and burden of youth mental health problems. *American Psychologist, 74*(3), 315–328. https://doi.org/10.1037/amp0000433

Humes, C. W., & Hohenshil, T. H. (1987). Elementary counselors, school psychologists, school social workers: Who does what? *Elementary School Guidance and Counseling, 22*(1), 37–45. https://www.jstor.org/stable/42873943?seq=1

Johnson, D. W., & Johnson, F. P. (1997). *Joining together: Group theory and skills* (6th ed.). Prentice-Hall.

Lambert, M. J., & Bergin, A. E. (1994). The effectiveness of psychotherapy. In A. E. Bergin & S. L. Garfield (Eds.), *Handbook of psychotherapy and behavior change* (4th ed., pp. 143–189). John Wiley.

Palmer, J. C. (2017, Nov). *Interdisciplinary research collaborations: A guide to creating new research teams.* American Psychological Association, Psychological Science Agenda. https://www.apa.org/science/about/psa/2017/11/tell-friends

Penn, M. L., & Kiesel, L. (1994). Toward a global world community: The role of black psychologists. *Journal of Black Psychology, 20*(4), 398–417. https://doi.org/10.1177/00957984940204002

Prilleltensky, I., & Prilleltensky, O. (2003). Synergies for wellness and liberation in counseling psychology. *Counseling Psychologist, 31*(3), 273–281. https://doi.org/10.1177/0011000003031003002

Proctor, R. W., & Vu, K.-P. L. (2019). How psychologists help solve real-world problems in multidisciplinary research teams: Introduction to the special issue. *American Psychologist, 74*(3), 271–277. http://dx.doi.org/10.1037/amp0000458

Thomas, M. L. (2006). The contributing factors of change in a therapeutic process. *Contemporary Family Therapy, 28*(2), 201–210. https://doi.org/10.1007/s10591-006-9000-4

Williams, J. M., & Greenleaf, A. T. (2012). Ecological psychology: Potential contributions to social justice and advocacy in school settings. *Journal of Educational and Psychological Consultation, 22*(1–2), 141–157. doi:10.1080/10474412.2011.649653

CHAPTER 22

STUDENT CHAPTER

The Journey Toward Letting Go of Fixing the Problem and Becoming an Ally

Jackie Tackett

As I read about the various journeys other students have taken down this road of multiculturalism and social justice, I cannot help but feel inspired in my own journey. Dr. Chung's description of her own story and the pain she suffered as a child really touched me (Chung & Bemak, 2012). However, her remarkable career in combating social justice issues is an example to everyone in this program. Although Dr. Bemak didn't experience racism first hand, he still learned to become an ally and deeply care about others. The students' narratives demonstrate how they integrated what they learned in this program and incorporated this into their lives. I identified with the White students' struggles with White identity because being from the United Kingdom and Caucasian carries with it shame and guilt for what my race has done to others in the past. I recalled similar reactions when reading Janet Helms's (1991) *Race Is a Nice Thing to Have* and the anger and frustration in the class discussion about racism. On some level I can identify with issues of prejudice. I am 60 and a woman. I grew up during the 1960s, when women were still struggling to be heard. I recall experiencing sexism throughout my life. However, I can see that we, as potential counselors, need to walk through this experience to really understand what social justice means.

Reflecting on my own journey, I believe this began 34 years ago, when I left the United Kingdom and traveled to the United States. As soon as I arrived at JFK airport in New York I sensed immediately that something was wrong. I could see it in the faces of the porters and other workers. This was not the "melting pot" portrayed to others, but something very different and not pleasant. I had a feeling of uneasiness, which has been with me ever since.

I settled in a small townhouse community in Northern Virginia. Our community was multicultural, and we have seen changes over the years. Although I was aware of the racism, I never considered taking action. I just went along with the status quo; even though I had friends who were African American, I really had no idea of the power of White privilege and how that affects the lives of others.

I started to realize the extent of the problem when, during undergrad, I took a course called "Social Determinates of Health." It was during this course that I realized some of the issues facing our poorest communities. I learned about internalized racism and how this affected the African American population, even those of higher economic status.

I did not really face my own White privilege until I was accepted into the counseling program at George Mason University. I chose this program because I was excited about its emphasis on multicultural and social justice counseling. I found that every course emphasized multicultural counseling. From these courses, I began to see how internalized racism has a profound effect on the mental health and welfare for people of color. This racism is insidious, and it infects every area of society with an underlying assumption that people of color are to be treated differently and not taken seriously. This made me feel extremely uncomfortable because I felt helpless: What could I do? My reaction was to try to fix things for my fellow students of color, but I could not. I felt frustrated, angry, and deeply sad. These feelings followed me into the multicultural counseling class. Did I really look at my own biases and beliefs when it came to issues of race? Deep down, I still did not want to admit to White privilege and what that entailed. By wanting to fix my classmates, this sent the message that I had White privilege because I had the power to fix their problems, which, in my opinion makes me a racist, because I am still holding on to White privilege. I still believed I was not racist, but unfortunately, I was just as guilty of committing microaggressions, such as feeling uncomfortable—even afraid—when I see a group of Black males on the street. I wrestled with the concepts of the Helms book and wanted to deny my own race. I did not want to be a part of society's institutionalized racism; this was for others, not me. As time went on in my training, I slowly realized, yes, I am White and I have privilege; I had obtained jobs because I am White. I had been granted a mortgage because I am White. I have never been refused service in a store because I am White. I never walked into a store and worried that employees would think I was stealing because I am White. I was not profiled by the police because I am White. By the end of the book and classes I was able to admit my own racial identity, I came to terms with what White privilege gives me at the expense of people of color. I now had a racial and cultural identity. My cultural identity is English, from the United Kingdom. I discovered that we have our own cultural practices, such as May Day, Father Christmas, Boxing Day, Guy Fawkes night, and Shrove Tuesday. In my family, every Sunday we visited my grandparents for tea, another cultural practice.

The class discussions were very powerful and exhausting. I was emotionally drained after every class. I felt confused, angry, sad, and wanted to shout out to the class "What do you want?" In each class, I could feel the anger coming from our classmates of color. I could not fix it; I just sat with their anger and listened, as I had not listened before. However, it was hard to find the words: anything that I could say would be trite. I finally shared that I was not in their position and could not possibly understand what they were going through, but I was there to listen and offer support. I am not sure that this went over well either. Several students were clearly angry; I felt that they could not hear me because they heard the same response their whole lives. These students continued to challenge the class by insisting we were not going deep enough. With every class I could feel their anger and pain. I felt helpless and sad. Finally, Dr. Chung stepped in and refocused the class by explaining how we can become allies together to fight racism. I realized that although I can never have the same experience, I can stand with students of color as an ally. I felt empowered by being able to stand with students of color against racism. Other White students came forward and we stood together. From there the class focused on what we can do to combat racism. We role-played how we could confront the people around us when they commit microaggressions or make racially bigoted statements. I finally realized that a safe space had been created for students of color to tell their stories, to explain what their lives were like, and for us, students of privilege, to really hear the experiences of students of color without comment and without trying to fix them. I can honestly say my worldview changed through being a part of this class.

The class on multiculturalism was not only powerful, but, more importantly, it also gave me the tools I needed for the social justice course. Being aware of White privilege and personal biases is not enough. People of color need a vehicle by which to tell their own story, to let others really witness their worldview.

In the social justice class, the focus has been on the issues we were most passionate about. When I told Dr. Chung that I was most passionate about racism, I did not know what was in store for me. I was assigned a character to present to the class that was so far from my own (Chung & Bemak, 2013), I was immediately filled with trepidation; how I was going to portray this character without being stereotypical? My character was an African American male who had been wrongly accused of rape and incarcerated for a number of years. As I researched the issue of false convictions, it was clear that the statistics support the fact that this population has been systematically targeted by the police. As I started to look at individual cases of wrongful incarceration, I became angry: I felt frustrated with a system that is clearly focused on punishing people of color whether they were guilty or not. I felt that just being a person of color carried with it a finding of guilty regardless of the evidence. Once again, I felt deeply sad at such a biased system. I also felt helpless because the problem is so widespread. As I read the stories of wrongful incarceration I felt deeply sad for those incarcerated and their families. How can we even begin to say our system is fair and just? It is far from this: it is only fair for people with privilege and money. One particular case spoke to me, Thomas Haynesworth. He was from the Richmond, Virginia, area and falsely accused of several rapes, not just one. He was convicted solely on the eyewitness testimony of two White women who, if the truth be known, could not identify the perpetrator other than he was a Black male.

As I did further research, I learned about the racism that is specifically inherent in the criminal justice system and has existed since the days of slavery. The Emancipation Proclamation really changed nothing because of White privilege. The same attitudes and beliefs prevailed, to this very day. I felt that slavery was merely forced underground. Slaves merely became indentured servants; emancipation changed nothing. What was particularly disturbing is the practice of lynching. This practice is abhorrent and is the epitome of White racists carrying out random killing to prove White privilege. I was not only horrified by this practice, but the level of my anger quickly rose against those committing such acts. What is worse, this practice permeated the legal system, as I learned that people of color received longer sentences than their White counterparts for rape and other sex crimes, specifically if those crimes were committed against a White woman. Until we challenge the criminal justice system, we cannot address social justice issues.

Going forward I feel even more impassioned about these issues. I have learned that confronting issues of racism is not always easy, and speaking out takes courage. Do I have the courage? I believe that through the program I found the courage to go forward and challenge the system. I learned I can do this one person at a time. Through class role-plays and presentations I found my voice. It is not easy, but now if I hear racial comments I feel I have the responsibility to challenge these comments, to be that ally. I have now spoken up several times with friends and family on issues of racism. In one instance, I challenged a good friend of mine who was convinced he did not have White privilege. I felt it was my duty step in and educate my friend on what White privilege means. He tried to argue his position, but I held my ground. My friend came to the point of admitting that there is White privilege in some instances. Did I change his position? Probably not. But as I learned from the social justice class, I planted the seed.

My practicum/internship is with a private agency. What sort of social justice issues will I face? Since the agency is for-profit and the clients have insurance, I can envision that there may be a client who cannot afford counseling, either through issues with insurance coverage or an inability to meet the high co-payments. I believe I can advocate for the client to get counseling services either free or at a greatly reduced rate. I can also see that clients may need outside services, and I can certainly help the client advocate to receive those services. As I learned, I am an ally; I am not there to fix the problem for the client.

Moving forward, I have considerable trepidation. I will be sad to leave the counseling program and, at the same time, excited by the prospect of moving forward in the counseling profession.

REFERENCES

Chung, R. C., & Bemak, F. P. (2012). *Social justice counseling the next step beyond Multiculturalism.* Sage.

Chung, R. C-Y., & Bemak, F. (2013). Use of ethnographic fiction in social justice graduate counseling training. *Counselor Education and Supervision, 52,* 56–68. https://doi.org/10.1002/j.1556-6978.2013.00028.x

Helms, J. E. (1992). *A race is a nice thing to have.* Microtraining Associates, Inc.

CHAPTER 23

CREATIVITY AND SOCIAL MEDIA AS A TOOL FOR SOCIAL JUSTICE ADVOCACY AND ACTION

Rita Chi-Ying Chung and Frederic P. Bemak

You can't use up creativity. The more you use, the more you have.

—Maya Angelou

Creativity is inventing, experimenting, growing, taking risks, breaking rules, making mistakes, and having fun.

—Mary Lou Cook

The worst enemy to creativity is self-doubt.

—Sylvia Plath

Creativity requires the courage to let go of certainties.

—Erich Fromm

Creativity is intelligence having fun.

—Albert Einstein

REFLECTION QUESTIONS

1. Do you recall a time when you were particularly creative? Describe what happened.
2. Do you think creativity is just letting yourself "go with the flow," or does it involve putting your whole self into your work to "make it happen"?

3. Is creativity something that has to be nurtured and learned, or is it part of human nature?
4. Do you believe you are a creative person? Why or why not?

Embedding social justice action into mental health work is often met with strong resistance. To address these barriers, it is important to develop creative strategies that go beyond our usual ways of promoting change and to utilize the rapid advances in technology. As mentioned in Chapter 14 about social change, individuals are frequently not open to change even when considering altering unhealthy aspects of their lives. The uncertainty that accompanies change causes greater stress and anxiety than living with what one knows as routine and comfortable, even when unhealthy components are attached to what is familiar. Thus, at times, when incorporating social justice activism into our work, it is important to move beyond traditional advocacy strategies to incorporate inventive social action approaches that include utilizing social media and other technological applications and platforms.

When we broach the issue of creativity and social action, often we hear students or colleagues lamenting that, when it comes to social justice mental health work, they are not imaginative or creative. Interestingly, when we explore these assertions we find untapped creativity based on beliefs that originality is only for those who are perceived as heroes making the mistake of holding high and sometimes unattainable standards by comparing themselves with the "giants" of social justice and human rights. For example, Irena Sendler, during World War II, smuggled Jewish children out of the Nazi concentration camps in coffins, toolboxes, and even under coats (Dawson, 2016). Irena Sendler's example is not only creative, but it is indeed a high standard of courage and risk-taking in addressing human rights violations.

An additional barrier to social justice creativity in mental health graduate training occurs when students downplay their abilities by comparing themselves to classmates and peers. Creativity in social justice mental health activism is not a competition: it is about accessing our own creative potential that can contribute to advocating for social change. We (Rita and Fred) continually ask ourselves, "How can we creatively educate others in psychology and counseling to surmount the barriers and succeed as social justice advocates?" We also realize that, because the world is forever changing, advocacy techniques that were once operative are no longer effective. For example, during the U.S. administration of the 45th U.S. president, when I (Fred) was speaking at a Muslim forum to address the U.S. and global perpetuation of xenophobia and discrimination against Muslims, I shared my belief of how social advocacy had to transform to adapt, saying, "What we understood yesterday about how negotiations work is no longer applicable. We are in a new era. Now we need to understand that there is no middle ground or compromise in negotiations with those holding opposing views. This requires us to approach the xenophobia and intolerance with a different mindset, a different set of skills, and different expectations." The point is that we need to be social justice savvy, adaptable, and creative in how we challenge injustices in our mental health work.

Creative advocacy means marketing your social justice message and framing or reframing the issue in a way that stakeholders and potential social justice allies can identify with, understand, and, most importantly, buy in to and have ownership of the idea. If there is proprietorship, then there is a much greater likelihood of commitment and motivation to advocate for change. For example, in a mental health clinic or agency, if one experiences misogynistic behavior from colleagues, we believe it is important to address those values, attitudes, and behaviors in a systemic manner. It requires challenging long-standing beliefs in a way that colleagues can hear, sometimes requiring originality in how to present the problem. Some of us in the mental health field do not possess the incredible creativity of artists, writers, poets, painters, musicians, dancers, actors, athletes, activists, or entertainers, yet we suggest that all of us have social justice creative potential that can be enacted in our mental health social justice–oriented work. We believe that we all have what we call a *social justice creative gene* that is conducive to being inventive. For some it is more apparent, for others less so, and for some it is still undeveloped. Being creative as a social justice advocate requires courage in tapping into our existing skills, resources, and knowledge to generate systemic change and to explore different social justice techniques and strategies.

Thus, social justice creativity requires us to consider extending our typically utilized professional and interpersonal skills such as listening, counseling, communication, and leadership, to think outside the box and look at our skill set differently. The question is, "How do we incorporate skills, such as technical (i.e., using social media), organizational (event planning), mechanical (i.e., fixing or building things), artistic (i.e., musical and art forms such as making collages), language (i.e., bilingual or multilingual), and hobbies (i.e., gardening, cooking, hiking) into social activism (Toporek & Ahluwalia, 2021)? For example, I (Fred) consulted for a mental health agency that began a biking and walking program for staff to stimulate race dialogues within the organization and deal with problems of unspoken discrimination. The biking and walking were based on the interests of a few staff and presented in a manner that was inclusive of all staff. In doing the biking and walking, other staff began to include other interests that helped address discrimination, such as sharing cultural food and reading materials related to race relations and racial justice. Forming partnerships and interests created a healthier organizational climate and buy-in by staff.

Infusing creativity into social justice work requires flexibility as well as an openness, courage, and confidence to give oneself permission to imagine and try new ideas. Noted throughout the literature by human rights and social justice leaders (e.g., Mahatma Gandhi, Martin Luther King Jr., Susan B. Anthony, Harvey Milk, Harriet Tubman, Nelson Mandela, Caesar Chavez, Malcolm X, Eleanor Roosevelt, W. E. B. Du Bois, Elie Wiesel, Rosa Parks, Malala Yousafzai, etc.) is the importance of taking chances and trying out ideas. Consider Martin Luther King Jr.'s 1967 address at the American Psychological Association (APA) meeting to the Society for the Psychological Study of Social Issues, calling for the creation of the International Association for the Advancement of Creative Maladjustment. In that address, he criticized adjusting to racial segregation, racial bigotry, and racial discrimination, disparaging the economic conditions that gave luxuries to so few people by taking basic necessities from so many (King, 1968). The call to establish such an association took courage, ingenuity, and confidence to introduce this new and innovative concept. Martin Luther King Jr.'s idea was to provoke the field of psychology and initiate an effort to generate change. It is important to acknowledge that many attempts to promote change, such as Martin Luther King Jr's, may introduce new ideas but begin with limited success. These experiences easily transfer to psychologists and counselors in the mental health field. As noted in Chapter 8 ("Unpacking the Psychological Barriers That Prevent Social Justice Action"), we suggested that social justice action failures should be acknowledged and worn as a *social justice failure badge of honor*, recognizing social action failures as attempts for change that plant social justice seeds with the potential to germinate into social change and as lessons to improve next steps. As I (Rita) say to psychology graduate students who get discouraged in doing social justice–oriented work when they meet with resistance, "Think back to when you were a child and wanted ice cream before dinner. You go to one parent who says no, you don't stop there; you then go to the other parent and then uncles, aunts, grandparents, and other care-providers. You were 'playing' the system with a cute innocent pouting face, saying something like: 'I've been good and so and so said I could have ice cream if I was good.' You weren't deterred when one, two, or three caretakers said no, you just kept trying."

To use creative approaches for social activism does not require proficiency in those strategies. For example, art activism is a good illustration of creative social justice–oriented work that can be employed in the mental health field. Examples of art activism can be seen in spoken art (i.e., storytelling, poetry, and song), visual art (i.e., theater, documentaries, and videos), and performing art (i.e., photography, crafts, murals, dance, knitting, etc.). An example of utilizing visual art is when we (Rita and Fred) were consulting in Myanmar on developing programs to prevent child trafficking and abuse. We utilized political theater, where children would write and perform their experiences in front of their entire village. Neither one of us or the children who performed their lived experiences had any acting training, but that was not the point. The goal of the performances was to use an active and visual technique to demonstrate to family members and villagers the children's experiences of human rights violations.

The villagers would gather in the center of the village, all sitting on the ground in groups of elders, men, women, and children, to watch the children perform. Watching the visual demonstration of child trafficking and abuse by children from their own village was a powerful and gripping experience for all, leaving some villagers in tears. The performance "hit home" for the villagers, who finally understood their children's painful experiences and their impact on the individual, family, and the entire village. The powerful and cathartic performances would be followed by us facilitating therapeutic dialogues that were essentially group therapy sessions among the villagers. Sessions began with the elders of the village speaking, followed by the men, then women, then children, followed by interactions between the groups. It may be helpful to think about creative social activism in terms similar to the Myanmar experience, creatively imagining how you can meet goals for social change and human rights and incorporate skills, interests, and hobbies into the intervention.

Another example of doing creative social justice–oriented work that applies to mental health professionals can be seen with food distribution. World-renowned chef José Andrés established a nonprofit organization called World Central Kitchen (WCK) that was created as a smart solution to hunger and poverty using food to empower communities and strengthen economies. WCK then evolved into using food as a tool for healing by working in post-disaster areas serving food to survivors. WCK social justice work continued during the COVID-19 pandemic shutdown of restaurants and the food industries by opening community kitchens, again using food as a healing tool (World Central Kitchen [WCK], 2020). Although neither of us (Rita and Fred) have the culinary training and skills, nor the resources of José Andrés, we did contact him to ask about collaborating with Counselors

Without Borders (CWB) by bringing mental health teams to provide psychological support at his food distribution centers. Although we did not work with him, we did take the idea of doing outreach mental health work to other disaster site food distribution centers in the United States and abroad (such as in Haiti with the United Nations World Food Programme).

Again, one does not need to be a well-known chef to incorporate cooking/food into social action work; instead, we can use food and cooking (or any other hobbies or skills) as a vehicle to bring people together to connect and join in healing and social change. This was evident when I (Rita) tapped into my culinary interests and skills, using food and cooking as a therapeutic technique when I worked with of group of refugee women. The women were struggling with healing and sharing their traumatic experiences. They frequently talked about their common interest in cooking and food. Thus, group therapy was transformed so that it was conducted in the lunch room of the mental health agency, where the refugee women would bring food to share with each other and exchange ideas on cooking and recipes. Throughout this process, a safe space was created and healing began as they shared about their pain, fears, and difficult past experiences.

Similarly, Ron Finley's (aka gangsta gardener) urban gardening was developed in Los Angeles (LA) in an act of defiance, planting food crops in empty lots owned by the City of Los Angeles (Weston, 2020). Finley lives in South Central LA, a predominantly Black and Latinx neighborhood that Finley calls a "food prison" that is known for "liquor stores, vacant lots, drive-throughs and drive-bys." Finley remarked, "I got tired of driving 45 minutes round trip to get an apple that wasn't impregnated with pesticides, so I began to plant a food forest in front of my house" (Weston, 2020). In an unusually creative way to protest and rebel about living in a food desert and to address issues of food insecurity, in 2010, Finley began planting a vegetable garden on the empty strip of land next to his house, between the footpath and the curb. This was illegal since the empty land was LA property.

He advocated to get the City law changed, arguing that the purpose of urban gardens was to (a) provide access and availability of free healthy food for residents, (b) educate residents about healthy eating, (c) create opportunities for healthy psychological self-growth, and (e) build community and reframe individual and group identity. Finley explained: "It is the most therapeutic and defiant act you can do . . . there are so many metaphors in that garden—we're cultivating ourselves, we're learning how to take care of things, we're learning that nothing is instantaneous." Finley went on to frame his work within the context of some of his community. "Let's all become gangsta gardeners. If you ain't a gardener, you ain't gangsta. Gardening is gangsta. Drugs, robbing—that's not gangsta. Building community— that's gangsta. I'm changing the vernacular." Balancing gardening with psychological growth and development in a community that needs both support and nutritious food is an inventive way to address multiple needs and psychological social justice issues. (For further information see Ron Finley's TED talk at https://www.ted.com/talks/ron_finley_a_guerrilla_gardener_in_south_central_la?language=en). Examples such as José Andrés and Ron Finley are important to help us think beyond traditional ways of doing social justice therapeutic work and healing. To further illustrate innovative ways of incorporating social justice into mental health work and to stimulate creative ideas, we share two examples. The first relates to the #MeToo movement and illustrates how to be creative when addressing sensitive issues such as male-dominated hierarchical values. In China, the #MeToo movement

was censored by the government. To get around government restrictions and the system, Chinese women used knowledge of their own culture and language and developed what appears to be to an innocuous, cute, feminine, silly concept. The homonym *mitu* #米兔 or "rice bunny" was created displaying a bowl of rice and a bunny rabbit. This logo was intentionally printed on pink-colored t-shirts to portray cuteness and innocence (The Conversation, 2018). For readers who are unfamiliar with the Chinese language, it is a nasal language utilizing different tones. So, "rice" in Chinese is *mi* and "bunny" is *tu*, which equals #mitu, sounding like the English language #metoo (see Box Text 23.1), which was promoted on social media in a huge movement that skirted censorship. Further discussion about social media and advocacy is presented in the next section of this chapter.

The second example is related to the Black Lives Matter (BLM) movement. Asian young adults in the United States were confronted by their family members about their support and involvement with BLM. The Asian young adults came together and wrote a letter to their elders in a culturally respectful manner outlining their concerns, explaining BLM and why it is important that the Asian community display solidarity with African Americans and other communities of color (Chan, 2016). The letter creatively and respectfully acknowledged their grandparents, parents, aunties, and uncles adjustment challenges in the United States; the sacrifices they made for their children; the racism and xenophobia they encountered; and the importance of being united with other immigrant groups and communities of color who have shared experiences. The letter was translated into various Asian languages and asked to be read out loud to their elders. It is written in a way that did not shame or denigrate elders for not understanding. Instead the letter was written in a culturally responsive manner that aligned the elders' experiences and those of BLM, resulting in acceptance and a change of values that was a "win-win" situation (see Box Text 23.2).

SOCIAL MEDIA AS A TOOL FOR ADVOCACY AND SOCIAL ACTIVISM

It is important to employ social media as a social justice advocacy tool and strategy since we are living in a time when there is a high reliance on technology in our personal and professional

BOX TEXT 23.2 LETTER TO ASIAN ELDERS (TRANSLATED INTO MULTIPLE ASIAN LANGUAGES)

Mom, Dad, Uncle, Auntie, Grandfather, Grandmother:

We need to talk.

You may not have grown up around people who are Black, but I have. Black people are a fundamental part of my life: they are my friends, my classmates and teammates, my roommates, my family. Today, I'm scared for them.

This year, the American police have already killed more than 500 people. Of those, 25% have been Black, even though Black people make up only 13% of the population. Earlier this week in Louisiana, two White police officers killed a Black man named Alton Sterling while he sold CDs on the street. The very next day in Minnesota, a police officer shot and killed a Black man named Philando Castile in his car during a routine traffic stop while his girlfriend and her 4-year-old daughter looked on. Overwhelmingly, the police do not face any consequences for ending these lives.

This is a terrifying reality that some of my closest friends live with every day.

Even as we hear about the dangers Black Americans face, our instinct is sometimes to point at all the ways we are different from them. To shield ourselves from their reality instead of empathizing. When a policeman shoots a Black person, you might think it's the victim's fault because you see so many images of them in the media as thugs and criminals. After all, you might say, we managed to come to America with nothing and build good lives for ourselves despite discrimination, so why can't they?

I want to share with you how I see things.

It's true that we face discrimination for being Asian in this country. Sometimes people are rude to us about our accents, or withhold promotions because they don't think of us as "leadership material." Some of us are told we're terrorists. But for the most part, nobody thinks "dangerous criminal" when we are walking down the street. The police do not gun down our children and parents for simply existing.

This is not the case for our Black friends. Many Black people were brought to America as slaves against their will. For centuries, their communities, families, and bodies were ripped apart for profit. Even after slavery, they had to build back their lives by themselves, with no institutional support—not allowed to vote or own homes and constantly under threat of violence that continues to this day.

In fighting for their own rights, Black activists have led the movement for opportunities not just for themselves, but for us as well. Many of our friends and relatives are only able to be in this country because Black activists fought to open up immigration for Asians in the 1960s. Black people have been beaten, jailed, even killed fighting for many of the rights that Asian Americans enjoy today. We owe them so much in return. We are all fighting against the same unfair system that prefers we compete against each other.

When someone is walking home and gets shot by a sworn protector of the peace—even if that officer's last name is Liang—that is an assault on all of us, and on all of our hopes for equality and fairness under the law.

For all of these reasons, I support the Black Lives Matter movement. Part of that support means speaking up when I see people in my community—or even my own family—say or do things that diminish the humanity of Black Americans in this country. I am telling you this out of love, because I don't want this issue to divide us. I'm asking that you try to empathize with the anger and grief of the fathers, mothers and children who have lost their loved ones to police violence. To empathize with my anger and grief, and support me if I choose to be vocal, to protest. To share this letter with your friends, and encourage them to be empathetic, too.

As your child, I am proud and eternally grateful that you made the long, hard journey to this country, that you've lived decades in a place that has not always been kind to you. You've never wished your struggles upon me. Instead, you've suffered through a prejudiced America, to bring me closer to the American Dream.

But I hope you can consider this: the American Dream cannot exist for only your children. We are all in this together, and we cannot feel safe until ALL our friends, loved ones and neighbors are safe. The American Dream that we seek is a place where all Americans can live without fear of police violence. This is the future that I want—and one that I hope you want, too.

With love and hope, Your daughters, sons, nieces, nephews and grandchildren

Source: https://www.youtube.com/watch?v=vrR-8_odGh4

lives. Not having our technological devices fully accessible wherever we are, even for a few hours, presents a challenge for some. The Pew Research Center (2019) found that 72% of people in the United States, from all age groups, use some form of social media to connect with one another, engage with news content, share information, and entertain themselves. Globally it is estimated that more than 4 billion people use social media (Kopel, 2021). With rapid advances and increased reliance on technology, we assume that the number of people using some form of social media nationally and globally will have increased after we write this chapter and even more so after the publication of this book. Further escalating the use of and dependence on technology are major national and worldwide events, such as the global COVID-19 pandemic, during which some countries and regions instituted stay at home policies, lockdowns, and quarantines; closed schools and businesses; and enforced social distancing. For some during this time, technology was the only form of communication to the outside world and a means to connect with others.

With globalization and worldwide communication technologies, we witness events as they happen, in real time, in towns, cities, states, countries, and continents around the world. Technology is a unique, simple, and rapid way to access a window to the world. Technology is changing the way we communicate and interact with each other and the world around us, giving us the ability to change our attitudes, values, and behaviors and motivating us to take social action as we experience real-time events. Although there is still a "digital divide," technology reaches multitudes of people. An example we have seen is in our work with refugees who are escaping from their war-torn home countries and using technology to navigate their perilous journey to a safe host country. Once in that country, they use technology to access services and locate family members. Due to their prevalent use of technology, they are known as "techfugees" (Bemak & Chung, 2021a, 2021b).

Consequently, the information we use on our technological devices creates huge (gargantuan) databases not only tracking what we buy, our political leanings, or our patterns of social media usage, but also being used to detect indicators of mental illness and psychological well-being (Kopel, 2021). Using artificial intelligence (AI), algorithms are analyzing these immense databases for language patterns and images in posts to identify signs of mental health issues, such as depression, anxiety, and suicide risk, as well as to evaluate mental health trends across entire populations (Kopel, 2021). Since some individuals use technology to express their psychological well-being or seek mental health support, current social media platforms, such as Snapchat and Pinterest, have created links and apps to connect users with mental health information and support (Kopel, 2021).

In fact, some countries, such as Canada, have taken steps to address mental health issues through social media channels. It should be noted that at the time of writing this book, using AI algorithms to analyze indicators of mental health and psychological well-being through social media posts is in its infancy with anticipated strides in this being further developed. Furthermore, social media has proved effective in interventions for human rights violations. This was seen when an adolescent girl who was kidnapped used a hand signal to successfully communicate with other drivers that she was distressed. The hand sign was created by the Canadian Women's Foundation (face your palm forward and with your thumb tucked in; then close your other fingers over your thumb to "trap" it) and is an international universal signal for help in case of domestic violence or other distress. The hand gesture popularized by Tik Tok represents distress or violence at home (Santucci, 2021). See Figure 23.1.

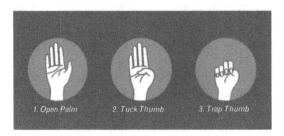

1) Tuck thumb in palm

2) Trap thumb with other fingers

3) Lift fingers back up (keep thumb in)

4) Repeat

FIGURE 23.1 Hand Signal for Help. https://candianwomen.org/signal-for-help/
https://professionallearning board.com/kids-use-this-hand-signal-for-help/

Regardless of changes in technology, it is here to stay and its use will grow. Given people's reliance on and use of technology, it is important that social justice–oriented mental health professionals keep pace with technological advances. It is noteworthy that social media has exponentially increased in the past several years as an effective advocacy and activism tool (Rehr, 2017) that can rapidly share information with a large global audience. Anyone with a smartphone or other technological device has the ability to record an event and disseminate it via the World Wide Web. Live streaming provides audiences with a minute-by-minute accounts of events, delivering viewers with updated information and fostering a personal connection with what is happening. This personal engagement has the potential to provide groundwork to move from a virtual world connection to social action, which was seen in the worldwide BLM protest movement after George Floyd was killed by U.S. police on May 25, 2020. We suggest that mental health social justice–oriented professionals have some responsibility, both personally and professionally, to their clients and colleagues to promote movement from the virtual world to social action.

Social media is a unique social justice advocacy tool since it has a wide range of inclusiveness in that it offers different methods of participating in social action for individuals who may not have access because of physical or health reasons or a preference for a different style of social activism. Social media against injustice has been used in multiple forums ranging from political change to advocacy. This can be seen when the 45th U.S. president used tweeting and social media to promote his political agenda, conspiracy theories, and false claims (Rehr, 2017). Since social media is here to stay, social justice–oriented psychologists and counselors must become more savvy in using it in their social action work.

There are numerous social media forums that we can utilize in our social justice–oriented work such as Twitter, Facebook, LinkedIn, YouTube, Instagram, TikTok, Snapchat, and Hashtag (Rehr, 2017), as well as other digital media such as blog, podcasts, vlogs, websites, and webpages. After the publication of this book we have no doubt that new social media platforms will be developed, and what we've just cited may be already outdated. Even so, we will focus on a few examples of social action via social media to provide encouragement for and ideas on how to apply social media in our social justice–oriented work. Even if the social media platforms we mention may be outdated by the time you read this book, we hope that the examples provide a foundation to stimulate ideas on how to build on updated technological devices, apps, and social media platforms.

SOCIAL MEDIA ACTIVISM EXAMPLES

Using *hashtags* as an advocacy tool is one example we want to highlight. Hashtags have been cited as one of the most powerful forms of social activism and a catalyst for social change. Issues that have high visibility can quickly inspire and mobilize large groups to become active while simultaneously reaching individuals who may have limited physical abilities (Khan-Ibarra, 2015). Four examples of hashtags on social media platforms that brought rapid national and global attention to social justice issues impacting the psychological well-being of individuals, families, and communities are #BlackLivesMatter, which heightened the awareness and consciousness of racial injustice in communities of color as a result of the numerous murders of and violence against innocent and unarmed Black men by law enforcement officers; the #MeToo hashtag, which brought attention and awareness to the prevalence of misogynistic behavior, sexual assault, violence, abuse, and harassment of women; the numerous hashtags on global warming (i.e., #globalwarming, #climatechange, #savetheplanet; #sustainability), which comprise a worldwide initiative that addresses the impact of global warming and climate change on the environment; and a number of hashtags (i.e., #MarchForOurLives, #NeverAgain, #EnoughisEnough, and #GunControlNow) to address U.S. gun violence and mass shootings to pressure federal and state lawmakers to create tougher gun access and control policies.

A closer examination of #MeToo demonstrates the influence of social media as a powerful social activism tool that leads to psychological well-being and justice for survivors of sexual violence, assault, abuse, and harassment. Within one week of launching #MeToo, Twitter reported more than 1.7 million women used #MeToo in more than 85 countries, while Facebook reported that within 24 hours there were more than 12 million posts, comments, and reactions (Thomson, 2018). With the national and global increase of awareness and understanding of sexual violence, #MeToo resulted in systemic change by moving the perception of the problem and responsibility from the individual to societal and cultural perspectives. Through #MeToo, survivors felt that they were not alone; they were given a space in which to speak out and be heard, leading to being empowered to call out and challenge perpetrator(s) to take responsibility for their violations. These actions are conducive to begin the psychological healing process for survivors.

The #MeToo movement did not stop at the individual level but continued to address injustice at a societal level, sparking the #TimesUp movement that focused on changing organizational laws and employment agreements and policies. It gave women a space in which to voice concerns and hold perpetrators of sexual abuse, assault, violence, and harassment accountable. The success of this social activism resulted in major corporations, such as Microsoft, changing sexual harassment policies, while U.S. state and national legislators strengthened sexual harassment policies (Thomson, 2018). #MeToo not only had widespread impact on both individuals and systems, but it also extended to fostering changes in prevention and intervention models for current and future victims of misogynistic behavior. One can view hashtags such as #MeToo as important examples of how technology and social media can fuel social movements that lead to a more just and psychologically healthy society (Deng, 2018).

CAUTION IN USING SOCIAL MEDIA ACTIVISM

We would like to offer a word of caution in using social media for social justice action. With our passion, emotions, excitement, and motivation to create a psychologically healthy environment for our clients' well-being, we may, at times, rush to educate and mobilize stakeholders to act. Before we act, we highly suggest that attention and care is necessary to ensure that we are providing accurate information and facts and getting permission to post information, photos, and other links. Checking and rechecking the sources of information to avoid misleading, unsubstantiated, and false information is essential when incorporating social media activism (Thomson, 2018). In fact, there are growing concerns about websites that appear legitimate but instead disingenuously provide misinformation or disinformation (Pappas, 2022). *Misinformation* may be incorrect information spread by someone who innocently believes it to be true; this is compared to *disinformation*, which is deliberately providing false information (Pappas, 2022). Regardless of misinformation or disinformation, we can all be vulnerable and misled, even when we are technologically savvy (Pappas, 2022). False information not only raises questions about one's credibility, but it is also counterproductive in promoting facts, truth, and justice. We say this remembering that our primary responsibility is to our clients; providing inaccurate information will not only affect our credibility, but, more importantly, may also result in additional harm that may impact clients' psychological well-being.

Interestingly, during his 2017–2021 U.S. presidency the 45th president threatened to "close down" social media networks after his tweets were monitored, deleted, and eventually banned from social media avenues because of his inaccurate and unsubstantiated messages of hate and intolerance inciting violence toward those who opposed him. He signed an Executive Order (May 28, 2020) restricting legal protections for social media companies' published content. The executive order aimed to empower federal regulators to penalize social media companies for suspending users or removing content, claiming that doing so violates free speech (Alaimo, 2020; Cellan-Jones, 2020). The executive order was prompted by Twitter flagging two of the past-President's tweets about mail-in election ballots as "potentially misleading" and used a fact-checking function to attach warnings to his tweets. Twitter stated: "We've taken action in the interest of preventing others from being inspired to commit violent acts, but have kept the tweet on Twitter because it is important that the public still be able to see the tweet given its relevance to ongoing matters of public importance" (Alaimo, 2020; Cellan-Jones, 2020). This is an illustration of the dangers of misusing social media at the expense and rejection of social justice values and change, and it certainly has relevance to social justice, mental health, psychological well-being, security, and safety.

It is also important to understand online technological resistance to social media advocacy. *Trolling* is a well-known practice that has the capability to undermine posts and derail important discussions and issues. Social media trolls follow trends and hashtags and purposefully disrupt and upset the site, creating disagreements, posting obstructive controversial ideas, and resorting to bullying to oppose ideas, with an intent to hijack the hashtag and prevent productive discussion (Thomson, 2018). Similarly, individuals can purchase tweets and even falsely use others' names to tweet people, again detracting from the focus of the social justice agenda. Behaviors such as these may result in undue stress on clients' mental health and require that psychologists and counselors be aware of such social media practices. Finally, as we utilize social media for social justice–oriented work it is vital that we are not misled or fooled by those who exhibit behavior that has been labeled "slacktivism" (Oxford Dictionaries, 2020), which describes those who support social and political change through internet/social media because it requires little effort, time, or commitment. As we discussed in Chapter 8 ("Unpacking the Psychological Barriers That Prevent Social Justice Action") doing social justice work requires actually "doing" and not being an "armchair social justice mental health advocate" who just talks the talk rather than walks the talk.

ADVOCACY STRATEGIES FOR DIFFERENT GENERATIONS

As we discuss creative advocacy and activism to promote healthy psychological well-being for our clients, their families, and communities, we also need to talk about how we do effective social justice work with and across different generations to ensure that our social justice work reaches a wide range of clients. There is no "one-size-fits-all" social justice advocacy strategy that promotes psychological well-being, hence we need to examine and investigate effective social justice techniques across different generations. To create healthy communities, members must "buy in" and be involved. Table 23.1 displays the characteristics of different generations and helps us to understand their respective psychology, history, psychopolitical, psychosocial, and lived experiences and how these major life events have impacted their worldviews, beliefs, values, and behaviors. The goal of Table 23.1 is to provide information that will lead to creative ideas on best advocacy strategies to use with different generations. It should be noted that Table 23.1 excludes the current Generation Alpha given their young age and a lack of information at present about this generation.

Recent generations have been brought up with and are comfortable using digital technology compared to older generations who are forced to learn technology as a growing aspect of their daily lives. For example, New Zealand has phased out using written checks to receive or make payments, resulting in a reliance on digital and online banking (Grant, 2021). This rapid growth and trend toward the increasing need for technological proficiency reinforces our premise that we, as social justice–oriented psychologists and counselors, must be technologically savvy and incorporate social media into the advocacy work we do. It is important to ensure that our social media advocacy is aligned with the target generation so that there is confluence with the generation's level of technological sophistication and access and their lived experiences. For instance, animation can be used as an effective tool in social justice education. However, animation has changed tremendously throughout the years, and, although many generations have been brought up with Disney characters, there is a huge difference between the original characters (i.e., Mickey and Minnie Mouse) and recent characters seen in the Lion King, Mulan, Coco, and Frozen. To do effective social justice work it is critical that we tailor our social media advocacy to connect with specific generations.

Applying the concept "children are our future" we now focus the discussion on GenZ (also called iGen or Gen Tech because of their reliance on social media and technology). According to U.S. Pew Research, GenZ is the most racially and ethnically diverse generation with just over half (52%) being non-Hispanic White, creating greater acceptance, openness, and empathy to diversity and inclusion, which is conducive to a more just and healthy society (Janfaza, 2020). GenZ has also come of age during a time of political divide, gun violence, mass shootings, global warming, heated immigration issues, and a COVID-19 global pandemic, and they are in the midst of a call for racial justice and protests to end racism and police brutality (Janfaza, 2020). They are fully aware of their political power: within their generation, 1 in 10 were eligible voters during the U.S. 2020 elections.

Recent generations such as the GenZers have been brought up using digital technology. Given their technological savvy and reliance on technology, it makes sense to incorporate

TABLE 23.1 The characteristics of the different generations

Generation	Life-shaping events	Characteristics	Values	Advocacy activities
Generation Z Born 1997 to 2012 Ages 7–22	Gun violence Opioid crisis Global warming Climate change	Tech-innate Accepting of others Concerned about cost of education Entrepreneurial and inventive spirit	Competitive Transparent Realists Individualistic	#MarchForOurLives Global Warming
Millennials Born 1981 to 1996 Ages 23–38	9/11 Reality TV AIDS Internet boom/ bust	Authentically confident Diversity and change valued Fully transparent, shares everything Socially, politically, and eco-conscious	Well-educated Technology savvy Meaningful work Community- focused	#BlackLivesMatter Occupy Wall Street DREAM Act
Generation X Born 1965 to 1980 Ages 39–54	Stagflation Gulf War High divorce rates Women working MTV	Work to live Focused on results Think globally Eager to learn Education necessary to succeed	Crave independence Skepticism Adapt to change Flexible	#MeToo Women's March
Baby Boomers Born 1946 to 1964 Ages 55–73	Man on the Moon Vietnam War Free love	Live to work Self- worth = work ethic Loyal to employer Goal-centric and process-oriented Need to know they are valued	Focused Disciplined Teamwork- focused Competitive Make a difference	Civil Rights Movement Vietnam War Women's Rights
Silent/ Traditionalists Born 1925 to 1945 Ages 74–94	World War II Depression FDR era	Conservative Disciplined Respect authority Patient, loyal, and hard working	Patriotic Risk-averse Trust the system	

Sources: Dimock, M. (2019, Jan 17). Defining generations: Where Millennials end and Generation Z begins. Pew Research Center.

https://www.pewresearch.org/fact-tank/2019/01/17/where-millennials-end-and-generation-z-begins/

Ghawi, D. (2018, Jul 16). Main characteristics per generation. Thrive Global. https://thriveglobal.com/stories/main-characteristics-per-generation/

social media in the advocacy work we do with members of these generations. Their openness to issues of justice, equity, diversity, and inclusion are all factors that promote a psychologically healthy society. Recent generations' awareness of the negative psychological impact of injustice encourages a willingness to act and fight for a healthier and just future. Consequently, the GenZers feel that they are the social media revolution in the forefront of social change and in a unique position to create a social justice transformation by utilizing their technological savviness and reliance on social media. They are globally connected and can mobilize diverse groups; are empathic and value diversity and inclusion; and are willing to mobilize and join others to advocate for social change knowing that issues such as global warming, racial injustice, xenophobia, and gender-based violence will directly impact their psychological well-being, security, and safety.

GenZers are already personally invested in social change, clearly understanding that social action can led to positively impacting their current and future lives. They have already demonstrated their influence and success in creating social change. For example, #MarchForOur Lives was created by GenZ students as a result of the February 14, 2018, shooting at Marjory Stoneman Douglas High School in Parkland, Florida, that killed 17 people (students and teachers). Utilizing technological skills and savviness, and knowing how to reach out to peers, a plan to march on Washington D.C. on March 24, 2018, using the #MarchForOurLives hashtag, spread swiftly via social media and reached more than 11.6 million people. The group's agenda was to demand legislation banning assault weapons, stop the sale of high-capacity magazines, and implement laws that require background checks on all gun purchases (Deng, 2018; Grinberg & Muadii, 2018).

Concurrently, utilizing their technological savviness, they started a GoFundMe campaign that raised more than $1.7 million in public donations in three days, along with $2 million in private donations from celebrities, such as Steven Spielberg and Oprah Winfrey (Grinberg & Muadii, 2018). They were also able to enlist companies like Microsoft to cut business ties with the National Rifle Association (NRA); get transportation to the march by the gun safety advocacy group Giffords (named for congresswoman Gabrielle Giffords who was shot and wounded); have the New England Patriots CEO donate his private jet for transportation to the march; secure sponsorship from Ben and Jerry's Ice Cream Company for travel grants to attend the march; receive free and discounted food from Chef José Andrés' ThinkFoodGroup to student marchers; and get support from various entertainers such as Miley Cyrus, Ariana Grande, Jennifer Hudson, Common, Demi Lovato, and Vic Mensa, who performed at the rally (Grinberg & Muadii, 2018).

At the same time #MarchForOverLives successfully collaborated with other gun safety advocacy groups and allies, building relationships that created a strong coalition of advocates. The influence and impact of using social media for social advocacy and change was evident when, on the day of the rally, #MarchforOverLives was tweeted 4 million times (Deng, 2018); it rapidly became a global march, with more than 800 groups marching across United States and internationally in London, Madrid, Rome, and Tokyo (Grinberg &Muadii, 2018). #MarchForOurLives is just one example of using social media in a way that is familiar to current generations and demonstrates the importance of communicating in a manner responsive to stakeholders' culture of communication. #MarchForOurLives created a space for psychological healing from the traumatic experiences of mass shooting and gun violence and resulted in empowerment by pushing for state and federal systematic change to prevent future gun violence and mass shooting scenarios. #MarchForOurLives is a good illustration of where psychologists and counselors can address highly charged issues in a responsive way with a targeted generation by aligning and cooperating with social media and advocacy groups to promote mental health support.

In summary, creative social activism requires us to know and understand our potential allies and engage with them through means that will align with their ways of communicating.

Collaborating with others is a key to creative social justice–oriented work. As Martin Luther King Jr. said, "There is power in numbers and there is power in unity." As social justice–oriented mental health professionals it is critical that we creatively partner with these generations and incorporate technology into our social action. The usage of modern-day technology will resonate with the next generations and foster effective partnerships in promoting a healthier and more just society.

GRADUATE-LEVEL UNIVERSITY TRAINING CREATIVE ASSIGNMENTS

We would like to end this chapter by providing a brief discussion of graduate-level university training assignments that promote and inspire creativity. We both (Rita and Fred) have used assignments that we developed and found effective in graduate training that were conducive to finding one's social justice creative gene (Bemak & Chung, 2011). For example, Box Text 23.3 features a Muslim student in my (Rita) social justice class who was motivated to do social action by educating people about the Muslim culture in the aftermath 9/11, an event that engendered global misperceptions of Muslims as terrorists. Given that he was a graduate student at that time with limited resources, he decided to take action by holding a sign that read "Meet a Muslim" in a busy urban tourist area in Washington D.C. on a Saturday afternoon. His social action idea demonstrated creativity and courage by putting himself "out there" and introducing himself to strangers in the large crowds that walked by him. The event was highly successful, with some people tooting their horns in support as they drove by in their cars and many stopping to shake his hand.

Ethnographic fiction (EF) (Chung & Bemak, 2013) was an assignment we developed to focus on social justice and mental health. EF can be incorporated in any multicultural social justice diversity-focused university class or agency-based training for mental health students or professionals. It is an assignment that provides students or professionals with an opportunity to "walk in another person's shoes." I (Rita) have been using this assignment since 2002, in a graduate program. Each semester, students' feedback showed how profoundly affected they were and how EF changed their lives as future social justice–oriented psychologists, counselors, and advocates. EF involves each student in the class being assigned at the beginning of the semester a client facing a social injustice. Students are assigned client characters who are completely different from their own lived experience with regards to race/ethnicity, gender, sexual orientation, age, religion, socioeconomic status, abilities, etc. Clients' social justice situations are based on contemporary social justice issues that include issues of poverty; discrimination; xenophobia; racial injustice; gender-based violence; refugees and immigrants; undocumented migrants; elderly abuse; gun violence; inequities in education, healthcare, and the criminal justice systems; transgender challenges; global warming; environmental racism; access to clean water; food insecurity; etc.

The assignment is in four parts: (a) a personal written paper about their client in the first person; (b) an 8-minute in class verbal presentation in the first person, introducing themselves as the client to the entire class, followed by an in-depth challenging Q&A session by the faculty and classmates for the purpose of assessing the student's degree of knowledge

BOX TEXT 23.3 MEET A MUSLIM

Source: With permission from Mohammad Biag.

and understanding of the client's lived experience and to further educate classmates about the injustices experienced by the client; (c) a creative assignment (that is not a presentation) to illuminate the client's situation, which can be in the form of puzzles, drawings, songs, collages, poems, etc. (see Box Text 23.4); and (d) the mental health professional's social justice action plan regarding the client's social justice situation that can be generalized to others experiencing similar issues. For more information on the EF assignment, see Chung and Bemak (2013), the video demonstration of EF (Chung & Bemak, 2014), and Chapter 22 by Jackie Tackett and Chapter 24 by Rodolfo Marenco, who in their narratives share their EF assignment experience.

Other creative social justice assignments we have used range from developing and implementing a tunnel of oppression on the university-wide campus that focuses on different social injustices; developing a multimedia gang prevention manual for school counselors; students' developing a 3–5 minute YouTube video on a social justice issues with the goal of educating others on the issue as well as providing resources on how to address the issue (e.g., students' YouTube video on hunger in America at https://www.youtube.com/watch?v=QrWUSDg_GoI); and bringing teams of students into the field on Counselors Without Borders work trips to give students an opportunity to provide counseling in

post-disaster situations, such as in Mississippi after Hurricane Katrina, in California during wildfires, and in Puerto Rico after Hurricane Maria. For further examples of what we call "classroom without walls" assignments, we refer readers to Bemak and Chung (2011).

SUMMARY

Although creativity is not discussed very much in human rights and social justice–oriented mental health work, we believe it is an important aspect to consider for psychologists and counselors. Tapping into our own strengths, interests, and hobbies and weaving them into our work adds an impactful dimension to social justice–oriented work. The rapid techno-logical advances and profound influence of social media necessitates that mental health professionals are both aware of and able to utilize these modern-day means of communica-tion and social engagement as effective social justice advocacy and activism tools. Including the use of technology in graduate level training of mental health professionals provides an excellent step in developing future social justice–oriented mental health professionals to be more technologically savvy and creative.

DISCUSSION QUESTIONS

1. Discuss and explore what skills you may have that could be used to do creative advocacy for clients.
2. What is your reaction to Ron Finley's creative gardening program in South Los Angeles?
3. What social justice action would you be interested in introducing through social media? Describe how you would do this.
4. If you can imagine introducing Ethnographic Fiction into mental health training, what would be two individual examples that you would develop for the training? Describe the injustices those two individuals are facing.

REFERENCES

Alaimo, K. (2020, May 28). Trump's dangerous move against Twitter. CNN. https://www.cnn.com/2020/05/28/opinions/trumps-executive-order-social-media-twitter-alaimo/index.html

Bemak, F., & Chung, R. C-Y. (2011). Applications in social justice counselor training: Classroom Without Walls. *Journal of Humanistic Counseling, Education, and Development, 50*(2), 204–219. doi:10.1002/j.2161-1939.2011.tb00119.x

Bemak, F., & Chung, R. C-Y. (2021a). Contemporary refugees: Challenges and a culturally responsive intervention model for effective practice. *Counseling Psychologist (Special Issue), 49*(2), 305–324. https://doi.org/10.1177/0011000020972182

Bemak, F., & Chung, R. C-Y. (2021b). A culturally responsive intervention model for modern day refugee: A multiphase model of psychotherapy, social justice, and human rights. In J.D. Aten & J. Hwang (Eds.), *Refugee mental health* (pp. 103–136). American Psychological Association.

Cellan-Jones, R. (2020, May 28). Twitter hides Trump tweet for "glorifying violence." BBC. https://www.bbc.com/news/technology-52846679A

Chan, R. (2016, Jul 14). How a group of Asian-Americans is spreading support for Black Lives Matter. Time. https://time.com/4404229/black-lives-matter-letter-alton-sterling-philando-castile/

Chung, R. C-Y., & Bemak, F. (2013). Use of ethnographic fiction in social justice graduate counseling training. *Counselor Education and Supervision, 52*, 56–68. https://doi.org/10.1002/j.1556-6978.2013.00028.x

Chung, R. C-Y., & Bemak, F. (2014). *Creative social justice training: Case study examples* [video]. Alexander Street Press, Proquest.

Dawson, M. (2016, Oct 2). Meet the female Schindler who saved 2,500 kids by posing them as gentiles. New York Post. https://nypost.com/2016/10/02/meet-the-female-schindler-who-saved-2500-kids-by-posing-them-as-gentiles/

Deng, O. (2018, Mar 30). March for our lives was born on social media. https://www.crimsonhexagon.com/blog/march-for-our-lives-was-born-on-social-media/

Grant, D. (2021, Apr 11). Banks phasing out use of cheques is simply poor form. https://www.stuff.co.nz/business/opinion-analysis/300272803/banks-phasing-out-use-of-cheques-is-simply-poor-form

Grinberg, E., & Muadii, N. (2018, Mar 26). How the Parkland students pulled off a massive national protest in only 5 weeks. CNN. https://www.cnn.com/2018/03/26/us/march-for-our-lives/index.html

Janfaza, R. (2020, Jun 22). "We're tired of waiting": GenZ is ready for a revolution. CNN. https://www.cnn.com/2020/06/16/politics/genz-voters-2020-election/index.html

Khan-Ibarra, S. (2015, Jan 13). The case for social media and hashtag activism. Huffington Post. https://www.huffingtonpost.com/sabina-khanibarra/the-case-for-social-edia_b_6149974.html

King Jr, M. L. (1968). The role of the behavioral scientist in the civil rights movement. *American Psychologist*, 23(3), 180–186. https://doi.org/10.1037/h0025715

Kopel, R. (2021, Sep 14). Mining social media reveals mental health trends and helps prevent self-harm: Patterns of word usage in online posts may point to individuals at high risk. Scientific American. https://www.scientificamerican.com/article/mining-social-media-reveals-mental-health-trends-and-helps-prevent-self-harm/

Oxford Dictionaries. (2020, Jun 26). Slacktivism. https://www.oxfordlearnersdictionaries.com/us/definition/english/slacktivism

Pappas, S. (2022, Jan 1). Fighting fake news in the classroom. *APA Monitor in Psychology*, 53(1), 87. https://www.apa.org/monitor/2022/01/career-fake-news

Pew Research Center. (2019, Jun 12). Social media fact sheet. https://www.pewresearch.org/internet/fact-sheet/social-media/

Rehr, D. K. (2017, Feb 8). How is social media being used in advocacy? Huffington Post. https://www.huffingtonpost.com/entry/how-is-social-media-being-used-in-advocacy_us_589a7b12e4b0985224db5bac

Santucci, J. (2021, Nov 5). Missing girl saved after she used hand signs from TikTok to ask for help from moving car, sheriff says. USA Today. https://www.usatoday.com/story/news/nation/2021/11/05/hand-signal-help-tiktok-helped-save-missing-girl-sheriff/6304765001/

The Conversation. (2018, Feb 5). From #MeToo to #RiceBunny: How social media users are campaigning in China. http://theconversation.com/from-metoo-to-ricebunny-how-social-media-users-are-campaigning-in-china-90860

Thomson, K. (2018, Jun 12). Social media activism and the #MeToo movement. https://medium.com/@kmthomson.11/social-media-activism-and-the-metoo-movement-166f452d7fd2

Toporek, R. L., & Ahluwalia, M. K. (2021). *Taking action: Creating social change through strength, solidarity, strategy, and sustainability*. Cognella.

Weston, P. (2020, Apr 28). "This is no damn hobby": The "gangsta gardener" transforming Los Angeles. Guardian. https://www.theguardian.com/environment/2020/apr/28/ron-finley-gangsta-gardener-transforming-los-angeles

World Central Kitchen. (2020). https://wck.org/

CHAPTER 24

STUDENT CHAPTER

Living in the Shoes of Another Person: Social Injustice and Advocacy Come Alive

Rodolfo E. Marenco

My name is Suzanne Johnson. I am a 16-year-old White female in my last year of high school. Yes, I am a senior. Big deal! The truth is that being a senior doesn't mean much to me, except perhaps for the fact that at least when I finish high school, my nightmare will be over. Yes, high school has been a nightmare for me. As a matter of fact, I think that my entire school experience has been a nightmare, a lie. I am tired of showing to others something I am not. I feel disgusted with myself, not for being a lesbian, but because I have kept it to myself all my life. I am tired of living the life of a heterosexual girl. I am tired of pretending I like guys. I wish I could just tell everyone the truth about me without having to worry about their rejection, without having to worry about losing my friends, my lifestyle, and even my parents. Sometimes I wish I would just finish it all for good. Yes, I have thought about ending my life on some occasions. I wonder why I had to be born in a world where my kind is not accepted by others. I wonder why it had to be me.

Ever since I was a child, I always felt I was different from other girls. In those days I didn't know I was a lesbian or what a lesbian was, but I knew enough about how girls were supposed to behave and feel to know that I needed to keep my feelings to myself. For this reason, I have always felt alone, isolated in my own world of who I really am. As I grew up in the safety of my upper-middle-class family, home never felt safe for me. Both my father and my mother are very conservative and on occasions I have heard them disapprove of LGBTQ people when they appear in the media. My father travels a lot in his job. He is in the military, and his job requires him to travel to different bases around the country very often. Being in the military, he has been trained to dislike those like me. My mom, on the other hand, is too busy to care about me. She lives in her own world of friends and shopping, spending the money my father makes. Besides, I think she is dealing with loneliness issues of her own by being married to a military man who is never home. I think that she is having an affair. No, I can't seek guidance from my parents; they would probably disown me if they knew they had a daughter who likes other girls. They would be ashamed of me. My worst fear is that they will someday find out. I can't even imagine what they will do. Would they throw me out of my home? I can't take that risk and cause them that much disappointment.

I have always been alone in my quest to find information about those like me. I am not friends with any lesbians in my school or in my neighborhood. All my friends are hetero-sexual, or at least act that way. Being the Captain of the soccer team has made me very popular among my peers. I guess many would like to be in my shoes and have as many friends as I have, but if only they knew. I even have a boyfriend in my effort to hide and con-ceal that I am lesbian. He even thinks that I am attracted to him, but I feel disgusted when he gets near me. The only way I can stand being with him is by drinking alcohol when I spend time with him, usually on Friday evenings after the football games.

This kind of life has to stop. I can't go through life always looking at myself through the eyes of others, measuring my soul by the tape of a world that looks on in. I am tired of lying. Yes, silence is a form of lying. I can't go around through life making excuses for those around me who do not accept those like me, or worrying over the reputation of those who decide to stick around me when I do decide to come out. I have the right to be a lesbian without receiving a cold shoulder and rejection. Until that day when I decide to come out, being a lesbian will continue to be lonely. On many occasions, I have had to just sit there, listening to stereotypic comments about lesbians, without the courage to say anything for myself out of fear, just listening to their jokes. It is painful to sit and watch while my friends, classmates, and peers tell lesbian jokes right in front of me.

Imagine that this was your life, that you were this girl you are reading about, and that you had been living this life without any guidance, with fear, without hope. This is what I had to do as an assignment for my social justice counseling class at George Mason University (GMU). The character you just read about, Suzanne Johnson, is not real. She was a product of my imagination who came to exist due to a class assignment to create a character adaptation. My assignment was to create and assume the character of a 16-year-old high school White female whose life experiences were like those you just read about (Chung & Bemak, 2013).

The assignment proved to be more challenging than anyone can imagine because not only was I being required to open up to experiences different from my own and to accept those who are very different from me, but I was also being forced to understand someone whose worldview I could not even begin to comprehend by trying to see the world from her own perspective, not mine. So, the question posed by this assignment was whether I, a Hispanic man who has raised his two heterosexual teenage children, would be able to com-prehend the worldview of a person so different from me and everything I am familiar with.

No, creating Suzanne Johnson's character was not an easy task, for when I created her, I was 37 years old, a Hispanic married heterosexual male, father of a 16-year-old boy and a 12-year-old girl. Before this assignment, I had never read any literature, nor had I ever had any real friendships with any members from the LGBTQ population. In addition to my ignorance about the topic, my ethnic culture and military background worked against me for this assignment. I was raised in El Salvador until the age of 19, and, after moving to the United States and spending 5 years in California, I moved to Virginia and joined the U.S. Army, where I served as an enlisted soldier for more than 9 years. Nevertheless, thanks to the guidance of my professor in the program and to the literature available on the topic, Suzanne Johnson came to be, and, even though she doesn't exist, she is very real because she exists in those who are like her and who, like her, have to cope with people who don't accept them, people who judge them, people like us.

Imagine living in a world where you are not accepted by those around you. Imagine living in constant fear of everyone around you, especially those closest to you: your classmates, your friends, your co-workers, your employer, your parents, your siblings, your spouse, all of the people who are meaningful to you and even those who are not. Imagine living in a constant struggle to be someone you are not, trying not to be who you are, and hiding your true self even from yourself. Imagine the disgust of doing things you despise and giving up doing things you would love to do. Imagine that one day you decide to confront everyone, and, as you reveal the true self you have been hiding from everyone for all of your life, you find yourself not only alone and rejected, but also becoming a target for judgment, hate, violence, social isolation, and social injustice. Would you be strong enough to remain truthful to yourself, or would you give in to social pressures? For me, this assignment was the first time I was forced to ask myself these questions.

The GMU program infused multiculturalism and social justice in all its courses. I not only received training on counseling techniques, but, in addition, I also got to explore how social justice and multiculturalism played a role and influenced the topics covered and discussed in the classroom and in our class assignments. On a personal level, what this meant for me as a Hispanic was that, as I learned new subjects in the classroom, it was within a context where my classmates and I became aware of how our different cultures and individual ethnic identities played a role and were affected by the topics we were learning. In other words, not only did we learn the topics required by the counseling program, but, in addition, we also learned how multiculturalism and social justice affect not only our clients but also our classmates and ourselves. Nowhere did this become more true than in the social justice and multicultural classes.

I am a Hispanic heterosexual male with a worldview typical of Latinos. *Machismo* is in my veins, and, as a result, so is prejudice against LGBTQ people. At age 37, after having spent the first 19 years of my life in my native country, I was as homophobic as I could be. The interesting thing is that I was not aware of my homophobia. As a counseling student, I have always tried to understand and accept those around me, and, before being confronted with my biases by the social justice counseling class and by the other classes taught in our program with a multicultural focus, I was sure that I had no problem accepting LGBTQ people. Thankfully, one thing that the GMU counseling program helped me to realize was that acceptance and tolerance are not enough when working with LGBTQ clients. If we are ever to become effective counselors with them, we don't only have to explore our own biases and prejudice against them, but we also must understand their worldview. This last item is where I've had the most problem with while in the program. The only reason I have been able to become aware of my ignorance when dealing with LGBTQ people and with any other population from a culture different from my own has been because of the assignments in my graduate program, the readings required by the program, and, most important, the guidance from professors who have made it a point to deliver their material with social justice and multiculturalism in mind.

I can't emphasize enough the importance of training counselors to become multiculturally competent and to understand the social injustice issues their clients have to face daily everywhere, at work, at home, on the streets, when relaxing while watching television, when going out for dinner to a restaurant, etc. The counseling profession owes it to clients to stop ignoring the issues that affect those very mental health problems we are trying to help our clients to resolve. These days, no longer can we call ourselves professional counselors and psychologists if we choose to live in denial to social justice issues that affect our clients. These days, the majority no longer has absolute power over the minorities because the psychology and counseling profession is full of minority people who will no longer let issues such as White privilege or discrimination due to gender, class, ethnicity, color of skin, and sexual preference go unchallenged. It is time for the profession to be accountable and to lead the mental health profession out of ignorance and social correctness. We owe it to our clients, and, most important of all, we owe to ourselves and to those we love to push for mental health advocacy and awareness. No longer can we be keepers and enforcers of the status quo and call ourselves helpers in the profession. Our ignorance hurts us, it hurts our clients, and it hurts the mental health profession.

Programs like the one offered at GMU are gold to the mental health profession. The leadership this program has shown by freeing us counselors from the chains of social correctness and denial are going to create change in our profession, I have no doubt. This is because, just like me, there are many of my classmates who feel like I do and who have been moved and motivated by our professors to be more than what social injustice allows us to be with our clients. We have been challenged, and we are reacting by becoming carriers of change in the profession, change that will benefit our clients, not only those who follow society's expectations, but all of our clients, including those society tries to ignore.

REFERENCE

Chung, R. C-Y., & Bemak, F. (2013). Use of ethnographic fiction in social justice graduate counseling training. *Counselor Education and Supervision, 52*, 56–68. https://doi.org/10.1002/j.1556-6978.2013.00028.x

CHAPTER 25

STUDENT CHAPTER

Somewhere Over the Rainbow

Nia Pazoki

The youngest of three siblings, I was born in 1990, in Iran. I experienced life after the Islamic Revolution. Growing up, I remember stories my mom, dad, and grandparents would share with me from the times before revolution in the 1970s; somewhere over the rainbow . . . each from their own perspectives, though. My grandfather would share his love of the Shah (the king) and the royal family ruling Iran before the revolution. My dad would share about how the economy was better, and "freedom" was my mom's angle. I remember my mom mumbling songs from "Googoosh," a Persian female singer and tell me how fun it was watching Googoosh performing live.

I was born and raised in Tehran, the heart of Iran. Growing up, my teachers described me as not being "an easy kid." I remember asking hundreds of questions, trying to make sense of the world that I was living in. Whenever I tried to challenge the ideas that were forced on us, I was considered to be a "rebel." Questions like how can a person be born as "Muslim" with no choice? Why were boys and girls separated in schools.? Why could boys play football in the streets, but girls couldn't? Why riding bikes on the streets was only illegal for girls but not boys? Why dogs are illegal? Or dancing? Or women singing? And my biggest question was: Why do women "only" have to cover themselves and not men? The given answer was always "Women should cover their bodies because they stimulate men!" I hated this justification because it was demeaning not only for women but also men.

My life during my adolescence was dark, like the clothes that I and other women wore. We were not allowed to listen to music, dance, or sing. Like so many other women, I was forced to live a dual life. My love of music, fashion, and color was restricted to the home. The boys that I grew up with could go out with their friends, have girlfriends, move to their own places, travel outside the country—so many activities that I couldn't take part in. Whenever I complained, I always heard the same response: they are boys, and you are not allowed as a girl. I would ask "So when would be my time to do all those activities and be free?" and the response was always the same one sentence: "When you get married and have a husband."

Throughout my life the idea of going with the flow never appealed to me. When I turned 18 and had to choose a major, I was encouraged to study medicine or engineering since they were the "valued" majors, so I chose architectural engineering, having no idea about my true passion. I felt I needed to study in another city to live with some freedom, so I chose Yazd. At first, it was exciting to live alone and study in Yazd, far from Tehran. But both the city and the university were very religious, and I soon felt suffocated and terrified. Girls had to wear *chadors*, which is a large piece of cloth that is wrapped around the head and upper body leaving only the face exposed. I remember getting harassed by the morality police so many times for not wearing the *chador* when talking to my male classmates.

After two years of studying architectural engineering, I felt I had wasted time, dropped out of college, and moved back to Tehran. My passion for serving people and kids led me volunteer at charity houses and work with refugee children. A year later I went back to school and started my studies in education at Sharif University of Technology. This was the best decision of my life. The field of education empowered me to be who I am today. Education provided me the freedom that I was always craving to navigate different angles and perspectives.

As I grew older, I still had so many human rights questions that remained un-answered . . . questions that had grown bigger and deeper. Like, why is being queer illegal? Or abortion? Why don't women have the right to divorce their husbands? Why is a married Iranian woman not allowed to leave the country without their husband's consent? Why are men allowed to have four wives at the same time? And so many other questions. At the age of 28, I left the country to seek answers to my infinite questions.

The trauma of growing up under the Islamic government can show up anywhere, even after leaving my country. When I attended the Whitecaps (Vancouver) versus Toronto soccer game I told a friend that, back in Iran, women were not allowed in the stadiums to watch sports games, reminding me of how, when back in Iran, I went to the stadium and stood behind closed doors while my guy friends went through the door. I also vividly re-member the day when I was stopped by the Canadian police for biking on the streets without wearing my helmet. I was so distressed and shaking so badly that the policeman had to help me to calm down. For me, it was a flashback to being stopped by the morality police in Iran who would enforce the women's government dress code where one could be arrested for showing a bit of hair or a few inches of your ankles or arms. This is what happened to Mahsa Zhina Amini, a 22-year-old Kurdish woman who was detained for wearing a "bad" *hijab* and subsequently died in custody. Her death sparked the 2022 uprising in Iran, creating large-scale civil unrest in the country that has risen to global attention.

Protesters are fighting not only for justice for Mahsa Amini and the rights of women, but for personal and political liberties and accountability from the Iranian government. The protests, led by women, have spread to more than 80 cities in Iran and have led to hundreds of arrests and violence against protesters, activists, journalists, and public figures. As a result of the protests, internet access in Iran remains limited as the Iranian government strictly regulates its usage. As anti-government protests roil cities and towns in Iran, tens of thou-sands of Iranians living abroad, from those who fled in the 1980s after Iran's 1979 Islamic Revolution to a younger generation of Iranians born and raised in Western countries, are marching on the streets around the world in Europe, North America, and beyond in support of this watershed moment at home. For the first time in my life, I can see no division between men and women in Iran. Everyone is fighting for one thing; "Woman, Life, Freedom." I think it is the first time in history that women have been both the spark and engine for human rights and an attempted counter-revolution.

Living in Canada and being away from home and witnessing all the protests, deaths, and arrests is one of the hardest experiences of my life. Like many Iranians outside of Iran, for the first few weeks, I was restless. I felt like I was a "walking dead" person, physically attending meetings, classes, and work but mentally with the people back in my country. I would check my phone every minute, and every time see news of Iran where children being abducted, raped, and murdered for exercising their basic human rights. Every new story felt like a stab in my heart. I never experienced this amount of anger and rage before in my life, becoming further enraged that the Western media coverage was not portraying the truth. This women-led revolution is not about religion or the poor economy of Iran, but rather about women and their basic human rights. What surprisingly shifted my perspectives and inspired me was a simple conversation with a friend. Since I have always rooted for "all women" around the world, I shared how disappointed I was in the idea of "feminism" and how sad it was to see that feminism was "Westernized," focusing solely women in the west. "Western feminism is a joke," I said. My friend asked me, "Why don't you do something about it then?" and I did.

"How do I turn my outrage into meaningful social action? How can I continue to mobilize people to support the Iranian women's struggle?" These were the questions that started circulating in my head while being away from my country during these dark times. I started by taking advantage of my social media platforms, posting, sharing, retweeting, and spreading the word to educate Iranians and non-Iranians on what truly is happening in Iran. I advocated to Canadian government officials to promote an international investigation of human rights violations by Iranian officials and promoted an Amnesty International petition at my university and surrounding community to end the protest bloodshed in Iran and initiate an investigation of violations of international law. I wrote to the United Nations and let them know that I oppose the inclusion of the Islamic Republic on the UN Commission on the Status of Women, which is supposed to champion gender equality and women's rights. With the privilege of having access to social media, I shared posts on my social media for Iranians based in Iran on how to access a virtual private network (VPN) manual to help them restore internet in Iran, so they could communicate with the world. In addition, I started donating to credible Iran-focused human rights organizations, such as Human Rights Activists News Agency (HRANA) and Amnesty International Iran.

My human rights advocacy and social justice action are all based on the hope of reaching somewhere over the rainbow.

CHAPTER 26

SELF-CARE

Feeding Your Soul

Rita Chi-Ying Chung and Frederic P. Bemak

> If you feel "burnout" setting in, if you feel demoralized and exhausted, it is best, for the sake of everyone, to withdraw and restore yourself.
>
> —Dalai Lama

> Our ultimate objective in learning about anything is to try to create and develop a more just society.
>
> —Yuri Kochiyama

REFLECTION QUESTIONS

1. When you are working hard, is it customary for you to take time out to re-energize?
2. If your answer to Question 1 was yes, what do you do to take care of yourself? If your answer was no, what holds you back from taking care of yourself?
3. Are there better ways that you could do self-care? Can you list five ways how self-care might help you improve your psychological well-being and improve your work life?

As we mention multiple times throughout this volume, social justice work is not easy: it requires a "tough, thick skin" so that criticism and insults do not easily upset us. Confronting resistance, injustice, volatile emotions, anger, and hostility necessitates that social justice advocates are able to take these obstacles in stride and accept this as part of the work to create social change. Even so, there are times when we will feel social justice fatigue, down-trodden, exhausted, beaten, and ready to give up. Developing that "tough, thick skin" to balance feelings of despair will help incorporate social justice work into our psychotherapy, counseling, teaching, and research.

The helping professions, by the nature of the work, are vulnerable to experiencing compassion fatigue and burnout. Social justice–oriented psychologists and counselors, similar to human rights and peace activists, are highly susceptible to social justice fatigue and activist burnout (Chen & Gorksi, 2015). Psychologists and counselors are trained to actively listen and understand clients' life challenges. When mental health professionals incorporate social justice and human rights work there is an added dimension of deeply understanding those social conditions, rooted in oppression and suffering, that society may disavow or even deny. Given this perspective social justice–oriented psychologists and counselors are in a challenging position. Expanding our work to include a profound understanding of the cultural, social, psychological, economic, historical, and political circumstances facing our clientele, combined with a passionate investment to "right the wrongs" and prevent and intervene in the injustices that impact our clients' quality of life, psychological well-being, and physical safety and security, we are faced with daunting questions about our role as professionals. This may indeed be a heavy burden to shoulder and may create added levels of stress that require special attention to self-care if we are to avoid social justice fatigue and burnout.

Burnout is viewed as an outcome of chronic fatigue; it is more severe and more debilitating than common fatigue. Even so, both conditions have overlapping characteristics resulting in acute or chronic tiredness and mental and physical exhaustion that interfere with daily activities (Burnett, Jr., 2017). Generally, burnout and fatigue are experienced by individuals, while social justice fatigue and activist burnout affects both individuals and the sustainability of the social justice movement (Chen & Gorksi, 2015). Graduate training programs for psychologists and counselors do not necessarily provide training about how to deal with burnout and self-care (Weir, 2021), resulting in many mental health professionals learning how to cope with stress on the job on their own. Thus, the question for social justice–oriented psychologists and counselors is, "How do I mitigate social justice fatigue and activist burnout to foster social justice sustainability to be an effective change agent?"

As mentioned earlier in the volume, after my (Rita) keynote address at the North Atlantic Region Association for Counselor Education and Supervision (NARACES) conference (Chung, 2011), I was asked, "How do I feed my soul?" I interpreted this question to mean, "How do I continue to be motivated to do social justice work when I am met with never-ending resistance." This indeed is an extremely important question. The practice of positive and healthy self-care is essential in combatting social justice fatigue, burnout, disillusionment, discouragement, disenchantment, and disappointment. We tell our clients, students, colleagues, friends, and family members to do self-care, and yet at times we neglect to practice self-care for ourselves. Some in the helping profession may dismiss self-care, viewing it as being selfish and self-indulgent. On the other hand, some may use the term "self-care" as an excuse to avoid or resist being engaged in social justice activities, believing that, "I can't be doing or be involved in social justice now, I need to do self-care." Compounding this situation are those of us who come from collectivistic cultures, where we have been socialized to focus on others versus ourselves, so that thinking about ourselves conflicts with our cultural backgrounds and may create additional stress and tension.

Self-care for psychologists and counselors has been well-documented with studies in health psychology, mindfulness, wellness, and well-being. There is a plethora of resources about how to do self-care, with ideas that range from having a self-care plan that outlines checklists of activities for the day, week, month, and year to utilizing self-care strategies such as cognitive techniques (i.e., mediation, journaling, reading for pleasure), emotional release (i.e., laughter, talking to friends, giving yourself permission to cry), physical activity (i.e., drinking plenty of water, yoga and regular exercise, turning off technological devices), spiritual practices (i.e., time to reflect, spend time outdoors, gardening), and social support activities (i.e., supportive relationship with supervisors, peers, family, and friends). It should be mentioned that research related to burnout for social justice activists found that mindfulness was helpful in dealing with stress and tension and helped to re-energize and refocus on the goals of social justice work (Gorksi, 2015). Resources on self-care are readily accessible on numerous websites and publications so there is no need to repeat them in this chapter. We strongly encourage you to access these resources and proactively practice social justice self-care. Rather than discussing different self-care techniques that have been expounded on at great length, we focus our discussion on collective social justice self-care and barriers to social justice self-care.

SOCIAL JUSTICE COLLECTIVE SELF-CARE

Given how taxing social justice work may be, we suggest that social justice self-care may require extending beyond our usual routines to reduce burnout and chronic fatigue. We may need to further adapt to highly stressful situations, incorporating flexibility and creativity in developing an expanded host of self-care techniques, keeping in mind that self-care is not just an individual endeavor but also involves advocating for others in our social and organizational lives to do intentional self-care (Weir, 2021). Fostering a climate of self-care for our colleagues rather than simply focusing on ourselves helps build a successful professional future for our organizations (Weir, 2021). For example, our organization Counselors Without Borders (CWB) has worked in numerous post-disaster situations in the United States and in other countries. In each situation, CWB was working in devastated post-disaster regions similar to a war zone, where our usual self-care strategies of going to a gym, jogging, socializing with friends at a nearby restaurant, watching a movie, or finding a quiet isolated place to meditate weren't possible. Destruction and danger were everywhere—there was no electricity, clean water, or technology access, there was limited food and lawlessness; and some areas were fraught with violence and rape.

In situations like this, it was important to use our ingenuity to develop new strategies for self-care for ourselves and the CWB team rather than be further stressed by the inability to utilize old means of coping. Developing innovative approaches to coping for our entire team was important in cultivating collective self-care. Besides our daily evening debriefing sessions with the team, we also sometimes sang together and at times we invited survivors of the disaster and mental health professionals from other organizations to join in (Bemak & Chung, 2011). There were times when many didn't know the song, some songs were not in English, some of us did not like to sing in public, some of us could not hold a tune, or singing may not have been "their thing." All of us went beyond those barriers to share the moment, sitting with people, clapping our hands, humming to the song, swaying our bodies to the music, seeing each other smile and laugh, and laughing ourselves. It was a tremendous release to deal with the day's tension, stress, pain, tears, and fears after listening to the horrific lived experiences of disaster survivors.

Similarly, some individuals benefit by having some "alone time" to regroup and re-energize, writing in a diary, meditating, or drawing. A few of the CWB team members who never drew started to draw pictures of the traumatic stories they heard from survivors, later sharing them with the team. This relates to the shift from individualistic to collectivistic self-care that we have found very helpful when doing social justice work. Although individual healing and regrouping are very important and helpful, when working on social change, it is vital to also take care of each other and rebuild together. We suggest that part of a shift in social justice self-care is to incorporate long-standing individual strategies into social or community healing strategies since we are working collectively to battle against injustices.

BOX TEXT 26.1 NEVER TOO LATE TO RIGHT WRONGS

Barnard College has made civil rights pioneer Dorothy Height an honorary alumna, 75 years after it rescinded her acceptance as a student because of her skin color. The college President Judith Shapiro named 92-year-old Height an honorary graduate—an accolade seldom bestowed by the school. "It not only reaffirms that I was a deserving person, it recognizes its old mistake. . . . This action shows the heart of a great institution," Height said in an interview with the Associated Press.

Height won admission to the college in 1929, after graduating with honors from an integrated Pennsylvania high school. But when she arrived alone from her home in Rankin, Pennsylvania, the college dean, noting her Black skin, told her Barnard had already reached its quota of "two Negro students per year," in Height's words. She said the experience left her crushed.

"I couldn't eat, I couldn't sleep for days," Height said.

"This really sharpened my determination to eliminate discrimination," Height said. "I learned that there is no advantage in bitterness, that I needed to go into action, which is something I have tried to follow since." Height served more than 30 years as the president of the National Council of Negro Women, an organization dedicated to uplifting Black women and their communities.

She also held leadership positions in the YWCA, where she advocated progressive policies embracing minorities. In 1964, she organized a series of informal dialogues between White and Black women from the North and South called "Wednesdays in Mississippi."

Source: Associated Press (2004, Jun 30). https://www.diverseeducation.com/leadership-policy/article/15080085/barnard-college-honors-dorothy-height-75-years-after-turning-her-away

CULTURE OF MARTYRDOM AS A BARRIER TO SOCIAL JUSTICE SELF-CARE

Barriers may exist to doing self-care for social justice and human rights activists. Chen and Gorski (2015) identified a "culture of selflessness" for individuals doing this type of work. Activists may question whether taking time for oneself is too selfish when others rely on you and feel guilt and shame in considering their own well-being: they are digging themselves into what we (Rita and Fred) call the "culture of martyrdom." For example, working in Haiti following the earthquake, the mental health needs were endless, with long lines of people lining up to see us. Taking a break after 6 hours of intensive trauma-based counseling was very important, yet it required us to leave literally hundreds right there in front of us, without receiving our services. It was clear that without rejuvenating we would not be effective as we continued our work each day.

This example poses the dilemma of self-care for the social justice–oriented mental health professional. How to do the work, facilitate the change, and promote a better world while ensuring one is in physical, psychological, and spiritual shape to meet the challenge? Since there is not a correct or perfect answer to this question, we pose the question to you to find an answer that fits into your lifestyle, values, and beliefs. Remember, the answer to self-care does not need to be picture-perfect, and it may change depending on your personal life and work environment. We encourage you to be adventurous and try new and creative self-care techniques and to do collective self-care by coordinating within your work site and with colleagues. If these self-care techniques work, that is wonderful, and you can build them into your repertoire. If not, be appreciative that you have tried to engage in that specific self-care technique and move on to experiment and develop another means for taking care of yourself, remembering that your psychological health is the gateway to effective social justice–oriented psychological work.

SUMMARY

In conclusion, as we close this chapter and end the volume reflecting on self-care and social justice, we are reminded of U.S. Supreme Court Justice Sonia Sotomayor's routines before sleep each night. Each night before going to bed, Justice Sotomayor asks herself two questions (Sotomayor, 2013). The first question she poses to herself is "What did I learn today?" If she doesn't have an answer to this, she gets up, opens her computer, and reads, ensuring she ends the day by acquiring some new piece of knowledge. The second question she poses to herself is "What act of giving and kindness did I do today?" If she finds that she hasn't done any act of kindness for the day she gets up and texts, emails, or writes a card to someone before sleeping. Justice Sotomayor explains how this nightly ritual gives meaning to each and every day and underscores her belief that "living is giving." The combination of growing, learning, and giving each day is conducive to social justice and human rights work. As you encounter challenges in creating social change and tackling social injustices and human rights violations, we encourage you to develop your own questions that will help you feed your soul and continue to grow and learn. By adopting Justice Sotomayor's value of living is giving, we hope this will help you keep centered and focused on the purpose of social justice work. We thank you for reading our volume and hope this has been helpful in your journey as a human rights and social justice–oriented mental health professional.

REFERENCES

Bemak, F., & Chung, R. C-Y. (2011). Post-disaster social justice group work and group supervision. *Journal for Specialists in Group Work, 36*(1), 3–21. https://doi.org/10.1080/01933922.2010.537737

Burnett, Jr., H. J. (2017). Revisiting the compassion fatigue, burnout, compassion satisfaction, and resilience connection among CISM responders. *Journal of Police Emergency Response, 7*(3). https://doi.org/10.1177/2158244017730857

Chen, C. W., & Gorksi, P. C. (2015). Burnout in social justice and human rights activists: Symptoms, causes and implications. *Journal of Human Rights Practice, 7*(3), 366–390. https://doi.org/10.1093/jhuman/huv011

Chung, R. C-Y. (2011). *Social justice counselors in action: Walking the talk.* North Atlantic Region, Association for Counselor Educators and Supervisors (NARACES) Conference 2010 Keynote Presentation (Invited). Alexander Street Press. ProQuest Company. https://alexanderstreet.com/preview/work/bibliographic_entity%7Cvideo_work%7C1779211

Sotomayor, S. (2013). *My beloved world.* Knopf.

Weir, K. (2021, Nov 1). The Ohio State University neuropsychologist is rethinking self-care to make it work in the real world. *American Psychological Association Monitor, 52*(8), 35. https://www.apa.org/monitor/2021/11/conversation-boxley

INDEX

American Psychological Association (APA) (*cont.*)
    psychological impact of U.S. policies, 79
    social justice and human rights, 59–60
    Task Force on Human Rights, 40*b*
    Task Force on Strategies to Eradicate Racism,
        Discrimination, and Hate, 6
Americans, ownership of stuff, 35*b*
American School Counselors Association (ASCA),
    33–34
Amini, Mahsa Zhina, 299
Andrés, José, 277–79, 288
Angelou, Maya, 90, 99–100, 243, 274
Annie E. Casey Foundation, 257
Anthony, Susan B., 276–77
apathy, 105–7
Ardern, Jacinda, 157, 197
Aristotle, 1
armchair social justice mental health advocates, 107,
    108
artificial intelligence (AI), 282
Asian elders, letter to, 280*b*–81*b*
Association for Adult Development and Aging
    (AADA), 33–34
Association for Counselor Education and
    Supervision (ACES), 33–34
Association for Lesbian, Gay, Bisexual, and
    Transgender (ALGBTIC) Issues in Counseling,
    33–36
Association for Multicultural Counseling and
    Development (AMCD), 33–34
Association for Specialists in Group Work (ASGW),
    33–34
Auden, W. H., 175
authentic collaborator, social justice leader, 211*b*,
    211–12
authentic empowerment, 10
    advocacy and, 246–48
    equity and, 249–50
    factors in, 246–48
    key factors for fostering, 247*b*
    social justice action and mental health, 174*f*
    term, 245–46
    See also empowerment
autocratic leadership, social justice, 205–6, 206*b*

Baby Boomers, characteristics of, 287*t*
badge of honor, fear of failure vs., 104
Baldwin, James, 94
Band-Aiding, 45, 63–65, 77
Banerjee, Abhijit, 65–66
banking concept, 44
    dynamics between therapists and clients, 77
    Freire's, 76–77, 91

Barman, Tanvi, 228*b*
Barnard College, 304*b*
Beers, Clifford, 37, 223
bees
    impact of loss of pollination, 41
    need for, 41*b*, 41
    pollination, 41
behavioral approach, model, 200
behavioral change, mental health, 144
bell curve, concept of, 31
Ben and Jerry's ice cream, 5, 288
benevolent leadership, social justice, 206*b*, 206
Bethune, Mary McLeod, 8
Bhutto, Benazir, 212–13
Big Lie, U.S. presidential election (2020), 3–4
Biko, Stephen Bantu, 8, 212–13
Black Lives Matter (BLM), 2, 103, 279, 281*b*, 283
#BlackLivesMatter, 283–84
blaming, 87
Bloomberg billionaire index, 65–66
Boko Haram, 204*b*
bullying, 87
bureaucratic leadership, social justice, 206*b*, 206–7
burnout, 302
bystanders/observers, witnessing acts of injustice,
    95–96

Cain, Kasey, 291*b*
Canadian Women's Foundation, 282
car vandalism, 61*b*
Centers for Disease Control and Prevention
    (CDC), 3
Central Intelligence Agency (CIA), 78–79
challenges system, social justice leader, 211*b*, 212
change
    Chinese character for crisis, 176*f*
    danger, 176*f*, 176–77
    difficulty of, 175–77
    effective agents, 185
    opportunity, 176*f*, 176–77
    principles of, 179–85, 180*b*
    process of, 183–84
    psychology of, 177–79
    resistance to, 187–90
    transtheoretical model (TTM) of, 177–79, 178*f*
    See also social change and social justice
change theory, interdisciplinary collaboration, 265
character assassination, 9, 87
Chavez, Cesar, 8, 212–13, 248, 276–77
Cherokee tale, 109
child abuse, 18*b*
Child Alone conference, 266*b*
child protective services (CPS), 18*b*

Chino Hills High School, 129*b*
Chinese proverb, 28, 91
"Chinese virus", 3, 103
Chino Valley Unified School District, 129*b*
Chobani Greek yogurt, 106*b*
Christchurch, New Zealand, terrorist attacks, 157
Cisco Youth Leadership Award, 125*b*
citizen advocacy, 229
civility, 87–91
civility guideline, American Psychological
    Association, 89*b*
clients' lived experiences, MPM application, 121–22,
    122*f*
climate activist, Thunberg, 201*b*
Clinton, Hillary, 67–68, 94, 203
cognitive-behavior therapy (CBT), 147–48
coining, healing method, 17, 18*b*
collaboration. *See* interdisciplinary collaboration
colonialism, European/White, 195
comfort with discomfort, authentic empowerment,
    247*b*, 248
common goals, authentic empowerment, 247*b*, 247
communitarian approach, social justice, 39–40
community-based participatory research, social
    justice principle, 45
compassion, social justice work, 17, 20
confidentiality, definition of, 143
contingency theory, model, 200
Cook, Mary Lou, 274
Cooke, Sam, 173
coronavirus (COVID-19), global pandemic, 2
Counseling Psychologist, The, 33
counseling skills and techniques, MPM application,
    122*f*, 122–23
counselor bias, 194
Counselors Without Borders (CWB), 25*b*–26*b*, 82,
    159, 277–78, 290–91
    mental health team, 183
    post-disaster regions, 303
    self-care of team, 303–4
courage, social justice leadership, 208–9
courageous risk taker, social justice leader, 211*b*,
    212
COVID-19 pandemic, 117, 224
    equal opportunity, 3
    hospitalization and death data, 3
    lockdown and social distancing, 264
    political countertransference, 86
    protection from, 87–88
    spreading hope through song during, 129*b*
    teddy bear hunts for kids during, 149*b*
    use and dependence on technology, 279–81
    xenophobia and, 103

CRC. *See* United Nations Child Rights Convention
    (CRC)
creative, social justice leader, 211*b*, 212
creativity
    advocacy, 275–76
    ethnographic fiction example, 289–90, 291*b*
    graduate-level university training, 289–91
    infusing into social justice work, 276–77
    "Meet a Muslim" action, 289, 290*b*
    social justice, 275, 276
    social justice work, 16–17, 20
"crisis"
    Chinese word for, 176*f*, 176–77
    See also change
critical conscientization, Freire on, 44
cross-agency, interdisciplinary collaboration, 265
cross-cultural identities, 194–95
cross-cultural skills, working with language
    translators/interpreters, 123–24
cross-disciplinary training, interdisciplinary
    collaboration, 265
Cruz, Philip Vera, 8
cuaranderismo, 156
cultural deficiency model, 31–32
cultural empowerment
    information guide and advocate, 153
    interdisciplinary collaboration, 152–53
    social and navigational capital, 151–53
cultural humility, concept of, 82–83
culturally diverse model, 32
culturally responsive interventions, 147
cultural self-awareness, MPM application, 122*f*,
    126–27
culture, mental health diagnoses, 149–51
culture of fear (COF), 9–10, 98
    age of anger, 103
    fear of failure *vs.* badge of honor, 104
    fear of litigation and ethical codes, 104–5
    psychological barrier, 102–5
culture of martyrdom, 83–84, 305
culture of selflessness, 305
Cyclone Nargis, Myanmar, 16, 25*b*

Dalai Lama, 212–13, 248, 301
danger, Chinese word for "crisis", 176*f*, 176–77
Davis, Angela, 59
decision-making, interdisciplinary collaboration,
    263–64
decolonization, 42–43
Diagnostic and Statistical Manual of Mental Disorders
    (DSM), 231
Disaster Cross-Cultural Counseling (DCCC) model,
    25*b*

George Mason University (GMU), 114, 170, 265, 271
   counseling program, 295, 296, 297
   social justice and counseling class, 63t
gestalt, 148–49
Giffords, Gabrielle, 288
Global Citizen Award, 125b
Global Citizen Business Leader Award, 106b
global warming, hashtags, 283–84
global wealth, 66
Goodall, Jane, 11–12
graduate-level university, creative assignments,
   289–91
grassroot advocacy, India, 125b
great man studies, leadership, 199
group psychotherapy and counseling, social justice-
   oriented, 146–47
guardians of injustice, 95
guide, not an expert, social justice leader, 211b, 213
guiding principles, interdisciplinary collaboration,
   262–66, 262t
Gurdon, Sir John, Nobel Prize, 100b

Haiti earthquake (2010), Counselors Without
   Borders (CWB), 25b, 159
hand signal for help, 282f, 282
Harris, Kamala, 67–68, 202
Hashtag, 283
hashtags, advocacy tool, 283–84
Haynesworth, Thomas, 272
healing methodologies
   accessing communities, 157–58
   integration of Western and Indigenous, 154–59
   true partnerships with traditional healers, 158–59
healing practice, collaborative partnership, and
   empowerment, 18b
HealthSetGo, 125b
healthy paranoia, 145–46
Height, Dorothy, 304b
Helms, Janet, 270
here and now advocacy, 229
historical successes, authentic empowerment, 247b,
   248
honeybees, need for, 41b, 41
hope
   authentic empowerment, 247b, 247
   interdisciplinary collaboration, 259–60
   MPM application, 125–26
   social justice work, 17–19, 20
   spreading, through song during COVID-19, 129b
human rights
   advocacy, 224–27
Human Rights Activists News Agency (HRANA),
   300

human services agencies, 258b
humble, lacking ego, social justice leader, 211b, 213
humility, social justice, 82–83
Hurricane Katrina, 290–91
   Counselors Without Borders (CWB), 25b
   Mississippi after, 17–19
Hurricane Maria, Puerto Rico, 25b, 290–91

identity
   positionality and, 84–86
   pride and comfort in one's, 194–96
immigrants, business supporting, 106b
imposter syndrome (IS), 9–10, 98–100
   stereotype threat (ST) and, 99–100
India, grassroot advocacy, 125b
Indigenous First Nation, 2
Indigenous healing methods, integration of Western
   and, 154–59
individual advocacy, 228–29
Instagram, 283
interdisciplinary collaboration, 257
   case study of interprofessional collaboration, 258b
   ecological context, 260
   fighting the opioid epidemic, 261b
   guiding principles for social justice, 262–66, 262t
   hope as key ingredient, 259–60
   need for and importance of social justice, 258–61
   realignment and sharing of power, 259
   recommended actions and strategies, 261–62
   social justice action and mental health, 174f
intergenerational trauma, 195
International Association of Marriage and Family
   Counselors (IAMFC), 33–34
International Classification of Diseases (ICD), 231
intersectionality, socioeconomic status, race/
   ethnicity, and gender, 67f, 67
interventions
   advocacy, 228–29
   cultural adaptation of traditional Western, 147–48
   culturally responsive, 147
   non-Western traditional, 148–49
introspection, social justice, 80–82
Itliong, Larry, 8

Journal for Social Action Counseling and Psychology
   (journal), 80

Kennedy, John F., 22–23, 173, 197, 212–13, 248
Kennedy, Robert, 207–8, 212–13
King, Coretta Scott, 76
King, Martin Luther, Jr., 1, 5–7, 8, 13, 21, 22, 45,
   105–7, 116, 140, 197, 212–13, 221, 248, 254,
   276–77, 288–89

Western healing methods, integration of Indigenous and, 154–59
Western interventions, cultural adaptation of traditional, 147–48
Western mental health, redefining traditional roles, 131–32
Western psychology, 118
    decolonization of, 42–43
Western psychotherapy and counseling, 146
Wheatley, Phillis, 212–13
White identity, 195
White privilege, 271, 272–73
    acknowledging, 171–72
    advocacy addict, 74–75
    term, 44–45
Wiesel, Elie, 276–77
Wilkins, Roger, 90
Wilson, Woodrow, 173

women, underrepresentation of, 68
women in refuge centers, flower gifts on Mother's Day, 154*b*
women of color
    Harris, 202
    leaders, 205
women's rights, Iranian women, 11
World Central Kitchen (WCK), 277–78
World Health Organization (WHO), 154
World War II, 14–15, 81*b*, 275
World Wide Web, 283

xenophobia, 5–7, 60–61, 275

Yamanaka, Shinya, Nobel Prize, 100*b*
Yousafzai, Malala, 204*b*, 276–77

Zinn, Howard, 44